T0242218

Lecture Notes in Computer Science 7593

Commenced Publication in 1973
Founding and Former Series Editors:
Gerhard Goos, Juris Hartmanis, and Jan van Leeuwen

Editorial Board

Vincent Guyot (Ed.)

Advanced Infocomm Technology

5th IEEE International Conference, ICAIT 2012
Paris, France, July 25-27, 2012
Revised Papers

Volume Editor

Vincent Guyot
Ecole Supérieure d'Informatique, Electronique, Automatique (ESIEA), France
E-mail: vincent.guyot@esiea.fr
and
Laboratoire d'Informatique de Paris 6 (LIP6), France
E-mail: vincent.guyot@lip6.fr

ISSN 0302-9743 e-ISSN 1611-3349
ISBN 978-3-642-38226-0 e-ISBN 978-3-642-38227-7
DOI 10.1007/978-3-642-38227-7
Springer Heidelberg Dordrecht London New York

Library of Congress Control Number: 2013937822

CR Subject Classification (1998): C.2, H.4, K.6.5, K.6, D.4.6, D.2

LNCS Sublibrary: SL 5 – Computer Communication Networks and Telecommunications

Typesetting: Camera-ready by author, data conversion by Scientific Publishing Services, Chennai, India

Printed on acid-free paper

Springer is part of Springer Science+Business Media (www.springer.com)

Preface

These are the post-proceedings of ICAIT 2012, the 5th IEEE International Conference on Advanced Infocomm Technology. The conference was held at the ESIEA IT School, Paris, France, during July 25–27, 2012. This 3-day event provided a platform for introducing advanced infocomm technologies that will shape the next generation of information and communication systems and technology platforms.

The call for papers requested anonymous submissions of full papers. There were 97 submissions from ICAIT 2012, from 19 countries and regions (Algeria, Australia, Brazil, Canada, China, France, India, Italy, Japan, Korea, Morocco, Pakistan, Portugal, Sweden, Taiwan, Tunisia, Turkey, UK, and USA), of which 32 papers were selected for presentation in eight sessions. All submissions were reviewed by at least three experts in the relevant fields.

Beside the regular selected papers sessions, the program also included four invited talks by Bezalel Gavish ("Energy-Based Limits on Computing Capacity and on Human Computing Ability"), Henri Binsztok ("Making a Breakthrough in Cloud Application Design"), Raouf Boutaba ("On Managing Heterogeneity in Production Cloud Computing Environments") and Yacine Ghamri-Doudane ("Towards Urban Vehicular Networking").

These proceedings gather the final versions of all papers revised after the conference. Since the revised versions were not checked for correctness of their scientific aspects, the authors bear the full responsibility for the content of their papers.

I am very grateful to all the Technical Program Committee members who dedicated much effort and valuable time to reading and selecting the papers, but also especially commenting on the papers so as to give the opportunity to their authors to produce better articles. I also thank the external experts and external reviewers who assisted the Technical Program Committee in evaluating various papers.

Submitting papers and reviews, dispatching of the reviews and notifications to authors was powered by the excellent web-based software OpenConf Peer Review & Conference Management System, from Zakon Group LLC.

I would like to thank everyone who submitted their papers to ICAIT 2012, including those whose submissions were not successfull, as well as the conference attendees from around the world, for their support, which made this conference a huge success.

Finally, I hope these proceedings will be helpful for your future research.

August 2012 Vincent Guyot

ICAIT 2012

5th IEEE International Conference on Advanced Infocomm Technology
ESIEA IT School, Paris, France
July 25–27, 2012

Organized by

Ecole Supérieure d'Informatique-Electronique-Automatique (ESIEA)
(http://www.esiea.fr/)
and
Université Pierre et Marie Curie (UPMC)
(http://www.upmc.fr/)

Sponsored by

Institute of Electrical and Electronics Engineers (IEEE)
(http://www.ieee.org/)
and
IEEE France Section
(http://www.ieeefrance.org/)

Organization

Program and General Chair

Vincent Guyot	ESIEA & UPMC, France

Steering Committee

Tulin Atmaca	RST, IT SudParis, France
Nadia Boukhatem	LTCI, IT ParisTech, France
Robert Erra	CVO, ESIEA, France
Eric Filiol	CVO, ESIEA, France
Maryline Laurent	LOR, IT SudParis, France
Elie Najm	SLS, IT ParisTech, France
Guy Pujolle	PHARE, LIP6-UPMC, France

Local Organizing Committee

Loica Avanthey	ATIS, ESIEA, France
Laurent Beaudoin	ATIS, ESIEA, France
Antoine Gademer	ATIS, ESIEA, France
Christophe Grenier	CGSecurity, France
Rami Langar	PHARE, LIP6-UPMC, France
Benoit Larroque	ESIEA, France
Aziza Lounis	PHARE, LIP6-UPMC, France
Thi-Mai-Trang Nguyen	PHARE, LIP6-UPMC, France
Stefano Secci	PHARE, LIP6-UPMC, France

Financial Chair

Ibrahim Hajjeh	Ineovation, France

International Advisory Committee

Hubert Van Den Bergh	ETH, Switzerland
Peter Chong	NTU, Singapore
A.K. Ghatak	ITT New Delhi, India
Ken T.V. Grattan	City University, UK
Gerd Keiser	Boston University, USA
Byoung Yoon Kim	Kaist, Korea

A.M.J. Koonen	Eindhoven University of Technology, The Netherlands
Jin Tong Lin	Beijing University of Post and Telecommunications, China
Jie Luo	YOFC, China
Muriel Medard	MIT, USA
Shum Ping	NTU, Singapore
David J. Richardson	University of Southampton, UK
Yikai Su	Shanghai Jiao Tong University, China
Ozan K. Tonguz	Carnegie Mellon University, USA
Do-Hong Tuan	Ho Chi Minh City University of Technology, Vietnam
Alex Ping Kong Wai	The Hong Kong Polytechnic University, China
Tak-Shing Yum	The Chinese University of Hong Kong, China
Bingkun Zhou	Chinese Academy of Sciences, China

Technical Program Committee

Tara Ali-Yahiya	LRI, University of Paris-Sud 11, France
Mohammed Badra	LIMOS, CNRS, France
Monique Becker	RST, IT SudParis, France
Zhisong Bie	Beijing University of Posts and Telecommunications, China
Arijit Biswas	Dolby, Germany
Mathieu Bouet	Thales Group, France
Lila Boukhatem	LRI, University of Paris-Sud 11, France
Khaled Boussetta	L2TI, University of Paris 13, France
Samia Bouzefrane	CEDRIC, CNAM, France
Pedro Braconnot-Velloso	UFF, Brazil
Fabien Bretenaker	CNRS-LAC, France
Herve Chabanne	MORPHO & IT ParisTech, France
Calvin-C-K Chan	The Chinese University of Hong Kong, Hong Kong
Hau-Ping Chan	City University of Hong Kong, Hong Kong
Nan-Kuang Chen	National United University, Taiwan
Chi Wai Chow	National Chiao Tung University, Taiwan
Shaowei Dai	RFNet Technologies Pte. Ltd., Singapore
Catalin Dima	LACL, UPEC, France
Xiaopeng Dong	Xiamen University, China
Xinyong Dong	China Jiliang University, China
Mauro Fonseca	PPGIa, PUC-PR, Brazil
Dominique Gaiti	UTT, France
Eric Gressier	CEDRIC, CNAM, France
Xiang Gui	Massey University, New Zealand
Jianzhong Hao	Institute for Infocomm Research, Singapore

Kokula-Krishna Hari-K	Techno Forum Research and Development Centre, India
Artur Hecker	LTCI, IT ParisTech, France
Tetsuya Kawanishi	National Institute of Information & Communications Technology, Japan
Josephine Kohlenberg	RST, IT SudParis, France
Yicheng Lai	Data Storage Institute, Singapore
Alan-Pak-Tao Lau	Hong Kong Polytechnic University, Hong Kong
Gyu Myoung Lee	IT SudParis, France
Gordon-Ning Liu	Huawei Technologies, China
Yunqi Liu	Shanghai University, China
Stephane Lohier	Institut Gaspard Monge, Université Marne-la-Vallee, France
Zhengqian Luo	Xiamen University, China
Leila Merghem-Boulahia	UTT, France
Dae Seung Moon	Samsung Electronics Hainan Fiberoptics-Korea Co. Ltd., Korea
Rola Naja	PRISM, UVSQ, France
Jean-Louis Rougier	LTCI, IT ParisTech, France
Michel Riguidel	LTCI, IT ParisTech, France
Kaouthar Sethom	ESTI, Tunis
Xuewen Shu	Aston University, UK
Promethee Spathis	NPA, LIP6-UPMC, France
Jean-Ferdy Susini	CEDRIC, CNAM, France
Weijun Tong	Yangtz Optical Fiber and Cable Co. Ltd., China
Vrizlynn L. L. Thing	Imperial College London, UK
An Tran	NICTA Ltd., Australia
Jian Wang	Huazhong University of Science and Technology, China
Lei Wei	MIT, USA
Yan-Ling Xue	East China Normal University, China
Lin Zhang	University of Southern California, USA

Table of Contents

Invited Talks

Energy Based Limits on Computing Capacity and on Human Computing Ability 1
Bezalel Gavish

Making a Breakthrough in Cloud Application Design 2
Henri Binsztok

On Managing Heterogeneity in Production Cloud Computing Environments 3
Raouf Boutaba

Towards Urban Vehicular Networking 4
Yacine Ghamri-Doudane

Contributed Papers

Session I: Fixed Mobile Convergence and Emerging Networks Technologies

Performance Evaluation of Fairness between High-Speed TCPs in Wireless Environment 5
Hiroki Mihara, Yuki Hayashi, and Miki Yamamoto

Evaluation of SIP Call Setup Delay for VoIP in IMS 16
Mohamed El Mahdi Boumezzough, Noureddine Idboufker, and Abdellah Ait Ouahman

MPLS-TP: OAM Discovery Mechanism 25
Mounir Azizi, Redouane Benaini, and Mouad Ben Mamoun

Supporting Data Center Management through Clustering of System Data Streams 33
Stefania Tosi, Sara Casolari, and Michele Colajanni

Session II: Performance and Quality of Service

Extension of Path Computation Element (PCE) Framework for Resource Provisioning Based on User Profile in Dynamic Circuit Network 47
Tananun Orawiwattanakul, Hideki Otsuki, Eiji Kawai, and Shinji Shimojo

Traffic Engineering Approaches in P2P Environments 61
Pedro Sousa

On Selective Placement for Uniform Cache Objects 75
Jong-Geun Park and Hoon Choi

Loss Probability and Delay of Finite-Buffer Queues with Discrete ON-OFF Markovian Arrivals and Geometric Service Times 83
Sheng-Hua Yang, Jay Cheng, Hsin-Hung Chou, and Chih-Heng Cheng

Improve Prefetch Performance by Splitting the Cache Replacement Queue 98
Elizabeth Varki, Allen Hubbe, and Arif Merchant

Session III: Fiber Technologies and Multimedia Processing

CO_2 Laser Writing of Long-Period Fiber Gratings in Polarization-Maintaining Fiber under Tension 109
Yunqi Liu, Jian Zou, Qiang Guo, and Tingyun Wang

SAVI - A Model for Video Workload Generation Based on Scene Length 116
Valter Klein Junior and Carlos Marcelo Pedroso

UNIVERSALLY: A Context-Aware Architecture for Multimedia Access in Digital Homes 128
Tayeb Lemlouma

Session IV: Communication Softwares and Services

A User-Centric Network Architecture for Sustainable Rural Areas 138
Farnaz Farid, Seyed Shahrestani, and Chun Ruan

A Relative Delay Measurement Method for Wideband Array with LFM Waveform 151
Yue-bin Chen, Fei Gao, Ji-hua Feng, and Wu-bang Hao

Signal Detection Based on Maximum-Minimum Eigenvalue in Rician Fading Channel 160
Sai-sai Feng, Yue-bin Chen, and Fei Gao

Collective Intelligence Based Place Recommendation System 169
Jehwan Oh, Ok-Ran Jeong, and Eunseok Lee

Providing Reliability for Transactional Mobile Agents 177
Linda Zeghache, Michel Hurfin, Izabela Moise, and Nadjib Badache

Session V: Security

On the Security of Lv et al.'s Three-Party Authenticated Key Exchange Protocol Using One-Time Key 191
Eun-Jun Yoon

Mechanisms to Locate Non-cooperative Transmitters in Wireless Networks 199
Éric Barthélémy and Jean-Marc Robert

Mantle: A Novel DOSN Leveraging Free Storage and Local Software 213
Antonino Famulari and Artur Hecker

Descriptional Entropy: Application to Security Software Analysis 225
Anthony Desnos and Robert Erra

Session VI: Sensor Technologies and Wireless Systems

Adaptative Delay Aware Data Gathering Strategy for Wireless Sensor Networks 231
Nour Brinis, Leila Azouz Saidane, and Pascale Minet

Overcoming the Deficiencies of Collaborative Detection of Spatially-Correlated Events in WSN 243
Martin Peres, Romain Perier, and Francine Krief

A Low-Complexity and High-Performance Beamforming Scheme for mmWave WPAN systems 258
Ying-Tsung Lin, Huan-Shun Yeh, and Sau-Gee Chen

Session VII: Energy-Aware Networks and Power Management

Energy Efficient Aggregation in Wireless Sensor Networks 264
Najet Boughanmi, Moez Esseghir, Leïla Merghem-Boulahia, and Lyes Khoukhi

Energy Optimization of Mesh Access Networks 274
Guy Pujolle and Khaldoun Al Agha

Predictive Sink Mobility for Target Tracking in Sensor Networks 283
Joseph Rahmé, Lila Boukhatem, and Khaldoun Al Agha

Session VIII: Mobile Ad-Hoc, Mesh and Vehicular Networks

Backhaul Topology Design and Weighted Max-Min Fair Capacity Allocation in Wireless Mesh Networks 296
Abdelhak Farsi, Nadjib Achir, Khaled Boussetta, Gladys Diaz, and Arturo Gomez

A Double Data Rate, Low Complexity 2 x 2 MIMO Scheme Based on a Combination of Alamouti System and Orthogonal Codes ... 310
Nizar Ouni and Ridha Bouallegue

GeoSUZ: A Geocast Routing Protocol in Sub-ZORs for VANETs 319
Salim Allal and Saadi Boudjit

Adaptive Contention Window for Zone-Based Dissemination of Vehicular Traffic 330
Arturo Gomez, Gladys Diaz, Khaled Boussetta, Nadjib Achir, and Abdelhak Farsi

Highway Preventive Congestion Control through Input Regulation in Vehicular Networks 340
Rola Naja

Author Index 357

Energy Based Limits on Computing Capacity and on Human Computing Ability

Bezalel Gavish

Southern Methodist University
http://www.cox.smu.edu/web/bezalel-gavish/

Abstract. Many forecasts and predictions have been made about the impact of the growth over time in processing capacity of computers. In this talk we introduce bounds on future processing capacity and analyze the possibilities for their realization in the long run. The analysis shows the existence of hard limits on the progress in processing capacity which in turn generates bounds on future computing capacity. The results show that it is unlikely that some of the predictions on computing capabilities will not be achieved in the long run. The capacity bounds are not based on architectural and engineering considerations, they stem from fundamental physical limitations, which generate the tight bounds. We show that the bounds will be reached much faster than expected when compared to using simple traditional forecasting methods.

Assuming that computational activities like, decision making, processing, vision, control, auditory and sensing activities of human beings require energy, the above energy based results generate upper bounds on the computational capacity (in the broadest sense) of human beings. The results are architecture independent and have direct impact on research on models of the brain and on the cognitive abilities of human beings. A byproduct of this line of research is providing some new conjectures on past and future human development.

V. Guyot (Ed.): ICAIT 2012, LNCS 7593, p. 1, 2013.

Making a Breakthrough in Cloud Application Design

Henri Binsztok

MLstate, Opa
http://www.opalang.org/

Abstract. Building a great product out of software research is generally not straightforward. In this talk, we will detail the lessons learned while making Opa – a new programming language for cloud applications that solve the impedance mismatch problem between client, server and database parts of the application. We developed the best technology we could and made our best efforts not to compromise.

After several years of hard work, we had built the breakthrough technology we dreamt of. Then, we figured out why few people were interested in it. We will detail the different steps we then followed to turn this new technology into a real product.

V. Guyot (Ed.): ICAIT 2012, LNCS 7593, p. 2, 2013.

On Managing Heterogeneity in Production Cloud Computing Environments

Raouf Boutaba

University of Waterloo

http://rboutaba.cs.uwaterloo.ca/

Abstract. The past few years have witnessed the rise of cloud computing, a paradigm that harnesses massive resource capacity of data centers to support Internet services and applications in a scalable, flexible, reliable and cost-efficient manner. However, despite its success, recent literature has shown that effectively managing resources in production cloud environments remains to be a difficult challenge. A key reason behind this difficulty is that both resources and workloads found in production environments are heterogeneous. In particular, large cloud data centers often consist of machines with heterogeneous resource capacities and performance characteristics. At the same time, real cloud workloads show significant diversity in terms of priority, resource requirements, demand characteristics and performance objectives. Consequently, finding an effective resource management solution that leverages resource heterogeneity to support diverse application performance objectives becomes a difficult problem.

The focus of this talk will be on understanding the research challenges introduced by resource and workload heterogeneity in production cloud environments. We will first provide a characterization of workload and resource heterogeneities found in production data centers, and highlight the key challenges introduced by them. We will then describe our recent work towards addressing some of these challenges. Finally, we will outline several key directions for future research.

V. Guyot (Ed.): ICAIT 2012, LNCS 7593, p. 3, 2013.

Towards Urban Vehicular Networking

Yacine Ghamri-Doudane

ENSIIE, Evry, France
http://www.ensiie.fr/~ghamri/

Abstract. Inter-Vehicle Communication (IVC) is attracting considerable attention from the research community and the automotive industry, where it is beneficial in providing Intelligent Transportation System (ITS) as well as assistance services for drivers and passengers. In this context, Vehicular Networks are emerging as a novel category of wireless networks, spontaneously formed between moving vehicles equipped with wireless interfaces that could have similar or different radio interface technologies, employing short-range to medium-range communication systems. The distinguished characteristics of vehicular networks such as high mobility, potentially large scale, and network partitioning introduce several challenges, which can greatly impact the future deployment of these networks. In this Keynote, we focus on IVC in urban environments. Our main goal is to discuss the feasibility of Vehicular Ad hoc Networking for road traffic estimation, vehicular data routing as well as information dissemination in urban environments. This will be discussed while considering the characteristics and constraints imposed by vehicular networks and their applications.

V. Guyot (Ed.): ICAIT 2012, LNCS 7593, p. 4, 2013.

Performance Evaluation of Fairness between High-Speed TCPs in Wireless Environment

Hiroki Mihara, Yuki Hayashi, and Miki Yamamoto

Faculty of Engineering Science, Kansai University,
3–3–35 Yamate-cho, Suita, Osaka, 564–8680 Japan
{k517040,k676440,yama-m}@kansai-u.ac.jp

Abstract. Among various TCP congestion controls proposed for high delay-bandwidth networks thus far, CUBIC and Compound TCP have been implemented as default congestion control in Linux and Microsoft Windows OS, respectively. CUBIC is loss-based high-speed congestion control. Compound TCP is constructed with NewReno TCP and delay-based high-speed congestion control. When these two versions of TCP shares bottleneck link, their aggressiveness and different behaviors might fall into unfair condition. In current network environment, bandwidth of wired networks is sufficiently large and a wireless access network can be one of the most likely bottleneck points. This wireless access network has different feature than wired networks, i.e. wireless caused loss which occurs independently of congestion. In this paper, we evaluate fairness among CUBIC and Compound TCP sessions sharing high-speed wireless channel. Our simulation results show that Compound TCP is seriously suffered by CUBIC with low loss rate and this unfair condition is relieved with increase of packet loss rate because loss based CUBIC is gradually degraded by wireless caused packet loss.

Keywords: CUBIC, Compound TCP, Wireless Network, Congestion Control.

1 Introduction

With rapid growth of network bandwidth especially in access line speed, it is well known that TCP NewReno obtains too low throughput and cannot effectively utilize wide bottleneck bandwidth [1]. To improve TCP throughput in high-speed network environment, e.g. high BDP (bandwidth delay product), various high-speed congestion controls have been proposed [2][3].

Several proposed high-speed TCP, e.g. CUBIC [4], BIC [5], HTCP [6], High-Speed TCP [7], TCP-Hybla [8] and Scalable TCP [9] have been implemented and available in Linux kernel version2.6.35.1 [10]. Especially, CUBIC is selected as a default congestion control in Linux. This means CUBIC is generally used as congestion control when an end user just uses Linux (without any manual setting). For Windows OS users of later versions than Vista and Windows Server 2008, Compound TCP [11] is implemented as a default congestion control. These two

V. Guyot (Ed.): ICAIT 2012, LNCS 7593, pp. 5–15, 2013.

OSs are now widely used, so CUBIC and Compound TCP are now dominant congestion controls in the current Internet.

CUBIC is loss-based congestion control with quite different congestion window control algorithm from the conventional loss-based TCP, TCP NewReno. Its window increase algorithm is basically binary increase (actually its rate increase is cubic function but its basic idea is based on binary increase of BIC) and rather aggressive than the conventional TCP (TCP NewReno) in high BDP region. Compound TCP is combined loss-based and delay-based congestion control. Its loss-based congestion control is the same one as TCP NewReno and congestion window size of delay-based algorithm is added to the window size of TCP NewReno. It is well known that when delay-based TCP shares bottleneck link with loss-based TCP, throughput of delay-based TCP is pessimistically low [12]. Delay-based TCP decreases its window size with small queue size but loss-based TCP decreases with full queue size. This aggressive behavior of loss-based TCP causes starvation of delay-based TCP throughput. When CUBIC and Compound TCP shares bottleneck link, delay-based window of Compound TCP will be shrunk and Compound TCP can obtain equivalent throughput to TCP NewReno. In high BDP region, Compound TCP might be able to obtain much smaller throughput than CUBIC.

High-speed TCP, including CUBIC and Compound TCP, is designed to behave like conventional TCP NewReno in low delay-bandwidth region. So, when they are used in low-speed wireless networks, CUBIC and Compound TCP will fairly share wireless channel bandwidth because both of them try to behave like TCP NewReno. With deployment of IEEE 802.11n and LTE, high delay-bandwidth environment is now emerging even in wireless networks. So, CUBIC and Compound TCP might work in aggressive mode in current wireless networks and unfairly share a bottleneck wireless channel. In wireless networks, there is another important factor affecting TCP performance, wireless caused packet losses. With our best knowledge, there have been no publications of fairness issue of high-speed TCP in wireless environment. In this paper, we would like to evaluate fairness issue between CUBIC and Compound TCP in high-speed wireless access networks. Our simulation results show that Compound TCP is seriously suffered by CUBIC with low loss rate and this unfair condition is relieved with increase of packet loss rate because loss based CUBIC is gradually more degraded by wireless caused packet loss than Compound TCP.

Remainder of the paper is structured as follows. Section II outlines two major high-speed TCP, Compound TCP and CUBIC. In this section, congestion window behavior of these two TCPs is explained in detail. Section III discusses high-speed TCP in wireless networks. In this section, we claim that fairness issues of these two TCPs are important and unrevealed technical issues. Section IV evaluates Compound TCP and CUBIC in wireless network environment. We use simple simulation model with burst packet loss which is generally observed in wireless networks. Finally, we conclude a paper in section V.

2 TCP for High Bandwidth Delay Product

In this section, we first show brief overview of CUBIC and Compound TCP. And we examine fairness issue of these two TCPs as our preliminary performance evaluation results.

2.1 CUBIC

CUBIC is loss-based congestion control and is modified from BIC so that RTT fairness issue is improved. In this subsection, we would like to first explain overview of BIC and show modification to CUBIC. When packet loss is detected, BIC decreases its window size by β (recommended value is 0.875). Window size where previous packet loss was detected is set to target window size (W_{max}). BIC uses binary search to target window size as its basic congestion window increase algorithm. When increments of window are larger than S_{max} and smaller than S_{min}, AI (Additive Increase) of S_{max} and S_{min} is applied, respectively. After current window size exceeds W_{max}, BIC increases its window size exponentially like Slow Start. When increments of window exceed S_{max}, increased algorithm is changed to AI. It has good scalability and TCP friendliness, which are important features that high-speed TCP should satisfy. However, for RTT fairness, which is also important feature for high-speed TCP, BIC still has unfairness among flows with different RTT.

To improve RTT fairness issue of BIC while keeping good features of scalability and TCP friendliness, CUBIC uses the following cubic function for its window increase algorithm.

$$W_{cubic} = C(t-K)^3 - W_{max}, \tag{1}$$

where C is control parameter (recommended value is 0.4[4]), t is elapsed time from previous loss detection, W_{max} is window size at previous packet loss detection, and K is equal to $\sqrt[3]{W_{max}\beta/C}$. This cubic function used for window increase phase in CUBIC is independent of RTT of flow and is computed only by elapsed time from previous loss detection (Fig. 1). So, it completely satisfies

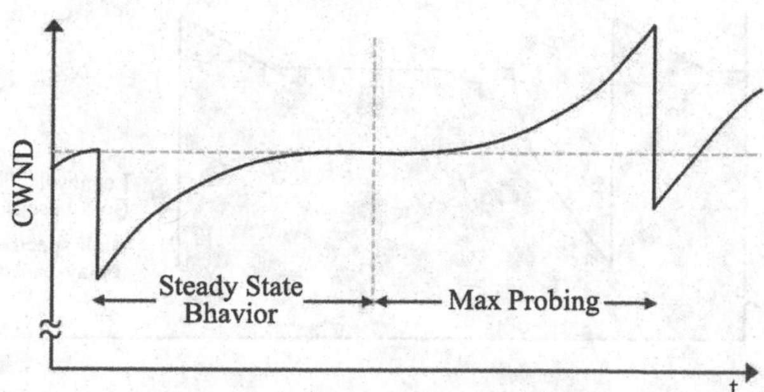

Fig. 1. Variation of CUBIC Window

RTT fairness. CUBIC is employed as default congestion control of Linux since its kernel version 2.6.35.1.

2.2 Compound TCP

Compound TCP is compound congestion control of loss-based and delay-based TCP. For loss-based TCP, Compound TCP employs TCP Reno. As it is well known that TCP Reno cannot effectively use bandwidth in high BDP environment[1]. So, delay-based TCP is applied in order to use leftover bandwidth unused by loss-based TCP. Compound TCP estimates queue size of the bottleneck link as follows,

$$Diff = (\frac{win}{RTT_{min}} - \frac{win}{RTT})RTT_{min}, \qquad (2)$$

where win is the sum of windows of loss-based and delay-based TCP, and RTT_{min} is the minimum value of measured RTT. Equation (2) is the same one as used in TCP Vegas. Compound TCP window algorithm is

$$win_{i+1} = \begin{cases} \{cwnd_i + 1\} + \{dwnd_i + (\alpha * win_i^k - 1)^+\} & Diff < \gamma \\ \{cwnd_i + 1\} + \{dwnd_i - \zeta * Diff\} & Diff \geq \gamma \\ \{\frac{cwnd_i}{2}\} + \{dwnd_i * (1 - \beta)\} & \text{Loss is detected} \end{cases} \qquad (3)$$

where $cwnd$ and $dwind$ is respective window size for loss-based and delay-based TCP, and α, β, k and λ are control parameters. Former parenthetic part of equation (3) shows window size of legacy TCP (TCP Reno) and latter part shows delay-based window. When queue size at the bottleneck link increases due to congestion, window size of delay-based TCP decreases and eventually becomes 0. After window size of delay-based TCP becomes 0, Compound TCP has only loss-based TCP window as shown in Fig. 2. In this region (heavy congestion region), Compound TCP has good TCP friendliness because it behaves as just TCP Reno. Microsoft Windows OS (Vista, 7, WindowsServer 2008) employs Compound TCP as its congestion control.

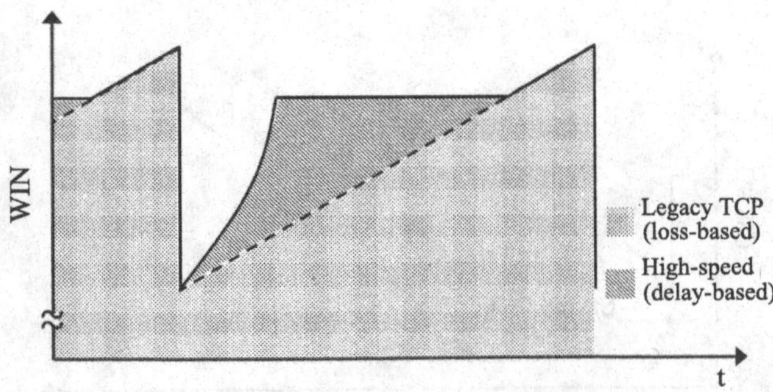

Fig. 2. Variation of Compound TCP Window

3 High-Speed TCP in Wireless Network

Compound TCP is implemented in Windows OS and the most-deployed TCP. CUBIC is implemented in Linux OS and the second-most used TCP [3]. So, in the current Internet, these two types of TCP frequently share the bottleneck link. With current trend of high-speed links in wired networks, a wireless access link which has generally lower bandwidth than wired links, might be the most likely bottleneck link when users access with wireless last mile access. Users do not care about what kind of access link they use, which means Compound TCP and CUBIC are generally used for transport layer congestion control also in wireless access. So, it is very important to understand how fairly Compound TCP and CUBIC share a wireless access link.

For design of high-speed TCP, response function is generally used for discussion in scalability, RTT fairness and TCP friendliness (with legacy TCP) in the congestion control. Response function for CUBIC, Compound TCP and legacy TCP is depicted in Fig. 3 (these response function is depicted by the equations in literatures [13][14]). Slope of response function in double logarithmic chart represents RTT-fairness. At the lower packet loss rate, a response function of high-speed TCP has intersection with legacy TCP, the higher TCP friendliness (to legacy TCP) it has. As shown in Fig. 3, response functions of Compound TCP (CTCP) and CUBIC are close to legacy TCP, which means these high-speed TCPs achieve TCP friendliness in low delay-bandwidth product region (in this region, packet loss rate is high). So, in wireless networks whose bandwidth was not so high, Compound TCP and CUBIC is said to work in low BDP

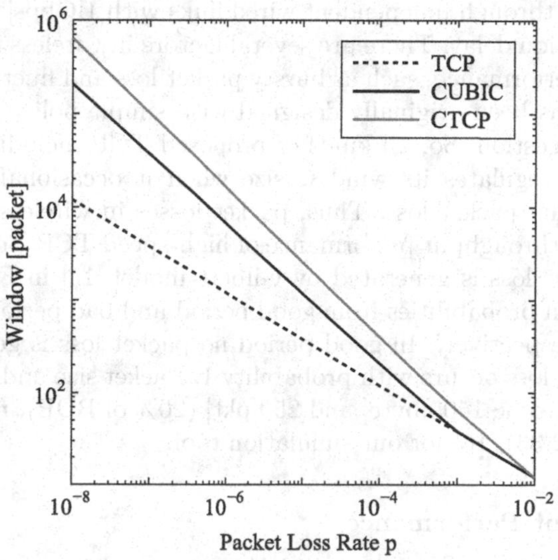

Fig. 3. Response Function

region. So, these two TCPs can fairly share bandwidth of wireless link because both of them has similar throughput to legacy TCP.

With remarkable growth of wireless networks, bandwidth of wireless channel is now still expanding as shown in LTE and IEEE 802.11n. This means Compound TCP and CUBIC will work in high BDP region even in wireless networks. Wireless networks have quite different features than wired networks. One of the most important technical feature which will affect TCP performance is packet loss due to wireless channel degradation (we call this packet loss gwireless lossh hereafter). When response function is derived for high-speed TCP, only packet loss due to congestion, i.e. buffer overflow in a droptail router, is taken into account. So, we cannot easily predict how fairly wireless bottleneck is shared by Compound TCP and CUBIC. Aim of the paper is revealing fairness issues of Compound TCP and CUBIC in wireless networks.

4 Fairness between CUBIC and CTCP in Wireless Networks

In this section, we evaluate fairness between CUBIC and Compound TCP in wireless networks. We mainly focus on how these two TCPs share a bottleneck link in bursty packet losses.

4.1 Simulation Model

Figure 4 shows our simulation model. We use simple model where two TCP sessions, one is a CUBIC session and the other is Compound TCP session, share a 150[Mbps] link. Before two sessions share 150[Mbps] wireless link at AP (access point), they come through independent wired links with 1[Gbps] bandwidth and 25[msec] propagation delay. There are several factors in wireless networks which will affect TCP performance, such as bursty packet loss and fluctuation of round trip time. TCP has been originally designed with simple policy that reason for packet loss is congestion. So, all kinds of proposed TCP including legacy TCP (TCP NewReno) regulates its window size when it occasionally observes (or implicitly finds out) packet loss. Thus, packet losses in wireless networks have great influence of throughput performance of high-speed TCP. So, we use simple model where burst loss is generated by Gilbert model [15] in Fig. 5. P and Q are state transition probabilities from good period and bad period and from bad to good period, respectively. In good period no packet loss is generated and in bad period packet loss occurs with probability 1. Packet size and buffer capacity in AP is assumed to be 1500[byte] and 250[pkt] (20% of BDP), respectively. We use ns-2 (release 2.33) [16] for our simulation tool.

4.2 Throughput Performance

Figure 6 shows throughput characteristics of CUBIC and Compound TCP. Total throughput of both TCPs is also depicted in this figure. Horizontal axis shows

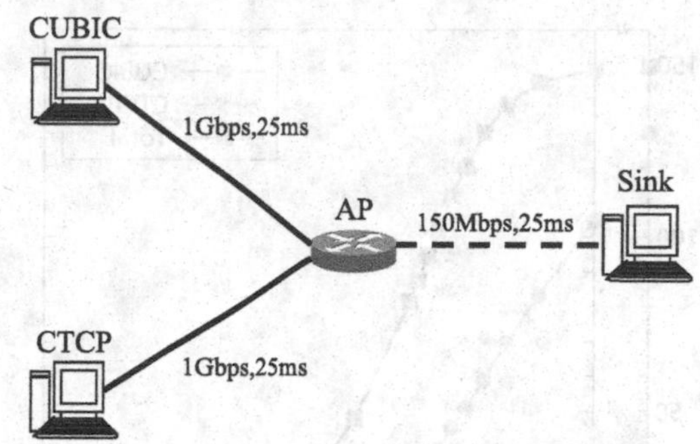

Fig. 4. Simulation Model

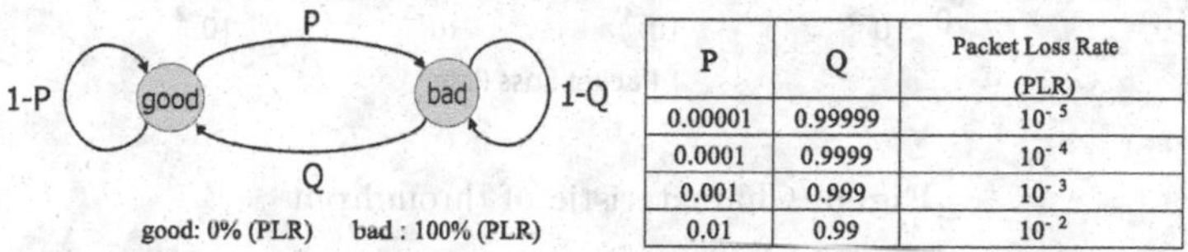

P	Q	Packet Loss Rate (PLR)
0.00001	0.99999	10^{-5}
0.0001	0.9999	10^{-4}
0.001	0.999	10^{-3}
0.01	0.99	10^{-2}

Fig. 5. Loss Model

packet loss rate in logarithmic scale. Vertical axis shows throughput of each TCP. Table 1 shows throughput of each TCP and fairness index [17].

As shown in Fig. 6, total throughput is significantly degraded with increase of packet loss rate. CUBIC throughput is gradually degraded. However, for Compound TCP, its throughput increases till it has maximum value at around $4.0 * 10^{-5}$ and decreases after that. Main reason for increase of Compound TCP throughput is bandwidth suppression by CUBIC occupancy is gradually resolved with decrease of CUBIC throughput. As shown in Table 1, fairness index is improved with increase of packet loss rate. So, with low loss rate, CUBIC significantly suppresses Compound TCP but this unfair situation is gradually resolved with increase of packet loss rate because CUBIC has moderate throughput.

In order to investigate the reason for these fairness dynamics, in the next section, we would like to show congestion window dynamics and queue behavior.

4.3 Congestion Window and Queue Length Dynamics

As described in response function in section III, CUBIC and Compound TCP work as high-speed TCP (aggressive increase of window) with low packet loss rate, such as packet loss rate below $1.0 * 10^{-4}$. In this section, we would like to carefully investigate and discuss about congestion window and queue length behavior in this low loss rate region, i.e. high BDP region. Figures 7, 8, 9 and 10 show congestion window and queue length dynamics for the case of no wireless loss, $1.0 * 10^{-5}$, $3.0 * 10^{-5}$ and $1.0 * 10^{-4}$ packet loss rates, respectively. Queue length at AP is depicted in these figures.

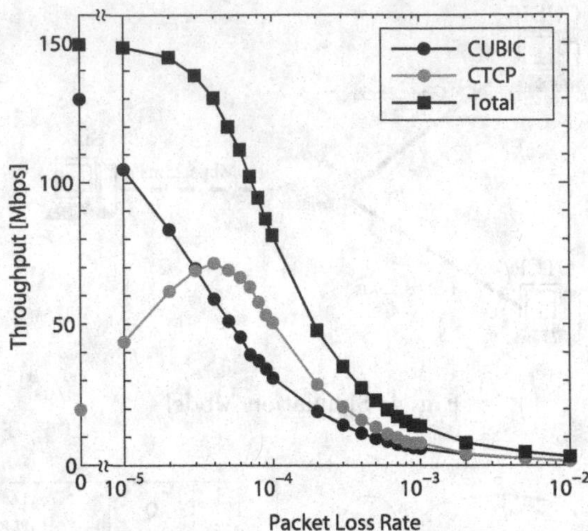

Fig. 6. Characteristic of throughput

Table 1. Throughput and Fairness Index to loss rate

	CUBIC[Mbps]	CTCP[Mbps]	Total [Mbps]	Fairness Index
no wireless loss	129.7	19.7	149.4	0.65
PLR 1.0*10^{-5}	104.7	43.6	148.3	0.85
PLR 3.0*10^{-5}	69.5	68.8	138.3	0.99
PLR 1.0*10^{-4}	30.9	50.4	81.3	0.94

As shown in Fig. 7, without wireless loss, CUBIC boosts its window size and window size of Compound TCP is significantly regulated. Delay-based part of Compound TCP regulates its window size with small queue size. However, CUBIC regulates its window size only with packet loss which occurs at large queue length. This gentle behavior of Compound TCP causes unfair condition.

When wireless loss happens even with low packet loss rate (say $1.0 * 10^{-5}$), as shown in Fig. 8, window size of CUBIC is degraded randomly with wireless caused loss. At this degraded timing of CUBIC, Compound TCP can increase its window size. This is because temporally regulated CUBIC decreases queue length of AP, which enables delay-based part of Compound TCP increase its window size. When packet loss rate increases to $3.0 * 10^{-5}$ (Fig. 9), randomly generated wireless loss decreases CUBIC window size so often that queue length cannot grow to buffer capacity. Decreased queue length makes delay-based part of Compound TCP increase its window size at the same level of CUBIC, which causes fair share of wireless link.

When packet loss rate is $1.0 * 10^{-4}$ (Fig. 10), wireless loss regulates both window sizes of CUBIC and Compound TCP too much. As shown in Fig. 10, queue length cannot grow, which means wireless bandwidth cannot be used efficiently

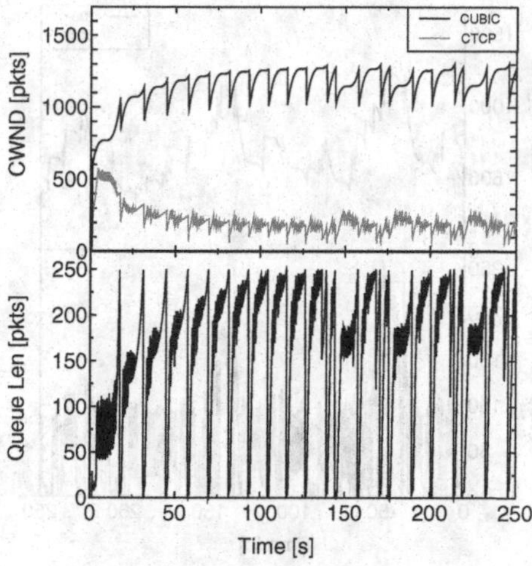

Fig. 7. Characteristic of Congestion Window and Queue Length (No Wireless Loss)

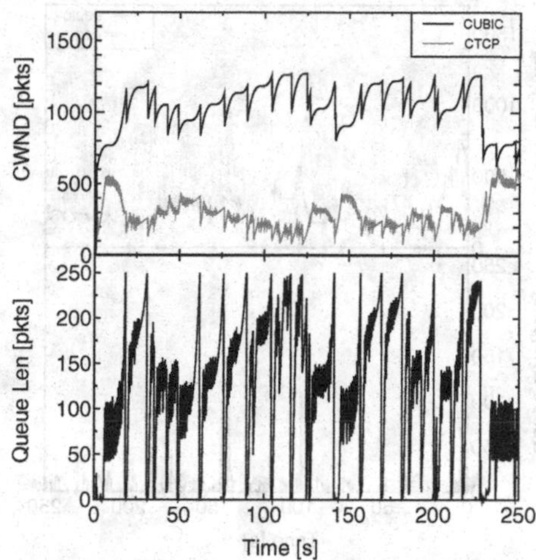

Fig. 8. Characteristic of Congestion Window and Queue Length (Packet Loss Rate $1.0 * 10^{-5}$)

(link bandwidth can be used efficiently when queue length grows moderately). With small queue size, delay-based part of Compound TCP boosts its window size, which causes larger window size of Compound TCP. So, fairness index is slightly degraded when compared with the case of $3.0 * 10^{-5}$ packet loss rate (as shown in Table 1).

In the current wireless networks, retransmission of layer 2 frame hides wireless channel degradation, which enables low packet loss rate observed in the network or transport layer. So, packet loss rate in wireless link will be in moderate region,

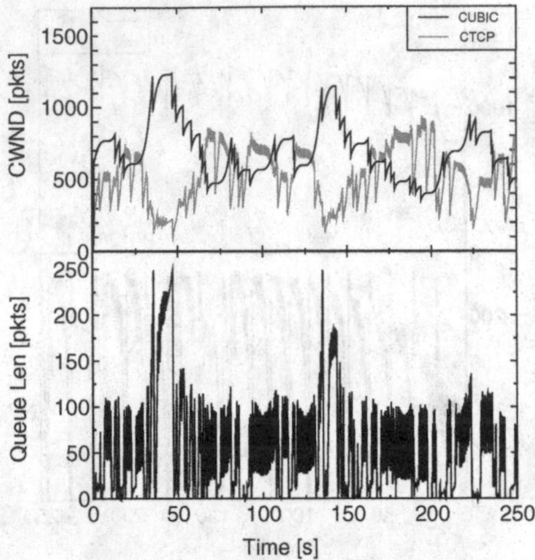

Fig. 9. Characteristic of Congestion Window and Queue Length (Packet Loss Rate $3.0 * 10^{-5}$)

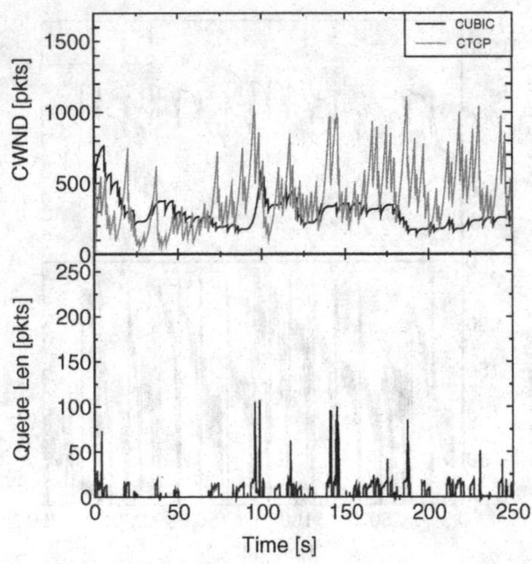

Fig. 10. Characteristic of Congestion Window and Queue Length (Packet Loss Rate $1.0 * 10^{-4}$)

which means CUBIC and Compound TCP will share wireless link fairly even in high BDP region.

5 Conclusion

To improve TCP throughput in high-speed network environment, various high-speed congestion controls have been proposed. Among them, CUBIC and Compound TCP have been implemented as default congestion control in Linux and

Microsoft Windows OS, respectively. Furthermore, high delay-bandwidth network is now emerging even in wireless networks with use of IEEE 802.11n and LTE. So, CUBIC and Compound TCP might work in aggressive mode in wireless environment. In this paper, we evaluate fairness issue of CUBIC and Compound TCP in high-speed wireless network. In the case of no wireless loss, CUBIC boosts its window size and window size of Compound TCP is significantly regulated. However, as a wireless loss increases, CUBIC decreases queue length of AP, which enables delay-based part of Compound TCP increase its window size. Therefore, CUBIC and Compound TCP share wireless link fairly even in high BDP region. It is important to investigate the variation of RTT as future work.

References

1. Floyd, S., Ratnasamy, S., Shenker, S.: Modifying TCP's Congestion Control for High Speeds (May 2002), `www.icir.org/floyd/papers/hstcp.pdf`
2. Yamamoto, M.: Research Trends in Congestion Control. IEICE Technical Report CS2011-32 (September 2011)
3. Afanasyev, A., Tilley, N., Reiher, P., Kleinrock, L.: Host-to-host congestion control for TCP. IEEE Communication Surveys and Tutorials 12(3), 304–342 (2010)
4. Rhee, I., Xu, L.: CUBIC: A New TCPFriendly HighSpeed TCP Variant. In: Proc. of the Third PFLDNet Workshop (February 2005)
5. Xu, L., Harfoush, K., Rhee, I.: Binary Increase Congestion Control(BIC) for Fast Long-Distance Networks. In: Proc. of IEEE INFOCOM (March 2004)
6. Leith, D., Shorten, R., Lee, Y.: H-tcp: A framework for congestion control in high-speed and long-distance networks. In: Proc. of PFLDNet Workshop (February 2005)
7. Floyd, S.: Highspeed tcp for large congestion windows. RFC 3649 (December 2003)
8. Caini, C., Firrincieli, R.: TCP Hybla: a TCP enhancement for heterogeneous networks. International J. Satellite Communications and Networking (August 2004)
9. Kelly, T.: Scalable TCP: improving performance in highspeed wide area networks. Computer Communications Review (April 2003)
10. linux-2.6.35.1, `http://www.kernel.org/pub/linux/kernel/v2.6/linux-2.6.35.1.tar.gz`
11. Tan, K., Song, J., Zhang, Q., Sridharan, M.: A compound TCP approach for high-speed and long distance networks. In: Proc. of IEEE INFOCOM (July 2005)
12. Mo, J., La, R.J., Anantharam, V., Walrand, J.: Analysis and Comparison of TCP Reno and Vegas. In: Proc. of IEEE INFOCOM (March 1999)
13. Rhee, I., Xu, L., Ha, S.: CUBIC for Fast Long-Distance Networks. IETF, Internet Draft, `draft-rhee-tcpm-cubic-02.txt`
14. Sridharan, M., Tan, K., Bansal, D., Thaler, D.: Compound TCP: A New TCP Congestion Control for High-Speed and Long Distance Network. IETF, Internet Draft, `draftsridharan-tcpm-ctcp-01.txt`
15. Gilbert, E.N.: Capacity of a burst-noise channel. Bell Systems Technical Jounal (September 1960)
16. Network Simulator ns-2, `http://www.isi.edu/nsnam/ns`
17. Jain, R., Chiu, D., Hawe, W.: A Quantitative Measure of Fairness and Discrimination for Resource Allocation in Shared Computer Systems. Digital Equipment Corporation. Technical Report TR-301 (September 1984)

Evaluation of SIP Call Setup Delay for VoIP in IMS

Mohamed El Mahdi Boumezzough, Noureddine Idboufker, and Abdellah Ait Ouahman

ENSA Marrakech, Cadi Ayyad University, Morocco
nasamehdi@gmail.com, {n_idboufker,aitouahman}@yahoo.fr

Abstract. IP Mulimedia Subsystem (IMS) is an architecture that can provide innovative solutions for multimedia services deployment regardless the type and network topology. New delivered value added services require significant changes to the multi-services IP network design, including the activation of multiple functions such as quality of service (QoS) capabilities, security mechanisms, multicast routing, etc. To ensure that services delivery meets the high expectations of end users, factors affecting QoS or user's quality of experience (QoE) must be properly considered. This paper will give a study of a the 'SIP Call Setup Delay' metric which will serve us to accomplish the QoE measurement in the case of VoIP sessions carried over IPv4 and IPv6 IMS networks.

Keywords: QoE, QoS, SIP, IMS, Call Setup Delay, IPv4, IPv6.

1 Introduction

The convergence phenomenon, modeled by the IMS (IP Multimedia Subsystem) architecture that started some years ago and that is accelerating will gradually remove the traditional boundaries between fixed and mobile communication systems. The success of IMS depends on satisfying the high expectations of end users. This led to the birth of the Quality of Experience (QoE). QoE is different from QoS which focuses on measuring performance from a network perspective. QoE is the term used to describe user perceptions of the service performance. On the other side, QoS is the ability of the network to provide a service at an assured service level.

The paper is organized as follows: we present the main components of the IMS architecture in Section 2. Then, we will introduce the concept of QoE and its correlation with QoS in section 3. In Section 4, we present our IMS testbed based on the "Open IMS Core". Section 5 describes our QoE evaluation of SIP Call Setup Delay and results. Finally, we present some conclusions in Section 6.

2 IMS Architecture

The IP multimedia subsystem (IMS) is rapidly becoming the de facto standard for real-time multimedia communications services. IMS standardization defines

V. Guyot (Ed.): ICAIT 2012, LNCS 7593, pp. 16–24, 2013.

open interfaces for session management, access control, mobility management, service control, and billing. This enables service providers to offer Session Initiation Protocol (SIP) communication services with more features and more flexibility than legacy services provide by circuit switched networks.

Fig. 1 presents a general overview of the IMS architecture [1] where one of its main characteristics is the separation between its different layers. Depending on the environment where IMS is being deployed, there are several access network alternatives like, for instance, UMTS (Universal Mobile Telecommunications System). The transport layer in IMS is in charge of providing IP connectivity to terminals, and allowing signaling and media exchange. The control layer constitutes the core of the IMS, and it is in charge of providing session control through call routing and policy enforcement. Finally, the service layer provides multimedia services to the overall IMS network.

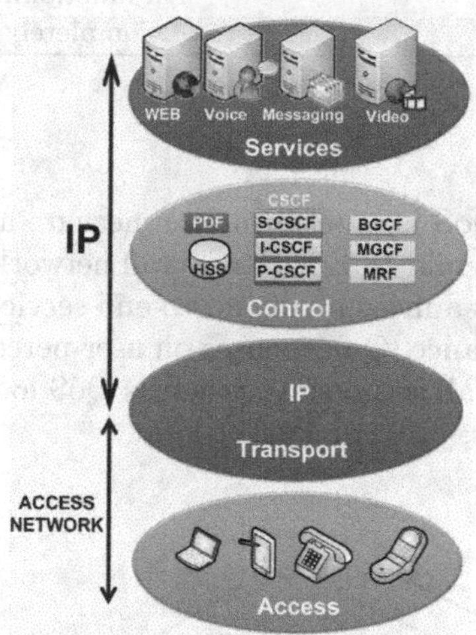

Fig. 1. IMS architecture overview

3 Introduction to QoE

3.1 Defining QoE

There are different definitions of QoE across current ETSI, ITU and other literature. ETSI TR 102 643 defines Quality of Experience as: "*A measure of user performance based on both objective and subjective psychological measures of using an Information and Communication Technologies service or product*" [2]. QoE takes into account technical parameters (e.g. QoS) and usage context variables (e.g. communication task) and measures both the process and outcomes of communication (e.g. user effectiveness, efficiency, satisfaction and enjoyment). Objective psychological measures do not rely on the opinion of the user (e.g. task completion time measured in seconds). While Subjective psychological measures are based on the user opinion (e.g. the perceived quality of a medium).

QoE is a concept comprising all elements of a subscriber's perception of the network and performance relative to expectations. The following table describes elements of user experience in the case of telephony service and the level of quality expectations for those elements [3].

Table 1. Elements of user experience for telephony services

Element of User's Experience	*Expectations for Level of Quality*
Reliability	Works every time
Availability	Always available
Call Completion	Completed successfully
Connect Latency	Rings in seconds
Voice Quality	Good as the PSTN
Speech Latency	Imperceptible
Services	All functioning properly
Billing	Completely accurate

3.2 QoE and QoS

As presented in Fig. 2, QoS is a performance measure at the packet level from a network point of view while QoE is the overall network performance from the user point of view. QoE is a measure of end-to-end service performance from the user perspective. For instance, QoE focuses on user-perceived effects [4], such as Call completion rate or Call setup time, whereas QoS focuses on network effects such as end-to-end delays, jitter or Packet loss.

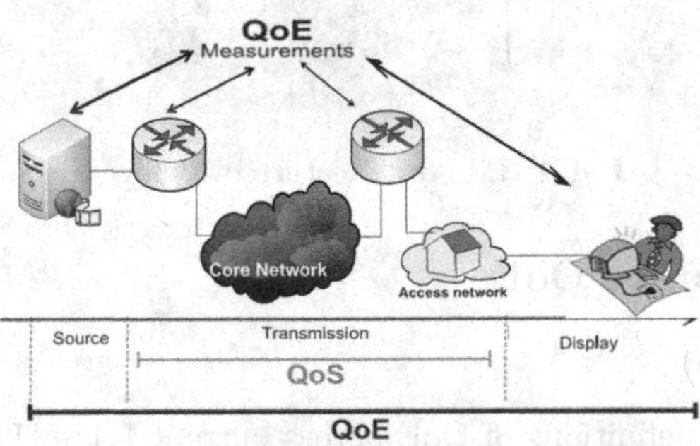

Fig. 2. QoE and QoS

3.3 Related Works

Some researches and development have been done in the field of QoE. Their main purposes can be classified in four categories: network planning, service and QoS provisioning, QoE and QoS monitoring and optimization. Four main approaches are used for QoE evaluation, which are:

1. QoE as an extension of QoS which use QoS perception models for network and service.
2. Objective cognitive schemas which use Human-Computer Interaction.
3. Subjective User Studies based on Marketing, and Business Models.
4. Subjective and Objective QoE which is an ITU-T Approach used for multimedia service and products.

4 IMS Testbed

4.1 Testbed Overview

The testbed is built based on the "Open IMS Core" [5] which is an Open Source implementation of IMS Call Session Control Functions (CSCFs) and a lightweight Home Subscriber Server (HSS). The figure below provides an overview of our experimental testbed.

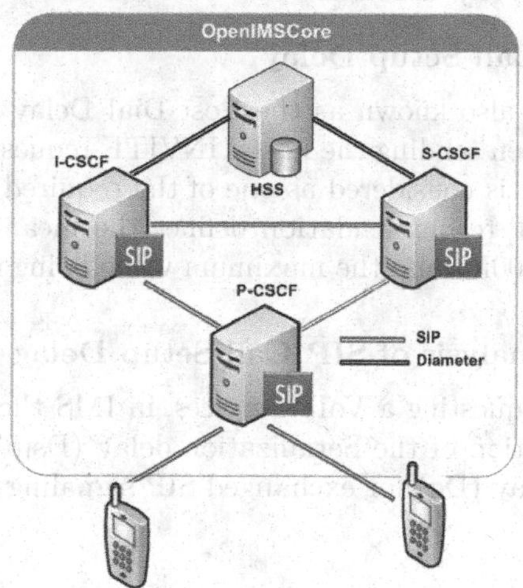

Fig. 3. Testbed Architecture

4.2 IMS Call Flow

The Fig. 4 depicts the SIP messages that are exchanged during VoIP Signaling at the IMS Access Network level. The signaling flows for call setup starts with a SIP invite request and finish with a 200 OK SIP response.

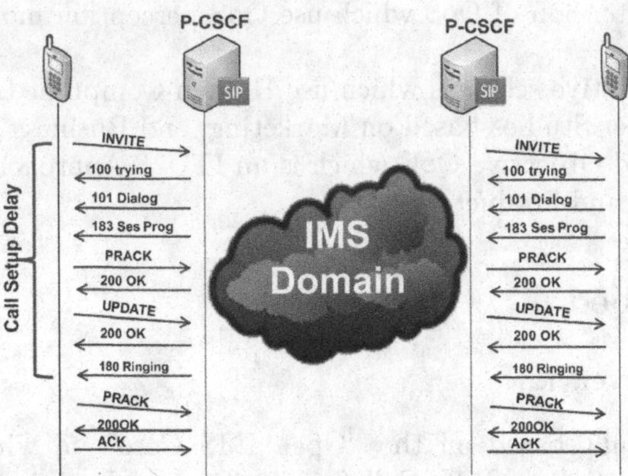

Fig. 4. Signaling flows for Call Setup in Access Network of IMS

5 Call Setup Delay Evaluation in IMS Environment

5.1 Definition of Call Setup Delay

The Call Setup Delay also known as the Post Dial Delay (PDD) is defined as the elapsed time between sending the initial INVITE request and receiving a 180 RINGING response. It is considered as one of the required parameters for QoE evaluation. The ITU-T recommendation defines the mean value of Call Setup Delay being equal to 800ms and the maximum value being equal to 1500 ms [6].

5.2 Theoretical Analysis of SIP Call Setup Delay

Theoretically, when requesting a VoIP services, in IMS the Call Setup Delay is defined as the summation of the Serialization delay (Dsip), Propagation delay (Dp) and Queuing delay (Dq) for exchanged SIP signaling messages during the call setup phase.

$$Dsip = Ds + Dp + Dq \ . \tag{1}$$

Where, the Serialization Delay is defined as the time it takes to send all the bits of a SIP message to the physical medium for transmission across the physical layer. The Propagation Delay is the time it takes for a SIP message bit to cross the physical link from end to end. Finally, the Queuing Delay is defined as the time the SIP message spends in the queue of the system.

In our SIP Call setup Delay's evaluation, we have only considered serialization delay, and we focused on the case where SIP signaling messages are exchanged via a Radio Access Network. The serialization delay formula is then defined as:

$$Ds = \frac{Msip}{Rlinq} \ . \tag{2}$$

Where, Msip is the length of SIP messages, and Rlink is transmission bit rate of Access link.

5.3 Numerical Results

For QoE evaluation, we need to define packet sizes for different SIP methods and responses. The table below lists the size for each SIP message established from packets captured by using Wireshark [7] in our experimental test bed. Also the number of exchanged messages, via the Radio Access Network for each SIP message is presented.

Table 2. Size and number of SIP messages

SIP message	*Numbers*	*Size(bytes)*
INVITE	2	1418
100 trying	2	555
101 Dialog	2	728
183 Session	2	1249
PRACK	2	1068
200 OK	2	451
200 OK with Session	2	917
UPDATE	2	1008
180 Ringing	2	740

Before transmitting SIP message, each message is encapsulated within a UDP datagram. This datagram is then encapsulated within an IPv4 or IPv6 packet. For this, the IPv4 layer adds 20 bytes header, and IPv6 adds 40 bytes header while UDP protocol adds an 8 byte header. Thus, table 3 shows the size of the SIP message including the UDP/IPv4 in the case VoIP calls over IPv4 and UDP/IPv6 header in the case VoIP calls over IPv6.

Table 3. Size of SIP messages including the UDP/IPv4 and UDP/IPv6 header

SIP message	*Size including UDP/IP4 header*	*Size including UDP/IP6 Header*
INVITE	1446	1466
100 trying	583	603
101 Dialog	756	776
183 Session	1277	1297
PRACK	1096	1116
200 OK	479	499
200 OK with Session	945	965
UPDATE	1036	1056
180 Ringing	768	788

By using equation number (2) and input data of table 3, table 4 shows the approximate Call Setup Delay for different values of bit rates in the case of VoIP calls transported over IPv4 and IPv6. Thus, for 9,6kbps bit rate the Call Setup

Delay is 13977 ms in the case VoIP calls over IPv4 and 14277 ms in the case VoIP calls over IPv6, while for 384kbps data speeds the Call Setup Delay value is then reduced to 349ms in the case VoIP calls over IPv4 and to 357ms in the case VoIP calls over IPv6.

Table 4. Call Setup Delay in IPv4 network versus IPv6 network

Speed(kbps)	*CSD IPv4(ms)*	*CSD IPv6(ms)*
9,6	13977	14277
14,4	9318	9518
56	2396	2447
128	1048	1071
220	610	623
260	516	527
384	349	357
1000	134	137

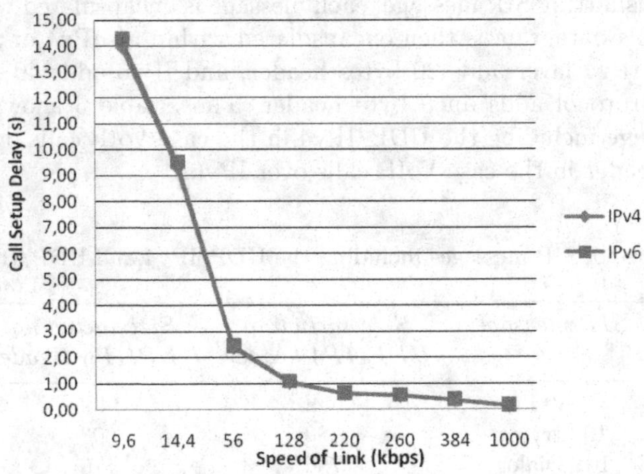

Fig. 5. Call Setup Delay for VoIP in IPv4 IMS and IPv6 IMS

Table 4 shows numerical results of the Call Setup Delay values depending on the version of the used IP protocol, the size of exchanged SIP messages, the number of these messages, and the bit rate of the wireless access link. By using results of table 4, Fig. 5 shows that the Call Setup Delay is conform to the ITU-T recommendation only for radio access link with a minimal bit rate equal to 128 kbps. Also, it is important to note that, for radio access links with a bit rate less than 128kbps, the obtained Call Setup Delay values when using IPv6 are

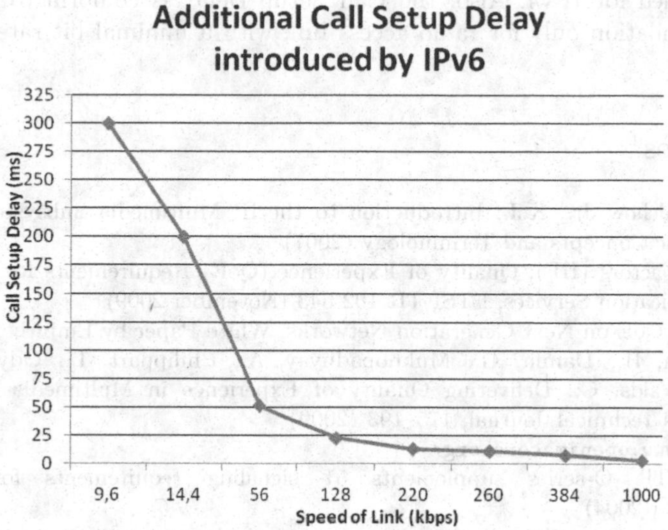

Additional Call Setup Delay introduced by IPv6

Call Setup Delay (ms)

325 300 275 250 225 200 175 150 125 100 75 50 25 0

9,6 14,4 56 128 220 260 384 1000

Speed of Link (kbps)

Fig. 6. Additional Call Setup Delay introduced by IPv6

greater than those obtained for IPv4. Thus, as shown in Fig. 6 from 128 kbps data speed, we can make VoIP calls over IPv6 in IMS without impacting the Call Setup Delay.

According to our results, we can propose various solutions in order to reduce SIP Call Setup Delay value. Our main propositions are:

- Compression of SIP messages using SigComp mechanism. This mechanism reduces the size of SIP messages and therefore contributes to the reduction of the Call Setup Delay.

- Optimization of SIP signaling flow in order to use a fewer number of SIP messages when establishing the VoIP session.

- Header compression contributes to the reduction of the total size of transmitted headers for each SIP message. The original headers should be decompressed at the reception end point.

6 Conclusion

QoE assessment is not an easy task. Indeed, their evaluation should take various parameters into consideration. The main challenges are development and standardization of objective and subjective QoE metrics.

In this paper, we presented an analytic model to evaluate the SIP Call Setup Delay for VoIP in IMS, we have measured SIP Call Setup Delay in IPv4 network and compared them with SIP Calls Setup Delays in the case of an IPv6 encapsulation. The results show that for radio access links with a bit rate less than 128kbps, the obtained Call Setup Delay values when using IPv6 are greater than those obtained for IPv4. Also, the Call Setup Delay is conform to the ITU-T recommendation only for radio access link with a minimal bit rate equal to 128 kbps.

References

1. (Ken) Salchow Jr., K.J.: Introduction to the IP Multimedia Subsystem (IMS): IMS Basic Concepts and Terminology (2007)
2. Human Factors (HF); Quality of Experience (QoE) Requirements for Real-time Communication Services, ETSI TR 102 643 (November 2009)
3. Assuring QoE on Next Generation Networks, White Paper by Empirix (2003)
4. Batteram, H., Damm, G., Mukhopadhyay, A., Philippart, L., Odysseos, R., Urrutia-Valds, C.: Delivering Quality of Experience in Multimedia Networks. Bell Labs Technical Journal, 175–193 (2009)
5. http://www.openimscore.org/
6. ITU-T TR Q-series supplements 51 signaling requirements for IP-QoS (December 2004)
7. http://www.wireshark.org/

MPLS-TP: OAM Discovery Mechanism

Mounir Azizi, Redouane Benaini, and Mouad Ben Mamoun

Data Mining & Network Laboratory, Department of Computer Science
Faculty of Science Mohammed V-Agdal University
Rabat, Morocco
mounir.azizi@gmail.com, {benaini,ben_mamoun}@fsr.ac.ma

Abstract. The present article is aimed to highlight issues happening when using multiple Operations, Administration and Maintenance (OAM) procedures for Multiprotocol Label Switching (MPLS) Transport Profile (MPLS-TP). We start by giving a quick review of what are MPLS-TP OAMs. Then we demonstrate how lack of interoperability of OAM solution is a real problem for operators. And finally, we suggest developing an OAM Discovery Mechanism (ODM) which can be adopted in order to help carriers to deal with mixed OAM environment.

Keywords: mpls-tp, OAM, Y.1731, 802.ag, 802.ah, MEP, MIP, MEG.

1 Introduction

MPLS-TP has a robust and a transport-like operations and management (OAM) capabilities. Carriers use OAM to provide reliable services with guaranteed service level agreements (SLA), while minimizing troubleshooting time and reducing operational expenses.

The general MPLS-TP OAM requirements are:

- Proactive (continuous) monitoring features, including continuity supervision, connectivity supervision, signal quality supervision (packet loss, frame delay, frame delay variation), alarm suppression, remote quality and continuity indication
- Proactive monitoring applications: Fault management, Performance/SLA monitoring, Protection switching
- Re-active/on-demand monitoring, including fault localization, signal quality measurement (throughput, ordering and error measurement, transfer delay, delay variation and jitter measurement)
- Communication channels, including protection switching head/tail-end coordination, network management, remote node management, service management [1].

There are two proposed standards for MPLS-TP OAM and no industry agreement on that. They are based on IETF (G.8113.2) and ITU-T (G.8113.1) recommendations. These two solutions propose using different format of Protocol Data Units (PDUs) and

V. Guyot (Ed.): ICAIT 2012, LNCS 7593, pp. 25–32, 2013.

are using different methods to satisfy MPLS-TP OAM Requirements [2]. European Advanced Networking Test Center (EANTC) has successfully conducted Multi-vendor Interoperability test for both proposed solutions (separately). Vendors implementing ITU-T OAM solution got less problem than IETF OAM solution. This is probably because of the luck of maturity of the second one and the Pre standard interpretation at this time [3] & [4].

As consequence, some equipments will run IETF based OAM solution; others will get ITU-T based one, and others will be supporting both of them with probably interworking functions (IWF). This make the MPLS transport Network very complex to operate and manual provisioning of OAM hard to do, which may increase Operating Expense (OpEx). In order to resolve this issue, we suggest using an automatic mechanism to discover which of OAM standard can be selected, to determine the Maintenance End Point-Identifier (MEP ID) without need to do manual provisioning, and to discover the OAM method that is supported by the MEP.

2 About MPLS-TP OAM

Three kind of OAM exist: Hop-by-hop (e.g. control plane based), Out-of-band OAM (e.g. User Datagram Protocol UDP return path) and In-band OAM (e.g. Pseudowire PW Emulation Edge-to-Edge PWE-3 Associated Channel ACh). Within the MPLS, the ACh is known as technique for in-band Virtual Circuit Connectivity Verification (VCCV) applicable only for PW, while Label Switched Path LSPs have no mechanism to differentiate user packets from OAM packets [5]. MPLS-TP extended the ACh to the Generic Associated Channel (G-ACh) and introduced a new label G-ACh Alert Label (GAL) to identify packets on the G-Ach as described in Figure.1. It is an in-band management channel on a PW or LSP that does not rely on routing, user traffic, or dynamic control plane functions. The OAM packets can then share the same path of user traffic, operate on a per-domain basis and/or across multiple domains, and are able to be configured in the absence of a control plane [6].

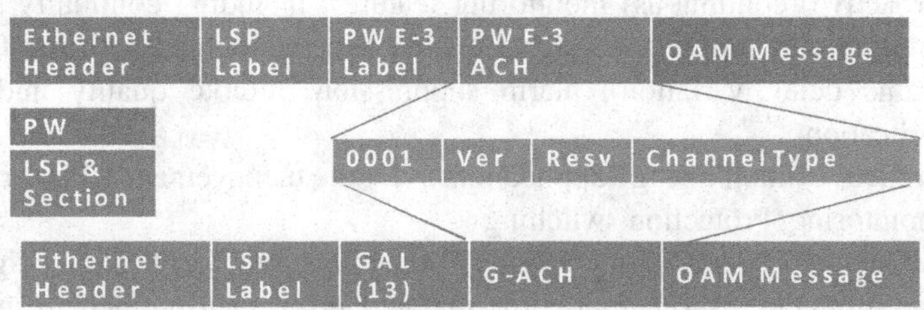

Fig. 1. Associated Channel for LSP, Section and PW

The network model of MPLS-TP OAM consists of:

- Different OAM Level (administrative domains). Each Level can be independently monitored by its own Ethernet Connectivity Fault Management (CFM) frames. The scope of OAM frames is limited to the domain in which the carried information is significant.

- Two plans: A "vertical plan" that represents the OAM entities across different administrative domains, and an "horizontal plan" that represents the OAM entities within a single administrative domain.

The Maintenance Entity Group (MEG) is the portion of the transport path that is being monitored or maintained. MEG endpoints are referred as management end points (MEPs) and intermediated nodes are referred as management intermediate points (MIPs). OAM message can be exchanged between MEPs, or from one MEP to other MIP. MEP handle OAM packet when it arrives at Label Edge Router (LER) because the label is popped and then the GAL is exposed which allow MEP to start processing by the corresponding OAM function. MIP can handle OAM packet using Time To Leave (TTL) mechanism. The TTL expiration causes the packet to be processed, and the existence of the GAL under the label for which the TTL expired causes the packet to be processed. MIPs cannot initiate OAM message, but may send an answer. There also some difference regarding the terminology used by ITU-T and IETF as show in "Table.1":

Table 1. IETF vs ITU-T Terminology

IETF	ITU-T
Maintenance Domain (MD)	Maintenance Entity (ME)
Maintenance Association (MA)	Maintenance Entity Group (MEG)
Maintenance Intermediate Point (MIP)	MEG Intermediate Point (MIP)
Maintenance Endpoint (MEP)	MEG Endpoint (MEP)
Maintenance Domain Level	MEG Level

2.1 ITU-T OAM Tools G.8113.1

ITU-T suggests reuse the same OAM Protocol Data Units (PDUs) and procedures defined in Ethernet OAM ITU-T Y.1731 [7]. Figure.2 shows that the presence of Y.1731 OAM PDU is identified by a single ACH channel Type. Within the OAM PDU, the OpCode field allows identifying the type of OAM frame.

<table>
<tr><td colspan="8">1</td><td colspan="8">2</td><td colspan="8">3</td><td colspan="8">4</td></tr>
<tr><td>1</td><td>2</td><td>3</td><td>4</td><td>5</td><td>6</td><td>7</td><td>8</td><td>1</td><td>2</td><td>3</td><td>4</td><td>5</td><td>6</td><td>7</td><td>8</td><td>1</td><td>2</td><td>3</td><td>4</td><td>5</td><td>6</td><td>7</td><td>8</td><td>1</td><td>2</td><td>3</td><td>4</td><td>5</td><td>6</td><td>7</td><td>8</td></tr>
<tr><td colspan="20">Tunnel Label GAL (13)</td><td colspan="3">TC</td><td>S</td><td colspan="8">TTL</td></tr>
<tr><td colspan="4">0001</td><td colspan="4">0000</td><td colspan="8">00000000</td><td colspan="16">Channel Type (Y.1731 OAM)</td></tr>
<tr><td colspan="3">MEL</td><td colspan="5">Version</td><td colspan="8">OpCode</td><td colspan="8">Flags</td><td colspan="8">TLV offset</td></tr>
<tr><td colspan="32">OAM PDU Payload area (Y.1731)</td></tr>
<tr><td colspan="4">End TLV</td><td colspan="28"></td></tr>
</table>

Fig. 2. ITU-T OAM Packet Format Definition

The ITU-T OAMs provide a set of mechanisms that meets the MPLS-TP OAM requirements. The methods and procedure supported are listed in "Table. 2":

Table 2. G.8113.1 OAM Functions [8]

OAM Function (IETF draft-bhh-mpls-tp-oam-y1731)				
Fault Management (FM)		**Performance Management (PM)**		**Other Applications**
Pro-active	Continuity check and Connectivity Verification (CC/CV)	Pro-active	Loss Measurement (LM)	Automatic Protection Switching (APS)
	Remote Defect Indication (RDI)			Management communication channel/ Signaling communication channel (MCC/SCC)
	Alarm Indication signal (AIS)		Delay Measurement (DM)	Vendor-specific (VS)
	Client signal Fail (CSF)			Experimental (EXP)
On-demand	Connectivity Verification (CV)	On-demand	Loss Measurement (LM)	Connectivity Verification (CV)
	Diagnostic test (DT)			Diagnostic test (DT)
	Locked Signal (LCK)		Delay Measurement (DM)	Locked Signal (LCK)

This OAM toolset claims to be mature and widely deployed. It is still under consensus of standardization. However G.8113.1 still requires a G-Ach codepoint to be assigned by IANA (IETF).

2.2 IETF OAM Tools G.8113.2

The IETF solution is based on the existing MPLS OAM toolset and provides the following functions: CC for proactive monitoring, CV for End-point verification, PM, FM and Diagnostics. This solution needs specifics extensions of Bidirectional Forwarding Detection (BFD) and LSP Ping and needs also to introduce new mechanisms for the function that are not available in MPLS such as loss and delay measurement. BFD and LSP should be able to run without IP (IP less).

Figure.3 shows how OAM packet format is structured:

<table>
<tr><td colspan="4">1</td><td colspan="12">2</td><td colspan="8">3</td><td colspan="8">4</td></tr>
<tr><td>1</td><td>2</td><td>3</td><td>4</td><td>5</td><td>6</td><td>7</td><td>8</td><td>1</td><td>2</td><td>3</td><td>4</td><td>5</td><td>6</td><td>7</td><td>8</td><td>1</td><td>2</td><td>3</td><td>4</td><td>5</td><td>6</td><td>7</td><td>8</td><td>1</td><td>2</td><td>3</td><td>4</td><td>5</td><td>6</td><td>7</td><td>8</td></tr>
<tr><td colspan="20">LSP Label</td><td colspan="3">TC</td><td>S</td><td colspan="8">TTL</td></tr>
<tr><td colspan="20">Tunnel Label (13)</td><td colspan="3">TC</td><td>S</td><td colspan="8">TTL</td></tr>
<tr><td colspan="4">0001</td><td colspan="4">version</td><td colspan="8">Reserved</td><td colspan="16">Channel Type</td></tr>
<tr><td colspan="32">ACH TLV Header</td></tr>
<tr><td colspan="32">OAM PDU Payload area (BFD, LSP Ping ...)</td></tr>
<tr><td colspan="4">End TLV</td><td colspan="28"></td></tr>
</table>

Fig. 3. IETF OAM Packet Format Definition

The methods and procedure supported are listed in "Table. 3":

Table 3. IETF MPLS-TP OAM Functions/RFCs

<table>
<tr><th colspan="3">Fault Management (FM)</th><th colspan="3">Performance Management (PM)</th></tr>
<tr><td rowspan="6">Pro-active</td><td>MPLS-TP Identifiers</td><td>RFC6370</td><td rowspan="9">Proactive PM OAM Functions and On demand PM OAM</td><td rowspan="2">Packet Loss Measurement (LM)</td><td rowspan="9">RFC6374
RFC6375</td></tr>
<tr><td>RDI – use BFD extension</td><td>RFC6428</td></tr>
<tr><td>AIS</td><td rowspan="3">RFC6427</td><td rowspan="3">Packet Delay Measurement (DM)</td></tr>
<tr><td>Link Down Indication (LDI)</td></tr>
<tr><td>Lock Report (LKR)</td></tr>
<tr><td>Config MPLS-TP OAM using LSP Ping</td><td>draft-absw-mpls-lsp-ping-mpls-tp-</td><td>Throughput measurement</td></tr>
<tr><td rowspan="3">On-demand</td><td>CV – use LSP Ping and BFD Extensions</td><td>RFC6426</td><td rowspan="3">Delay variation measurement (use DM)</td></tr>
<tr><td>Loopback Message/Replay (LBM/LBR)</td><td rowspan="2">RFC6435</td></tr>
<tr><td>Lock Instruct (LI)</td></tr>
</table>

IETF has overcome the luck of MPLS OAM by extending BFD and LSP Ping, and also by creating new tools in order to satisfy Transport-like OAM expectations.

3 OAM Discovery Mechanism

Both of proposed standards are satisfying MPLS-TP OAM requirements but are not subject of interoperability. The OAM Discovery Mechanism, which we propose in this paper, allows discovering the nature of each Maintenance End Point in order to swap the equipment supporting both standards to the appropriate OAM method. ODM can also be used to advertise supported OAM Functions by the MEP, and MEP-ID which are actually manually provisioned. In this chapter, we present briefly how OAM service are working, and we explain how ODM will run as preamble for MPLS-TP End-to-End OAM service operation.

3.1 The Reference Model

The reference model of MPLS-TP OAM is based in some important functional components: Maintenance Entity (ME), Maintenance End Group (MEG), Tandem Connection Monitoring (TCM), MEG End Points (MEPs), MEG Intermediate Points (MIPs), and Server MEP [9].

Maintenance Domain (MD) defines the part of the network that is managed and monitored. MEPs are the edges of MD. MD has a ME level from 0 to 7 in order to accommodate different deployment scenarios. The MA allows monitoring of a service instance within a MD, and each MA inside the MD inherits its ME level. A MEP terminates OAM frames in the MEG of the level it is configured for. Whether it drops or passes through packets from MEGs on different levels depends on the "direction" of the MEP (up or down) as show in Figure.4.

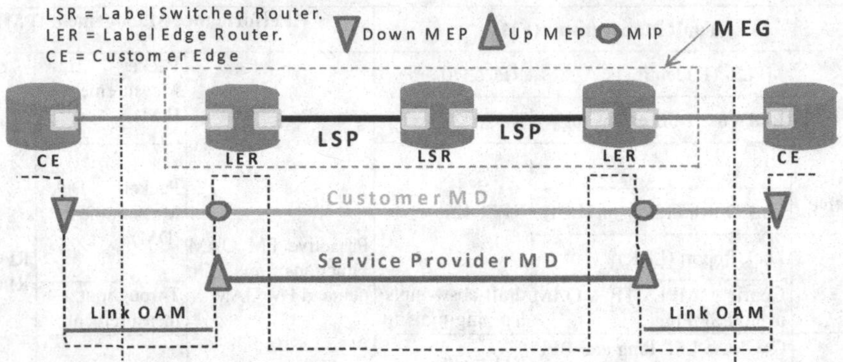

Fig. 4. Service OAM above MPLS-TP Domain

Most of functions ("Table.2" and "Table.3") needed for service layer OAM run between MEPs. Some requirements to set up these maintenance domains and association, most important are: local and remote MEP Identifier MEP ID, MA Identifier MAID and MD level [10]. Some other parameters are also needed like Continuity Check Message CCM interval Rate which is used for Pro-active OAM functions like CC/CV, RDI and Packet Loss Measurement. Any OAM discovery mechanism has to take in consideration these requirements. Other parameters need to be present represented by optional Type-Length-Value TLV to be able to offer negotiation facilities to both MEP. Thanks to TLV, MEPs can choose which OAM standard type will be selected. We also suggest adding a new TLV option where MEPs can use authentication to set up maintenance operation. This is can be very useful when Multiple Service Providers are interconnected to offer a service, especially for MEPs existing at boundaries of a network.

3.2 OAM Discovery Mechanism

ODM is a mechanism which permits two MEPs inside the same MEG to negotiate some options needed to set up maintenance operations. ODM prevent manual provisioning of Remote MEP ID and allow Vendors who are supporting both MPLS-TP OAM Standards (Y.1731 based one, and BFD/LSP based one) to select the appropriate method. Just like MPLS-TP OAM packet, ODM can be distinguished from user packets by using the G-ACh and GAL constructs. It is also mandatory that ODM have to be supported by each node that is member of a maintenance operation association.

ODM session starts by initiating a discovery message others remote MEP. This discovery message contains parameters like local MEP ID, MEG ID, MD level, Password if authentication enabled, and OAM Standard supported/preferred. The remote MEPs inside same MD and sharing same level will respond to the discovery message by discovery answer message with its corresponding parameters. The MEP that initiated ODM discovery process decide of which OAM standard is used and both sender/receiver MEP have the required parameter to set up a maintenance operation association as illustrated in Figure.5.

To make ODM suitable for large deployments, we propose to run it in two different modes: Active mode, where the MEP is responsible of initiating discovery process. After the discovery process has been initiated, both sides participate in discovery; and Passive mode, where a MEP does not initiate the discovery process but it is able to respond. Therefore, ODM establishment process will not start of all MEP inside same MD are in passive mode. The diagram bellow indicates the prerequisites to make ODM running as shown in Figure.6.

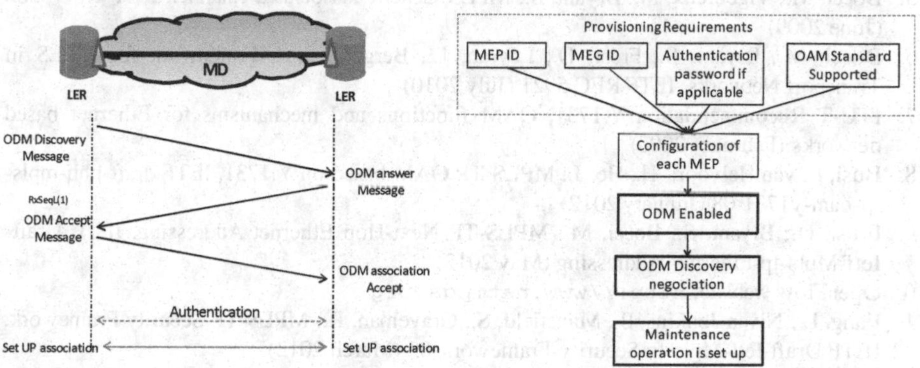

Fig. 5. ODM Establishment Process

Fig. 6. ODM functional diagram

Next step is to work on an openflow based testbed which is an MPLS capable open source solution [11].

4 Conclusion

It is important to say that having two OAM solutions from two different organizations standard IETF and ITU-T is not the solution, but unfortunately this is becoming reality and service provider and industry have to co-exist them sometimes by implementing interworking functionalities which are cost effective. ODM is not resolving interoperability MPLS-TP OAM problem, but it facilitates OAM discovery and automatic provisioning. ODM introduce also security aspect in MPLS-TP OAM which was the big absent of both Y.1731 and BFD/LSP OAM worlds. We proposed ODM while security and MEP identification are still under discussion and not fully standardized yet. Another work has to be done to handle security and how authentication can be elaborated [12]. There is also other area to develop regarding ODM, which is especially the case of MIP.

References

1. Vigoureux, M., Ward, D., Betts, M.: Requirements for Operations, Administration, and Maintenance (OAM) in MPLS Transport Networks. IETF RFC 5860 (May 2010)
2. Busi, I., Allan, D.: Operations, Administration, and Maintenance Framework for MPLS-Based Transport Networks. IETF RFC 6371 (September 2011)
3. Evolving Universal Services - Carrier Ethernet World Congress 2010 Multi-Vendor Interoperability Test, http://www.eantc.de/fileadmin/eantc/downloads/events/2007-2010/CEWC2010/EANTC-CEWC2010-WhitePaper-v1_2.pdf
4. Progressing Advanced MPLS & Carrier Ethernet Solutions - Public Multi-Vendor Interoperability Test, http://www.eantc.de/fileadmin/eantc/downloads/events/MPLS2011/EANTC-MPLSEWC2011-WhitePaper-1_0.pdf
5. Bocci, M., Vigoureux, M., Bryant, S.: MPLS Generic Associated Channel. IETF RFC 5586 (June 2009)
6. Bocci, M., Bryant, S., Frost, D., Levrau, L., Berger, L.: A Framework for MPLS in Transport Networks. IETF RFC 5921 (July 2010)
7. ITU-T Recommendation Y.1731, OAM functions and mechanisms for Ethernet based networks (February 2008)
8. Busi, I., van Helvoort, H., He, J.: MPLS-TP OAM based on Y.1731. IETF draft-bhh-mpls-tp-oam-y1731-08 (Junuary 2012)
9. Frost, D., Bryant, S., Bocci, M.: MPLS-TP Next-Hop Ethernet Addressing. IETF Draft-Ietf-Mpls-tp-Ethernet-Addressing (May 2012)
10. OpenFlow website, http://www.netfpga.org
11. Fang, L., Niven-Jenkins, B., Mansfield, S., Graveman, R.: MPLS-TP Security Framework. IETF Draft-Ietf-Mpls-tp-Security-Framework-03 (March 2012)

Supporting Data Center Management through Clustering of System Data Streams

Stefania Tosi, Sara Casolari, and Michele Colajanni

Department of Information Engineering
University of Modena and Reggio Emilia
{stefania.tosi,sara.casolari,michele.colajanni}@unimore.it

Abstract. Aggregating large data sets related to hardware and software resources into clusters is at the basis of several operations and strategies for management and control. High variability and noise characterizing data collected from system resources monitoring prevent the application of existing solutions that are affected by low accuracy and scarce robustness.

We present a new algorithm which extends the clustering method to data center management because it is able to find groups of related objects even when correlation is hidden by high variability.

Our experimental evaluation performed on both synthetic and real data shows the accuracy and robustness of the proposed solution, and its ability in clustering servers with correlated functionality.

Keywords: data clustering, high variability, correlation index, data management.

1 Introduction

Clustering aims to partition data into groups based on their similarity. There is a huge literature on clustering models applied to data related to almost any scientific field and to pursue a large range of different purposes [1][2]. For example, clustering can be used to improve marketing by customer segmentation, to determine homogeneous groups of web users, to structure large amounts of text documents, or to develop thematic maps from satellite images [3]. Many clustering models have been proposed [1][2]. Although definitions of similarity vary from one clustering model to another, most of these models use distances (e.g., Euclidean distance [4] or cosine distance [5]) or correlation indexes (e.g., Pearson product moment [6] or Spearman and Kendall ranks [7][8]) as their measure of similarity. In summary, distance-based approaches require similar data to have close values in order to be clustered in the same group; correlation-based approaches denote that two data are similar if they exhibit some degree of dependency.

In both instances, the similarity measure has a high impact on the quality of resulting clusters. The better the accuracy and robustness of the measure in finding similarities, the more accurate and robust the clustering model is. Existing distance measures and correlation indexes are accurate and robust in disclosing similarity except when data exhibit high variability. In highly variable contexts, data assume values far apart from each other and therefore distance functions are inadequate in finding similarity. Moreover, existing correlation indexes fail in capturing correlations when relationships

V. Guyot (Ed.): ICAIT 2012, LNCS 7593, pp. 33–46, 2013.

among data are hidden by high variability. In these scenarios, the most popular correlation indexes, such as the Pearson coefficient [6], the Spearman rank [7], the Kendall rank [8], and the Local Correlation index [9], are unable to capture correlations even when they exist.

In this paper, we propose a new correlation index that is able to disclose similar data even when they are characterized by high variability. The accuracy and robustness of the proposed correlation index is achieved through an original approach that separates trend patterns from perturbation patterns, and evaluates correlation by computing the similarity of trend patterns. Trends allow us to reveal how a generic time series may be similar to the other one. Therefore, the basic idea is that, when dealing with highly variable data, it is convenient: (i) to extract from data all the information about trends by removing perturbations that mask the presence of possible correlations between the measures; (ii) to measure how close the extracted trends are.

On the basis of the closeness of the extracted trends, clustering models can group data presenting similarity also in highly variable contexts, such financial stock markets [10], geophysical processes [11], network traffic [12], workloads [13] and data centers resource metrics [14]. Data related to these contexts may have strong correlations masked by perturbations related to the nature of the applications. For example, in Internet-based services, network traffic volume and response times change in accordance with the volume of user requests [15], but these relationships are masked by perturbations. Nevertheless, when correlations exist, the proposed index is able to identify them and clustering algorithms can cluster data accordingly. The results are demonstrated on synthetic and real data characterized by high variability.

The remainder of this paper is organized as follows. Section 2 defines the problem of correlation clustering for highly variable datasets. Section 3 presents the proposed algorithm. Section 4 evaluates the performance in capturing correlations and clustering data referring to synthetic and real scenarios. We conclude the paper in Section 5 with some final remarks.

2 Problem Definition

Let us define the clustering process for time series in a formal way. We assume that the dataset $\boldsymbol{X} = \{\mathbf{x}_1, \ldots, \mathbf{x}_N\}$ collects all the time series of a monitored process, where a time series $\mathbf{x}_j = [x_{j1}, \ldots, x_{jn}]$ is a vector collecting a time-ordered discrete sequence of data points that can be sampled once. We are interested in partitioning the time series into K clusters $\mathcal{C} \equiv \{\mathcal{C}_1, \ldots, \mathcal{C}_K\}$ $(K \leq N)$, such that:

1. $\mathcal{C}_i \neq \varnothing, i = 1, \ldots, K$;
2. $\bigcup_{i=1}^{K} \mathcal{C}_i = \boldsymbol{X}$;
3. $\mathcal{C}_i \cap \mathcal{C}_j = \varnothing, i, j = 1, \ldots, K$ and $i \neq j$.

Cluster creation requires the selection of a similarity measure, according to which data are grouped so that the similarity between data within a cluster is larger than the similarity between data belonging to different clusters. The *correlation index*, ρ, measures the similarity between two time series $\mathbf{x}_i$ and $\mathbf{x}_j \in \boldsymbol{X}$. The absolute value of the correlation index ranges between 0 and 1. When $\rho = 0$, there is no correlation between the two time series, while $\rho = 1$ indicates a complete correlation between $\mathbf{x}_i$ and $\mathbf{x}_j$. The literature offers several guidelines for the best interpretation of the value of the correlation index [16][6], but all criteria depend on the context and purposes of the analysis. As this paper does not refer to a specific scenario, we prefer to adopt the most general interpretation indicating a *strong correlation* when $\rho > 0.5$, and a *weak correlation* for $\rho \leq 0.5$ (e.g., [16]). Different choices for the threshold do not impact the main conclusions of this paper.

This paper proposes a new similarity measure for correlation clustering in datasets exhibiting a high degree of variability where existing models (e.g., [6][9][7][8]) are affected by several problems. In accordance with [12], high variability is a phenomenon by which a set of observations takes values that vary over orders of magnitude, with most observations taking values around the time series trend (i.e., *trend pattern*) and some observations departing from it with appreciable frequency, even taking extremely large values with non-negligible probability (i.e., *perturbation pattern*). Trend patterns represent the tendency of a time series that may be related to the other time series, while perturbation patterns consist of random observations hiding trends. A high standard deviation is the most typical trademark of a highly variable dataset. This characteristic implies a trend pattern that is hard to identify because it is masked by perturbations. In this paper, we use standard deviation as a measure of data variability.

The ability of a correlation model in detecting similarity among correlated time series is measured in terms of *accuracy*. The ability in guaranteeing a stable correlation index when conditions do not change is measured in terms of *robustness*. In the case of highly variable time series, the most popular correlation models are affected by two main problems:

1. low accuracy, since they are unable to detect similarities even among correlated time series;
2. low robustness, since they do not guarantee a stable evaluation of the correlation index, even when the relationships between the time series do not change.

The problems of correlation indexes affect the performance of correlation clustering models. Indeed, existing correlation indexes as similarity measures for clustering in highly variable data cause low clustering accuracy and low clustering robustness. In practice, time series with strong correlation may be clustered in different sets; similarly, uncorrelated time series may be assigned to the same cluster. Moreover, using existing correlation indexes may cause quite different clustering results for different evaluations even when the similarity between time series does not change.

For these reasons, in highly variable contexts there is the need of a new similarity measure able to disclose correlations in an accurate and robust way.

3 Clustering of Highly Variable Datasets

In this section, we present a clustering model aiming to disclose groups of similar datasets in highly variable contexts. It modifies the complete-linkage clustering model [17] by adopting a measure of similarity based on a novel correlation index, namely *CoHiVa* (*Co*rrelation for *Hi*ghly *Va*riable data), that is able to capture correlation between time series even when it is hidden by perturbations.

The proposed clustering algorithm is based on the following steps:

1. Start with N singleton clusters $\{\mathcal{C}_1, \ldots, \mathcal{C}_N\}$, where $\mathcal{C}_i = \mathbf{x}_i$.
2. Compute the NxN similarity matrix $\mathcal{D}$ containing the CoHiVa correlation indexes $\rho(\mathbf{x}_i, \mathbf{x}_j)$ between all pairs of time series $\mathbf{x}_i$, $\mathbf{x}_j$ in $\boldsymbol{X}$ by the following procedure:
   (a) extract from time series $\mathbf{x}_i$, $\mathbf{x}_j$ all main patterns, that correspond to trend patterns and perturbation patterns;
   (b) remove errors contaminating the collected time series;
   (c) select the trend patterns by discarding highly variable patterns containing information about perturbations;
   (d) compute the CoHiVa correlation index between $\mathbf{x}_i$, $\mathbf{x}_j$ by evaluating the similarity between their trend patterns.
3. Find the most correlated pair of clusters in the current clustering:
$$\rho(\mathbf{x}_r, \mathbf{x}_s) = \max_{1 \leq i,j \leq N, i \neq j} \rho(\mathbf{x}_i, \mathbf{x}_j). \tag{1}$$
4. Combine cluster $\mathcal{C}_r$ and cluster $\mathcal{C}_s$ to form a new cluster, denoted as $\mathcal{C}_{(r,s)}$.
5. Update the similarity matrix $\mathcal{D}$ by deleting the rows and columns corresponding to clusters $\mathcal{C}_r$ and $\mathcal{C}_s$ and by adding a row and a column corresponding to the early created cluster. The similarity between the new cluster $\mathcal{C}_{(r,s)}$ and a generic old cluster $\mathcal{C}_k$ is defined as:
$$\rho(\mathbf{x}_k, \mathbf{x}_{(r,s)}) = \max(\rho(\mathbf{x}_k, \mathbf{x}_r), \rho(\mathbf{x}_k, \mathbf{x}_s)). \tag{2}$$
6. Repeat steps 3)-4)-5) until all objects are in one cluster.

This algorithm results in an organized tree according to the similarity matrix build through CoHiVa. Cutting the tree at a given height will give a partitioning clustering at a selected precision.

The steps for the computation of the similarity matrix are detailed below.

a) Pattern Extraction. Let us consider a time series $\mathbf{x} \equiv [x_1, \ldots, x_n]$ of a dataset $\boldsymbol{X}$. The first goal is to identify the main patterns in $\mathbf{x}$, where patterns correspond to trends (i.e., periodic and seasonal components) and perturbations. To this end, we apply the Singular Value Decomposition (SVD) [9] to the auto-covariance matrix of the time series. Among the spectral decomposition techniques, SVD is considered as the baseline technique for separating existing patterns without any assumption about the statistical characteristics of the datasets [18][19]. In practice, we estimate the full auto-covariance matrix of the time series $\mathbf{x}$ that is defined as:

$$\boldsymbol{\Phi}(x) = \mathbf{x} \otimes \mathbf{x}, \tag{3}$$

where $\boldsymbol{\Phi}(x)$ is the auto-covariance matrix of $\mathbf{x}$.

Then, we compute the SVD of the auto-covariance matrix $\boldsymbol{\Phi}(x)$ as follows:

$$\boldsymbol{\Phi}(x) = \mathbf{U}(x)\boldsymbol{\Sigma}(x)\mathbf{V}(x)^T, \tag{4}$$

where $\mathbf{U}(x) \in \mathbb{R}^{t \times p}$, $\boldsymbol{\Sigma}(x) \in \mathbb{R}^{p \times p}$ and $\mathbf{V}(x) \in \mathbb{R}^{t \times p}$.

The columns $\mathbf{v}_i$ of $\mathbf{V}(x) \equiv [\mathbf{v}_1, \ldots, \mathbf{v}_p]$ are the right singular vectors of $\boldsymbol{\Phi}(x)$. Similarly, the columns $\mathbf{u}_i$ of $\mathbf{U}(x) \equiv [\mathbf{u}_1, \ldots, \mathbf{u}_p]$ are the left singular vectors of $\boldsymbol{\Phi}(x)$. Finally, $\boldsymbol{\Sigma}(x) \equiv \text{diag}[s_1, \ldots, s_p]$ is a diagonal matrix with positive values s_i, called the singular values of $\boldsymbol{\Phi}(x)$.

b) Removing Errors. The singular vectors corresponding to small singular values are only composed by errors [20] that usually contaminate the measured variables. The contribution of these errors must be discarded by eliminating the singular vectors corresponding to the smallest singular values [21]. By retaining just the principal vectors corresponding to the highest k singular values $(k < p)$ we can reconstruct a *k-dimensional approximation* of the correlation matrix:

$$\bar{\boldsymbol{\Phi}}(x) \equiv \bar{\mathbf{U}}(x)\bar{\boldsymbol{\Sigma}}(x)\bar{\mathbf{V}}(x)^T, \tag{5}$$

where $\bar{\mathbf{U}}(x) \equiv [\bar{\mathbf{u}}_1, \ldots, \bar{\mathbf{u}}_k]$, $\bar{\mathbf{V}}(x) \equiv [\bar{\mathbf{v}}_1, \ldots, \bar{\mathbf{v}}_k]$ and $\bar{\boldsymbol{\Sigma}}(x) \equiv \text{diag}\,[\bar{s}_1, \ldots, \bar{s}_k]$.

Literature on SVD gives little importance to the problem of dynamically selecting the appropriate number of principal vectors that capture the patterns (e.g., [9][18]). A common approach is to choose a fixed number of principal vectors independently of data characteristics, but this choice is unsuitable to time varying contexts where the statistical properties of data continuously change. Hence, we choose a threshold-based method that takes into account the characteristics of the considered data as in [22]. We select the principal vectors contributing to 90% of variation, and discard singular vectors contributing for less than 10%. The variable number of principal vectors used to capture the main patterns of the time series is denoted by k.

c) Selection of Trend Patterns. We now analyze the main patterns of $\mathbf{x}$ in order to understand the embedded information. The goal is to retain just trend patterns. However, in contexts characterized by high variability it is expected that the extraction includes also some perturbation patterns among the k principal vectors [23]. As these last patterns prevent the identification of trends and their possible correlations, we have to discard them. The idea is to build a new matrix based on a subspace of $\hat{k} \leq k$ principal vectors that captures just trend patterns.

To remove perturbation patterns from $\bar{\mathbf{U}}(x)$, we compute the Hurst exponent H of the k principal vectors by means of the R/S analysis of Hurst [24]. The Hurst exponent provides a measure of whether the data has pure random variability or even some underlying trends [25]. For each principal vector $\bar{\mathbf{u}}_i \in \bar{\mathbf{U}}(x)$ of length t, we define its cumulative deviate series $Z_n = \sum_{j=1}^{n}(\bar{u}_j - m)$, where $n = 1, 2, \ldots, t$, $\bar{u}_j$ is the j−th element of the i−th principal vector and m is the mean of $\bar{\mathbf{u}}_i$.

To define the rescaled range $\frac{R(t)}{S(t)}$, we compute the range as following:

$$R(t) = \max\left(Z_1, Z_2, \ldots, Z_t\right) - \min\left(Z_1, Z_2, \ldots, Z_t\right), \tag{6}$$

and the standard deviation as:

$$S(t) = \sqrt{\frac{1}{t}\sum_{j=1}^{t}\left(\bar{u}_j - m\right)^2}. \tag{7}$$

The *Hurst exponent* H is defined in terms of the asymptotic behavior of the rescaled range as a function of the time span of a time series as follows [24]:

$$\mathrm{E}\left[\frac{R(t)}{S(t)}\right] = Ct^H \quad \text{as } t \to \infty, \tag{8}$$

where $E[\frac{R(t)}{S(t)}]$ is the expected value of the rescaled range, t is the number of observations in a time series, and C is a constant.

If the estimated Hurst exponent H_i of a principal vector $\bar{\mathbf{u}}_i \in \bar{\mathbf{U}}(x)$ is close to 0.5, then we can conclude that $\bar{\mathbf{u}}_i$ contains perturbations. On the other hand, if the Hurst exponent remains far from 0.5, then we can assume that $\bar{\mathbf{u}}_i$ is a trend principal vector. Our model builds up a new $\hat{\mathbf{U}}(x)$ matrix containing only the $\hat{k}$ trend principal vectors $\hat{\mathbf{u}}_j$, $j = 1, \ldots, \hat{k}$ as follows:

$\forall \bar{\mathbf{u}}_i \in \bar{\mathbf{U}}(x), \quad i = 1, \ldots, k$:

$$\hat{\mathbf{u}}_j \equiv \bar{\mathbf{u}}_i \quad \text{if} \quad H_i < 0.5 - \frac{\delta}{2} \quad \text{or} \quad H_i > 0.5 + \frac{\delta}{2}, \tag{9}$$

where δ is a two-sided 95% confidence interval empirically computed depending on the number of samples [25].

This separation approach allows us to remove perturbation patterns in the time series and to focus only on trends. By focusing on the $\hat{k}$ trend principal vectors, we are able to construct a new approximation of the $\boldsymbol{\Phi}(x)$ matrix that we name *trend approximation*. Given $\hat{\mathbf{U}}(x) \equiv [\hat{\mathbf{u}}_1, \ldots, \hat{\mathbf{u}}_{\hat{k}}]$, the corresponding singular values and the right singular vectors form the matrices $\hat{\boldsymbol{\Sigma}}(x) \equiv \mathrm{diag}\,[\hat{s}_1, \ldots, \hat{s}_{\hat{k}}]$ and $\hat{\mathbf{V}}(x) \equiv [\hat{\mathbf{v}}_1, \ldots, \hat{\mathbf{v}}_{\hat{k}}]$, respectively. Through these matrices, the trend approximation of the correlation matrix using only trend patterns is given by:

$$\hat{\boldsymbol{\Phi}}(x) \equiv \hat{\mathbf{U}}(x)\hat{\boldsymbol{\Sigma}}(x)\hat{\mathbf{V}}(x)^T. \tag{10}$$

The matrix $\hat{\boldsymbol{\Phi}}(x)$ approximates the trend behavior of $\boldsymbol{\Phi}(x)$ by removing error information and perturbation patterns that affect the identification of the trends of the time series.

d) Computation of the CoHiVa Index. After the extraction of the main trends from the time series, we evaluate whether they are correlated or not by computing how close their trends are. As example, we compute the correlation index of the time series $\mathbf{x}_i$ and $\mathbf{x}_j$ by measuring their trend similarity. When the matrices $\hat{U}(x_i)$ and $\hat{U}(x_j)$ are similar, the time series $\mathbf{x}_i$ and $\mathbf{x}_j$ follow similar (linear or non-linear) trends, and we can consider that the original time series are correlated. In geometric terms, if two time series are correlated, then the trend principal vectors of each set should lie within the subspace spanned by the trend principal vectors of the other set. For this reason, we project the trend principal vectors of the time series $\mathbf{x}_i$ into the trend principal vectors of $\mathbf{x}_j$, as following:

$$\rho(\mathbf{x}_i, \mathbf{x}_j) = \frac{1}{\hat{k}(x_i) + \hat{k}(x_j)}(\|\hat{\mathbf{U}}(x_i)^T\hat{\mathbf{U}}(x_j)\| + \|\hat{\mathbf{U}}(x_j)^T\hat{\mathbf{U}}(x_i)\|), \tag{11}$$

where $\hat{k}(x_i)$ and $\hat{k}(x_j)$ are the amounts of trend principal vectors of $\boldsymbol{\Phi}(x_i)$ and $\boldsymbol{\Phi}(x_j)$, respectively, while $\hat{\mathbf{U}}(x_i)$ and $\hat{\mathbf{U}}(x_j)$ are the trend principal vectors matrices collecting them.

4 Performance Evaluation

We evaluate the performance of our proposal on several synthetic datasets (Section 4.1), as well as on real datasets referring to the system resource measures monitored on a distributed system (Section 4.2). Performance are evaluated in terms of accuracy and robustness in finding correlation and accordingly clustering datasets characterized by high variability.

4.1 Synthetic Datasets

We initially evaluate the performance of the proposed correlation index in finding correlation on synthetic settings, and we compare it against the results of several state-of-the-art alternatives. As terms of comparison, we consider the following correlation indexes: the Pearson product moment (Pearson) [6], the Spearman rank (Spearman) [7], the Kendall rank (Kendall) [8], and the Local Correlation index (LoCo) [9].

We collect performance over 1000 independent generations of synthetic data, that are quite useful because we have full control on their actual degree of correlation. As a consequence, we can exactly evaluate the performance of all indexes. We generate datasets of correlated time series taking values in the range $[0,1]$. In order to evaluate the ability of the correlation indexes in capturing correlations for different levels of variability, we introduce perturbations from $N(0,\sigma)$, where $\sigma \in \{0.01, 0.05, 0.1, \ldots, 0.5\}$ is the standard deviation that quantifies the intensity of perturbations added to data [26]. Despite the intensity of perturbation, we expect the optimal correlation index to be close to $\rho = 1$ for any evaluation.

The first set of experiments evaluates the accuracy of the correlation indexes when datasets are characterized by different intensities of perturbations. We define the *accuracy* of a correlation index as its ability in capturing correlation when data present some relationship. For example, in the synthetic scenario considered in this section, an accurate correlation index should obtain a value close to 1.

In Figure 1, we report the average correlation results of 1000 independent generations of synthetic data for different σ values. We remind that we consider a strong correlation when $\rho > 0.5$, and a weak correlation for $\rho \leq 0.5$ [16]. As expected, we see a decrease of all correlation indexes for increasing values of σ, but the impact of perturbations is quite different for the considered indexes. When the dispersion is low ($\sigma \leq 0.2$), all indexes are able to capture the strong correlation among data. When the dispersion increases ($\sigma > 0.2$), the Kendall rank is the first losing its ability of detecting data correlation. In higher variable contexts ($\sigma > 0.3$), only the CoHiVa index captures the strong data correlation, because its values are always higher than 0.65.

The accuracy of a correlation index must be combined with information about its *robustness*. Generally speaking, the robustness of a correlation index assesses the reliability of its results across different evaluations. We quantify the robustness in terms

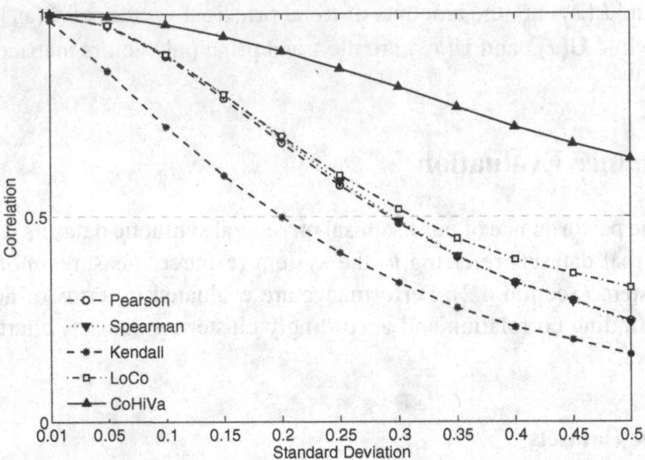

Fig. 1. Analysis of accuracy of correlation indexes

of *coefficient of variation* (CoV) for different experimental evaluations. The coefficient of variation is defined as the ratio of the standard deviation to the mean of the correlation index over all the experiments. A lower CoV denotes a better robustness of the correlation index.

We evaluate the robustness of the results obtained so far. Table 1 reports the CoV of each considered correlation index, where the columns refer to the increasing values of perturbation intensity, σ, while the rows report the correlation indexes. The CoV of all correlation indexes increases when σ increases. Compared to existing solutions, the CoHiVa index is able to keep the lowest CoV for any σ value. Thanks to a CoV always lower than 0.15, the proposed correlation index guarantees a high robustness in capturing correlations also among highly variable data. On the contrary, state-of-the-art indexes show scarce robustness for medium-high values of σ ($\sigma \geq 0.3$). All indexes have CoV values above the 0.15, even reaching values around 0.5 for high perturbation intensities. These results evince that they cannot be used to capture correlations among highly variable time series.

Table 1. Coefficient of variation of correlation indexes

	σ					
	0.01	**0.1**	**0.2**	**0.3**	**0.4**	**0.5**
Pearson	0.0232	0.0299	0.0914	0.1992	0.3437	0.4817
Spearman	0.0227	0.0304	0.0905	0.2036	0.3496	0.4874
Kendall	0.0371	0.0486	0.1098	0.2170	0.3606	0.4936
LoCo	0.0220	0.0284	0.0835	0.1653	0.2452	0.2735
CoHiVa	0.0073	0.0086	0.0217	0.0498	0.0888	0.1343

These analyses confirm that the most popular correlation indexes are affected by scarce accuracy and robustness when data exhibit high variabilities. The main result is that the proposed CoHiVa index is able to improve state of the art when data are characterized by high variability, and to guarantee analogous performance of existing solutions when time series are less variable.

4.2 Real Datasets

We evaluate the performance of a clustering model using CoHiVa as similarity measure for clustering real datasets, and compare it against different solutions. To this purpose, we refer to datasets coming from the resource monitoring of a locally distributed multi-tier system. Partitioning data coming from the monitoring of system resource metrics into clusters of related objects allows to disclose dependencies among servers, and to group servers performing similar tasks. To consider these groups as unique entities may reduce the effort of supporting management decisions in large data centers. Since system resource metrics are characterized by high variability due to system instability, variable offered load, heavy-tailed distributions, hardware and software inter-actions [14], it becomes necessary to rely on an accurate and robust model for generating clusters in a highly variable context.

The architecture of the considered multi-tier system is described in Figure 2. The four application servers are deployed through the Tomcat servlet container and are connected to two MySQL database servers. The Web switch node, running a modified version of the Apache Web server, decides whether to serve or to refuse HTTP requests by using the implementation presented in [14]. If a request is admitted into the system, the dispatcher forwards it to the two Apache-based HTTP servers.

We evaluate the accuracy and robustness of a clustering model in finding groups of related servers performing similar tasks, even when collected resource measures present high variability. In a supervised setting, we define the *accuracy* of a clustering model

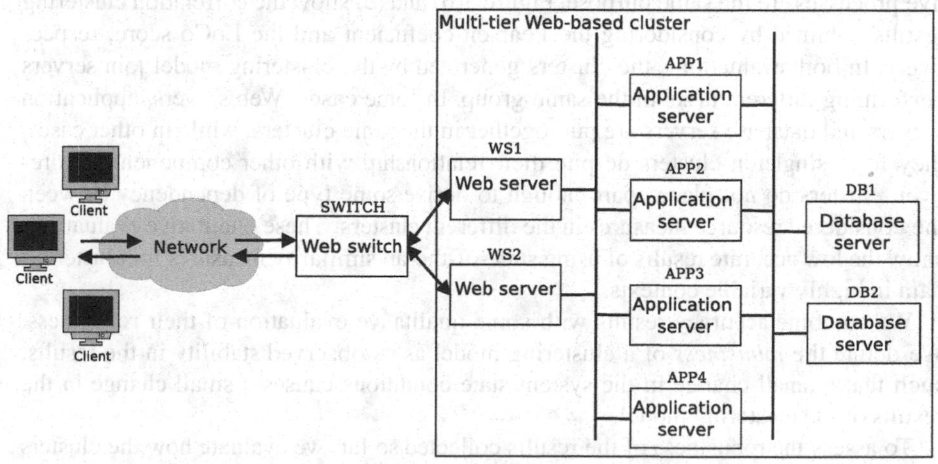

Fig. 2. Architecture of a multi-tier Web cluster

as its observed ability in clustering datasets that present similar degrees of correlation among their time series. For example, in the scenarios considered in this section, an accurate clustering model should group the two Web servers in a unique cluster, disjointed from the one of the four application servers, as well as from the one containing the two MySQL database servers. We expect the Web switch to form a singleton cluster.

In the following, we apply a complete-linkage clustering model for grouping the 9 servers of the architecture according to the correlation computed between a subset of their resource measures. We qualitatively compare the accuracy of the clustering model when it bases on three different similarity measures: the CoHiVa index, the Pearson product moment, and the LoCo score. In particular, we build 9 datasets $\mathcal{X} \equiv \{\boldsymbol{X}_1, \ldots, \boldsymbol{X}_9\}$, each one collecting the time series (i.e., the system resource measures) of one server in the architecture. We choose a subset of resource measures and compute three 9x9 similarity matrices $\mathcal{D}_C$, $\mathcal{D}_P$, and $\mathcal{D}_L$, containing the pair-wise distances between all the datasets in $\mathcal{X}$ on the basis of the data correlations in the subset computed through CoHiVa, Pearson, and Loco, respectively. The generation of the similarity matrix $\mathcal{D}_C$ follows the steps detailed in the previous section, while $\mathcal{D}_P$ and $\mathcal{D}_L$ contain the correlation results of two of the state-of-the-art models that achieved the best trade-off between accuracy and robustness on synthetic settings (i.e., the Pearson product moment and the LoCo score).

Figure 3 shows the results of a complete-linkage clustering model in grouping servers by using similarity matrices containing the correlation distances between network packet rate, CPU%, and number of active processes. In Figure 3(a), we appreciate how the clustering model using the CoHiVa correlation index as similarity measure is able to accurately group the 9 servers basing on their similarity. As desired, we obtain four clusters, one grouping the Web servers, one containing the application servers, one for the database servers, and one comprising the Web switch. Moreover, the four clusters place in clearly distinct portions of the clustering space generated through CoHiVa, thus manifesting that different typologies of servers present different levels of dependency between the CPU% and network packet rate, and between CPU% and number of active processes. To the same purpose, Figure 3(b) and (c) show the correlation clustering results obtained by considering the Pearson coefficient and the LoCo score, respectively. In both evaluations, the clusters generated by the clustering model join servers performing different tasks in the same group. In some cases, Web servers, application servers and database servers are put together in the same clusters; while in other cases, they form singleton clusters despite their relationship with other components. Moreover, clusters do not place apart enough to derive some type of dependency between the considered resource measures in the different clusters. These qualitative evaluations show the low accurate results of using state-of-the-art similarity measures for clustering data in highly variable contexts.

We combine accuracy results with some qualitative evaluation of their robustness. We define the *robustness* of a clustering model as its observed stability in the results, such that a small change in the system state conditions causes a small change in the results of the clustering model.

To assess the robustness of the results collected so far, we evaluate how the clusters generated by the complete-linkage clustering model evolve at consecutive evaluations.

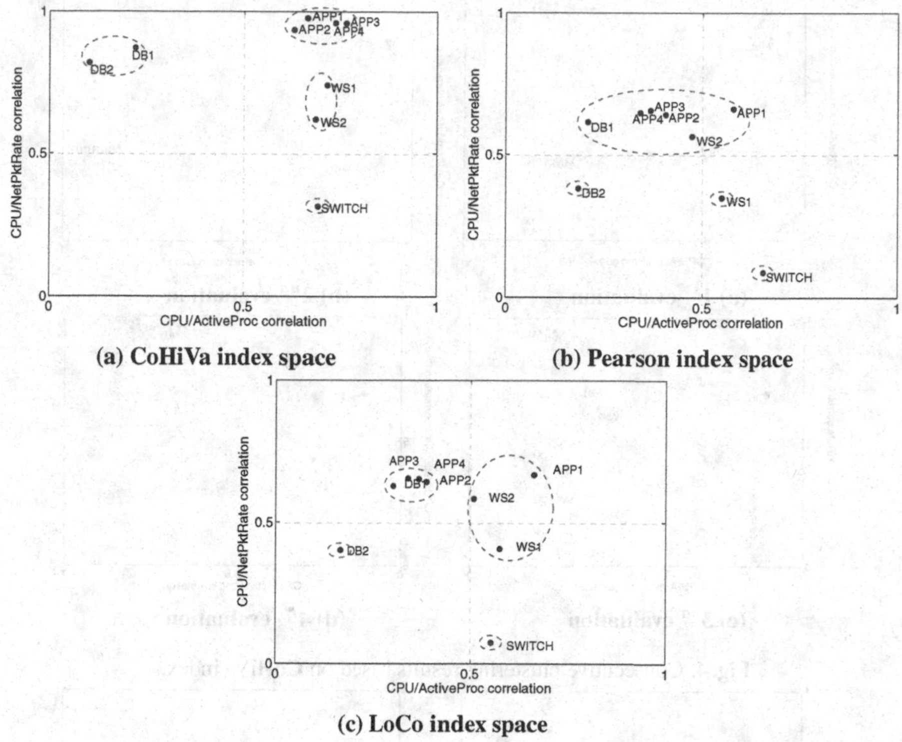

(a) CoHiVa index space

(b) Pearson index space

(c) LoCo index space

Fig. 3. Results of a clustering model using different similarity measures

As a summary of a larger set of experiments, we report the clusters obtained by the model across four consecutive evaluations by using the CoHiVa index and Pearson product moment as similarity measures.

By using CoHiVa as similarity measure, Figure 4 shows that the clustering model maintains stable results during the four consecutive evaluations. In all the plots in the figure, similar servers are grouped together, while separated from servers performing different tasks. Furthermore, the clusters place in the same portion of the space across all four evaluations. As evaluations are carried out under unchanged system conditions, the stability of the results confirm that the use of CoHiVa as similarity measure brings to robust clustering outcomes. On the contrary, the results achieved by the clustering model using the Pearson index significantly change from an evaluation to the other, as we can evince by comparing the plots in Figure 5. In consecutive evaluations, clusters change in the number and type of servers they contain, as well as in their positioning in the space. This solution provides low robust results that are useless for supporting any strategic management decision.

The reported evaluations demonstrate that CoHiVa is a good choice as similarity measure to be used by clustering models to find correlation-connected clusters when dealing with highly variable data.

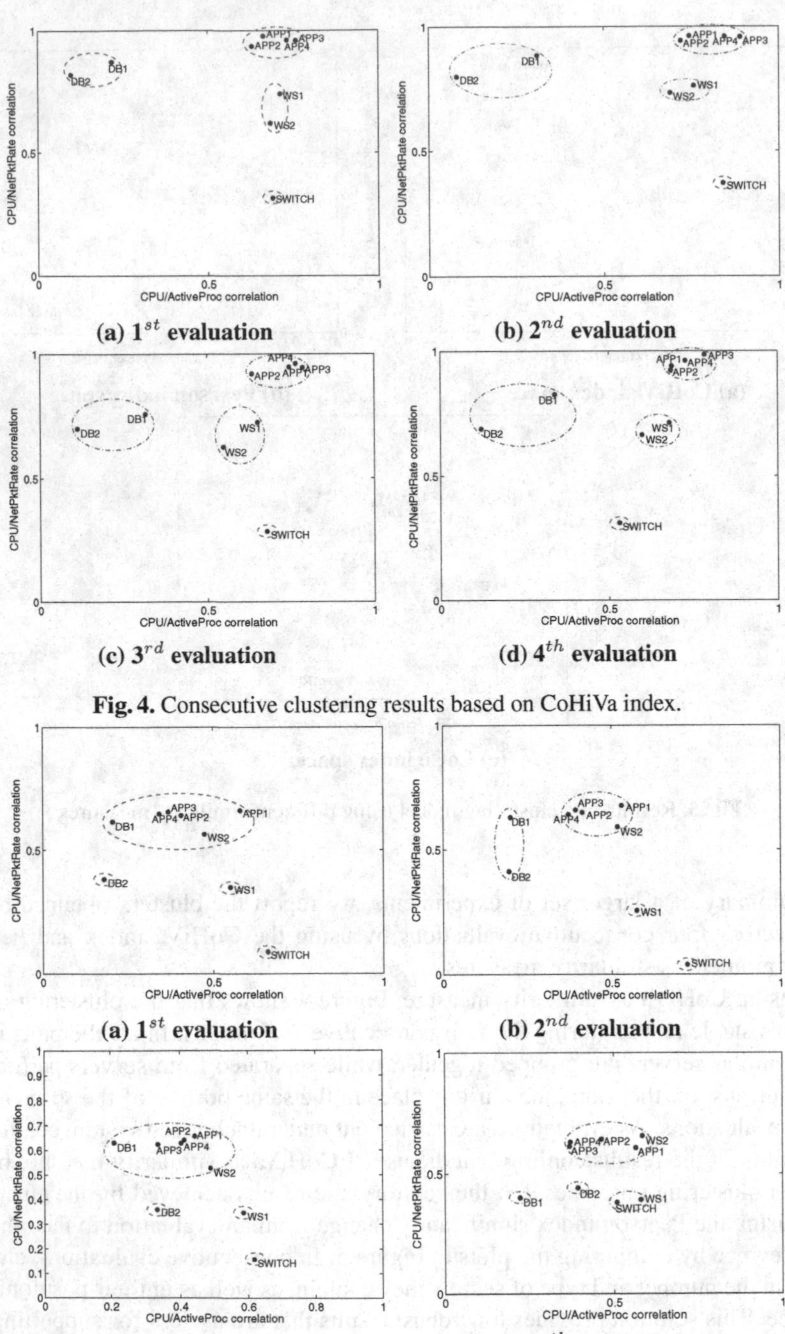

Fig. 4. Consecutive clustering results based on CoHiVa index.

Fig. 5. Consecutive clustering results based on Pearson index

5 Conclusion

Relying on an accurate and robust similarity measure is crucial for clustering models to guarantee a good partitioning of data into clusters of similar objects. However, when similarity between data is hidden by high variability, the accuracy and robustness of common-used similarity measures are limited. This paper proposes a new correlation index able to disclose the presence of similarity also between highly variable data. It is based on the extraction of the main patterns of the time series, the removal of perturbations, and the selection of just the trend patterns. This approach makes the proposed correlation index a good similarity measure to be used by clustering models to discover correlation-connected data also in highly variable domains. Evaluations carried out on synthetic and real datasets demonstrate the accuracy and robustness of the proposal, that improves the state of the art both in correlation and cluster analysis.

Acknowledgments. The authors acknowledge the support of MIUR-PRIN project DOTS-LCCI Dependable Off-The-Shelf based middleware systems for Large-scale Complex Critical Infrastructures.

References

1. Liao, T.W.: Clustering of time series data - a survey. Pattern Recognition 38 (2005)
2. Xu, R., Wunsch, D.: Survey of clustering algorithms. IEEE Trans. on Neural Networks 16 (2005)
3. Böhm, C., Kailing, K., Kröger, P., Zimek, A.: Computing clusters of correlation connected objects. In: Proc. of the 2004 ACM SIGMOD International Conference on Management of Data, Paris, France (2004)
4. MacQueen, J.B.: Some methods for classification and analysis of multivariate observations. In: Proc. of the Fifth Berkeley Symposium on Mathematical Statistics and Probability. University of California Press (1967)
5. Steinbach, M., Karypis, G., Kumar, V.: A comparison of document clustering techniques. Technical Report TR 00-034, University of Minnesota - Department of Computer Science and Engineering, Minneapolis (2000)
6. Cohen, J.: Applied multiple regression/correlation analysis for the behavioral sciences. L. Erlbaum Associates (2003)
7. Spearman, C.: The proof and measurement of association between two things. The American Journal of Psychology 100 (1904)
8. Kendall, M.G.: Rank correlation methods. Charles Griffin & Company Ltd. (1962)
9. Papadimitriou, S., Sun, J., Yu, P.S.: Local correlation tracking in time series. In: IEEE International Conference on Data Mining, Los Alamitos, CA, USA (2006)
10. Hamao, Y., Masulis, R., Ng, V.: Correlations in price changes and volatility across international stock markets. Review of Financial Studies 3 (1990)
11. Taqqu, M.S.: Random processes with long-range dependence and high variability. Journal of Geophysical Research 92 (1987)
12. Willinger, W., Alderson, D., Li, L.: A pragmatic approach to dealing with high-variability in network measurements. In: Proc. of the 4th ACM SIGCOMM Conference on Internet Measurement, Taormina, Sicily, Italy (2004)

13. Bennani, M.N., Menasce, D.A.: Assessing the robustness of self-managing computer systems under highly variable workloads. In: Proc. of the First International Conference on Autonomic Computing, Washington, DC, USA (2004)
14. Andreolini, M., Casolari, S., Colajanni, M.: Models and framework for supporting run-time decisions in web-based systems. ACM Trans. on the Web 2 (2008)
15. Ghosh, S., Squillante, M.S.: Analysis and control of correlated web server queues. Computer Communications 5244 (2004)
16. Buda, A., Jarynowski, A.: Life-time of correlations and its applications. Wydawnictwo Niezalezne (2010)
17. Sørensen, T.: A Method of Establishing Groups of Equal Amplitude in Plant Sociology Based on Similarity of Species Content. Biologiske Skrifter. E. Munksgaard (1948)
18. Papadimitriou, S., Yu, P.S.: Optimal multi-scale patterns in time series streams. In: Proc. of the 2006 ACM SIGMOD International Conference on Management of Data, Chicago, IL, USA (2006)
19. Papadimitriou, S., Sun, J., Faloutsos, C.: Streaming pattern discovery in multiple time-series. In: Proc. of the 31st International Conference on Very Large Data Bases, Trondheim, Norway (2005)
20. Bakshi, B.R.: Multiscale pca with application to multivariate statistical process monitoring. AIChE Journal 44 (1998)
21. Abrahao, B., Zhang, A.: Characterizing application workloads on cpu utilization in utility computing. Technical Report HPL-2004-157, Hewlett-Packard Labs (2004)
22. Khattree, R., Naik, D.: Multivariate data reduction and discrimination with SAS software. SAS Institute Inc. (2000)
23. Lakhina, A., Papagiannaki, K., Crovella, M., Diot, C., Kolaczyk, E.D., Taft, N.: Structural analysis of network traffic flows. In: Proc. of the Joint International Conference on Measurement and Modeling of Computer Systems, New York, NY, USA (2004)
24. Hurst, H.E.: Long-term storage capacity of reservoirs. Trans. of the American Society of Civil Engineers 116 (1951)
25. Weron, R.: Estimating long range dependence: finite sample properties and confidence intervals. Physica A 312 (2002)
26. Brockwell, B.L., Davis, R.A.: Time Series: Theory and Methods. Springer (1987)

Extension of Path Computation Element (PCE) Framework for Resource Provisioning Based on User Profile in Dynamic Circuit Network

Tananun Orawiwattanakul, Hideki Otsuki, Eiji Kawai, and Shinji Shimojo

The National Institute of Information and Communications Technology
KDDI Building, 1-8-1 Otemachi, Chiyoda-ku, Tokyo, Japan, 100-0004
{tananun,eiji,eiji-ka,sshinji}@nict.go.jp

Abstract. Dynamic circuit network (DCN) refers to an on-demand virtual circuit (VC) service in which a user makes a request for a circuit in advance via a Web page. On-demand Secure Circuits and Advance Reservation System (OSCARS) is well-known DCN software. All requests in DCN/OSCARS are guaranteed bandwidth. Therefore, the quality of service (QoS) can be determined by the request blocking probability (RBP). Several QoS provisioning mechanisms, such as the bandwidth allocation policy (BAP) and preemption, have been proposed in the literature in order to ensure low RBPs for high-priority users. This paper proposes the extension of path computation elements (PCEs) in OSCARS version (v.) 6, called the UP-PCE, which considers the user attributes in its computation. Our extended OSCARS with the UP-PCE can determine two mechanisms: the control of the available topology and the BAP.

Keywords: dynamic circuit network (DCN), advance bandwidth reservation, constraint-based shortest path (CSPF).

1 Introduction

Reliable high-speed data transmission is required by many e-science projects and multimedia applications. Consequently, dynamic circuit network (DCN) has been developed as one of the future Internet technologies. DCN enables authorized users and applications to reserve bandwidth in advance in order to guarantee its availability via a Web page and an application program interface (API), respectively. On-demand Secure Circuits and Advance Reservation System (OSCARS) [1]-[2] is a project funded by the U.S. Department of Energy (DOE) for providing a DCN service (layers 2 and 3) in the Energy Sciences Network (ESnet) [3]. OSCARS provides Java-based open-source DCN software that offers advance network resources with provisions for both intra- and inter-domain connections, and it is has been utilized in many networks, e.g., Internet2, and JGN-X (the Japanese future Internet testbed) [4].

OSCARS uses multiprotocol label switching (MPLS) as a transport mechanism, but it can be cooperative with other controllers that run on other network environments [2], such as the Dynamic Resource Allocation via GMPLS Optical Networks (DRAGON) in Generalized multiprotocol label switching (GMPLS) controlled networks. In addition,

V. Guyot (Ed.): ICAIT 2012, LNCS 7593, pp. 47–60, 2013.

OSCARS can be utilized as an alternative to provide inter-domain communications for networks which lack a standard inter-domain capability, such as, OpenFlow [5]. Consequently, OSCARS plays a key role as an important tool for future Internet technologies.

OSCARS guarantees bandwidth for all requests by using a Resource Reservation Protocol (RSVP) and an admission control mechanism. Typically, MPLS-Traffic Engineering (MPLS-TE) is used to determine a path based on the Constraint-based Shortest Path First (CSPF) algorithm for a virtual circuit (VC) in MPLS networks. CSPF is an algorithm for determining an optimal path under multiple constraints. Nevertheless, the Path Computation Elements (PCEs) of the OSCARS perform the CSPF algorithm for circuit traffic in the OSCARS instead of MPLS-TE, because DCN involves several additional constraints that are beyond the scope of MPLS-TE, such as the future availability of link resources and policies. In CSPF, the network elements that cannot satisfy constraint conditions are excluded from path computation. The typical constraints in DCN/OSCARS are the requested bandwidth and the virtual local area network (VLAN) identifier (ID).

This paper proposes an extension of the CSPF algorithm that considers resource control policies as constraints. We developed our proposal by introducing an extension of the new PCE module, called the User Profile PCE (UP-PCE), in OSCARS version (v.) 6 to determine user attributes. The UP-PCE is able to differentiate among requests and it determines two policies: (1) policy for control of available topology and (2) bandwidth allocation policy (BAP).

Section 2 describes the research motivation and our proposal. Section 3 describes the architecture of DCN/OSCARS with the extended UP-PCE. Section 4 presents the development of UP-PCE, and Section 5 concludes this paper.

2 Research Motivation

OSCARS guarantees bandwidth for all requests; consequently, the request blocking probability (RBP) is mainly used to determine the quality level of a DCN/OSCARS service. RBP equals the number of rejected requests divided by the total number of requests arriving at the system. Several studies have proposed methods to decrease the RBP for all requests based on the DCN/OSCARS architecture, e.g., continuous and parallel bandwidth scheduling [6], anycast routing [7], and the Flexible Reservation Algorithm (FRA) [8]. Although these algorithms decrease the RBP, when the network eventually becomes congested, the quality of service (QoS) provisioning mechanisms are required to differentiate among services. Two main QoS mechanisms have been studied in the literature, namely BAP [10], and preemption [11]. In BAP, a certain amount of network resources is reserved for high-priority users. When the system cannot grant bandwidth for these users, the preemption mechanism allows the high-priority users to preempt network resources that were previously reserved by low-priority users.

Connections in DCN are dynamically driven by the users. The main role of the network administrator is to manage user accounts, and define authorization and resource control policies. Authorization in OSCARS is primarily performed on the basis of the determination of user attributes, so that it is understandable to both users and administrators. Note that a user attribute is a description of a user, e.g., name or organization. In OSCARS, the resources are allocated and managed during the service request process; therefore, the request can be differentiated according to the attributes of the requesters (users and applications). Some software modules in OSCARS determine the user attributes and the incoming request to impose some restrictions, such as the maximum requested bandwidth and time as given in [9]. The PCEs, which are the main components for resource allocation in OSCARS, should also determine the user attributes so that they can differentiate among requests. Several resource control policies studied in the literature, e.g., QoS mechanisms (BAP and preemption), and topology control (zoning topology (northern route) and unauthorized path), can be realized in DCN/OSCARS, if the PCEs determine the user attributes during path computation.

The administrator in our extended OSCARS with the UP-PCE can define the resource policies as attributes, which are called the User-PCE attributes, via the Web page. A User-PCE attribute consists of constraint-name and constraint-value, which indicate the resource policy's name and the constraints for resources, respectively. When creating a user account, the administrator assigns the User-PCE attributes according to the user profile, and he/she can change the User-PCE attributes at any time though the Web page. Our developed UP-PCE determines the User-PCE attributes and processes the corresponding resource control policies by pruning the unsatisfied-constraint elements from a topology graph. The policies are defined according to the User-PCE attributes rather than individual grants; consequently, the number of policies is small. At this stage, two policies can be defined: (1) topology control policy (unauthorized ports) and (2) BAP (the threshold of the reserved bandwidth ratio of ports available for use by the user).

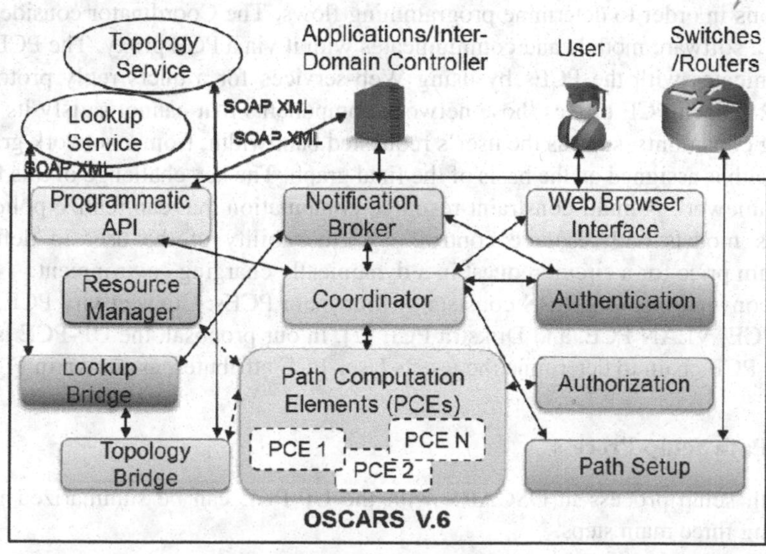

Fig. 1. Architecture of OSCARS v.6

In this paper, we define the constraint for topology control as the unauthorized ports, because we intend to control the use of some paths that have low-bandwidth capacity in networks. Our proposal supports connections made by a user via a Web page. We intend to extend the UP-PCE to support connections made by applications through Simple Object Access Protocol (SOAP) based Extensible Markup Language (XML) messages in our future work. Our proposal in this paper is based upon intra-domain connections. The UP-PCE for inter-domain requests is described in Section 3.3.

3 Proposed Architecture of OSCARS with UP-PCE

Figure 1 presents the conventional architecture of OSCARS software v. 6, which consists of 11 distinct pluggable modules [2]. Our main modifications of OSCARS for the UP-PCE are the Coordinator and PCE modules. This section describes the path setup process in OSCARS with the UP-PCE. Several steps and functions of the modules are skipped for the sake of brevity.

3.1 Path Computation Elements (PCEs)

The PCE is an entity, e.g., a software component, which determines the path according to a network graph algorithm and constraints (CSPF). In OSCARS v.6, the PCE framework allows the execution of PCEs in any arbitrary sequence, such as on the basis of a chain or tree. This enables the OSCARS administrator to develop and deploy new PCEs into the conventional chain. Several PCEs can be used to compute a path with specific constraints, and they are executed independently. The administrator can define the execution process of PCEs as workflow in a configuration file (pce-configuration.xml). The Coordinator module processes an incoming request and conditions in order to determine programming flows. The Coordinator considers each PCE as a software module and communicates with it via a PCE proxy. The PCE proxy communicates with the PCEs by using Web-services for a query/reply protocol. In OSCARS, each PCE prunes those network components that cannot satisfy its corresponding constraints, such as the user's requested bandwidth, from a network graph.

The path is assigned on the basis of the final graph. The key challenge of this flexible PCE framework is multi-constraint resource computation that can realize policies for business models and resource control, e.g., the ability of the user to define the maximum price for a circuit request in a dynamically charging environment.

The conventional OSCARS consists of four main PCEs: Connectivity PCE, Bandwidth PCE, VLAN PCE, and Dijkstra PCE [7]. In our proposal, the UP-PCE is added into the PCE chain to determine the user's User-PCE attributes, as shown in Fig. 2.

3.2 Path Setup Process

The path setup process in OSCARS with the UP-PCE can be summarized into the following three main steps.

(1) Request for a Connection:

(1.1) The network administrator creates the User-PCE attributes for processing in the UP-PCE. There are two resource policies:

- Unauthorized ports: constraint-name = "unauthz-linkid*" and constraint-value = a set of the port IDs that the user is not authorized to use. Note that the port IDs must be assigned correspondingly to those connected ports in the network topology.
- Threshold of reserved bandwidth ratio: constraint-name = "bandwith-policy*" and constraint-value = threshold of the reserved bandwidth ratio as a percentage of the ports that the user can utilize.

Next, the administrator assigns an account to a user, and the User-PCE attributes are then assigned to the user with restrictions on to the use of network resources. The administrator can define multiple User-PCE attributes but only a single attribute for each policy should be assigned to the user.

(1.2) The user logs in to the OSCARS via a Web interface and requests a connection by specifying the source (*S*), the destination (*D*), an amount of bandwidth (*BW*), the start time (t^{Start}), and the end time (t^{End}). The request can be described as $R = (S, D, BW, t^{Start}, t^{End})$. The user is able to specify the VLAN ID of *S* and *D* for L2-VCs, and in such a case, the request can be described as $R = (S, D, BW, t^{Start}, t^{End}$, VLAN ID).

(1.3) Communications between the PCE proxy and PCEs take place via a SOAP-based XML message exchange. *PCEDataContent* is one of the data types in messages, and it contains the path constraints and the *Topology* element. Three types of constraints are defined in *PCEDataContent* to instruct PCEs which constraints they should determine

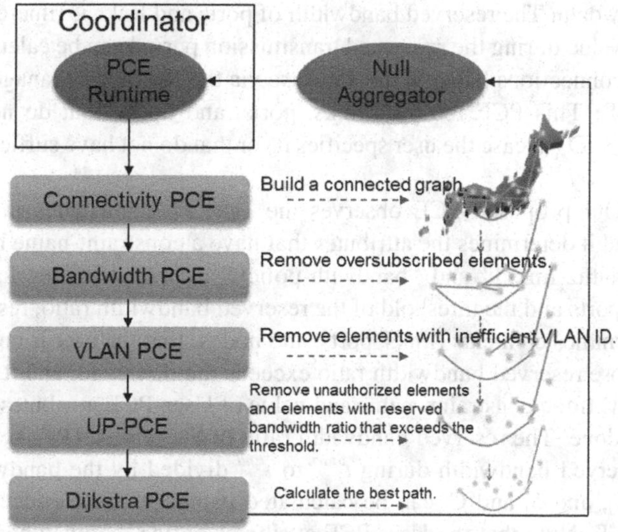

Fig. 2. PCE chain in OSCARS V.6 with UP-PCE

in order to remove or to modify appropriate elements from the topology graph. *UserRequestConstraint* specifies the user's requirements, such as *BW*, t^{Start}, and t^{End}. *RequestConstraint* specifies the requirements of the inter-domain controllers along the path, including the current domain. *OptionalConstraint* is an optional constraint in the case that new constraints need to be added. We modified *UserRequestConstraint* so that it includes the User-PCE attributes as its parameters. The Coordinator is responsible for adding *UserRequestConstraint* to the request. In some cases, the User-PCE attribute is NULL; for example, the network operator does not assign the User-PCE attributes to the user (no restrictions on resource utilization), and the request is made by applications via API. The *Topology* element in *PCEDataContent* contains a network graph, which will be modified and pruned by the PCEs. The Coordinator sends a query message consisting of *PCEDataContent* to PCEs via the PCE proxy.

(2) Determination of Paths and Resources:
The request is subsequently processed through the PCE modules. Figure 2 shows the PCE chain in our proposal. Each PCE retrieves constraints and a network graph (*Topology*) from *PCEDataContent.* The PCE Runtime agent controls the ordering of the PCE execution. The processes in the PCEs are as follows.

- **Connectivity PCE:** This PCE is initially called by the PCE Runtime. It builds an initial connected graph by pooling topology data from the Topology Bridge.
- **Bandwidth PCE:** This PCE determines which links, ports, and nodes have insufficient bandwidth for *BW* during the requested transmission period (from t^{Start} to t^{End}), and it prunes them from *Topology*. The available bandwidth of the network element i (A_i) during the requested period equals the bandwidth capacity (C_i) minus the maximum reserved bandwidth (S_i), $A_i = C_i - S_i$. The bandwidth capacity of ports and links are in the topology data. The reserved bandwidth of ports and links is time-dependent, and its maximum value during the requested transmission period can be calculated from the details of the connections listed in the database via the Resource Manager.
- **VLAN PCE:** This PCE removes links, ports, and nodes that do not support the required VLAN ID (in case the user specifies it) or that do not have sufficient VLAN ID for allocation.
- **UP-PCE:** Our proposed PCE observes the User-PCE attributes in *UserRequestConstraint*, and it determines the attributes that have a constraint-name beginning with the term "unauthz-linkid" and "bandwith-policy" as the attributes for determining unauthorized ports and the threshold of the reserved bandwidth ratio, respectively. The UP-PCE determines elements (links, ports, and nodes) that the user is not authorized to utilize, or whose reserved bandwidth ratio exceeds the threshold, and it removes them from *Topology*. If the constraint- name and value of User-PCE attributes are NULL, no processing is done. The reserved bandwidth ratio of the port e_i, ($R_i(e_i)$), is equal to the maximum reserved bandwidth during t^{Start} to t^{End} divided by the bandwidth capacity, $R_i(e_i) = S_i / C_i$, and S_i and C_i can be calculated using the same process done in the Bandwidth PCE. Note that the User-PCE attributes define the unauthorized ports and

the threshold of the reserved bandwidth ratio of ports. However, the other elements, i.e., links and nodes, may be removed from a topology graph, because a port contains links; therefore, when the UP-PCE removes a port, all links within that port are also removed. A node contains ports. If all ports in a node are removed, the node should be removed too. Figure 3 shows the pseudocode of the UP-PCE.

- **Dijkstra PCE:** This PCE computes the end-to-end path based upon some criteria. The NullAggregator module sends the result from Dijkstra PCE to PCE Runtime. We assume that there is sufficient bandwidth for this request. The Resource Manager updates this request in a database.

(3) Path Establishment:

The Path Setup module communicates with the switches along the assigned path by using RSVP to set up and tear down the MPLS label-switched path (LSP) prior to t^{Start} and t^{End}, respectively.

PARAMETERS:
$G_i(V_i, E_i)$ = a network graph of Domain i
V_i = set of nodes in domain $i = \{v_1, v_2, \ldots\}$
E_i = set of ports in domain $i = \{e_1, e_2, \ldots\}$
E_i^m = set of ports in domain i that belong to the node v_m =
$\{e_1^m, e_2^m, \ldots\}$, $E_i^m \sqsubseteq E_i$
P_i = set of unauthorized ports for the user in domain i, $P_i \sqsubseteq E_i$
$R(e_j^m)$ = the reserved bandwidth ratio of port e_j^m
T = the threshold of reserved bandwidth ratio

INPUT: $G_i(V_i, E_i)$, P_i, $R(e_j^i(m))$, and T
OUTPUT: Pruned $G_i(V_i, E_i)$
ALGORITHM:
Search for all nodes in a domain i
For each node v_m, search for all ports
  If $((e_j^m \in P_i)$ or $(R(e_j^m) \geq T))$
    $E_i^m \leftarrow E_i^m \backslash \{e_j^m\}$
    $E_i \leftarrow E_i \backslash \{e_j^m\}$
  End If
End search for all ports
If $|E_i^m| = 0$
  $V_i \leftarrow V_i \backslash \{v_m\}$
End If
End search for all nodes

Fig. 3. Pseudocode of UP-PCE

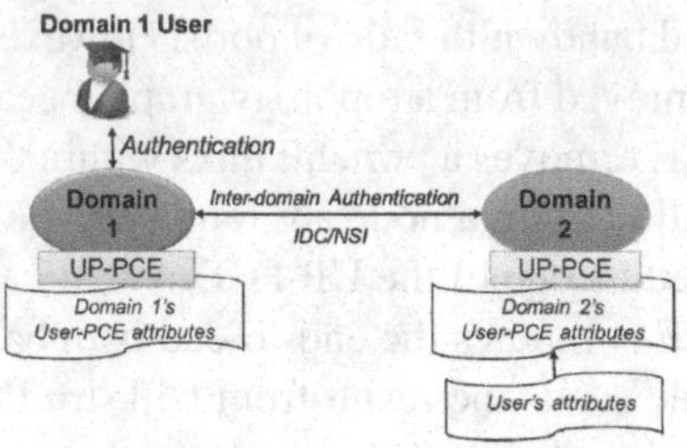

Fig. 4. Inter-domain connections

3.3 Inter-Domain Connections

The proposal described in this paper assumes intra-domain connections. Let us consider an inter-domain connection request (Fig. 4), in which the other inter-domain controllers can communicate with OSCARS by using the Dante, Internet2, CANARIE, and ESnet (DICE) InterDomain Controller (IDC) protocol [12] (as utilized in Internet2's Interoperable On-demand Network (ION)), and the Open Grid Forum's (OGF) network standard interface (NSI) [13]. The user authenticates him/herself with his/her home domain, but the authentication across domains is performed between the DCN controllers. Generally, the IDC/NSI attributes that are exchanged between domains are agreed upon in advanced, and each controller considers all connections from different users to be connections that were made by the corresponding controller. The process in PCEs in each domain is independent but it should follow the service level agreement (SLA) that exists between peer domains. However, in an identity federation environment resource allocation policies in each domain along an inter-domain path should be defined based on user attributes, such as, project name and role, or an agreement between the user's home organization and a corresponding DCN provider domain. Our proposed UP-PCE can be extended to support resource allocation policies based on the user attributes for an inter-domain request by extending inter-domain messages to carry the attributes of the originating user, e.g., project name and role of users, and converting the incoming user attributes to the local User-PCE attributes according to the pre-defined matching rules. Note that the user attributes must be understood by co-operating domains.

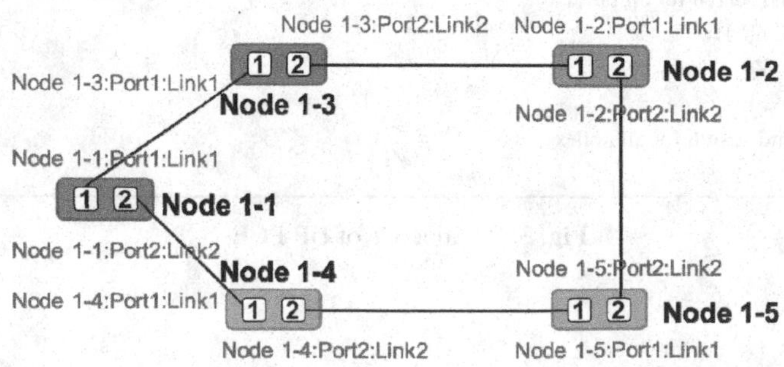

Fig. 5. Five-node ring test topology

4 Development

We developed the UP-PCE as a prototype based on OSCARS v.6 (a beta version, SDK-01.11.11). The latest version of OSCARS can be found in [14]. The UP-PCE can be added as a new software module, as presented in Section 3. At this stage, however, we extended the Bandwidth PCE to determine the UP-PCE's algorithm in order to decrease the time and the number of processing jobs, because both PCEs perform similar basic jobs, e.g., retrieving data from a database to calculate the reserved bandwidth in ports. The UP-PCE should be added as a new module if more complex constraints are to be determined. Currently, OSCARS v.6 contains scripts to run a client test program for an entire system, and we performed a test based on adapted scripts. Note that the database in MySQL consisted of five databases: information_schema, authn, authz, mysql, and rm. The assigned path can be verified from the data in the pathElems table in the rm database.

The test was conducted based on a ring topology consisting of five nodes, as shown in Fig. 5. Each node consisted of two ports and each port consisted of one link. All ports and links were assumed to have the same capacity of 1 Gbps. The ID of each element is presented by using a Uniform Resource Name (URN) beginning with the prefix "urn:ogf:network" and it contains the parent elements' ID. For example, a link ID "urn:ogf:network:domain=testdomain-1:node=node1-1:port= port1:link=link1" contains a domain ID, a node ID and a port ID, according to the hierarchy structure.

In this paper, the ID of network elements is written in a short term for simplicity, e.g., port ID = "node-1-3:port2". The test topology was written in XML format and was fed into a system. Our test was conducted as follows. We initially logged into the system by using an administrator account. Figure 6 shows a screen shot of the creation of an account. The username and password were registered for authentication. The details of the user, such as the first and last names, and the organization name, were maintained for records. The typical attributes regarding authorization in OSCARS, which are called AuthZ attributes, are OSCARS-user, OSCARS-engineer, OSCARS-admin, OSCARS-service, OSCARS-operator, OSCARS-site-administrator, and OSCARS-publisher. The description and authorization details of attributes can be found in [9]; for example, OSCARS-user can create a reservation, but only OSCARS-administrator can assign a new user account. The administrator could create, view, and modify the User-PCE attributes as he/she did for the AuthZ attributes. The User-PCE attributes were assigned to the user with restrictions on resource utilization.

To show a simple implementation of our proposal, we added two User-PCE attributes (Fig. 6): (1) Attribute-name = yaresourcename (constraint-name = unauthz-linkid1 and constraint-value = node-1-3:port2$node-1-2:port1) (2) Attribute-name = yabandwidth-priority (constraint-name = bandwith-policy1 and constraint-value = 80). In our development, a set of unauthorized ports was assigned as a string in which each port ID was separated by "$". Next, we created two accounts: user 1 (AuthZ attributes: OSCARS-user) and user 2 (AuthZ attributes: OSCARS-user; and User-PCE attributes:

yaresourcename, and yabandwidthpriority). Consequently, there were no restrictions on user 1 in utilizing network resources. In contrast, user 2 was not authorized to use the path between the nodes 1-3 and 1-2 (the port IDs “node-1-3:port2” and “node-1-2:port1”) and the ports with a reserved bandwidth ratio that exceeded 80%.

None of the requests in our test specified VLAN Tag, and a request made by the user account i can be presented as R = *User i*-(S, D, BW, t^{Start}, t^{End}). There were two test scenarios: unauthorized ports and BAP. We assumed that the test started at 0:00 for the sake of simplicity, and the time at which we sent a request for a connection to the system was not presented.

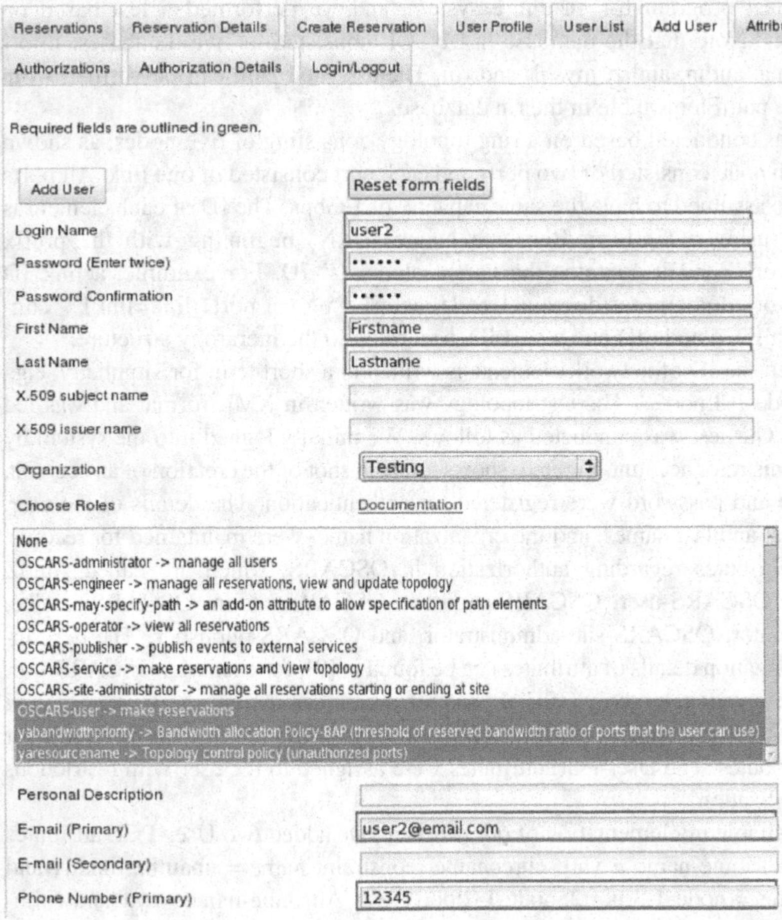

Fig. 6. Creation of an account

```
mysql> select * from pathElems where pathID=657;
+------+--------+-----------+----------------------------------------------------------------------
-----+
| id   | pathId | seqNumber | urn
     |
+------+--------+-----------+----------------------------------------------------------------------
-----+
| 1601 |    657 |         0 | urn:ogf:network:domain=testdomain-1:node=node-1-1:port=port1:link=l
ink1 |
| 1602 |    657 |         1 | urn:ogf:network:domain=testdomain-1:node=node-1-3:port=port1:link=l
ink1 |
| 1603 |    657 |         2 | urn:ogf:network:domain=testdomain-1:node=node-1-3:port=port2:link=l
ink2 |
| 1604 |    657 |         3 | urn:ogf:network:domain=testdomain-1:node=node-1-2:port=port1:link=l
ink1 |
| 1605 |    657 |         4 | urn:ogf:network:domain=testdomain-1:node=node-1-2:port=port2:link=l
ink2 |
+------+--------+-----------+----------------------------------------------------------------------
-----+
5 rows in set (0.60 sec)
```

(a) Assigned path for request *R1* (with no restrictions on resource utilization)

```
mysql> select * from pathElems where pathID=661;
+------+--------+-----------+----------------------------------------------------------------------
-----+
| id   | pathId | seqNumber | urn
     |
+------+--------+-----------+----------------------------------------------------------------------
-----+
| 1617 |    661 |         0 | urn:ogf:network:domain=testdomain-1:node=node-1-1:port=port1:link=l
ink1 |
| 1618 |    661 |         1 | urn:ogf:network:domain=testdomain-1:node=node-1-1:port=port2:link=l
ink2 |
| 1619 |    661 |         2 | urn:ogf:network:domain=testdomain-1:node=node-1-4:port=port1:link=l
ink1 |
| 1620 |    661 |         3 | urn:ogf:network:domain=testdomain-1:node=node-1-4:port=port2:link=l
ink2 |
| 1621 |    661 |         4 | urn:ogf:network:domain=testdomain-1:node=node-1-5:port=port1:link=l
ink1 |
| 1622 |    661 |         5 | urn:ogf:network:domain=testdomain-1:node=node-1-5:port=port2:link=l
ink2 |
| 1623 |    661 |         6 | urn:ogf:network:domain=testdomain-1:node=node-1-2:port=port2:link=l
ink2 |
+------+--------+-----------+----------------------------------------------------------------------
-----+
7 rows in set (0.00 sec)
```

(b) Assigned path for request *R2* (with restrictions on resource utilization)

Fig. 7. Assigned path retrieved from MySQL database

4.1 Unauthorized Ports

We ran the test scripts to request two connections *R1* = *User 1*-(Node 1-1:Port1:Link1, Node 1-2:Port2:Link2, 10 Mbps, 21:00, 21:05) and *R2* = *User 2*-(Node 1-1:Port1:Link1, Node 1-2:Port2:Link2, 10 Mbps, 21:01, 21:06), using the accounts user 1 and user 2. The assigned paths were then retrieved from the rm database and the pathElems table, as shown in Figs. 7 (a) and 7 (b). Note that the pathIDs 657 and 661 in the pathElems table were the assigned paths for requests *R1* and *R2*, respectively. User 1 had no restrictions on available ports; consequently, the PCEs allocated the shortest path (2 hops) from Node 1-1 to Node 1-3 to Node 1-2, as presented in Fig. 7 (a). In contrast, user 2 was not authorized to use the path between Node 1-3 and Node 1-2, so the UP-PCE pruned all ports and links of the unauthorized ports from the service topology. The PCEs allocated the alternative 3-hop path to user 2's request (from Node 1-1 to Node 1-4 to Node 1-5 to Node 1-2), as shown in Figure 7 (b).

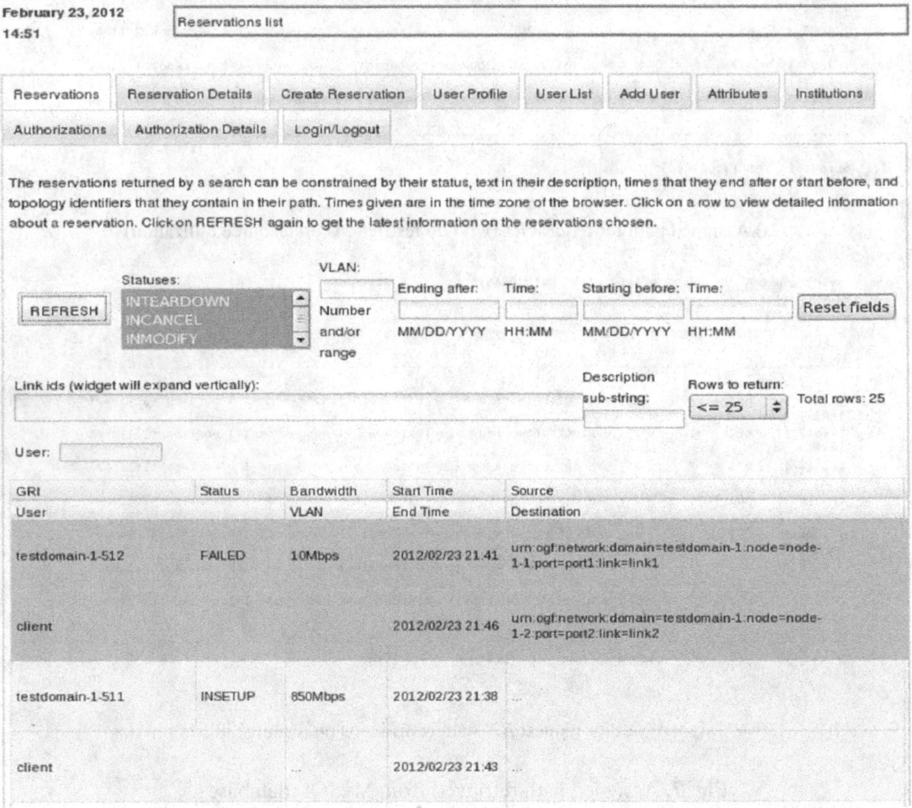

Fig. 8. Reservation list page showing the reservation statuses of *R3* and *R4*

4.2 Bandwidth Allocation Policy (BAP)

User 2 was also not authorized to use the link that had a reserved bandwidth that exceeded 80%. As described in the previous subsection, only the corresponding 3-hop path (from Node 1-1 to Node 1-4 to Node 1-5 to Node 1-2) could be allocated for user 2's request from node 1-1 to node 1-2. The functioning of BAP was confirmed by initially making request *R3* = *User2*-(Node 1-1:Port1:Link1, Node 1-2:Port2:Link2, 850 Mbps, 21:38, 21:43). Next, request *R4* = *User2*-(Node 1-1:Port1:Link1, Node 1-2:Port2:Link2, 10 Mbps, 21:41, 21:46) was created. Figure 8 shows the status of reservations, in which the reservation IDs for *R3* and *R4* were 511 and 512, respectively. The results in Fig. 8 show that request *R3* was accepted while request *R4* was denied, because although the network had sufficient bandwidth for request *R4*, the reserved bandwidth ratio of the ports along the path equaled 0.85 (850/1000) (85%), which exceeded the threshold for user 2.

5 Conclusion

This paper extends PCEs in OSCARS in order to determine the user attributes and the corresponding resource policies in its computation. This approach realizes efficient resource control and service differentiation in DCN. In addition, it is simple to implement in the practical networks because the network administrator can define the constraint-value of the attributes and assigns the corresponding attributes to users via a webpage. Our future work includes the extension of our proposal to support requests via API, the control of topology by assigning different virtual topology data according to the user attributes, and the determination of other QoS provisioning schemes, e.g., preemption.

References

1. Guok, C.P., Robertson, D., Thompson, M., Lee, J., Tierney, B., Johnston, W.: Intra and Interdomain Circuit Provisioning Using the OSCARS Reservation System. In: Proceedings of the 3rd International Conference on Broadband Communications, Networks, and Systems, ICST (2006)
2. Johnston, W., Guok, C.P., Chaniotakis, E.: Motivation, Design, Deployment and Evolution of a Guaranteed Bandwidth Network Service. In: Proceedings of the TERENA Networking Conference (2011)
3. Energy Sciences Network, `http://www.es.net`
4. JGN-X: New Generation Network Testbed, `http://www.jgn.nict.go.jp`
5. Monga, I., Ganguly, S.: Openflow with OSCARS: Bridging the Gap between Campus, Data Centers and the WAN. In: A Demonstration in the Summer 2011 ESCC/Internet2 Joint Techs Conference (2011), `http://events.internet2.edu/2011/jt-uaf/agenda.cfm?go=session&id=10001853`
6. Angu, P., Ramamurthy, B.: Continuous and Parallel Optimization of Dynamic Bandwidth Scheduling in WDM networks. In: Proceedings of the Global Telecommunications Conference (Globecom), pp. 1–6 (2010)
7. Boddie, M., Entel, T., Guok, C., Lake, A., Plante, J., Pouyoul, E., Ramaprasad, B.H., Tierney, B., Triay, J., Vokkarane, V.M.: On Extending ESnet's OSCARS with a Multi-Domain Anycast Service. In: Proceedings of the 16th Conference on Optical Network Design and Modeling (ONDM) (2012)
8. Balman, M., Chaniotakisy, E., Shoshani, A., Sim, A.: A Flexible Reservation Algorithm for Advance Network Provisioning. In: Proceedings of the ACM/IEEE International Conference for High Performance Computing, Networking, Storage and Analysis (2010)
9. OSCARS Authorization Policy, `http://www.es.net/services/virtual-circuits-oscars/documentation/Authorization-Policy/`

10. Zhao, Z., Weber, S., de Oliveira, J.C.: Admission Control and Preemption Policy Design of Multi-Class Computer Networks. In: Proceedings of the 44th Conference on Information Sciences and Systems, CISS (2010)
11. Szviatovszki, B., Szentesi, A., Juttner, A.: Minimizing Re-routing in MPLS Networks with Preemption-aware Constraint-based Routing. The International Journal of Computer and Communications 25(11–12), 1076–1084 (2002)
12. The Dante, Internet2, CANARIE, and ESnet (DICE) InterDomain Controller (IDC) Protocol, http://www.controlplane.net/
13. Network Services Interface (NSI) Working Group, Open Grid Forum, http://ogf.org/gf/group_info/view.php?group=nsi-wg
14. OSCARS-IDC, On-Demand Secure Circuits and Advance Reservation System, http://code.google.com/p/oscars-idc/

Traffic Engineering Approaches in P2P Environments

Pedro Sousa

Centro Algoritmi, Department of Informatics
University of Minho, Braga, Portugal
pns@di.uminho.pt

Abstract. Nowadays, P2P applications proliferate in the Internet with distinct utilization contexts, being also an attractive model for the deployment of advanced Internet services. However, there are several undesirable effects that are caused by such applications, raising coexistence problems with Internet Service Providers (ISPs). In this context, using as case study BitTorrent like applications, this work explores a collaborative framework allowing that advanced efforts could be carried on between P2P applications and network level entities. In order to illustrate such framework, several Traffic Engineering (TE) mechanisms are devised in order to align some P2P dynamics with particular objectives pursued by network administrators. The simulation results show that both the proposed framework and corresponding illustrative mechanisms are viable and can effectively foster future research efforts within this field.

1 Introduction

The nature of Internet applications has greatly evolved in the last years and there is an increasing usage of P2P overlay networks [1], where peers form self-organized network infrastructures. Within this class of applications, BitTorrent [2][3] is a common example of one of the most popular solutions [7], being responsible for a large amount of the total Internet traffic [8].

Thus, the massive use of P2P applications and their inherent operating models opened new application opportunities in areas as content distribution, distributed file systems, games, virtual reality, software updates, etc. However, it is also true that ISPs are facing serious coexistence problems with the P2P operational paradigm. In fact, P2P usually generates high variability and distortion in traffic patterns, along with excessive and unpredictable loads in crucial links. Moreover, P2P behaviors many times preclude the use of classical Traffic Engineering (TE) techniques for network optimization [9][10]. As consequence, this results in several coexistence problems between network providers and P2P based applications [12]. In order to deal with that, ISPs often resort to caching devices [15][16] to reduce bandwidth consumption, or inspection tools to detect and control P2P traffic [17]. Nevertheless, P2P applications are permanently fostering the battle to surpass some of these mechanisms and there is a wide range of P2P approaches with distinct selfish behaviors, adaptation strategies

V. Guyot (Ed.): ICAIT 2012, LNCS 7593, pp. 61–74, 2013.

and peering solutions [18][19]. In this perspective, this work assumes the inherent advantages of devising collaborative approaches between P2P and network level entities (e.g. ISPs). For that purpose, using a BitTorrent-like P2P approach as case study, this work proposes a framework able to enrich the decisions adopted by P2P applications, also taking into account specific requirements imposed by the underlying network level. Within this context, and resorting to a highly reconfigurable P2P tracker, several illustrative TE mechanisms are explored by considering some mathematical foundations from the graph theory field. The explored models constitute preliminary approaches to deal with P2P swarms involving a high number of peers, aiming to raise the network level with some control and estimation capabilities to better accommodate such P2P traffic aggregates in the underlying infra-structure.

The paper is organized as follows: Section 2 describes the rationale of the proposed framework along with illustrative tracker configurations; Section 3 presents the experimental platform and obtained simulation results; finally, Section 4 draws the main conclusions related to the proposed solution.

2 Proposed Framework and Illustrative Configurations

In order to illustrate the proposed framework (see Figure 1) we assume the specific case of BitTorrent-like applications, considering that such system principles could be used to develop proprietary applications offered by content/service providers to their end-users. Additionally, the application scenario adopted within the proposed collaborative system assumes that the tracker is the only entity able to provide peering information. Thus, client side software provided to end-users is not able to exchange peer identities with other peers, meaning that the tracker fully controls the peering informations provided to the clients. In BitTorrent classical systems, new peers wishing to join a specific swarm contact a tracker which then provides the clients with a random sample of peers. This sample is used by the peers for establishing new P2P connections with other peers in the swarm to obtain a given shared resource. After this stage, several BitTorrent rules will drive the data transfer processes among the peers. These additional details about the BitTorrent protocol regarding pieces selection algorithms and choking strategies to determine which peers to choke/unchoke can be found in [1,2]. In this perspective, the P2P tracker main role is to keep track of the current peers participating in a given swarm and dynamically provide random peer samples to newly arrived peers in the swarm.

The proposed architecture, depicted in Figure 1, assumes an ISP networking domain, consisting of several core routers (which in this work context may also express possible Points of Presence (PoPs) of the ISP), interconnected by several links. At the P2P application level, peers are distributed among several end-users areas, which access ISP infrastructure through the corresponding PoP. The P2P tracker is able to use alternative configurations, which could be defined by the administrator (or other external entities) and might be programmed and activated using appropriate configuration commands. Distinct configuration strategies adopted by the tracker may require distinct types of information, depending

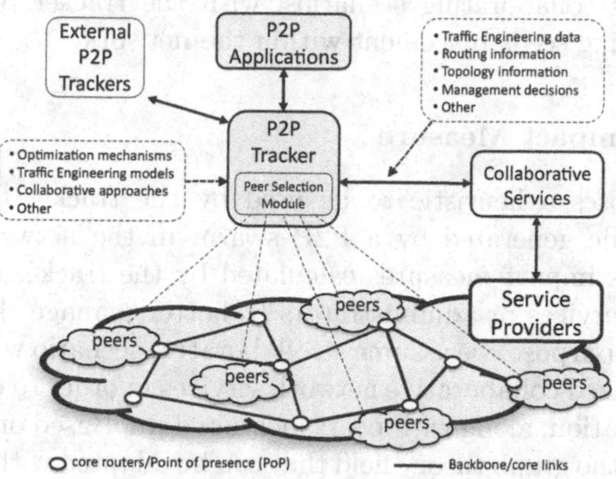

Fig. 1. Illustrative description of the proposed operational scenario

on their objectives and operation modes. Moreover, if required, the tracker may also integrate additional intelligent optimization (e.g. [11,14]) or forecasting (e.g. [4]) mechanisms to deal with high complex optimization problems. The external collaborative services, mainly controlled by the network providers, are expected to provide useful information for the P2P system. Examples of possible external information sources may include: network level entities/services able to provide privileged network level information (e.g. topology inputs, routing information, peers location, or other TE data); Provider Portals (e.g. as defined in [13]); administrative services providing specific management policies to the tracker; or any other entity able to interact with the tracker providing valuable information. These interoperation possibilities between the P2P applicational level and network level entities present incentives attracting both sides. Service level entities (e.g. content providers) can benefit from gathering underlying network information and network providers might also try to influence application level peering decisions in order to improve their network resources usage. In this perspective, and depending on the defined objectives, distinct advanced TE mechanisms could be implemented at the P2P tracker.

Some examples of possible configurations useful for TE purposes will be presented in the following sections. Within the context of P2P swarms involving a considerable number of peers, the objective at this stage is to explore how some simple mathematical foundations from the graph theory field can be adapted and used as underpinning models to gather preliminary snapshots of the global P2P application and corresponding traffic aggregates dynamics. If such estimation efforts could be effectively accomplished, the studied models will be then able to be enriched and improved in the future with additional modeling capabilities. The first two examples of the presented illustrative mechanisms focus on providing some preliminary estimation approaches able to achieve qualitative measures about the impact of P2P traffic in network links, also allowing that ISPs may divert traffic from specific links of their infrastructures. The third example could be useful for other collaborating scenarios, with the tracker providing useful information regarding seeds placement within the network.

2.1 P2P Link Impact Measure

This section proposes a heuristic to be used by the tracker to estimate the impact of the traffic generated by a P2P swarm in the network links of the ISP. Such P2P link impact measures calculated by the tracker can be used by external network services or administrators to better manage their networking resources. For that purpose, we assume a collaborative scenario where the tracker can contact authorized collaborative network services in order to collect topology and routing information, along with peers location data. Based on that, there are some aspects from the graph theory field that can be adapted within this context. As example, several graph measures [5,6] could constitute valuable inputs to be adapted in order to devise estimation techniques of P2P link impacts values.

To illustrate such concepts we assume that the tracker may resort to a network representation using a mathematical model which represents ISP nodes (routers) and transmission links by a set of nodes (N) and links (L), respectively, in a simple graph $G = (N, L)$. For simplicity, we consider network scenarios with symmetric links, which can be modeled by an undirected graph. Each pair of nodes in the graph ($x, y \in N$) is connected by a given path comprising one or more links, according to a given routing strategy adopted at the network domain (e.g. as shortest-path based mechanisms). Also, each link ($l \in L$) has specific attributes, such as an assigned weight for routing purposes, used by the ISP to compute shortest-paths among the nodes. Moreover, we also assume that the location (area) of end-users peers participating in the swarm is denoted by the corresponding ISP PoP/core router, a, with $a \in A$ and $A \subseteq N$. In order to compute the P2P link impact values, the tracker will evaluate a P2P betweenness centrality measure for each one of the links, taking into account the locations of the swarm peers (identified by the corresponding ISP router/PoP). For a particular link, l, and a specific pair of end-users areas, $i, j \in A$, the metric takes into account the ratio between the number of shortest paths from i to j, $nsp_{i,j}$, and the number of shortest paths from i to j that pass through link l, $nsp_{i,j}(l)$, resulting that link l will be assigned with a partial impact value of $\frac{nsp_{i,j}(l)}{nsp_{i,j}}$ for the particular case of i, j peering adjacencies. It is then possible to sum all the partial impact values involving link l, and obtain a reference value within the interval $[0, 1]$ by considering all the possible area peering adjacencies, i.e. $|A| \cdot (|A| - 1)$. In the case of P2P swarms where end-user areas show a considerable unbalanced distribution of the number of peers (also reflected in the number of peers from each area that are included in the random samples returned by the tracker) an additional weighting factor could be introduced, $w_{i,j}$, for each specific i, j[1]

[1] $w_{i,j}$ factor considers the ratio between the number of peers involved in the area peering adjacency i, j over the total number of peers involved in all possible area peering adjacencies. In order to preserve the original form of the betweenness measure, this ratio is multiplied by $|A| \cdot (|A| - 1)$ for normalization purposes.

case. This will increase the importance of shortest paths connecting areas having a higher number of peers. Thus, links presenting higher betweenness centrality values have a higher probability of being traversed by traffic of the corresponding BitTorrent P2P swarm. For the case of a tracker returning random samples to the contacting peers, Equation 1 presents the normalized P2P betweenness centrality value for link l, within the interval $[0, 1]$, which is from this point on designated as P2P link Impact Measure I (IM_I).

$$IM_I(l) = \frac{\sum_{i,j \in A, i \neq j} \frac{nsp_{i,j}(l)}{nsp_{i,j}} \cdot w_{i,j}}{|A| \cdot (|A| - 1)}, l \in L \quad (1)$$

The devised P2P link impact measure can be further enhanced taking into account some common application level dynamics assumed by the BitTorrent protocol. In fact, due to the inherent characteristics of the transport protocols used by BitTorrent (e.g. TCP), peers usually have a considerable probability of establishing peering connections with nearest peers in the network, taking advantage of lower RTTs . In this perspective, in Equation 1, when considering a given shortest path between areas i and j (assuming the context of peers in area i trying get data from peers in area j) it is also possible to assign a preference value[2] ($p_{i \leftarrow j} \in [0, 1]$ with $\sum_{j \in A, j \neq i} p_{i \leftarrow j} = 1$) to such shortest paths, which implicitly expresses how close is area j from area i. This value is then multiplied by the number of possible external peering adjacencies that could be made by peers in area i, i.e. $|A| - 1$. The resulting value is then used as a weighting factor when accounting the shortest path between areas i and j. Equation 2 expresses an alternative P2P betweenness centrality value for link l, from this point on designated as P2P link Impact Measure II (IM_{II}). The IM_{II} or IM_I impact measures could be then announced to network services or administrators which may require the tracker to change its behavior according to a given objective.

$$IM_{II}(l) = \frac{\sum_{i,j \in A, i \neq j} [(|A| - 1) \cdot p_{i \leftarrow j}] \cdot \frac{nsp_{i,j}(l)}{nsp_{i,j}} \cdot w_{i,j}}{|A| \cdot (|A| - 1)}, l \in L \quad (2)$$

2.2 Protecting Links from P2P Traffic

This configuration mode allows that the tracker could be configured in order to protect specific network links from excessive levels of P2P traffic. In a context of TE efforts, external network level services or administrators are now able to inform the tracker about the link(s) that it should protect, i.e. requiring that the tracker reduces their P2P impact values. For that purpose, and taken the example of a given set of protected links, $K \subseteq L$, the tracker objective is to

[2] If required, in highly heterogeneous scenarios, the estimation model could be enriched by also reflecting in this parameter the relative quality of the average upload capacities of area j peers, when compared with other peers in the domain.

minimize the P2P impact values of links $k \in K$, e.g. induce peering adjacencies constrained by one of the illustrative objective functions expressed in Equation 3, depending on the adopted P2P link impact measure. To achieve this objective, the tracker should change its random behavior and carefully select which peers should integrate the peer samples returned to requesting clients.

$$\min\Big(\sum_{k \in K, K \subseteq L} IM_I(k)\Big) \;\; OR \;\; \min\Big(\sum_{k \in K, K \subseteq L} IM_{II}(k)\Big) \tag{3}$$

The underpinning optimization concept is that the P2P tracker be able to induce peering adjacencies that should now avoid traversing network paths including the protected links. It is possible that under some peering configurations achieved by the tracker the previously presented P2P link impact equations need to be adapted in consonance with the new conditions[3].

2.3 Seeds Placement Strategies

This tracker configuration example could be used when network level services, in collaboration with content providers, are intended to have an active participation in the definition of the swarm structure, namely as regards to seeds placement. In this context, and as will be illustrated in Section 3.3, this mechanism can be used with distinct objectives, such as benefit some peers areas in the swarm, or to achieve a more efficient usage of networking resources. For that purpose, the tracker should be able to provide valuable information to network administrators about the correct positioning of the seed(s) given a pre-defined criteria. Assuming that the tracker has the objective of finding the more appropriate seed locations for a given set of end-users areas Z (with $Z \subseteq A$), it is possible to resort to the notion of closeness centrality to compute the mean length of the shortest paths (lsp) between the candidate seed locations (any network node/PoP within the ISP infrastructure) and the considered areas. As before, for unbalanced distributions of the number of peers in the areas, an weighting factor could be introduced, w_i, for each specific area[4]. Equation 4 expresses then a closeness centrality measure for location n, from this point on designated as P2P Closeness Measure (CM), and candidate locations with lower CM values are expected to better serve the considered areas.

$$CM(n) = \frac{\sum_{i \in Z, Z \subseteq A} lsp_{n,i} \cdot w_i}{|Z|}, n \in N \tag{4}$$

[3] As an example, if peers in some area are not able to contact peers in other specific areas, then the number of all possible area adjacencies will be no longer $|A| \cdot (|A| - 1)$ as assumed in Equations 1 and 2, for normalization purposes.

[4] The w_i factor considers the ratio between the number of peers in area i over the total number of peers in all areas. Taking into account the original form of the closeness measure this ratio is multiplied by $|Z|$ for normalization purposes.

3 Experiments and Results

For testing purposes, the ns-2 [21] simulator was used to develop the proposed architecture and test some of the devised tracker configurations. A packet-level simulation approach was adopted for that purpose, using a simulation patch [20] implementing a BitTorrent-like protocol. This patch was extended to integrate a prototype with the major components of the framework presented in Figure 1, also including the illustrative tracker configurations previously described.

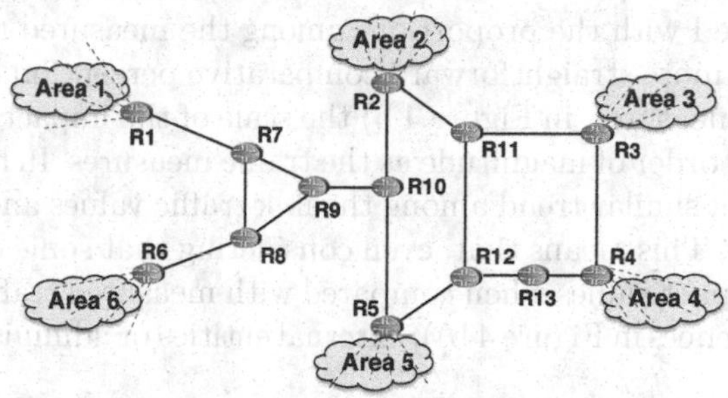

Fig. 2. Network topology used to collect illustrative results

Figure 2 illustrates the network topology adopted to present some illustrative results. At the top level the Internet Service Provider consists of several core routers (for this work context they can also be viewed as possible Points of Presence (PoPs)), interconnected by several links. For P2P application level simulation, six end-users areas with participating peers are assumed. Each area is composed by a second level of nodes/access links. Most of the parameters controlling the BitTorrent-like protocol could be configured, such as the number of seeds and leechers per domain, their arrival processes into the swarm group, tracker related configurations, the use (or not) of superseeding, chunk size, file size, among others. In the selected examples the results were taken from a simulation scenario assuming nearly 50 leechers per area, i.e. a total number of 300 peers. The file size is 50 MB and the chunk size 256 KB. The maximum size of the peer sample returned by the tracker is 25. At the end-users areas the peers have, on average, an upload capacity of 1 Mbps and a download capacity which is considered to be eight times higher than this value. In order to improve the heterogeneity of each area, the propagation delays of the access links were randomly generated in the interval of 1-50 ms. In this illustrative scenario, the ISP links were considered to be able to support a maximum share of 50 Mbps for P2P traffic and their propagations delays are at least two times higher than the values considered for access links. In the following sections, and for each particular tracker configuration example, five simulations ($s_1, ..., s_5$) were made and the corresponding mean values taken for analysis.

3.1 P2P Link Impact Measures

This section illustrates a scenario where the P2P tracker evaluates qualitative P2P impact measures for the network links of the domain. In this specific example a single seed in considered to exist on each end-user network area. The values presented in Figure 3 a) report the cumulative values of P2P traffic traversing each link, for each one of the simulation instances, with the corresponding mean values presented in Figure 3 b). As observed, the P2P traffic resulting from the swarm behavior has a major impact in some specific links of the network domain. The estimated P2P link impacts, using the IM_I technique[5], are presented in Figure 4 a), where it is visible an acceptable match when the proportions over such link impact values are compared with the proportions among the measured traffic values. In order to provide a more straightforward comparative perception between impact values and traffic measures, in Figure 4 b) the scale of the impact values was converted to the same order of magnitude as the traffic measures. In this perspective, Figure 4 b) shows a similar trend among the link traffic values and the forecasted link impact values. This means that, even considering that some distortions exist among the link impact values when compared with measured traffic (given by the plotted lines differences in Figure 4 b)), external entities or administrators can rely

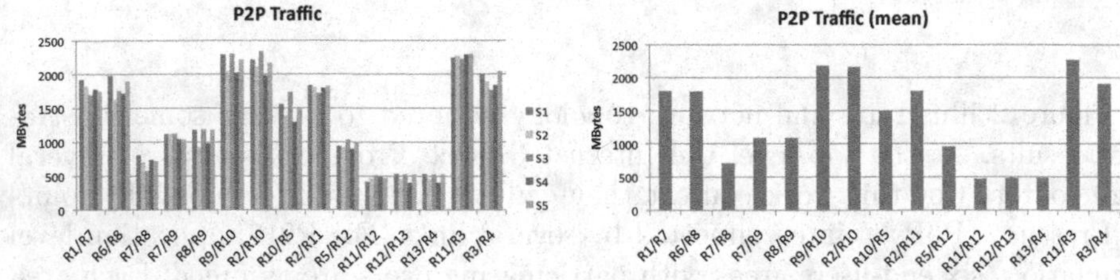

Fig. 3. P2P traffic traversing each link a) on each simulation b) mean values

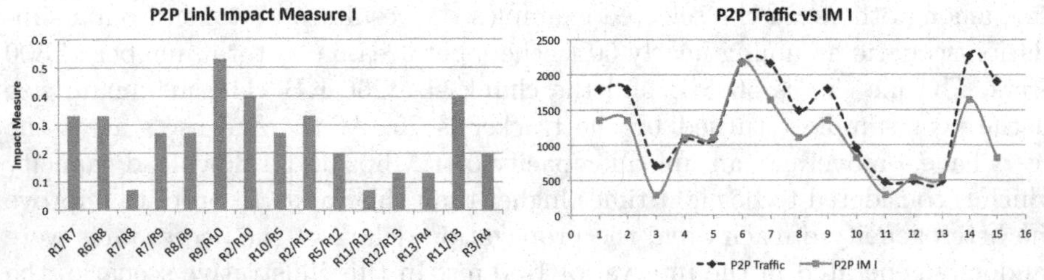

Fig. 4. a) P2P link impact measure IM_I b) IM_I vs observed traffic values

[5] For this scenario, the estimation model considers all i, j paths with $w_{i,j} = 1$.

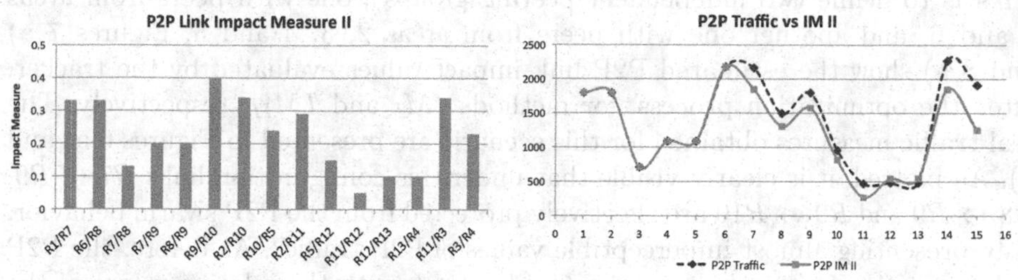

Fig. 5. a) P2P link impact measure IM_{II} b) IM_{II} vs observed traffic values

on trackers that use the IM_I technique to nearly forecast the qualitative impact of P2P traffic in the network domain. The estimation of the P2P link impact measures can be further enhanced using the IM_{II} method. In this context, Figure 5 a) presents the P2P link impact estimations using the IM_{II} model[6], with the comparative values presented in Figure 5 b). As shown, a more accurate match between the link impact values and the proportions among real traffic measures is now obtained.

3.2 Protecting Links from P2P Traffic

The results included in this section illustrate a tracker configuration protecting specific links of the network from excessive P2P traffic, using a similar simulation scenario. In this specific case, the tracker was informed (e.g. by the network administrator) that it should protect the following links: $R7 \leftrightarrow R9$, $R8 \leftrightarrow R9$ and $R9 \leftrightarrow R10$ (see Figure 2). For that purpose, the tracker will try to reduce the betweenness centrality values associated with such links in order to decrease the corresponding P2P traffic. After this optimization process the tracker will verify which are the most appropriate peering adjacencies to follow, and will apply such knowledge when returning peer samples to the requesting peers. In this specific case the tracker will find that the best way to protect the mentioned

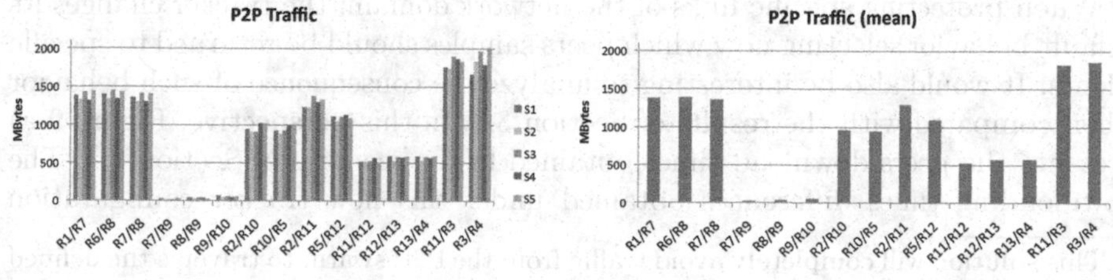

Fig. 6. P2P traffic traversing each link a) on each simulation b) mean values

[6] $p_{i \leftarrow j}$ was set to 0.4 for the nearest area and 0.15 for the other areas.

links is to define two independent peering groups[7], one with peers from areas 1 and 6, and another one with peers from areas 2, 3, 4 and 5. Figures 7 a) and 8 a) show the estimated P2P link impact values evaluated by the tracker, after the optimization process, for methods IM_I and IM_{II}, respectively. The real traffic measures obtained for this scenario are presented in Figures 6 a) and b). As plotted, it is clearly visible that under this configuration links $R7 \leftrightarrow R9$, $R8 \leftrightarrow R9$ and $R9 \leftrightarrow R10$ are effectively protected from the P2P swarm behavior, only presenting almost imperceptible values of P2P traffic[8]. As before, the P2P link impact measures show an acceptable match with the relative values of the traffic gathered in simulation, with the IM_{II} method providing more accurate estimations, as depicted by Figures 7 b) and 8 b).

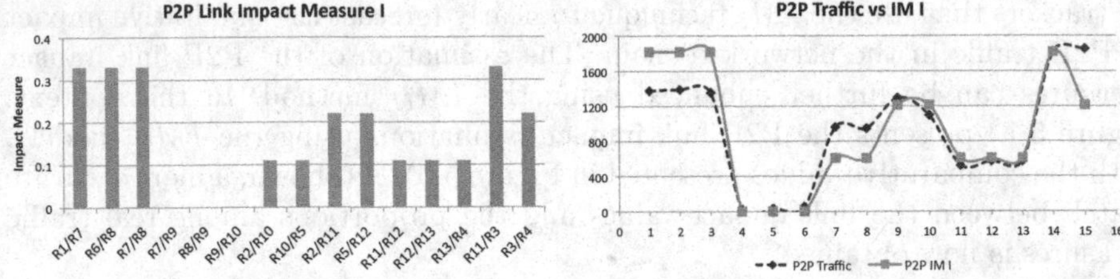

Fig. 7. a) P2P link impact measure IM_I b) IM_I vs observed traffic values

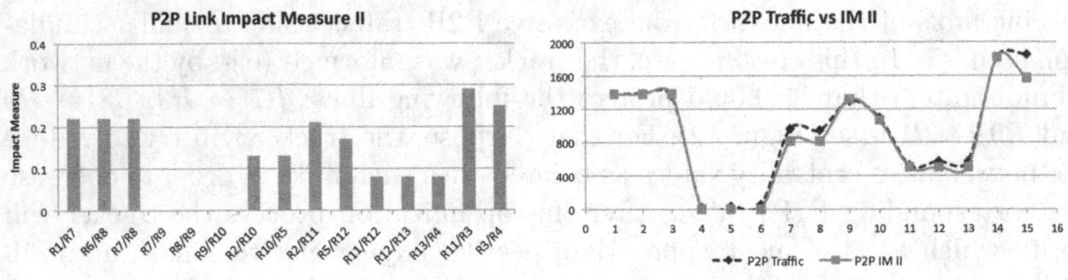

Fig. 8. a) P2P link impact measure IM_{II} b) IM_{II} vs observed traffic values

When protecting specific links of the network domain, the tracker changes its default behavior selecting now which peers samples should be returned to specific clients. It would also be interesting to analyze the consequence of such behavior when compared with the results of Section 3.1. In this perspective, Figure 9 a) presents the peers download times obtained in the scenario of Section 3.1. The downloading times differences obtained under this new tracker configuration

[7] This solution will completely avoid traffic from the P2P swarm to traverse the defined links, i.e. impact measures equal to zero. However, other not so severe solutions could also be defined by the tracker.

[8] The residual values are due to the implemented algorithm at the tracker, with an initial phase where no constraints are applied to the peering adjacencies.

are plotted in Figure 9 b). As observed, some peers from areas 1 and 6 obtained slightly higher download times (roughly an 8% increase), while peers from the other areas experience download times which may increase or decrease in the same order of magnitude. Overall, such values do not significantly affect the overall service quality meaning that the objective of protecting specific network links was accomplished, in this case, with lower costs from the end-users P2P service quality perception.

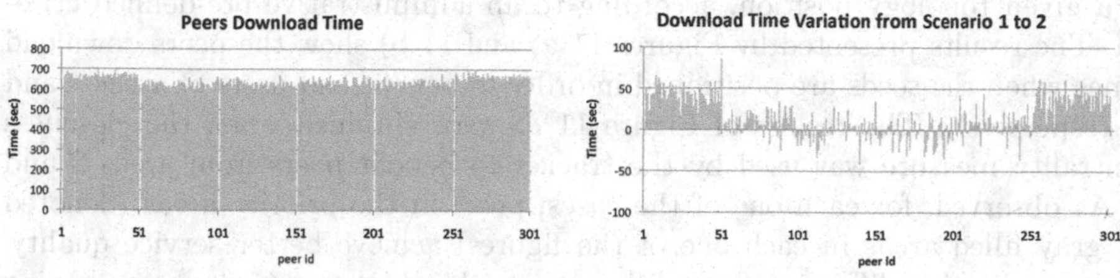

Fig. 9. a) Peers download time in Scenario 1 b) variations observed in Scenario 2

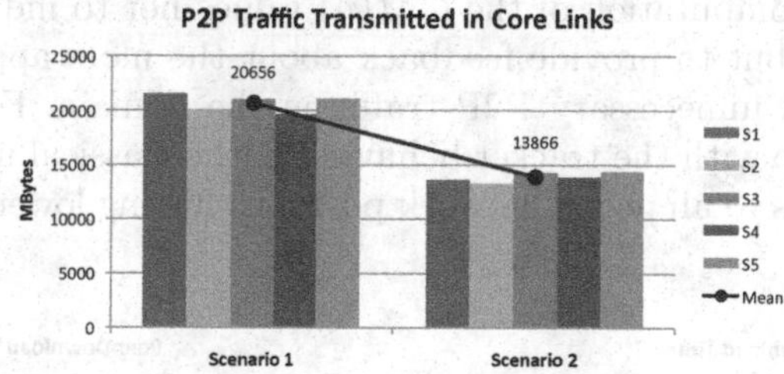

Fig. 10. Overall P2P traffic transmitted in the network domain links

Figure 10 also compares both scenarios as regards to the overall P2P traffic transmitted in the network. As observed, when the tracker was configured to protect some specific links (scenario 2) there is a clear decrease in the overall P2P traffic traversing the network domain (around a 32% decrease), representing a significative advantage from the operator perspective. This is justified by a side-effect resulting from the peering adjacencies induced by the tracker in Scenario 2, which forces nearing peers to participate in the data exchanges, thus avoiding unnecessary connections among distant peers. This example proves that intelligent tracker decisions can effectively improve network resource usage without significantly degrading end-users service quality.

3.3 Seed Placement Influence

The results included in this section assume that the network level is able to participate in the P2P swarm configuration, namely being responsible for the placement of P2P seeds in the network. As explained, within the devised method, the tracker resorts to $CM(n)$ measures to devise appropriate placements for a given seed(s) and provide such information to the network level administrators responsible to place them in the pointed positions. In the next examples the tracker was required to devise the placement of two high upload capacity seeds in a given topology position, according to an administrative pre-defined criteria. The results presented by Figures 11 a) and 11 b) show the peers download times when the seeds are positioned in order to benefit end-users of areas 1 and 3, respectively. The results of Figure 11 c) were obtained when the closeness centrality measure was used by the tracker to benefit peers from areas 2 and 5. As observed, for each one of the cases, peers in the priority areas (denoted by gray filled areas in each one of the figures) achieve better service quality, i.e. a qualitative differentiation with peers within higher priority areas having lower downloading times. In each one the three illustrative cases presented before the tracker indication was to place the seeds in network positions R1, R3 and R10, respectively (see Figure 2). In another distinct perspective, the tracker can also resort to the computation of the $CM(n)$ values not to induce service quality differentiation, but to provide feedback about the more appropriate seed(s) placement to avoid unnecessary P2P traffic in the domain. For that purpose, assuming a scenario with the tracker behaving in the classical mode, i.e. returning random samples to all peers, network positions having lower global closeness

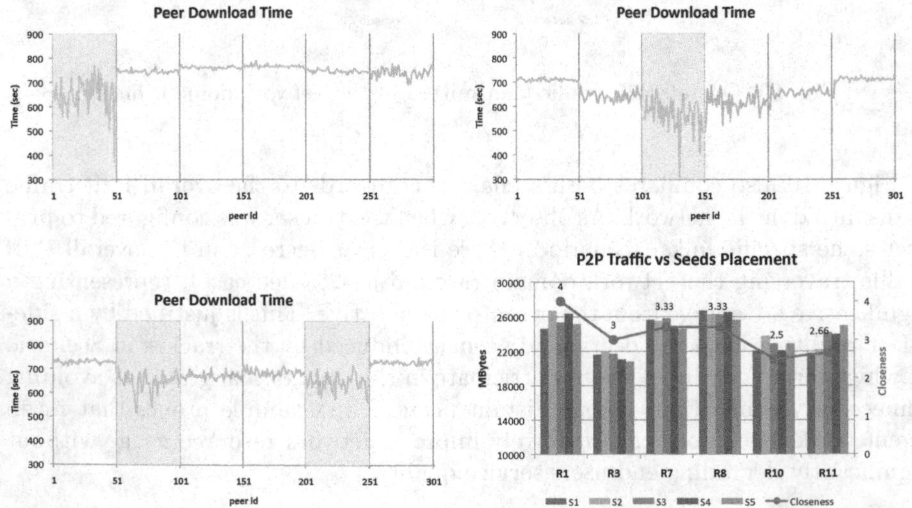

Fig. 11. Peers download times with seeds placed at a) R1 b) R3 c) R10; d) P2P traffic traversing the domain for distinct seeds placements

centrality values, $CM(n)$, are expected to be better candidates for seed positions. Figure 11 d) illustrates this by showing the centrality values of distinct candidate seed positions and the overall P2P traffic traversing the domain when seeds are placed in such positions. As observed, network locations having lower $CM(n)$ values show a tendency to originate lower amounts of P2P traffic.

4 Conclusions

This work explored the concept of a collaborative framework involving P2P applications and network level entities to underpin the development of advanced TE mechanisms. Taken the example of BitTorrent applications, several illustrative tracker configurations were explored being able to provide useful auxiliary information to network administrators, and better accommodate P2P traffic within the network infrastructure, e.g. by protecting specific links from excessive P2P traffic. Resorting to simulation, both the framework and the devised mechanisms were tested successfully. Even considering the inherent difficulties of controlling application level P2P dynamics and obtain precise impact estimations, it has been demonstrated that there is a wide range of possible fruitful collaboration efforts that could be made between the P2P and network levels. As future work, there are still many other TE related mechanisms that could be developed using the proposed framework. Moreover, some of the preliminary TE mechanisms proposed here can be further enhanced by also considering other network level specificities. In such cases, the tracker may gather additional information from the network level (e.g. congestion levels, packet loss, etc.) to further improve the modeling capabilities and the effectiveness of the devised TE mechanisms.

Acknowledgments. This work is partially funded by FEDER Funds through the Programa Operacional Fatores de Competitividade COMPETE and by National Funds through the FCT - Fundação para a Ciência e a Tecnologia (Portuguese Foundation for Science and Technology) within project FCOMP-01-0124-FEDER-022674.

References

1. Lua, K., Crowcroft, J., Pias, M., Sharma, R., Lim, S.: A survey and Comparison of Peer-to-peer Overlay Network Schemes. IEEE Communications Surveys & Tutorials, 72–93 (2005)
2. Choen, B.: Incentives Build Robustness in BitTorrent. In: Proc. 1st Workshop on Economics of Peer-to-Peer Systems, Berkeley (June 2003)
3. Bharambe, A., Herley, C., Padmanabhan, V.: Analyzing and Improving a BitTorrent Networks Performance Mechanisms. In: Proc. IEEE INFOCOM (2006)
4. Cortez, P., Rio, M., Rocha, M., Sousa, P.: Multi-scale Internet traffic forecasting using neural networks and time series methods. Expert Systems: The Journal of Knowledge Engineering 29(2), 143–155 (2012)
5. Opsahl, T., Agneessens, F., Skvoretz, J.: Node Centrality in Weighted Networks: Generalizing degree and shortest paths. Social Networks 32(3), 245–251 (2010)

6. Narayanan, S.: The Betweenness Centrality of Biological Networks. MSc Thesis, Faculty of the Virginia Polytechnic Inst. and State University (2005)
7. Karagiannis, T., et al.: Is P2P Dying or Just Hiding? In: Proc. Globecom, Dallas, TX, USA (November 2004)
8. Schulze, H., Mochalski, K.: Internet Study 2007: The Impact of P2P File Sharing, Voice over IP, Skype, Joost, Instant Messaging, One-Click Hosting and Media Streaming such as YouTube on the Internet, Tech. report (2007)
9. Keralapura, R., Taft, N., Chuah, C., Iannaccone, G.: Can ISPs Take the Heat from Overlay Networks? In: Proc. HotNets-III, San Diego, CA (November 2004)
10. Qiu, L., Yang, Y.R., Zhang, Y., Shenker, S.: SelFIsh Routing in Internet-like Environments. In: Proc. of SIGCOMM, Karlsruhe, Germany (August 2003)
11. Sousa, P., Cortez, P., Rio, M., Rocha, M.: Traffic Engineering Approaches using Multicriteria Optimization Techniques. In: Masip-Bruin, X., Verchere, D., Tsaoussidis, V., Yannuzzi, M. (eds.) WWIC 2011. LNCS, vol. 6649, pp. 104–115. Springer, Heidelberg (2011)
12. Xie, H., Krishnamurthy, A., Silberschatz, A., Yang, Y.R.: P4P: Explicit Communications for Cooperative Control between P2P and Network Providers, http://www.dcia.info/documents/P4P_Overview.pdf
13. Xie, H., et al.: P4P: Provider Portal for Applications. In: Proc. SIGCOMM 2008 Conference, Seattle, Washington, USA, August 17–22 (2008)
14. Sousa, P., Rocha, M., Rio, M., Cortez, P.C.: Efficient OSPF Weight Allocation for Intra-domain QoS Optimization. In: Parr, G., Malone, D., Ó Foghlú, M. (eds.) IPOM 2006. LNCS, vol. 4268, pp. 37–48. Springer, Heidelberg (2006)
15. Shen, G., Wang, Y., Xiong, Y., Zhao, B., Zhang, Z.: HPTP: Relieving the Tension between ISPs and P2P. In: Proc. of IPTPS, Bellevue, WA (February 2007)
16. Wierzbicki, A., Leibowitz, N., Ripeanu, M., Wozniak, R.: Cache Replacement Policies Revisited: The case of P2P traffic. In: Proc. of GP2P (2004)
17. Spognardi, A., Lucarelli, A., DiPietro, R.: A Methodology for P2P File-Sharing Trafc Detection. In: Proc. Second International Workshop on Hot Topics in Peer-to-Peer Systems 2005 (HOT-P2P 2005), pp. 52–61 (July 2005)
18. Karagiannis, T., Rodriguez, P., Papagiannaki, K.: Should Internet Service Providers fear Peer-assisted Content Distribution? In: Proc. Proceedings of the Internet Measurement Conference, Berkeley, CA (October 2005)
19. Madhyastha, H., et al.: iPlane: An Information Plane for Distributed Services. In: Proc. of OSDI Conference, Seattle, WA (2006)
20. Eger, K., et al.: Efficient Simulation of Large-Scale P2P Networks: Packet-level vs. Flow-level Simulations. In: Proc. 2nd Workshop on the Use of P2P, GRID and Agents for the Development of Content Networks (2007)
21. ns-2 The Network Simulator, http://www.isi.edu/nsnam/ns/

On Selective Placement for Uniform Cache Objects

Jong-Geun Park[1] and Hoon Choi[2]

[1] Electronics & Telecommunications Research Institute (ETRI), Daejeon 305-700, Republic of Korea
queue@etri.re.kr

[2] Dep't of Computer Science & Engineering, Chungnam National University, Daejeon 305-764, Republic of Korea
hc@cnu.ac.kr

Abstract. For several decades, numerous studies for the cache replacement algorithms have been performed in order to enhance cache performance. But, as the performance of a new algorithm has improved, the complexity of the algorithm has gradually increased. In the end, in most of practices, the LRU algorithm has been still successfully used, because of its good hit ratio, low complexity of O(1), and so on.

For most of cache replacement algorithms, all references are always cached without any limitation. But, in the reference stream which follows the well-known Zipf-like nature of popularity, such as Web server/proxy and P2P file sharing environments, a large fraction of the total reference stream are arbitrarily singly or rarely accessed objects. These unpopular objects tend to cause unnecessary replacement of popular ones. Thus, to account for this, a mechanism such as the cache placement policy needs to be considered.

In this paper, we proposed the recency-based cache placement strategy to effectively capture the popularity of a newly referenced object, and showed the superiority of the cache placement policy by performance comparison with simulation experiments. Finally we concluded that simply combining with the cache placement policy enables to raise the hit ratio without need of complex replacement algorithms.

Keywords: Cache Placement Policy, Cache Replacement Policy, Uniform Cache Object.

1 Introduction

Generally the caching strategy exploits the principle of locality by proving an expensive, small and fast memory. Due to the constraints of cache size, however, eventually a cache will be full and a problem that which data object should be replaced arises. Moreover, an efficient cache management that increases hit ratios by only several percentage points would be equivalent to a several-fold increase in cache size [1]. Therefore, the finding a better cache management algorithm is an important and ongoing research work.

V. Guyot (Ed.): ICAIT 2012, LNCS 7593, pp. 75–82, 2013.

So far, most of studies have been focused on finding a good cache replacement algorithm. Generally the goal of the cache replacement policy in a uniform sized caching environment is to reduce cache misses by replacing an object with the least likelihood of re-reference in the near future. So the design goal of cache replacement policies is to find a victim object of which likelihood of re-reference is the lowest.

The Zipf-like nature of popularity distribution for Web proxies and P2P file sharing environments is a well-known feature. In the references which follows the Zipfian popularity property, a large fraction of the total reference stream are arbitrarily singly or rarely accessed objects, and it may result in unnecessary replacement of an popular object by an unpopular one. Thus, to account for this, a mechanism such as the cache placement policy needs to be considered that de-emphasizes accesses made to unpopular objects.

In this paper, we proposed the recency-based cache placement strategy to effectively capture the popularity of a newly referenced object, and showed the superiority of the cache placement policy by performance comparison with simulation experiments. Finally we concluded that simply combining with the cache placement policy enables to raise the hit ratio without need of complex replacement algorithms.

The remainder of the paper is organized as follows. In Section 2, we summarize typical cache replacement and placement algorithms. And then, we introduce the recency-based cache placement policy in the Section 3. In Section 4, the performance comparisons among LRU, LRU-2, 2Q, LRFU and RBP-LRU are presented and discussed. Finally the conclusion follows in Section 5.

2 Related Works

2.1 Cache Replacement Policies

Among the various replacement algorithms, the Least Recently Used (LRU) algorithm has been successfully used in practice. The LRU is based on the temporal locality of the reference seen in request streams. Temporal locality refers to repeated accesses to the same object within short time periods and implies that recently referenced objects are likely to be re-referenced in the near future. Due to the property of temporal locality, a lot of variants of the LRU have been proposed and analyzed. In certain applications, however, the LRU and its simple variants have difficulties in deciding an optimal victim object since they do not consider enough reference information including frequency and size information of the object. For example, once an object has been accessed, the LRU guarantees it a long cache sojourn time, even though the object has never been referenced before.

The Least Frequently Used (LFU) algorithm makes use of frequency information as a main decision factor. But, frequency-based algorithms should track the frequency values for all objects in the system, and calculate their priorities to evict the most unpopular object, eventually which causes logarithmic complexity. In addition, the stale objects frequently accessed in the past can stay in the cache for a long time, which causes cache pollution. An aging policy is often used to cope with this problem. Therefore, the LFU was pushed into a corner until 1993, when the LRU-K replacement algorithm [2] was developed by revisiting the LFU [3].

After that, several replacement strategies considering both recency and frequency information have been proposed. When a cache slot is needed for a new referenced object, the LRU-K strategy evicts an object whose elapsed time from the backward K-th reference epoch, so called Backward K-distance, is the maximum of all objects in the cache. The Backward K-distance of an object i at time t, $b_{i,K}(t)$, is defined as (1).

$$b_{i,K}(t) = \begin{cases} x, & \text{if } \tau_{i,-K} = t - x, (0 \leq x \leq t); \\ \infty, & \text{if } N_i(t) < K \end{cases} , \tag{1}$$

where $\tau_{i,-k}$ is the backward k-th referenced time to an object i, and $N_i(t)$ is the total number of references to an object i among reference streams up to time t. The LRU-K also requires the logarithmic complexity of O($log_2 N$) to compute the priorities and incurs an O(KN) space overhead to keep the history of the last K references for all objects in the system. Therefore, the LRU-K achieves significant improvement in hit ratio, but it does not beat the LRU owing to its complexity.

The 2Q algorithm [4] is a successor of the LRU-K algorithm, the goal of which is to satisfy similar cache replacement performance as LRU-2 while maintaining low complexity, as in the LRU. So, in the 2Q algorithm, the buffer cache is partitioned into a special buffer, the A1 queue, which contains objects referenced once; and a main buffer, the Am queue, in which re-referenced objects staying in the A1 buffer can be cached.

The Least Recently/Frequently Used (LRFU) strategy [5] inherits the benefits of the LRU and LFU policies in a unified scheme, and allows a flexible trade-off between the recency and frequency of the references. The LRFU policy associates the Combined Recency and Frequency (CRF) value with each object that quantifies the likelihood that the object will be referenced in the near future. The CRF value of an object i at time t is defined as (2).

$$C_t(i) = \sum_{k=1}^{n} F(t - \tau_{i,k}) , \tag{2}$$

where $F(x)$ is a monotonically non-increasing weighting function to reflect the influence of the recency and frequency factors of the past references of an object, and $\tau_{i,k}$ are the k-th referenced time to an object i. The LRFU policy replaces the object with the minimum CRF value and outperforms LRU, LFU, LRU-K and 2Q in the hit ratio, but also requires the logarithmic complexity of O($log_2 N$) to sort the CRF values.

The comparison of cache replacement algorithms which we mentioned above are summarized in Table 1. Finally, the characteristics of various replacement algorithms for Web caches are well classified and described in [6].

Table 1. Comparison of cache management algorithms

Algorithm	Estimation of Reference Potential	Time Complexity	Space overhead	Advantages	Weaknesses
LRU	Last reference time	O(1)	O(1)	Simplest algorithm	Do not consider frequency
LFU	Reference frequency	$O(log_2 N)$	$O(N)$	Consider popularity	Time complexity; Cache pollution
LRU-K	Backward K-th reference time	$O(log_2 N)$	$O(KN)$	Recency & frequency	Time complexity; Space overhead; Parameter tuning
2Q	Division cache into A1 and Am buffer	O(1)	O(1)	Simplicity; Recency & frequency	Parameter tuning
LRFU	All past references	$O(log_2 N)$	$O(N)$	Recency & frequency	Time complexity; Parameter tuning
RBP-LRU	Last reference time	O(1)	$O(N)$	Simplicity; Admission control	Parameter tuning

2.2 Selective Cache Placement Policy

The cache placement policy is also called as cache admission policy or selective caching. The selective caching is not a new concept and has been studied in the past for CPU caching, for example, a mechanism to dynamically decide whether an instruction causes conflicts and should be excluded from the cache [7]. However, in most of the cache replacement algorithms for the Web mentioned above, it is taken for granted that every requested object should be necessarily placed into the cache without validating whether it is popular or sufficiently valuable. Though a new object may be referenced rarely in near future, it can evict more popular object and results in additional cache misses and costs. Therefore, the cache performance can be enhanced by prohibiting unpopular objects from entering into the cache as a preventive action.

One of previous studies for object cache placement algorithm is the Window-based Frequency Estimation (WFE) placement policy [8]. The basic idea behind the WFE algorithm is to estimate the popularity of an object by running a sliding window on the past requests. The size of sliding window is a fixed constant, W , which is the number of past references used to evaluate the popularity. The estimate of the actual popularity is the number of references to the new object among past W references. Thus, the WFE policy permits placement of an object into the cache if its estimated frequency is above a given threshold value. The weakness of the WFE is that two parameters, the size of window and the threshold value, should be tuned for the optimal performance. The WFE placement algorithm is simply evaluated through distribution-driven simulation experiments between the Greedy-Dual Size (GDS) [9] and the GDS with WFE placement algorithm.

3 LRU Replacement with Cache Placement Control

The cache replacement algorithms only focus on evicting the most unpopular object from the cache in order to make a room for a newly referenced object. Thus any object can be cached without any restrictions even though it will never be re-referenced during its staying in the cache. If we can filter out unpopular objects to be cached in, we can raise the hit ratio by keeping higher popular objects in the cache.

The recency-based selective cache placement (RBP) policy incorporates both the recency and frequency information of a referenced object, like LRU-K, 2Q, and LRFU. The RBP policy only admits either an object that the elapsed time after its last referenced epoch is less than the time window, W, or when the cache is not yet full. Let $I_{i,n}(t)$ be an indicator random variable that indicates whether the n-th reference to an object i at time t is admitted or not. Then, the RBP policy allows an object i to be cached only if $I_{i,n}(t) = 1$ in (3).

$$I_{i,n}(t) = \begin{cases} 1, \text{ if } \ (t - \tau_{i,n-1}) \leq W; \\ 0, \text{ otherwise} \end{cases}, \tag{3}$$

where $\tau_{i,n-1}$ is a time epoch of the $(n-1)$-th reference to an object i.

As if the LRU-K considers the backward K-th reference, the RBP can extend to the elapsed time from the backward K-th reference. However, it incurs K times space overhead, and does not guarantee the performance improvements. Thus, in the RBP policy, we just consider only the last reference time of the referenced object. The time complexity of the RBP policy is just O(1), but additional space to keep the last reference time for all objects in the system is necessary. But, more important issue of the RBP policy is to find the optimal size of time window in order to get the best performance of the RBP policy. Therefore, an on-line adaptive window size decision considering characteristics of recent reference streams is additionally necessary.

In this paper, we consider the LRU replacement with the RBP policy (RBP-LRU). The LRU is the simplest algorithm, but it does not make use of frequency information. However, this can be compensated by the RBP policy. Therefore, the RBP-LRU can achieve high hit ratio with low complexity.

4 Simulation Experiments

In this section, we discuss the results from simulation experiments and compare the performance among LRU, LRU-2, 2Q, LRFU, and RBP-LRU policies to evaluate the effectiveness of the proposed simple LRU replacement with recency-based cache placement control. In all our experiments, we tried to represent the best result for tunable algorithms such as 2Q, LRFU, and RBP-LRU while changing their parameters.

4.1 Experiment Setup

We used two different types of traces: artificially generated trace from the Zipf's distribution with parameter $\alpha = 1.0$, and the real Web server access trace from the ClarkNet [10]. The ClarkNet-HTTP trace contains two weeks of HTTP logs from a busy Internet service provider for the Metro Baltimore-Washington DC area. It is one of traces which are available from the Internet Traffic Archive. The Internet Traffic Archive is a moderated repository to support widespread access to traces of Internet network traffic, sponsored by ACM SIGCOMM.

The artificial Zipf's distributed trace was generated from the Zipf's distribution with parameter $\alpha = 1.0$ for distinct 10,000 objects and the inter-reference time between consecutive references follows the Exponential distribution with mean 1.0 for 1,000,000 time duration.

The ClarkNet-HTTP trace contains requests to a WWW server from clients for two weeks period from Aug. 28 to Sep. 10, 1995. From them, we filtered out certain requests such as cgi-bin requests; requests with 302 Found or 304 Not Modified HTTP status code which does not cause to transmit real object data. Thus the total 2,914,808 requests to 27,670 unique objects were obtained.

The cache size used in the simulation experiments were chosen by taking a fixed percentage of the total number of unique objects in each trace, which is equivalent to having an infinite size of cache. The percentages are 0.05%, 0.5%, 5.0%, 10.0%, and 20.0%, which are relative to the infinite cache size (total number of unique objects).

In the simulation experiments, we did not count the number of cache hit or cache miss during initial certain period to explicitly exclude the effects of the startup transient period. The transient periods for the artificial Zipf's distributed trace and the ClarkNet-HTTP trace are 50,000 and 86,400, respectively.

4.2 Simulation Results

Figure 1 shows the comparison results of the hit ratio of each cache management algorithms as a function of the cache size for both traces. In our experiments, the weighting function of the LRFU, $F(x)$, was set to $(\frac{1}{2})^{\lambda x}$, as the range of control parameter λ covering both the LFU and LRU is between 0 and 1.

For the artificial Zipf's distributed trace, the LRFU is the best performed algorithm, but the its relative performance improvement over the RBP-LRU is less than 1.5%. The parameter, λ, of the LRFU was set to 0, which means the LRFU policy replaces the same object as the LFU policy does. The hit ratio decreases as the λ value increases. The relative enhancement of the RBP-LRU with respect to the LRU is at most 183.6% when the cache size is 0.05%, and then the gap of the hit ratio between the RBP-LRU and the LRU is gradually decreased when the cache becomes large. For the 2Q algorithm, the tuning parameter, we set Kin to 1 (minimum size) and Kout to 50% of the number of page slots in the cache for the best performance.

For the real ClarkNet-HTTP trace, the λ of the LRFU was set to 0.0001, and Kin and Kout of the 2Q algorithm were also set to 1 and 50% of the cache size, respectively. The LRFU is also the best algorithm among the others compared in our simulation experiments. The gap of hit ratio between the LRFU and the RBP-LRU is not significant. For the small cache, the LRFU enhances the hit ratio as much as 27.8% with respect to the RBP-LRU policy, but the gap

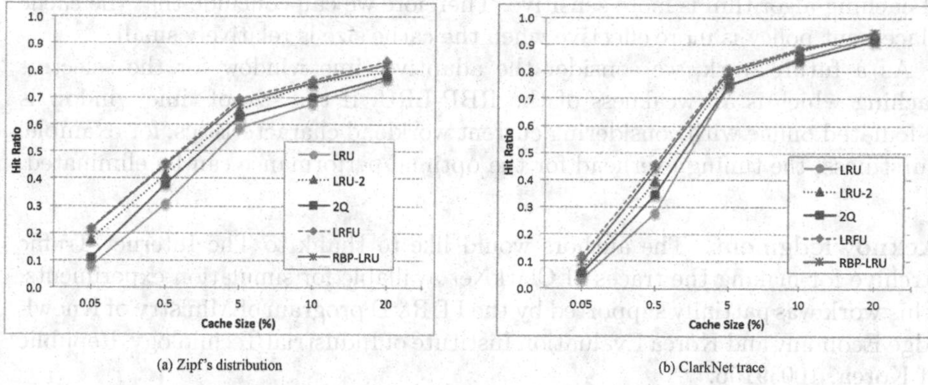

Fig. 1. Comparison the hit ratio of the RBP-LRU policy with other replacement algorithms using generated Zipf trace and real ClarkNet-HTTP trace

decreases as the cache size increases. The relative improvement of the RBP-LRU over the LRU replacement is at most 192.9% when the cache is small. Also this gap is gradually decreases as the cache size increases.

As a consequence, the LRFU consistently outperforms the others for both traces, but the results for both the LRFU and the RBP-LRU policy are nearly equivalent for all cache sizes. Thus, we can achieve the relative higher performance enhancement just by adopting of the recency-based cache placement with the simplest LRU replacement without requiring calculation of complex decision functions for replacement, in comparison with other well-known cache replacement algorithms for uniform cache objects. Furthermore, the RBP-LRU policy achieves higher improvement with respect to the others when the cache is relatively small. This is because the RBP-LRU is more effective for small cache which tries to keep the high popular objects in the cache by preventing an unpopular object from staying in the cache for a long time.

5 Conclusion

A number of cache management algorithms have been proposed and evaluated for several decades. As the performance of algorithms increases, however, the complexity of them also increases. In this paper, we used the recency-based cache placement control policy which allows only recently referenced objects in time window to be cached. From the simulation experiments, we observed that the LRFU outperforms consistently for all cache sizes, but the hit ratios of the LRFU and RBP-LRU policy are closed. It means that we can achieve performance enhancement as high as the LRFU can, just by combining the simplest LRU replacement with the recency-based cache placement policy, which does not require complex decision functions for replacement. Furthermore, the RBP-LRU policy can achieve higher enhancement when the cache is relatively small, since the responsiveness of caching algorithm is more sensitive. Therefore we can conclude that the cache placement policy is more effective when the cache size is relatively small.

As a future work, we consider the adaptive time window for the selective caching which is an weakness of the RBP-LRU. If the size of time window is calculated online with considering current workload characteristics, for example, burstiness, the tuning overhead for the optimal performance can be eliminated.

Acknowledgment. The authors would like to thank to The Internet Traffic Archive for making the traces of ClarkNet available for simulation experiments. This work was partially supported by the IT R&D program of Ministry of Knowledge Economy and Korea Evaluation Institute of Industrial Technology, Republic of Korea, 10039156.

References

1. Jin, S., Bestavros, A.: Popularity-aware greedy dual-size web proxy caching algorithms. In: Lai, T.H. (ed.) Proc. of the 20th International Conference on Distributed Computing Systems (ICDCS 2000), Taipei, Taiwan, pp. 254–261 (2000)
2. O'Neil, E.J., O'Neil, P.E., Weikum, G.: The LRU-K page replacement algorithm for database disk buffering. In: Buneman, P., Jajodia, S. (eds.) Proc. of the 1993 International Conference on Management of Data (ACM SIGMOD 1993), Washington, D.C, pp. 297–306 (May 1993)
3. Wiseman, Y.: Lecture notes for advanced operating systems, `http://u.cs.biu.ac.il/~wiseman/2os/2os/os2.pdf`
4. Johnson, T., Shasha, D.: 2Q: A low overhead high performance buffer management replacement algorithm. In: Bocca, J.B., Jarke, M., Zaniolo, C. (eds.) Proc. of the 20th International Conference on Very Large Data Bases (VLDB 1994), Washington, D.C, pp. 439–450 (1994)
5. Lee, D., Choi, J., Kim, J., Noh, S.H., Min, S.L., Cho, Y., Kim, C.S.: LRFU: A spectrum of policies that subsumes the least recently and least frequently used policies. IEEE Transactions on Computer 50(12), 1352–1361 (2001)
6. Podlipnig, S., Bszrmnyi, L.: A survey of web cache replacement strategies. ACM Computing Survey 35(4), 374–398 (2003)
7. Bahn, H., Koh, K., Min, S.L., Noh, S.H.: Efficient replacement of nonuniform objects in web caches. IEEE Computer 35(6), 65–73 (2002)
8. Hosseini-Khayat, S.: Improving object cache performance through selective placement. In: Fahringer, T. (ed.) Proc. of the 24th IASTED International Conference on Parallel and Distributed Computing and Networks (PDCN 2006), pp. 262–265. IASTED/ACTA Press (2006)
9. Cao, P., Irani, S.: Cost-aware www proxy caching algorithms. In: Proc. of the USENIX Symposium on Internet Technologies and Systems (USITS 1997), pp. 193–206 (December 1997)
10. ClarkNet-HTTP, `http://ita.ee.lbl.gov/html/contrib/ClarkNet-HTTP.html`

Loss Probability and Delay of Finite-Buffer Queues with Discrete ON-OFF Markovian Arrivals and Geometric Service Times

Sheng-Hua Yang, Jay Cheng, Hsin-Hung Chou, and Chih-Heng Cheng

Department of Electrical Engineering &
Institute of Communications Engineering
National Tsing Hua University, Hsinchu 30013, Taiwan, R.O.C.
s100064804@m100.nthu.edu.tw, jcheng@ee.nthu.edu.tw
{d9564808,d9764512}@oz.nthu.edu.tw

Abstract. Discrete-time queues are commonly used in the performance analysis of many computer and communications systems. As the independent and identically distributed (i.i.d.) arrival traffic model frequently adopted (due to its analytical tractability) in the literature does not capture some important properties of real-world traffics, such as self-similarity, long-range dependence, and burstiness, it is more realistic to model the arrival traffic as a time-correlated process.

A widely used time-correlated arrival traffic model is the ON-OFF traffic model as it is capable of capturing the burstiness of real-world traffics. In particular, it is commonly adopted for modeling voice traffics, where the talker is speaking (resp., silent) in the *ON* (resp., *OFF*) periods. In this paper, we present the performance analysis of a finite-buffer queue with ON-OFF Markovian arrival traffic and geometric service times, called ON-OFF/Geom/1/B queue in this paper. We derive closed-form expressions for the packet loss probability and the average packet delay. The closed-form expressions are given in term of the buffer size of the queue, the characterizing parameters of the ON-OFF Markovian traffic, and the service rate.

Keywords: Average packet delay, discrete-time queues, ON-OFF Markovian traffic, packet loss probability, time-correlated arrival processes.

1 Introduction

Discrete-time queues are commonly used in the performance analysis of many computer and communications systems where time is slotted and synchronized [1]–[3]. In the literature, it is not unusual to see that the arrival traffic to a discrete-time queue is modeled as a independent and identically distributed (i.i.d.) process, i.e., the numbers of packets arriving in different time slots are independent and identically distributed, due to its analytical tractability [4]–[6]. However, the i.i.d. arrival traffic model does not capture some important properties of real-world traffics, such as self-similarity, long-range dependence, and

V. Guyot (Ed.): ICAIT 2012, LNCS 7593, pp. 83–97, 2013.

burstiness [7]–[10]. Therefore, it is more realistic to model the arrival traffic to a discrete-time queue as a time-correlated process, i.e., the numbers of packets arriving in different time slots are correlated.

A widely used time-correlated arrival traffic model is the ON-OFF traffic model [9]–[18] as it is capable of capturing the burstiness of real-world traffics (we note that continuous-time ON-OFF traffic model is considered in [9]–[15] and discrete-time ON-OFF traffic model is considered in [16]–[18]). Specifically, the ON-OFF traffic is characterized by alternating *ON* and *OFF* periods, where packets arrive at a constant rate in the *ON* periods and there are no packet arrivals in the *OFF* periods. In particular, it is commonly adopted for modeling voice traffics, where the talker is speaking (resp., silent) in the *ON* (resp., *OFF*) periods.

The performance analysis of various kinds of queueing systems with ON-OFF arrival traffic has been studied intensively in the literature [10]–[18]. In [10], a multiplexer fed by voice traffics or by mixed voice and data traffics is considered, where each single voice source is modeled as a continuous-time ON-OFF traffic, and approximation and simulation results of the loss probability and the first and second moments of the packet delay are given. In [11]–[15], various communications systems with the same ON-OFF traffic model as that in [10] are designed to meet certain quality of service (QoS) requirements, such as packet loss probability and average packet delay. In [16] and [17], a multiplexer with discrete-time ON-OFF traffics is considered, and the mean buffer occupancy is derived in [16] and the asymptotic tail probability distribution of the buffer occupancy and approximated loss probability are given in [17]. In [18], a loss probability and delay analysis is performed for a special hybrid optical packet switch, called OpCut switch, with ON-OFF Markovian traffic (a special type of ON-OFF traffic).

In this paper, we consider a single-server queue with finite buffer size B and i.i.d. geometric service times with discrete-time ON-OFF Markovian arrival traffic, called ON-OFF/Geom/1/B queue in this paper. The main contribution of this paper is to provide closed-form expressions for packet loss probability and average packet delay for ON-OFF/Geom/1/B queues. The closed-form expressions are given in term of the buffer size of the queue, the characterizing parameters of the ON-OFF Markovian traffic, and the service rate.

The rest of this paper is organized as follows. In Section 2, we introduce the ON-OFF Markovian traffic model. In Section 3, we present our derivations of the packet loss probability and the average packet delay. In Section 4, we show our numerical results on the packet loss probability and the average packet delay. This paper is concluded in Section 5.

2 ON-OFF Markovian Traffic Model

Under the discrete-time ON-OFF Markovian traffic model, there is always a packet arrival when the arrival process is in the *ON* state and there are no packet arrivals when the arrival process is in the *OFF* state. Furthermore, given that the the arrival process is in the *ON* state at time $t-1$, the probability that it will go to the *OFF* state at time t is α, where $0 < \alpha < 1$, while the probability that it will stay in the *ON* state at time t is $1-\alpha$, and this is independent of everything else. Similarly, given that the the arrival process is in the *OFF* state at time $t-1$, the probability that it will go to the *ON* state at time t is β, where $0 < \beta < 1$, while the probability that it will stay in the *OFF* state at time t is $1-\beta$, and this is also independent of everything else.

Let $a(t)$ be the number of arrival packets at time t, i.e., $a(t) = 1$ if the arrival process is in the *ON* state and $a(t) = 0$ if the arrival process is in the *OFF* state. It is not difficult to see that the arrival process $\{a(t), t \geq 1\}$ is a homogeneous two-state discrete-time Markov chain with the following state transition probabilities:

$$P(a(t) = 0|a(t-1) = 1) = \alpha, \tag{1}$$
$$P(a(t) = 1|a(t-1) = 1) = 1-\alpha, \tag{2}$$
$$P(a(t) = 1|a(t-1) = 0) = \beta, \tag{3}$$
$$P(a(t) = 0|a(t-1) = 0) = = 1-\beta, \tag{4}$$

for all $t \geq 1$.

It is easy to see that under the discrete-time ON-OFF Markovian traffic model, the burst length ℓ_b of a burst of arrival packets follows the geometric distribution with parameter $1-\alpha$, i.e., $P(\ell_b = n) = \alpha(1-\alpha)^{n-1}$ for $n \geq 1$. Also, it is clear that the unique steady state probabilities π_0 and π_1 of the Markov chain $\{a(t), t \geq 1\}$ can be obtained from (1)–(4) as $\pi_0 = \frac{\alpha}{\alpha+\beta}$ and $\pi_1 = \frac{\beta}{\alpha+\beta}$. As such, we see that the arrival rate λ of the arrival traffic in steady state is given by

$$\lambda = \lim_{t\to\infty} P(a(t) = 1) = \pi_1 = \frac{\beta}{\alpha+\beta}. \tag{5}$$

Furthermore, for the special case that $\alpha + \beta = 1$, we have

$$\begin{aligned}
&P(a(t) = 1)\\
&= P(a(t-1) = 0) \cdot P(a(t) = 1|a(t-1) = 0)\\
&\quad +P(a(t-1) = 1) \cdot P(a(t) = 1|a(t-1) = 1)\\
&= P(a(t-1) = 0) \cdot \beta + P(a(t-1) = 1) \cdot (1-\alpha)\\
&= P(a(t-1) = 0) \cdot \beta + P(a(t-1) = 1) \cdot \beta\\
&= \beta, \text{ for all } t \geq 1.
\end{aligned}$$

Therefore, in this case the ON-OFF Markovian traffic model degenerates to the well-known i.i.d. Bernoulli traffic model with arrival rate β.

3 Loss Probability and Delay Analysis

In this section, we derive the packet loss probability and the average packet delay for the ON-OFF/Geom/1/B queues.

As mentioned in Section 1 that the service times of packets are i.i.d. geometric random variables, we can assume the service times are geometrically distributed with parameter γ, where $0 < \gamma < 1$, i.e., the service time of a packet is n with probability $\gamma(1-\gamma)^{n-1}$ for $n \geq 1$. It is clear that the service rate is γ. Furthermore, the server can be viewed as having i.i.d. time-varying capacity $c(t)$, where $c(t) = 1$ with probability γ and $c(t) = 0$ with probability $1-\gamma$. In other words, the process $\{c(t), t \geq 1\}$ of the service capacity is an i.i.d. Bernoulli process with parameter γ, and this is independent of everything else. As a practical scenario, the server could be viewed as resources that are also shared by some other network elements in the same network, and could be regulated by certain resource management or congestion control schemes. In the case that the queue is allotted to use the server for a fraction of time that is equal to γ, it is reasonable to assume that the service capacity at each time is equal to 1 with probability γ and is equal to 0 with probability $1-\gamma$.

Let $q(t)$ be the number of packets in the system at time t (at the end of the tth time slot). Assume the system is initially empty, then we can see that the evolution of buffer occupancy follows the following well-known Lindley equation:

$$q(t) = \min\{[q(t-1) + a(t) - c(t)]^+, B\}, \tag{6}$$

where $x^+ = \max\{x, 0\}$.

We note that throughout this paper, we denote $\bar{\alpha} = 1-\alpha$, $\bar{\beta} = 1-\beta$, $\bar{\gamma} = 1-\gamma$, and we assume that the system is initially empty at time 0. From (6), it is easy to see that $q(t)$ is uniquely determined by $q(t-1)$, $a(t)$, and $c(t)$ for all $t \geq 1$. As we assume that the arrival process $\{a(t), t \geq 1\}$ is a homogeneous two-state discrete-time Markov chain that is independent of everything else, and the service capacity process $\{c(t), t \geq 1\}$ is an i.i.d. Bernoulli process that is also independent of everything else, it then follows that the process $\{(a(t), q(t)), t \geq 1\}$ is a homogeneous discrete-time Markov chain. In Section 3.1, we obtain the steady state probabilities for the Markov chain $\{(a(t), q(t)), t \geq 1\}$ and use them to derive the packet loss probability and the average packet delay in Section 3.2.

3.1 Steady State Probabilities of the Markov Chain $\{(a(t), q(t)), t \geq 1\}$

In this section, we obtain the steady state probabilities for the Markov chain $\{(a(t), q(t)), t \geq 1\}$. For this, we need to first calculate the state transition probabilities as follows.

As we assume that the system is initially empty at time 0 and we know that $q(t)$ is uniquely determined by $q(t-1)$, $a(t)$, and $c(t)$ for all $t \geq 1$, it is easy to deduce that $q(t)$ depends on $a(1), a(2), \ldots, a(t)$ and $c(1), c(2), \ldots, c(t)$ for all $t \geq 1$. Since we assume that the arrival process $\{a(t), t \geq 1\}$ is a homogeneous two-state discrete-time Markov chain with state transition probabilities given by (1)–(4) that is independent of everything else, and the service capacity process $\{c(t), t \geq 1\}$ is an i.i.d. Bernoulli process with parameter γ that is also independent of everything else, it follows from (6) that

$$\begin{aligned} &P(a(t) = 1, q(t) = i+1 | a(t-1) = 0, q(t-1) = i) \\ &= P(a(t) = 1 | a(t-1) = 0, q(t-1) = i) \\ &\quad \times P(q(t) = i+1 | a(t) = 1, a(t-1) = 0, q(t-1) = i) \\ &= P(a(t) = 1 | a(t-1) = 0) \cdot P(c(t) = 0) \\ &= \beta\bar{\gamma}, \text{ for } i = 0, 1, \ldots, B-1. \end{aligned} \tag{7}$$

Similarly, we have

$$\begin{aligned} &P(a(t) = 1, q(t) = i+1 | a(t-1) = 1, q(t-1) = i) \\ &\quad = P(a(t) = 1 | a(t-1) = 1) P(c(t) = 0) \\ &\quad = \bar{\alpha}\bar{\gamma}, \text{ for } i = 0, 1, \ldots, B-1, \end{aligned} \tag{8}$$

$$\begin{aligned} &P(a(t) = 0, q(t) = i-1 | a(t-1) = 0, q(t-1) = i) \\ &\quad = P(a(t) = 0 | a(t-1) = 0) P(c(t) = 1) \\ &\quad = \bar{\beta}\gamma, \text{ for } i = 1, 2, \ldots, B, \end{aligned} \tag{9}$$

$$\begin{aligned} &P(a(t) = 0, q(t) = i-1 | a(t-1) = 1, q(t-1) = i) \\ &\quad = P(a(t) = 0 | a(t-1) = 1) P(c(t) = 1) \\ &\quad = \alpha\gamma, \text{ for } i = 1, 2, \ldots, B, \end{aligned} \tag{10}$$

$$\begin{aligned} &P(a(t) = 0, q(t) = i | a(t-1) = 0, q(t-1) = i) \\ &\quad = P(a(t) = 0 | a(t-1) = 0) P(c(t) = 0) \\ &\quad = \bar{\beta}\bar{\gamma}, \text{ for } i = 1, 2, \ldots, B, \end{aligned} \tag{11}$$

$$\begin{aligned} &P(a(t) = 0, q(t) = i | a(t-1) = 1, q(t-1) = i) \\ &\quad = P(a(t) = 0 | a(t-1) = 1) P(c(t) = 0) \\ &\quad = \alpha\bar{\gamma}, \text{ for } i = 1, 2, \ldots, B, \end{aligned} \tag{12}$$

$$\begin{aligned} &P(a(t) = 1, q(t) = i | a(t-1) = 0, q(t-1) = i) \\ &\quad = P(a(t) = 1 | a(t-1) = 0) P(c(t) = 1) \\ &\quad = \beta\gamma, \text{ for } i = 0, 1, \ldots, B-1, \end{aligned} \tag{13}$$

$$\begin{aligned} &P(a(t) = 1, q(t) = i | a(t-1) = 1, q(t-1) = i) \\ &\quad = P(a(t) = 1 | a(t-1) = 1) P(c(t) = 1) \\ &\quad = \bar{\alpha}\gamma, \text{ for } i = 0, 1, \ldots, B-1. \end{aligned} \tag{14}$$

Furthermore, we have

$$
\begin{aligned}
&P(a(t)=0,q(t)=0|a(t-1)=0,q(t-1)=0)\\
&\quad=P(a(t)=0|a(t-1)=0,q(t-1)=0)\\
&\qquad\times P(q(t)=0|a(t)=0,a(t-1)=0,q(t-1)=0)\\
&\quad=P(a(t)=0|a(t-1)=0)\cdot 1=\bar{\beta}, &(15)\\
&P(a(t)=0,q(t)=0|a(t-1)=1,q(t-1)=0)\\
&\quad=P(a(t)=0|a(t-1)=1)\cdot 1=\alpha, &(16)\\
&P(a(t)=1,q(t)=B|a(t-1)=0,q(t-1)=B)\\
&\quad=P(a(t)=1|a(t-1)=0,q(t-1)=B)\\
&\qquad\times P(q(t)=B|a(t)=1,a(t-1)=0,q(t-1)=B)\\
&\quad=P(a(t)=1|a(t-1)=0)\cdot 1=\beta, &(17)\\
&P(a(t)=1,q(t)=B|a(t-1)=1,q(t-1)=B)\\
&\quad=P(a(t)=1|a(t-1)=1)\cdot 1=\bar{\alpha}. &(18)
\end{aligned}
$$

The rest of the state transition probabilities are all zero.

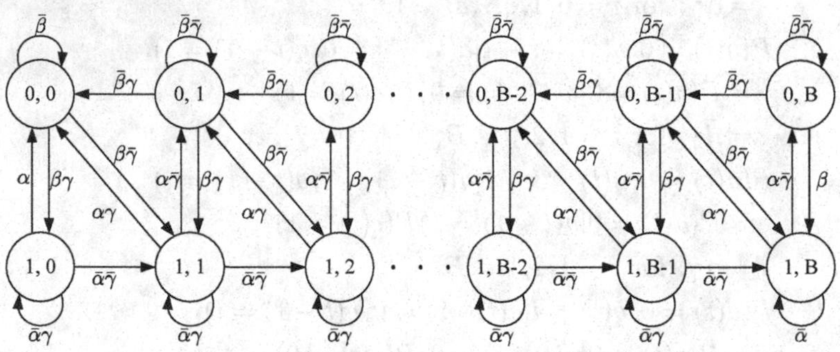

Fig. 1. The state transition diagram for the homogeneous Markov chain $\{(a(t),q(t)),t\geq 1\}$

Clearly, the Markov chain $\{(a(t),q(t)),t\geq 1\}$ is a homogeneous Markov chain as its state transition probabilities in (7)–(18) are independent of time t. In Figure 1, we show the state transition diagram for the homogeneous Markov chain $\{(a(t),q(t)),t\geq 1\}$. It is easy to see from the state transition diagram in Figure 1 and $0<\alpha,\beta,\gamma<1$ that any two states can communicate with each other, and hence the Markov chain $\{(a(t),q(t)),t\geq 1\}$ is irreducible. Also, we have from (11), (14), (15), (18), and $0<\alpha,\beta,\gamma<1$ that

$$
\begin{aligned}
P(a(t)=k,q(t)=i|a(t-1)=k,q(t-1)=i)>0,&\\
\text{for } k=0,1 \text{ and } i=0,1,\ldots,B.&
\end{aligned}
$$

It follows that the Markov chain $\{(a(t), q(t)), t \geq 1\}$ is aperiodic. As the Markov chain $\{(a(t), q(t)), t \geq 1\}$ is finite, irreducible, and aperiodic, it is well known [19] that there exist unique steady state probabilities $\boldsymbol{\pi} = (\pi_{0,0}, \pi_{1,0}, \pi_{0,1}, \pi_{1,1}, \ldots, \pi_{0,B}, \pi_{1,B})$ for the Markov chain $\{(a(t), q(t)), t \geq 1\}$, where

$$\pi_{k,i} = \lim_{t\to\infty} P(a(t) = k, q(t) = i), \text{ for } k = 0, 1 \text{ and } i = 0, 1, \ldots, B. \quad (19)$$

From the state transition diagram in Figure 1 and (7)–(18), we see that the steady state probabilities $\boldsymbol{\pi}$ could be obtained in closed form from the following global balance equations subject to $\sum_{i=0}^{B}(\pi_{0,i} + \pi_{1,i}) = 1$:

$$\pi_{0,0} = \bar{\beta}\pi_{0,0} + \alpha\pi_{1,0} + \bar{\beta}\gamma\pi_{0,1} + \alpha\gamma\pi_{1,1}, \quad (20)$$

$$\pi_{1,0} = \beta\gamma\pi_{0,0} + \bar{\alpha}\gamma\pi_{1,0}, \quad (21)$$

$$\pi_{0,i} = \bar{\beta}\bar{\gamma}\pi_{0,i} + \alpha\bar{\gamma}\pi_{1,i} + \bar{\beta}\gamma\pi_{0,i+1} + \alpha\gamma\pi_{1,i+1}, \text{ for } i = 1, 2, \ldots, B-1, \quad (22)$$

$$\pi_{1,i} = \beta\bar{\gamma}\pi_{0,i-1} + \bar{\alpha}\bar{\gamma}\pi_{1,i-1} + \beta\gamma\pi_{0,i} + \bar{\alpha}\gamma\pi_{1,i}, \text{ for } i = 1, 2, \ldots, B-1, \quad (23)$$

$$\pi_{0,B} = \bar{\beta}\bar{\gamma}\pi_{0,B} + \alpha\bar{\gamma}\pi_{1,B}, \quad (24)$$

$$\pi_{1,B} = \beta\bar{\gamma}\pi_{0,B-1} + \bar{\alpha}\bar{\gamma}\pi_{1,B-1} + \beta\pi_{0,B} + \bar{\alpha}\pi_{1,B}. \quad (25)$$

The closed-form expressions for $\pi_{k,i}$, $k = 0, 1$ and $i = 0, 1, \ldots, B$, are given in Theorem 1 below.

Theorem 1. *The steady state probabilities* $\boldsymbol{\pi}$ *of the Markov chain* $\{(a(t), q(t)), t \geq 1\}$ *are given by*

$$\pi_{0,0} = u \cdot \alpha\gamma(1 - \bar{\alpha}\gamma)(\alpha\gamma + \bar{\beta}\bar{\gamma}), \quad (26)$$

$$\pi_{1,0} = u \cdot \alpha\beta\gamma^2(\alpha\gamma + \bar{\beta}\bar{\gamma}), \quad (27)$$

$$\pi_{0,i} = u \cdot \alpha\beta\bar{\gamma}^2\rho^{i-1}, \text{ for } i = 1, 2, \ldots, B-1, \quad (28)$$

$$\pi_{1,i} = u \cdot \alpha\beta\gamma\bar{\gamma}\rho^{i-1}, \text{ for } i = 1, 2, \ldots, B-1, \quad (29)$$

$$\pi_{0,B} = u \cdot \alpha\beta\bar{\gamma}^2(\alpha\gamma + \bar{\beta}\bar{\gamma})\rho^{B-1}, \quad (30)$$

$$\pi_{1,B} = u \cdot \beta\bar{\gamma}(1 - \bar{\beta}\bar{\gamma})(\alpha\gamma + \bar{\beta}\bar{\gamma})\rho^{B-1}, \quad (31)$$

where

$$\rho = \frac{\bar{\gamma}(\bar{\alpha}\gamma + \beta\bar{\gamma})}{\gamma(\alpha\gamma + \bar{\beta}\bar{\gamma})}, \quad (32)$$

and u *is a normalization constant that can be obtained by solving* $\sum_{i=0}^{B}(\pi_{0,i} + \pi_{1,i}) = 1$ *and is given by*

$$u = \begin{cases} \frac{\alpha\gamma - \beta\bar{\gamma}}{\alpha\gamma + \bar{\beta}\bar{\gamma}} \big\{\alpha\gamma^2[(\beta - \bar{\alpha})(\alpha\gamma - \beta\bar{\gamma}) + \alpha] \\ \qquad + \beta\bar{\gamma}^2[(\alpha - \bar{\beta})(\alpha\gamma - \beta\bar{\gamma}) - \beta]\rho^{B-1}\big\}^{-1}, & \text{if } \rho \neq 1, \\ \frac{(\alpha+\beta)^2}{\alpha^2\beta(1 + B(\alpha+\beta))}, & \text{if } \rho = 1. \end{cases} \quad (33)$$

Proof. The proof is omitted due to space limit. ■

For the special case that $\rho = 1$, we obtain from (32) that $\gamma = \frac{\beta}{\alpha+\beta}$ and the steady state probabilities in (26)–(31) can be simplified as follows:

$$\pi_{0,0} = \frac{\alpha(1+\beta)}{(\alpha+\beta)(1+B(\alpha+\beta))}, \tag{34}$$

$$\pi_{1,0} = \frac{\beta^2}{(\alpha+\beta)(1+B(\alpha+\beta))}, \tag{35}$$

$$\pi_{0,i} = \frac{\alpha}{1+B(\alpha+\beta)}, \text{ for } i = 1, 2, \ldots, B-1, \tag{36}$$

$$\pi_{1,i} = \frac{\beta}{1+B(\alpha+\beta)}, \text{ for } i = 1, 2, \ldots, B-1, \tag{37}$$

$$\pi_{0,B} = \frac{\alpha^2}{(\alpha+\beta)(1+B(\alpha+\beta))}, \tag{38}$$

$$\pi_{1,B} = \frac{\beta(1+\alpha)}{(\alpha+\beta)(1+B(\alpha+\beta))}. \tag{39}$$

3.2 Packet Loss Probability and Average Packet Delay

In this section, we use the steady state probabilities obtained in Section 3.1 for the Markov chain $\{(a(t), q(t)), t \geq 1\}$ to derive the packet loss probability and the average packet delay.

Packet Loss Probability. Let $P_\ell(\alpha, \beta, \gamma, B)$ be the packet loss probability in steady state, namely, the probability that there is a loss packet at a time slot in steady state. Since there is a loss packet at time t if and only if the buffer is full at time $t-1$, there is a packet arrival at time t, and the service capacity is equal to 0 at time t, i.e., $q(t-1) = B, a(t) = 1, c(t) = 0$. As we assume that the arrival process $\{a(t), t \geq 1\}$ and the service capacity process $\{c(t), t \geq 1\}$ are independent of everything else and we know from (6) that $q(t)$ depends on $a(1), a(2), \ldots, a(t)$ and $c(1), c(2), \ldots, c(t)$ for all $t \geq 1$, it then follows that the packet loss probability in steady state is given by

$$\begin{aligned}
P_\ell(\alpha,\beta,\gamma,B) &= \lim_{t\to\infty} P(q(t-1)=B, a(t)=1, c(t)=0) \\
&= \lim_{t\to\infty} P(q(t-1)=B, a(t)=1)P(c(t)=0) \\
&= \lim_{t\to\infty} \bar{\gamma}[P(q(t-1)=B, a(t)=1, a(t-1)=0) \\
&\qquad + P(q(t-1)=B, a(t)=1, a(t-1)=1)] \\
&= \lim_{t\to\infty} \bar{\gamma}[P(a(t-1)=0, q(t-1)=B) \\
&\qquad \times P(a(t)=1|a(t-1)=0, q(t-1)=B) \\
&\qquad + P(a(t-1)=1, q(t-1)=B) \\
&\qquad \times P(a(t)=1|a(t-1)=1, q(t-1)=B)] \\
&= \lim_{t\to\infty} \bar{\gamma}[P(a(t-1)=0, q(t-1)=B) \\
&\qquad \times P(a(t)=1|a(t-1)=0) \\
&\qquad + P(a(t-1)=1, q(t-1)=B) \\
&\qquad \times P(a(t)=1|a(t-1)=1)] \\
&= \bar{\gamma}(\pi_{0,B}\beta + \pi_{1,B}\bar{\alpha}).
\end{aligned} \tag{40}$$

If $\rho \neq 1$, then we have from (40), (30), and (31) that

$$\begin{aligned}
&P_\ell(\alpha,\beta,\gamma,B) \\
&= u \cdot \bar{\gamma}(\alpha\gamma + \bar{\beta}\bar{\gamma})[\alpha\beta^2\bar{\gamma}^2 + \bar{\alpha}\beta\bar{\gamma}(1-\bar{\beta}\bar{\gamma})]\rho^{B-1} \\
&= u \cdot \beta\bar{\gamma}^2(\alpha\gamma + \bar{\beta}\bar{\gamma})[\alpha\beta\bar{\gamma} + \bar{\alpha}(1-\bar{\beta}\bar{\gamma})]\rho^{B-1}, \text{ if } \rho \neq 1,
\end{aligned} \tag{41}$$

where ρ is given by (32) and u is given by (33). On the other hand, if $\rho = 1$, then we have $\gamma = \frac{\beta}{\alpha+\beta}$ and it follows from (40), (38), and (39) that

$$\begin{aligned}
P_\ell(\alpha,\beta,\gamma,B) &= \frac{\alpha^2\beta + \bar{\alpha}\beta(1+\alpha)}{(\alpha+\beta)(1+B(\alpha+\beta))}\bar{\gamma} \\
&= \frac{\alpha\beta}{(\alpha+\beta)^2(1+B(\alpha+\beta))}, \text{ if } \rho = 1.
\end{aligned} \tag{42}$$

We now show how the packet loss probability behaves as the buffer size goes to infinity. If $\rho > 1$, then we see from (41) and (33) that the asymptotic average packet delay $P_\ell(\alpha,\beta,\gamma,\infty)$ is given by

$$\begin{aligned}
P_\ell(\alpha,\beta,\gamma,\infty) &= \lim_{B\to\infty} P_\ell(\alpha,\beta,\gamma,B) \\
&= \frac{(\alpha\gamma - \beta\bar{\gamma})[\alpha\beta\bar{\gamma} + \bar{\alpha}(1-\bar{\beta}\bar{\gamma})]}{(\alpha-\bar{\beta})(\alpha\gamma-\beta\bar{\gamma}) - \beta} > 0, \text{ if } \rho > 1.
\end{aligned} \tag{43}$$

If $\rho < 1$, then we see from (41) and (33) that

$$\lim_{B\to\infty} \frac{P_\ell(\alpha,\beta,\gamma,B)}{\rho^{B-1}} = \frac{\beta\bar{\gamma}^2(\alpha\gamma-\beta\bar{\gamma})[\alpha\beta\bar{\gamma}+\bar{\alpha}(1-\bar{\beta}\bar{\gamma})]}{\alpha\gamma^2[(\beta-\bar{\alpha})(\alpha\gamma-\beta\bar{\gamma})+\alpha]}, \text{ if } \rho<1. \tag{44}$$

Finally, if $\rho = 1$, then we see from (42) that

$$\lim_{B\to\infty} B \cdot P_\ell(\alpha,\beta,\gamma,B) = \frac{\alpha\beta}{(\alpha+\beta)^3}, \text{ if } \rho = 1. \tag{45}$$

Therefore, it follows from (43)–(45) that the packet loss probability is lower bounded from a positive constant when $\rho > 1$, decreases exponentially to zero with B as B goes to infinity when $\rho < 1$, and decreases inverse linearly to zero with B as B goes to infinity when $\rho = 1$.

Average Packet Delay. Let $P_b(\alpha,\beta,\gamma,B)$ be the packet blocking probability in steady state, namely, the probability that an arrival packet is blocked in steady state. It follows from (5) that the packet blocking probability in steady state is given by

$$\begin{aligned} P_b(\alpha,\beta,\gamma,B) &= \lim_{t\to\infty} P(q(t-1)=B, c(t)=0 | a(t)=1) \\ &= \lim_{t\to\infty} \frac{P(q(t-1)=B, c(t)=0, a(t)=1)}{P(a(t)=1)} \\ &= \frac{P_\ell(\alpha,\beta,\gamma,B)}{\lambda}. \end{aligned} \tag{46}$$

Therefore, it follows from (46) and (5) that the effective arrival rate to the queue is given by

$$\begin{aligned} \lambda_{\text{eff}} &= \lambda(1 - P_b(\alpha,\beta,\gamma,B)) \\ &= \lambda - P_\ell(\alpha,\beta,\gamma,B) \\ &= \frac{\beta}{\alpha+\beta} - P_\ell(\alpha,\beta,\gamma,B) \end{aligned} \tag{47}$$

Let $N(\alpha,\beta,\gamma,B)$ be the average number of packets in the system in steady state. Then we can see that

$$\begin{aligned} N(\alpha,\beta,\gamma,B) &= \sum_{i=1}^{B} i \lim_{t\to\infty} P(q(t)=i) \\ &= \sum_{i=1}^{B} i \lim_{t\to\infty} (P(a(t)=0, q(t)=i) + P(a(t)=1, q(t)=i)) \\ &= \sum_{i=1}^{B} i(\pi_{0,i} + \pi_{1,i}). \end{aligned} \tag{48}$$

If $\rho \neq 1$, then we have from (48) and (28)–(31) that

$$\begin{aligned} N(\alpha,\beta,\gamma,B) &= u\cdot\beta\sum_{i=1}^{B-1} i(\alpha\bar{\gamma}^2+\alpha\gamma\bar{\gamma})\rho^{i-1} \\ &\quad + u\cdot B\beta\bar{\gamma}(\alpha\bar{\gamma}+1-\bar{\beta}\bar{\gamma})(\alpha\gamma+\bar{\beta}\bar{\gamma})\rho^{B-1} \\ &= u\cdot\alpha\beta\bar{\gamma}\frac{1-B\rho^{B-1}+(B-1)\rho^B}{(1-\rho)^2} \\ &\quad + u\cdot B\beta\bar{\gamma}(1+\alpha\bar{\gamma}-\bar{\beta}\bar{\gamma})(\alpha\gamma+\bar{\beta}\bar{\gamma})\rho^{B-1}, \text{ if } \rho\neq 1, \end{aligned} \tag{49}$$

where ρ is given by (32) and u is given by (33). On the other hand, if $\rho = 1$, then we have from (48) and (36)–(39) that

$$\begin{aligned} N(\alpha,\beta,\gamma,B) &= \sum_{i=1}^{B-1} i\frac{\alpha+\beta}{1+B(\alpha+\beta)} + \frac{B(\alpha^2+\beta(1+\alpha))}{(\alpha+\beta)(1+B(\alpha+\beta))} \\ &= \frac{B^2(\alpha+\beta)^2+B(\alpha^2-\beta^2+2\beta)}{2(\alpha+\beta)(1+B(\alpha+\beta))}, \text{ if } \rho=1. \end{aligned} \tag{50}$$

Let $D(\alpha,\beta,\gamma,B)$ be the average packet delay in steady state. As the effective packet arrival rate in steady state is given in (47), it follows from Little's formula [20] that the average packet delay in steady state is given by

$$\begin{aligned} D(\alpha,\beta,\gamma,B) &= \frac{N(\alpha,\beta,\gamma,B)}{\lambda_{\text{eff}}}, \\ &= \frac{N(\alpha,\beta,\gamma,B)}{\frac{\beta}{\alpha+\beta}-P_\ell(\alpha,\beta,\gamma,B)}, \end{aligned} \tag{51}$$

where $N(\alpha,\beta,\gamma,B)$ is given in (49) and $P_\ell(\alpha,\beta,\gamma,B)$ is given in (41) if $\rho \neq 1$, and $N(\alpha,\beta,\gamma,B)$ is given in (50) and $P_\ell(\alpha,\beta,\gamma,B)$ is given in (42) if $\rho = 1$.

As in the case of loss probability, we now show how the average packet delay behaves as the buffer size goes to infinity. If $\rho < 1$, then $P_\ell(\alpha,\beta,\gamma,\infty) = 0$ as mentioned in the analysis of loss probability. Hence, we see from (51), $P_\ell(\alpha,\beta,\gamma,\infty) = 0$, (49), and (33) that $D(\alpha,\beta,\gamma,\infty)$ is given by

$$\begin{aligned} &D(\alpha,\beta,\gamma,\infty) \\ &= \lim_{B\to\infty} D(\alpha,\beta,\gamma,B) \\ &= \frac{\bar{\gamma}(\alpha+\beta)(\alpha\gamma-\beta\bar{\gamma})}{\gamma^2(1-\rho)^2(\alpha\gamma+\bar{\beta}\bar{\gamma})[(\beta-\bar{\alpha})(\alpha\gamma-\beta\bar{\gamma})+\alpha]} < \infty, \text{ if } \rho < 1. \end{aligned} \tag{52}$$

If $\rho > 1$, then we see from (51), (49), and that (33)

$$\lim_{B\to\infty} \frac{D(\alpha,\beta,\gamma,B)}{B}$$
$$= \frac{1}{\frac{\beta}{\alpha+\beta} - P_\ell(\alpha,\beta,\gamma,\infty)}$$
$$\times \frac{(\alpha+\beta)(\alpha\gamma-\beta\bar{\gamma})[\frac{\alpha}{\rho-1} + (1+\alpha\bar{\gamma}-\bar{\beta}\bar{\gamma})(\alpha\gamma+\bar{\beta}\bar{\gamma})]}{\beta\bar{\gamma}(\alpha\gamma+\bar{\beta}\bar{\gamma})[(\alpha-\bar{\beta})(\alpha\gamma-\beta\bar{\gamma})-\beta]}, \text{ if } \rho > 1. \tag{53}$$

Finally, if $\rho = 1$, then $P_\ell(\alpha,\beta,\gamma,\infty) = 0$ as mentioned in the analysis of loss probability. As such, we see from (51), $P_\ell(\alpha,\beta,\gamma,\infty) = 0$, and (50) that

$$\lim_{B\to\infty} \frac{D(\alpha,\beta,\gamma,B)}{B} = \frac{\alpha+\beta}{2\beta}, \text{ if } \rho = 1. \tag{54}$$

Therefore, it follows from (52)–(54) that the average packet delay is upper bounded by a positive constant when $\rho < 1$ and grows linearly to infinity with B as B goes to infinity when $\rho \geq 1$. This suggests that ρ plays the role of traffic intensity in a single server queue. Indeed, it can be seen from (32) that $\rho \gtreqqless 1$ if and only if $\frac{\beta}{\alpha+\beta} \gtreqqless \gamma$. As we know from (5) that $\lambda = \frac{\beta}{\alpha+\beta}$ is the arrival rate of the arrival traffic to the queue and we can view γ as the service rate of the queue, it is natural to expect that the average packet delay is upper bounded when $\lambda < \gamma$, i.e., $\rho < 1$, and grows to infinity as the buffer size goes to infinity when $\lambda \geq \gamma$, i.e., $\rho \geq 1$.

4 Numerical Results

In this section, we show our numerical results on the packet loss probability and the average packet delay. In Figure 2 (resp., Figure 3), we show the numerical results on the the packet loss probability $P_\ell(\alpha,\beta,\gamma,B)$ (resp., average packet delay $D(\alpha,\beta,\gamma,B)$) given by (41) and (42) (resp., (51)) for $\rho = 0.5, 0.8, 0.98, 1$, and 1.02 when $\beta = 0.5$ and $\gamma = 0.8$

From Figure 2, we observe that the packet loss probability decreases exponentially with B for sufficiently large B when $\rho = 0.5, 0.8$, and 0.98 as expected from (44), decreases inverse linearly with B for sufficiently large B when $\rho = 1$ as expected from (45), and approaches a lower bound 0.00507 for sufficiently large B when $\rho = 1.02$ as expected from (43). From Figure 3, we observe that the average packet delay approaches an upper bound 1.5000 (resp., 5.2500 and 61.500) for sufficiently large B when $\rho = 0.5$ (resp., $\rho = 0.8$ and $\rho = 0.98$) as expected from (52), and increases linearly with B for sufficiently large B when $\rho = 1$ and $\rho = 1.02$ as expected from (53) and (54).

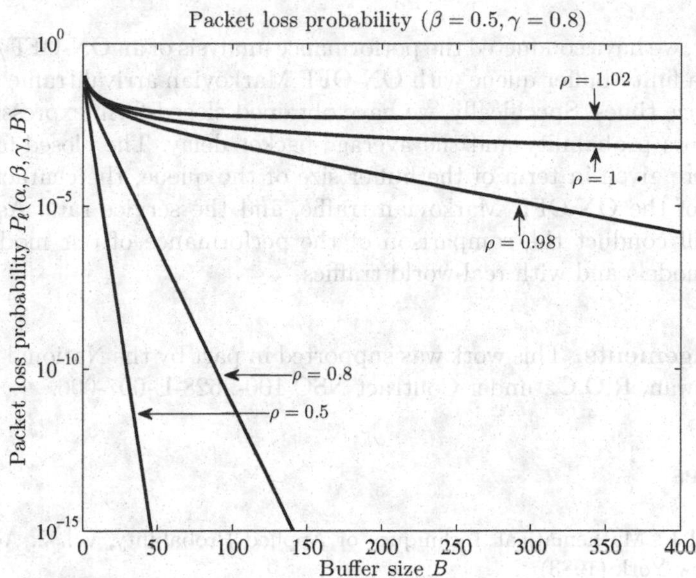

Fig. 2. Packet loss probability $P_\ell(\alpha, \beta, \gamma, B)$ for $\rho = 0.5, 0.8, 0.98, 1$, and 1.02 when $\beta = 0.5$ and $\gamma = 0.8$

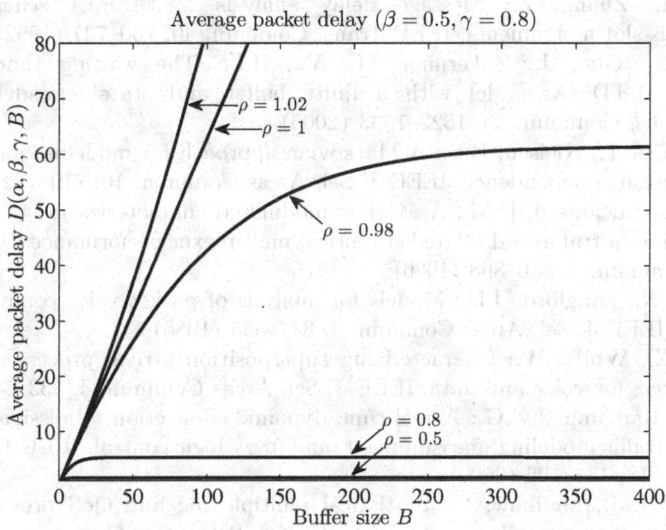

Fig. 3. Average packet delay $D(\alpha, \beta, \gamma, B)$ for $\rho = 0.5, 0.8, 0.98, 1$, and 1.02 when $\beta = 0.5$ and $\gamma = 0.8$

5 Conclusion

In this paper, we have conducted the performance analysis of an ON-OFF/Geom/ $1/B$ queue, a finite-buffer queue with ON-OFF Markovian arrival traffic and geometric service times. Specifically, we have obtained closed-form expressions for the packet loss probability and the average packet delay. The closed-form expressions were given in term of the buffer size of the queue, the characterizing parameters of the ON-OFF Markovian traffic, and the service rate. As future work, we will conduct the comparison of the performance of our model with other used models and with real-world traffics.

Acknowledgements. This work was supported in part by the National Science Council, Taiwan, R.O.C., under Contract NSC 100-2628-E-007-006.

References

1. Hunter, J.J.: Mathematical Techniques of Applied Probability, vol. 2. Academic Press, New York (1983)
2. Bruneel, H., Kim, B.G.: Discrete-Time Models for Communication Systems Including ATM. Kluwer Academic Publishers, Boston (1993)
3. Takagi, H.: Queueing Analysis, A Foundation of Performance Evaluation, vol. 3. North-Holland, Amsterdam (1993)
4. Rubin, I., Zhang, Z.: Message delay and queue-size analysis for circuit-switched TDMA systems. IEEE Trans. Commun. 39, 905–914 (1991)
5. Rubin, I., Zhang, Z.: Message delay analysis for TDMA schemes using contiguous-slot assignments. IEEE Trans. Commun. 40, 730–737 (1992)
6. Neuts, M., Guo, J., Zukerman, M., Vu, H.L.: The waiting time distribution for a TDMA model with a finite buffer and state-dependent service. IEEE Trans. Commun. 53, 1522–1533 (2005)
7. Andersen, A.T., Nielsen, B.F.: A Markovian approach for modeling packet traffic with long-range dependence. IEEE J. Sel. Areas Commun. 16, 719–732 (1998)
8. Heffes, H., Lucantoni, D.M.: A Markov modulated characterization of packetized voice and data traffic and related statistical multiplexer performance. IEEE J. Sel. Areas Commun. 4, 856–868 (1986)
9. Daigle, J.N., Langford, J.D.: Models for analysis of packet voice communications systems. IEEE J. Sel. Areas Commun. 4, 847–855 (1986)
10. Sriram, K., Whitt, W.: Characterizing superposition arrival processes in packet multiplexers for voice and data. IEEE J. Sel. Areas Commun. 4, 833–846 (1986)
11. Ren, Q., Ramamurthy, G.: A real-time dynamic connection admission controller based on traffic modeling, measurement, and fuzzy logic control. IEEE J. Sel. Areas Commun. 18, 184–196 (2000)
12. Chaskar, H.M., Madhow, U.: Statistical multiplexing and QoS provisioning for real-time traffic on wireless downlinks. IEEE J. Sel. Areas Commun. 19, 347–354 (2001)
13. Sheu, S.-T., Sheu, T.-F.: A bandwidth allocation/sharing/extension protocol for multimedia over IEEE 802.11 ad hoc wireless LANs. IEEE J. Sel. Areas Commun. 19, 2065–2080 (2001)

14. Sze, H.P., Liew, S.C., Lee, J.Y.B., Yip, D.C.S.: A multiplexing scheme for H.323 voice-over-IP applications. IEEE J. Sel. Areas Commun. 20, 1360–1368 (2002)
15. Wang, Y., Chan, S., Zukerman, M., Harris, R.J.: Priority-based fair scheduling for multimedia WiMAX uplink traffic. In: Proceedings IEEE International Conference on Communications (ICC 2008), Beijing, China, pp. 301–305 (2008)
16. Bruneel, H.: Queueing behavior of statistical multiplexers with correlated inputs. IEEE Trans. Commun. 36, 1339–1341 (1988)
17. Sohraby, K.: On the theory of general ON-OFF sources with applications in high-speed networks. In: Proceedings IEEE International Conference on Computer Communications (INFOCOM 1993), San Francisco, CA, USA, pp. 401–410 (1993)
18. Guo, Z., Zhang, Z., Yang, Y.: Performance modeling of hybrid optical packet switches with shared buffer. In: Proceedings IEEE International Conference on Computer Communications (INFOCOM 2011), Shanghai, China, pp. 1692–1700 (2011)
19. Resnick, S.I.: Adventures in Stochastic Processes. Birkhaüser, Boston (1992)
20. Gross, D., Shortle, J.F., Thompson, J.M., Harris, C.M.: Fundamentals of Queueing Theory, 4th edn. John Wiley & Sons, New York (2008)

Improve Prefetch Performance by Splitting the Cache Replacement Queue

Elizabeth Varki, Allen Hubbe*, and Arif Merchant**

University of New Hampshire, EMC, Google
varki@cs.unh.edu
Allen.Hubbe@emc.com
aamerchant@google.com

Abstract. The performance of a prefetch cache is dependent on both the prefetch technique and the cache replacement policy. Both these algorithms execute independently of each other, but they share a data structure - the cache replacement queue. This paper shows that even with a simple prefetch technique, there is an increase in hit rate when the LRU replacement queue is split into two equal sized queues. A more significant performance improvement is possible with a sophisticated prefetch technique and by splitting the queue unequally.

Keywords: prefetching, caching, replacement policies, disk array, RAID.

1 Introduction

A prefetch technique is the software responsible for identifying access patterns in the cache workload and loading data blocks from these patterns into the cache before the blocks are requested. For example, if a file is being read sequentially, the prefetch technique associated with the file system cache may prefetch several blocks contiguous to the requested file block. Thus, a prefetch technique is responsible for leveraging the *spatial* locality of reference in the cache workload.

The task of a prefetch technique is to determine what data blocks to prefetch and when to prefetch the blocks. The prefetch technique, however, does not control when a prefetched block is evicted from the cache. The replacement policy is the cache software that determines which block is evicted from the cache when a new block is to be loaded into a full cache. Therefore, it is the replacement policy that is responsible for keeping a prefetch block in the cache until it is requested.

The goal of cache software is to ensure that the cache contains blocks that will be requested in the near-future. The cache software essentially consists of two algorithms, namely, the prefetch technique and the replacement policy. The two algorithms are standalone - capable of executing independently of each other

* This work was done while Allen was in UNH.
** This work was done before Arif joined Google.

V. Guyot (Ed.): ICAIT 2012, LNCS 7593, pp. 98–108, 2013.

- the prefetch technique does not decide when a prefetched block is evicted; the replacement policy does not decide when a block is prefetched. The two algorithms together determine the contents of the cache.

Both the prefetch technique and the replacement policy have a say in the contents of the cache via the replacement queue. The cache replacement queue orders cache blocks by eviction priority and it is the meta-data used by caching software. Even though the prefetch technique and the replacement policy are distinct standalone algorithms, they share this data structure. The prefetch technique controls what prefetch blocks are inserted into the replacement queue and when they are inserted, while the replacement policy controls where a prefetch block is placed in the replacement queue. The cache replacement queue encapsulates the combined impact of the two algorithms, and ultimately determines the performance of the prefetch cache.

Contribution: This paper shows that the performance of a prefetch cache can be improved by merely splitting the single replacement queue into two queues. The replacement policy should be aware of the two queues and of the prefetched blocks. This paper demonstrates the Split queue approach using the sequential prefetch technique and the LRU replacement policy.

2 Sequential Locality

Prefetching is carried out by caches at all levels of the memory hierarchy; this papers discusses prefetching in the context of file system and storage caches. The operating system maps user read requests for bytes into read requests for blocks. Therefore, the unit of measurement used is blocks: a cache size is C blocks; the cache workload consists of user requests, where each request is for a single block.

Workload: We explain Split using an example workload that displays sequential locality:

$< 1001, 64, 1002, 72345, 65, 323, 66 >$

The workload is a sequence of block numbers that represent user requests; the position in the sequence represents the relative time at which the request arrives at the cache. That is, requests for blocks 1001, 64, 1002, 72345, 65, 323, 66 arrive at times t_1, t_2, t_3, t_4, t_5, t_6, t_7, respectively.

At first glance, it is difficult to see the sequentiality in the workload. There are two interleaved *streams* of sequential requests: $< 1001, 1002 >$, $< 64, 65, 66 >$. The lone requests $< 72345 >$, $< 323 >$ may also be considered as streams - they represent the start of streams whose future requests arrive after the observation period. Thus, the example workload has four streams, namely, stream 1: $< 1001, 1002 >$, stream 2: $< 64, 65, 66 >$, stream 3: $< 72345 >$, and stream 4: $< 323 >$. To make it easier to identify the sequentiality in the workload, we represent block numbers in a stream as follows: stream 1: $< 1, 1a >$, stream 2: $< 2, 2a, 2b >$, stream 3: $< 3 >$, and stream 4: $< 4 >$. Thus, each block number is mapped to its stream number and its sequential position within the stream. Using this new notation, the example workload is written as follows:

< 1, 2, 1a, 3, 2a, 4, 2b >
A number i in the workload represents the first request from stream i; the variable ia represents the next request in stream i, and so on.

Sequential prefetch techniques are broadly classified into two types [5]: *Prefetch on Miss (PM)* and *Prefetch Always (PA)*. The PM technique generates synchronous prefetch requests for blocks contiguous to the missed block whenever a user request misses in the cache. The basic PA technique generates prefetch requests whenever a user request arrives at the cache. A synchronous prefetch request is generated when a read request misses in the cache. If this synchronously prefetched block gets a hit, then an asynchronous prefetch request is generated for the next block.

There are several versions of PA. In a common version of PA, implemented in Linux and BSD, a synchronous prefetch request is generated on every miss, but an asynchronous prefetch request is not generated on every hit. Several blocks are prefetched at a time, and one of the prefetched blocks in each stream is marked as a *trigger* block. An asynchronous prefetch for this stream is initiated only when the trigger block gets a hit.

Reconsider the example workload: The maximum number of sequential prefetch hits possible is three - for blocks 1a, 2a, 2b. We now present examples that illustrate that for a given workload, the prefetch technique determines (1) the order in which blocks are inserted into the cache, and (2) the number of prefetch hits that can be achieved. The examples assume that (1) the cache is large enough so that no blocks are evicted, and (2) prefetched blocks are instantaneously loaded into the cache.

Let the first prefetch technique ensure that for each user request, the next two contiguous blocks are prefetched. For the example workload, the order in which requests - user requests or prefetch requests - arrive at the cache is:
<1, *1a, 1b*, 2, *2a, 2b*, 1a*, *1c*, 3, *3a, 3b*, 2a*, *2c*, 4, *4a, 4b*, 2b*, *2d*>.
The requests in italics are the prefetched requests. The * represents a prefetch hit.

Now, consider a second technique that prefetches 2 blocks on miss, and prefetches 2 blocks on hit of last cached block of the corresponding stream. For the example workload, the order in which user/prefetch requests arrive at the cache is:
< 1, *1a, 1b*, 2, *2a, 2b*, 1a*, 3, *3a, 3b*, 2a*, 4, *4a, 4b*, 2b*, *2c, 2d* >.

With a PM technique, where 1 block is prefetched on each miss, the order of requests is:
< 1, *1a*, 2, *2a*, 1a*, 3, *3a*, 2a*, 4, *4a*, 2b, *2c* >.
Note that with this last technique, the workload only gets 2 prefetch hits.

Replacement policy becomes relevant when the cache is too small to hold all the blocks. For the example workload, consider a cache of size 4 blocks. Table 1 demonstrates the ordering of the LRU replacement queue with the first prefetch technique. The example workload does not display *temporal* (rereference) locality, so a prefetch block is moved out of the cache as soon as it receives a hit.

The LRU policy is designed for workloads that display temporal locality, but even so, the prefetch cache achieves the maximum prefetch hit rate of 3. However, in general, it can be argued that the prefetch cache would perform better if the replacement policy is aware of prefetching and sequential locality. Consequently, file system and storage caches often implement a prefetch aware version of LRU - all blocks of a stream are placed contiguously in the replacement queue and moved as a unit [3]. When a block gets a hit, all prefetched blocks from the stream are moved to the MRU end of the replacement queue. The least recently used stream blocks are evicted from the cache when a new stream is to be inserted. This version of LRU, called StreamLRU, is presented in Table 2. The computational complexity of StreamLRU is the same as that of LRU.

Note that for the example workload and this prefetch technique, LRU gets 3 prefetch hits while StreamLRU only gets 2 hits. In general, however, StreamLRU gets more prefetch hits than LRU since StreamLRU recognizes the temporal locality of streams and keeps the most recently used stream blocks in the cache. In fact, for the second prefetch technique presented earlier - prefetch 2 blocks on miss, prefetch 2 blocks on hit of last stream block - LRU gets 2 prefetch hits, while StreamLRU gets 3 prefetch hits.

3 Split

This is a how-to section that explains the mechanics of Split queue with respect to sequential prefetch and LRU. The next section presents experimental evidence of Split's superior performance when the workload displays sequential locality. Section 5 presents the intuition behind Split and explains why the Split queue is better than the single queue.

Split divides the single replacement queue into two queues, the Up queue and the Down queue - a block evicted from the LRU end of the Up queue is inserted into the MRU end of the Down queue; all evictions from the prefetch cache are from the LRU end of the Down queue. When two blocks of a stream are prefetched, the earlier (*i.e.*, first) block of the stream is inserted into the Up

Table 1. LRU, 1st prefetch technique: ensures that for each request the next 2 contiguous blocks are loaded

Prefetch cache size = 4, LRU							
hits			h1		h2		h3
workload	**1**	**2**	**1a**	**3**	**2a**	**4**	**2b**
rep.Queue	1a	2a	1c	3a	2b	4a	2d
	1b	2b	2a	3b	2c	4b	4a
		1a	2b	1c	3a	2b	4b
		1b	1b	2a	3b	2c	2c
eject				**2b**	**1c**	**3a**	
				1b		**3b**	

Table 2. StreamLRU, 1st prefetch technique: ensures that for each request the next 2 contiguous blocks are loaded

Prefetch cache size = 4, StreamLRU							
hits			h1				h2
workload	**1**	**2**	**1a**	**3**	**2a**	**4**	**2b**
rep.Queue	1a	2a	1b	3a	2b	4a	2c
	1b	2b	1c	3b	2c	4b	2d
		1a	2a	1b	3a	2b	4a
		1b	2b	1c	3b	2c	4b
eject				**2a**	**1b**	**3a**	
				2b	**1c**	**3b**	

Table 3. SplitLRU, 1st prefetch technique: ensures that for each request the next 2 contiguous blocks are loaded. Split gives the same number of hits as LRU and more hits than StreamLRU.

Prefetch cache size = 4, SplitLRU							
hits			h1		h2		h3
workload	**1**	**2**	**1a**	**3**	**2a**	**4**	**2b**
rep.Up Q	1a	2a	1b	3a	2b	4a	2c
		1a	2a	1b	3a	2b	4a
rep.Down Q	1b	2b	1c	3b	2c	4b	2d
		1b	2b	2a	1b	3a	4b
eject				**1c**	**3b**	**2c**	**3a**
				2b		**1b**	

Table 4. SplitLRU, 2nd prefetch technique: ensures that 2 contiguous blocks are prefetched on miss and on hit of last cached stream block. Split gives the same number of hits as StreamLRU and more hits than LRU.

Prefetch cache size = 4, SplitLRU							
hits			h1		h2		h3
workload	**1**	**2**	**1a**	**3**	**2a**	**4**	**2b**
rep.Up Q	1a	2a	1b	3a	2b	4a	2c
		1a	2a	1b	3a	2b	4a
rep.Down Q	1b	2b	2b	3b	2c	4b	2d
		1b		2a	1b	3a	4b
eject				**2b**	**3b**	**2c**	**3a**
						1b	

queue; if any block is evicted from the LRU end of the Up queue then this block is inserted into the MRU end of the Down queue; finally, the later (*i.e.*, second) block of the newly prefetched stream is inserted into the MRU end of the Down queue. Split, like StreamLRU, assumes that the replacement policy recognizes streams, but unlike StreamLRU (and like LRU), Split does not require that all stream blocks be placed together in the replacement queue.

Table 3 demonstrates Split LRU using the example workload and the first prefetch technique presented in the last section. In the example, when a request arrives for prefetched block $1a$, the block $1a$ is removed from the prefetch cache (since it is now referenced). The prefetch cache contains block $1b$. Since the replacement policy is prefetch aware LRU, block $1b$ is moved from the Down queue to the insertion end of the Up queue, and the newly prefetched block $1c$ is inserted into the insertion end of the Down queue. When a request arrives for block 3, blocks $3a, 3b$ are prefetched; block $3a$ is inserted into the Up queue which results in block $2a$ being evicted from the Up queue; this block is inserted into the Down queue, and then the second block from stream 3, $3b$, is inserted into the Down queue.

Table 4 demonstrates Split LRU using the example workload and the second prefetch technique presented in the last section. Due to space limitations, LRU and StreamLRU's performance with this second prefetch technique is not shown. With this prefetch technique too, Split achieves the maximum prefetch hit rate of 3.

4 Experimental Evaluation

We developed a simulator to evaluate Split; the front end model is our cache simulator, while the back end storage model is the Disksim 4.0 simulator. Table 5 gives the setup used for our experiments. The replacement policy is LRU, and the prefetch technique is the 2nd one presented in Section 2: prefetch the next 2 contiguous blocks on miss and on hit of last cached stream block.

Table 5. Storage simulator setup

Disksim parameter	Value
disk type	cheetah9LP
disk capacity	17783240 blocks
mean disk read seek time	5.4 msec
maximum disk read seek time	10.63 msec
disk revolutions per minute	10045 rpm

Workload: Sequential prefetching is effective only if the workload has some sequential locality. The workload used in our experiments contains no re-references to ensure that all hits are prefetch block hits. Our cache workload generator

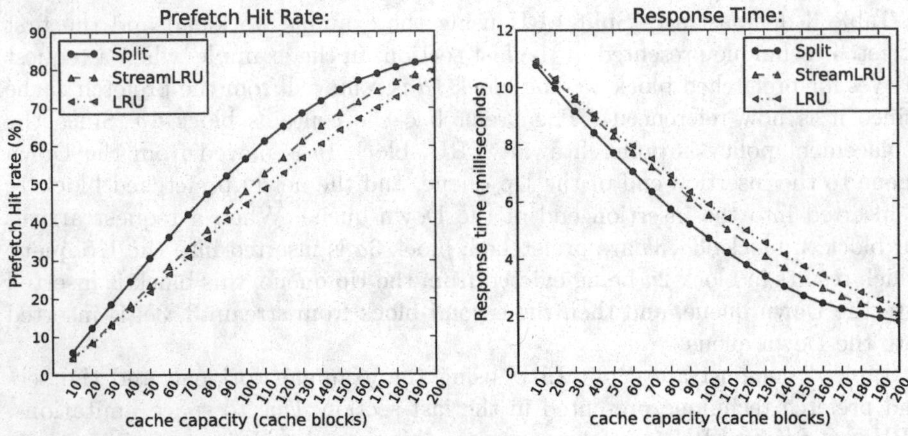

Fig. 1. Workload with 90 multiple sequential sequences and 10 random sequences

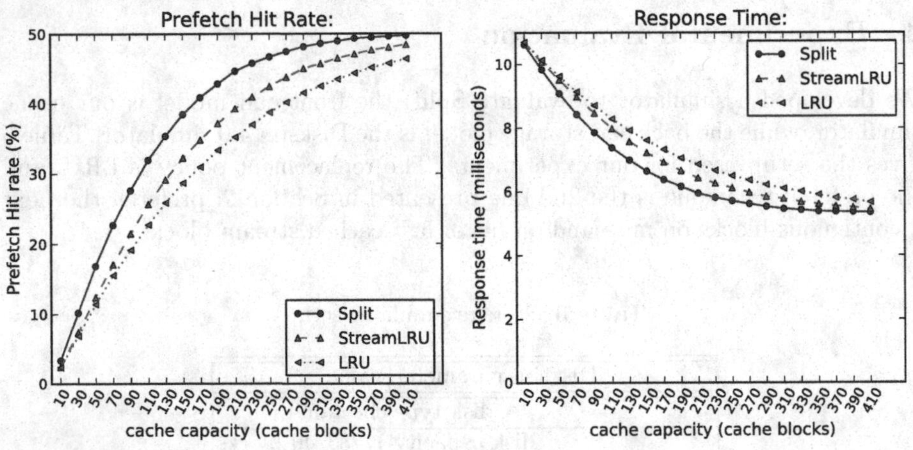

Fig. 2. Workload with 50 single sequential and 50 random sequences

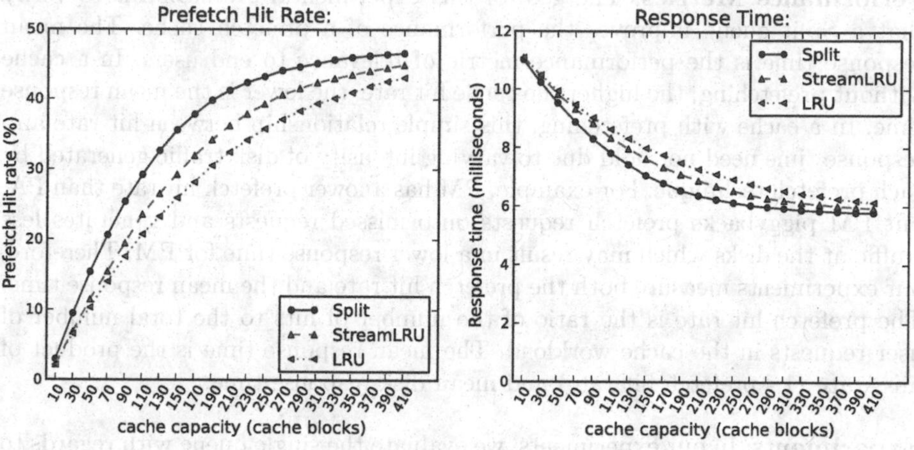

Fig. 3. Workload with 10 single sequential, 40 multiple sequential, 50 random sequences

is composed of sequence generators; we have three types of sequence generators - single sequential, multiple sequential, and random. Example output from the three types of sequence generators:

single sequential: < 234, 235, 236, 237, ... >; a single sequence of requests for contiguous blocks.

multiple sequential: < 100, 101, 102, 103, ..., 4567, 4568, 4569, ..., 95489, 95490, 95491, ... >; two or more subsequences of requests for contiguous blocks; the number of requests in each subsequence is drawn from a Poisson distribution.

random sequence: < 45, 1982, 99999, 247, 8174, ... >; a single sequence of requests for random blocks.

Each of our experiment's workload traces is composed of a total of 100,000 requests from 100 independent, concurrent sequence generators; all generators start up at the beginning of the simulation. For each sequence, the request interarrival times are drawn from an exponential distribution. Therefore, the final workload submitted to our cache simulator are interleaved requests from the 100 sequence generators. An example of a workload containing the above 3 interleaved sequences is:

< 100, 45, 234, 235, 101, 236, 102, 103, 104, 1982, 99999, 237, 238, 105, 4567, 247, 8174, 4568, ... >.

Note that from the perspective of PA or PM, this example workload contains several (more than 3) interleaved streams: < 100, 101, 102,... >, < 234, 235, ... > < 45 >, < 1982 >, < 9999 >, ... Each request from the random sequence is viewed by a prefetch technique as a start of a stream, and therefore, each random request results in a (wasted) prefetch. The last request in a subsequence of a multiple sequential stream also results in a wasted prefetch.

Performance Metrics: The goal of this experimental evaluation is to verify that a Split queue improves the performance of a prefetch cache. The mean response time is the performance metric of relevance to end users. In a cache without prefetching, the higher the cache hit rate, the lower is the mean response time. In a cache with prefetching, this simple relationship between hit rate and response time need not hold due to varying intensity of disk traffic generated by each prefetch technique. For example, PM has a lower prefetch hit rate than PA, but PM piggybacks prefetch requests onto missed requests and generates less traffic at the disks which may result in a lower response time for PM. Therefore, our experiments measure both the prefetch hit rate and the mean response time. The prefetch hit rate is the ratio of the number of hits to the total number of user requests in the cache workload. The mean response time is the product of miss rate (1 - prefetch hit rate) and mean disk response time.

Experiments: In our experiments, we evaluate the single queue with regards to both LRU and streamLRU since streamLRU is the version of LRU that recognizes prefetch blocks. We measure hit rate and response time for a fixed workload as the cache size varies. The cache size is increased until the maximum prefetch hit ratio for the workload is achieved. The workload has no rereferences of blocks, so a prefetch block is evicted from the cache as soon as it gets a hit (similar to the examples presented in the last section).

In the first experiment shown in Figure 1, the workload consists of 90 interleaved multiple sequential sequences and 10 random sequences. From the prefetch technique's viewpoint, every random request is the start of a new stream, every start of a new subsequence in a multiple sequential sequence is a new stream. Therefore, there are more than 100 streams in the workload from the viewpoint of the prefetch technique. The cache size is varied from 10 to 200 blocks. When the cache size is 110 blocks, the hit rate of Split is approximately 27% greater than that of LRU and StreamLRU; resulting in a 23% decrease in response time of Split.

In the next experiment (Figure 2), the workload is generated by 50 single sequential sequence generators and 50 random sequence generators. Therefore, the maximum hit rate for this workload is 0.5. Since 2 blocks are prefetched into the cache for every random request, the cache contains a lot of useless blocks. The maximum hit rate is achieved when the cache approaches 400 blocks. The greater the randomness in the workload, the larger is the cache size required to achieve the maximum prefetch hit rate. In the last experiment - Figure 3 - the workload consists of 40 multiple sequential sequences, 10 sequential sequences, and 50 random sequences. Again, Split queue performs better than the single queue. When the cache size is 150 blocks, the hit rate of Split is 38% greater than that of LRU and SplitLRU. The Split queue achieves maximal performance for the workload before the single queue.

5 Analysis

In all our experiments, the Split queue performs better than the single queue. In order to understand why the Split queue performs better than the single queue, it is necessary to explain sequential (spatial) locality in relation to the actions of a prefetch technique. In order to amortize the cost of prefetching - reduce the traffic at the disks - several blocks are prefetched at a time. Not all these blocks are expected to receive user requests immediately. In fact, the sequential access pattern dictates that blocks are accessed contiguously, in sequence. Therefore, when there are 2 prefetched blocks, as in our examples and experiments, the first block is expected to receive an user request before the second block. Split incorporates this characteristic by inserting the 1st block in the Up queue and the 2nd block in the Down queue. Even if the 2nd block gets evicted, the first block remains in the cache longer than it would in the single queue approach; if the first block gets a prefetch hit, there is time to prefetch the 2nd block.

The Split queue performs better than the single queue since it incorporates both the temporal and spatial locality of streams. By evicting blocks from the least recently used stream, StreamLRU incorporates the temporal locality of streams. For the workloads considered, StreamLRU performs better than LRU, but their performances are close, almost statistically identical. This is somewhat surprising given that LRU does not recognize streams. A possible reason for the similarity between LRU and StreamLRU's performance may be found by looking at the replacement queues in Tables 1 and 2 (Section 2): when user request for 3 is processed, LRU's replacement queue contains streams 3, 1, 2, while StreamLRU's replacement queue only contains 3 and 1. Since LRU does not keep stream blocks together, it is possible for LRU's replacement queue to hold more streams than StreamLRU's replacement queue. In general, the Split queue holds more streams than the single queue and consequently, Split performs better.

Summarizing, this paper shows that given a prefetch technique and LRU, performance is improved by simply splitting the replacement queue. Prior work has shown that the performance of a prefetch technique cannot be studied in isolation of the replacement policy and vice versa [1] [2] [4]. The intuition behind Split is the recognition that this dependency is a result of the shared data structure - the cache replacement queue - that both algorithms update. Instead of targeting the prefetch technique or the replacement policy, Split manipulates the queue to maximize performance. In fact, the Split queue is a single queue with the 2nd prefetched block being inserted midway in the replacement queue.

6 Conclusion

The impact of prefetching and caching is encapsulated in the cache replacement queue. This paper shows that by splitting the queue, the performance of a prefetch cache improves, without changing the prefetch technique or the replacement policy. In the experiments, the lengths of the Up and Down queue are equal. By setting the Up queue to twice the length of the Down queue, we have found that there is a greater improvement of Split's performance. This paper analyzes the Split queue with a basic prefetch technique that prefetches at most 2 blocks. The Split queue improves performance more significantly if more blocks are prefetched per stream. Incorporating a combination of the above - increasing length of Up queue and using a more sophisticated prefetch technique that varies the amount of prefetch may result in greater improvement of performance.

We plan to evaluate the Split queue approach with other replacement policies. The Split policy is evaluated here for single-level caches. However, the Split policy with its 2-queue structure is naturally geared for multiple-level cooperative caches and it would be interesting to analyze Split in a multiple-level setting. Other issues that could be addressed include analysis of traffic generation by the policies, theoretical analysis of Split, and prefetch cache sizing based on hit rates in Up and Down queues.

References

1. Bhatia, S., Varki, E., Merchant, A.: Sequential prefetch cache sizing for maximal hit rate. In: 18th Annual IEEE/ACM International Symposium on Modeling, Analysis and Simulation of Computer and Telecommunication Systems, pp. 89–98 (2010)
2. Butt, A.R., Gniady, C., Hu, Y.C.: The performance impact of kernel prefetching on buffer cache replacement algorithms. IEEE Transactions on Computers 56(7), 889–908 (2007)
3. Gill, B.S., Modha, D.S.: SARC: Sequential prefetching in adaptive replacement cache. In: Proc. of USENIX 2005 Annual Technical Conference, pp. 293–308 (2005)
4. Jiang, S.: Dulo: An effective buffer cache management scheme to exploit both temporal and spatial localities. In: USENIX Conference on File and Storage Technologies (FAST) (2005)
5. Li, M., Varki, E., Bhatia, S., Merchant, A.: TaP: Table-based prefetching for storage caches. In: 6th USENIX Conference on File and Storage Technologies (FAST 2008), pp. 81–97 (2008)

CO_2 Laser Writing of Long-Period Fiber Gratings in Polarization-Maintaining Fiber under Tension

Yunqi Liu, Jian Zou, Qiang Guo, and Tingyun Wang

Key Lab of Specialty Fiber Optics and Optical Access Networks, School of Communication and Information Engineering, Shanghai University, Shanghai 200072, China
yqliu@shu.edu.cn

Abstract. We demonstrate CO_2 laser writing of long-period fiber gratings (LPFGs) in a panda polarization-maintaining (PM) fiber under external tension. The transmission spectrum of the LPFGs depends on the irradiation direction of the writing beam with respect to the principal axes of the fiber. When the irradiation direction is along the fast axis of the PM fiber, the transmission spectra of the LPFG has two more rejection bands, compared to the transmission spectra of the LPFG written in the PM fiber without tension. Our results provide a better understanding of the formation of LPFGs written by CO_2 laser.

Keywords: Long-period fiber grating (LPFG), CO_2 laser, polarization-maintaining (PM) fiber.

1 Introduction

Long period fiber grating (LPFG) is a passive mode coupling device which couples light from the guided core mode to the cladding modes of a single-mode fiber (SMF) and provides distinct attenuation bands in the transmission spectrum [l]. The unique characteristics of LPFG make it attractive for applications in sensing strain, temperature, bending and refractive index of surrounding medium, et al [2]. Among the methods reported for the fabrication of LPFGs, the CO_2 laser writing method is particularly flexible, as it can be applied to practically any fibers and can be computer controlled to generate complicated grating profiles without using any masks [3]–[5]. It is well known that the absorption of the CO_2 laser radiation in the fiber results in residual stress relaxation in the core [6] and asymmetric index distribution induced by CO_2 laser exposure can lead to light couplings to both symmetric and asymmetric cladding modes and thus produce complicated transmission spectra [7]. For a polarization-maintaining (PM) fiber, the presence of boron-doped stress-applying parts (SAPs) in the cladding area has obvious effect on the index changes induced by the stress changes due to CO_2 laser exposure. The fabrication of CO_2 laser written LPFGs in a bow-tie PM fiber has been demonstrated recently, and the results verified that the grating formation should be the combined effect of direct stress relaxation in the core and the indirect modification of the stress distribution in the core due to stress relaxation in the SAPs of the PM fiber [5]. When a LPFG was written in the PM fiber by CO_2 laser, the writing efficiency was

V. Guyot (Ed.): ICAIT 2012, LNCS 7593, pp. 109–115, 2013.

found to be dependent on the irradiation direction of the writing beam with respect to the principal axes of the fiber. The highest efficiency was obtained when the irradiation direction is along the slow axis of the fiber [5].

Besides, recent studies [8], [9] show that freezing of tensile inelastic stresses into the glass network structure (frozen-in viscoelasticity) can take place during the fiber drawing process, which can lower the refractive index of the fiber cladding significantly. Refractive-index changes due to frozen-in viscoelasticity can be induced by heating treatment of a post-draw fiber under tension, which has been demonstrated for the fabrication of LPFGs in the conventional SMF [10]. The CO_2 laser writing efficiency can be enhanced with the amount of axial tension applied along the fiber [10]. In this paper, we demonstrate CO_2 laser writing of LPFGs in a panda PM fiber under applied axial tension, and show that the transmission spectra of LPFGs depends on the irradiation direction of the writing beam with respect to the principal axes of the PM fiber.

2 Experimental Results and Discussion

The PM fiber used in our experiments was a commercial panda fiber (YOFC, PM1010-A), which had a beat length of 2.63 mm at the wavelength 1550 nm. The writing source we used was a focused pulsed CO_2 laser (CO_2-H10, Han's Laser). The pulse frequency and average power were fixed at 5 kHz and 0.6 W, respectively. The fiber was mounted on a stage and tensioned with two equal weights hanging on both ends of the fiber. The laser beam was focused on the exposed fiber (with its jacket removed) to a spot of ~30 μm, which was computer programmed to scan across the fiber point-wise in the transverse direction at a particular speed. Transverse scanning was advanced along the fiber at steps, with each step equal to the grating period. A scanning cycle was completed when the specified number of periods was reached. The transverse scanning speed was used to control the total CO_2 laser energy irradiated on the fiber. We measured the transmission spectrum of the LPFGs with a broadband source and an optical spectrum analyzer (OSA), and monitored in particular the resonance wavelength and the contrast of the grating on the completion of every laser scanning cycle. A polarizer and a polarization controller were inserted between the light source and the PM fiber for controlling the polarization state of the input light.

Firstly, Two LPFGs, with CO_2 laser being irradiated along the slow axis and the fast axis of PM fiber, respectively, were fabricated without tension. The grating pitch was 460 μm and the grating length was 27.6 mm (60 periods). The CO_2 laser energy density was set to be 4.7 J/mm^2. Figure 1 shows the transmission spectra of the LPFGs written along the slow and fast axes, respectively. Because the experimental results for the two polarized modes of the fiber are similar, only the transmission dips corresponded to the slow axis (slow mode) are presented. When we irradiated the fiber along the fast axis (LPFG 1), the grating was fabricated by 12 laser scanning cycles. The resonance wavelength and contrast of LPFG 1 were 1495.8 nm and 22.5 dB for the transmission dip corresponding to fast axis, respectively. When the laser was irradiated along the slow axis (LPFG 2), the resonance wavelength was

1503.4nm, and the contrast of the grating reached to the highest value (16 dB) after 4 laser scanning cycles as the same laser energy density was used. The writing efficiency was so high that the grating is easy to be over-coupled due to the high CO_2 laser doses. In order to write a LPFG with high grating contrast, we can use a lower CO_2 laser energy intensity to reduce the grating writing efficiency.

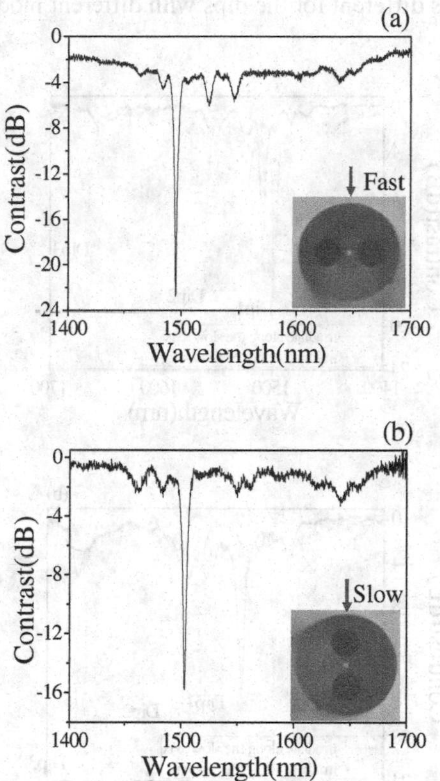

Fig. 1. Transmission spectra (slow mode) of two LPFGs written in PM fiber (Λ=460 μm, without tension): (a) Irradiation along the fast axis, and (b) Irradiation along the slow axis. The optical image in the inset shows the fast and slow axes of the fiber and the irradiation direction (arrow).

Then we wrote another two LPFGs with the same grating pitch and grating length in the PM fiber under an applied tension of 200 g. Due to the generation of inelastic frozen-in strains in the fiber by the CO_2 laser irradiation, there is an enhancement in the writing efficiency of LPFG with a fiber under tension [10]. The CO_2 laser energy density was reduced to be 3.3 J/mm^2. As shown in Figure 2, when CO_2 laser irradiation is along the fast axis of the fiber, there are two new grating dips emerging at longer wavelengths, Dip 2 (1521 nm) and Dip 3 (1664.4 nm). After 7 scanning cycles, the original transmission dip, Dip 1 (1498.4 nm), reaches the peak strength, as the red line shown in Fig. 2(a). However, in the case of irradiation being along the slow axis of the fiber, the transmission spectra only has one rejection band, which is consistent with the transmission spectra of the LPFGs written without tension. The black line of Fig. 2(a) shows the transmission spectrum of the LPFG, where the only grating dip (1508.8 nm) reaches the peak strength after one scanning cycle. Fig. 2(b) shows the transmission spectra of LPFGs after the same scanning cycles (10 cycles). At this time, both Dip 1 and Dip 2 have been over-coupled, and the Dip 3 reaches to a higher value (23.8 dB) as shown in the red line. The linewidth of the grating dips varied from 10 nm to 15 nm, which is different for the dips with different mode orders.

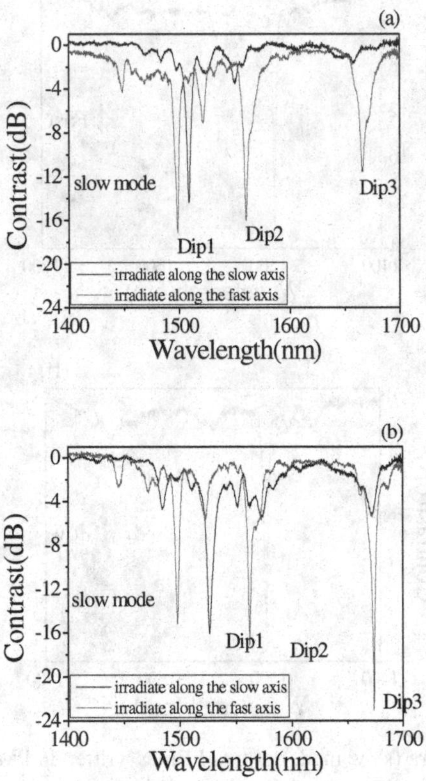

Fig. 2. Transmission spectra of LPFGs written in the PM fiber under tension (Λ=460 μm, 200 g tension), the black line (irradiation along the slow axis) and the red line (irradiation along the fast axis): (a) Dip 1 reaches the peak strength, and (b) with the same scanning cycles

The spectrum of LPFG obtained with CO_2 laser irradiation being along the slow axis still have no obvious transmission dips at the wavelengths of Dip 2 or Dip 3, and the contrast of the original transmission dip (Dip 1) reaches to a high value again, which indicates that the LPFG couples light from the guided core mode to the cladding modes again after the cladding modes fully re-coupled back into the core mode [11]. The formation of the original transmission dip (Dip 1), which emerges in all the cases, should be the combined effect of direct stress relaxation in the core and the indirect modification of the stress distribution in the core due to stress relaxation in the SAPs of the fiber [5]. While the formation of the new transmission dips, Dip 2 and Dip 3 could be attributed to the generation of inelastic frozen-in strains in the fiber by the CO_2 laser irradiation [10]. The writing efficiency of different grating dips has large difference, which leads to the contrast difference of grating dips for the same LPFG. By controlling the applied tension and the CO_2 laser energy density, the resonance wavelength of the grating could be adjusted in the accuracy of nanometer.

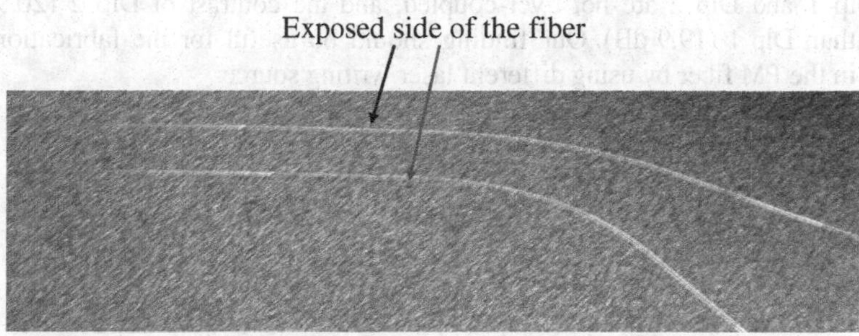

Fig. 3. LPFGs written in an axially stressed PM fiber curve naturally with the exposed side of the fiber bending outward when the weight applied to the fiber is removed and the fiber was set free: the LPFG the red arrow points to (irradiation along the fast axis) is more curved than the one the black arrow points to (irradiation along the slow axis)

As shown in the inset optical image of Fig. 1(b), one of the SAPs is brought close to the irradiating CO_2 laser beam, when the irradiation is along the slow axis. Most of the CO_2 laser energy is absorbed by the SAP. No enough laser energy can be use for the frozen-in strain, which is believed to account for the formation of new transmission dips. So no new transmission dips can be observed, as shown in Figure 2. Compare to the situation of CO_2 laser irradiation being along the fast axis, where the SAPs are far away from the writing beam. The laser writing beam can interact in the core and cladding of the PM fiber as the same way as in a convention SMF under tension, which can induce the inelastic frozen-in strain and then form two more rejection bands. Besides, recent results show that the frozen-in tensile strain induced on the exposed side is stronger than that on the other side. When the gratings was released in space by removing the applied weight, the unexposed side recoiled more than the exposed side, which make the fiber curve naturally with the exposed side of the fiber bending outward [10]. Fig. 3 shows the pictures of the LPFGs written in an axially stressed PM fiber curve naturally with the exposed side of the fiber bending outward when the weight applied to the fiber is removed and the fiber was set free. We find that the LPFG (irradiation along the fast axis) is more curved than the one (irradiation along the slow axis), which confirms the above assumption that the writing beam induces the inelastic frozen-in strains and then makes the spectrum emerge two more rejection bands when CO_2 laser irradiation is along the fast axis, but does not in the case of CO_2 laser irradiation being along the slow axis.

Several LPFGs with the same grating pitch and grating length were fabricated in the PM fiber under different applied tension in the case of CO_2 laser irradiation being along the fast axis. Fig. 4(a) shows the dependence of the grating contrast of Dip 2 when the Dip 1 begins to be over-coupled on applied weights. Only when the applied tension is above 100 g, obvious new grating dips can be observed in the transmission spectra of the LPFGs and the gap of the writing efficiency between the new dip (Dip 2) and the original dip (Dip 1) decreases with the increase of applied weights. When the largest weight, 400 g, which was close to the maximum load that the fiber could bear without breaking, was applied in the fiber, the writing efficiency of Dip 2 is slightly larger than the efficiency of Dip 1. Fig. 4 (b) shows transmission spectra of the LPFG written by 5 scanning cycles of CO_2 laser at an energy density of 2.6 J/mm^2. Both Dip 1 and Dip 2 are not over-coupled, and the contrast of Dip 2 (20.9 dB) is greater than Dip 1 (19.9 dB). Our finding should be useful for the fabrication of the LPFGs in the PM fiber by using different laser writing source.

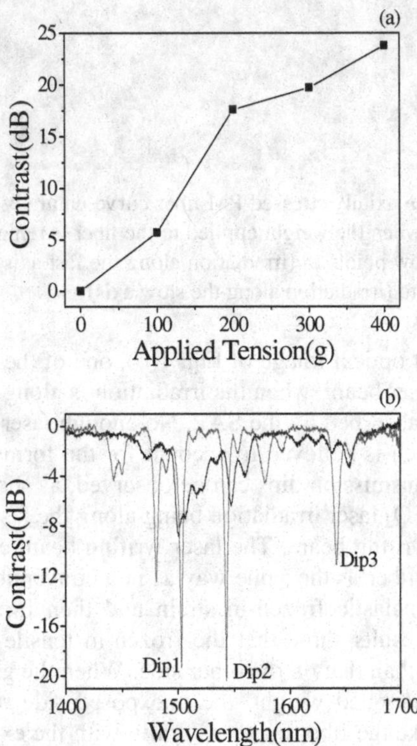

Fig. 4. (a) Dependence of the grating contrast of Dip 2 on applied weights when the Dip 1 begins to be over-coupled, and (b) Transmission spectra of LPFGs (Λ=460 μm, 400 g tension), the black line (irradiation along the slow axis) and the red line (irradiation along the fast axis)

3 Conclusion

In summary, we have investigated the writing of LPFGs in the PM fiber under tension by CO_2 laser. When the irradiation direction is along the fast axis of the fiber, the transmission spectrum of LPFG has two more rejection bands, compared to the transmission spectrum of LPFG written in the PM fiber without tension. Comparing to the situation of irradiation along the slow axis, we find that the generation of the new dips is due to the generation of inelastic frozen-in strains in the fiber by the CO_2 laser irradiation. The CO_2 laser written LPFGs could find wide application in fiber sensors and optical communications.

Acknowledgement. This work was jointed supported by the National Natural Science Foundation of China (61077065), the New Century Excellent Talents in University, Ministry of Education of China (NCET-10-0082), Project of Shanghai Science and Technology Commission (09530500600), the Shanghai Shuguang Program (08SG40), and the Shanghai Leading Academic Discipline Project (S30108).

References

1. Vengsarkar, A.M., Lemaire, P.J., Judkins, J.B., Bhatia, V., Erdogan, T., Sipe, J.E.: Long-period fiber gratings as band-rejection filters. J. Lightw. Technol. 14(1), 58–64 (1996)
2. James, S.W., Tatam, R.P.: Optical fibre long-period fiber grating sensors: characteristics and application. Mcas. Sci. Technol. 14(5), 49–61 (2003)
3. Rao, Y.J., Wang, Y.P., Ran, Z.L., Zhu, T.: Novel fiber-optic sensors based on the long-period fiber grating written by high-frequency CO_2 laser pulses. J. Lightw. Technol. 21(5), 1320–1327 (2003)
4. Liu, Y., Lee, H.W., Chiang, K.S., Zhu, T., Rao, Y.J.: Glass structure changes in CO_2 laser writing of long-period gratings in boron-doped single-mode fibers. J. Lightw. Technol. 27(7), 857–863 (2009)
5. Lee, H.W., Liu, Y., Chiang, K.S.: Writing of long-period gratings in conventional photonic-crystal polarization-maintaining fibers by CO_2 laser pulses. IEEE Photon. Technol. Lett. 20(2), 132–134 (2008)
6. Kim, B.H., Park, Y., Ahn, T.-J., Kim, D.Y., Lee, B.H., Chung, Y., Peak, U.C., Han, W.-T.: Residual stress relaxation in the core of optical fiber by CO_2 laser irradiation. Opt. Lett. 26, 1657–1659 (2001)
7. Grubsky, V., Feinbery, J.: Fabrication of axially symmetric long-period gratings with a carbon dioxide laser. IEEE Photon. Technol. Lett. 18(21), 2296–2298 (2006)
8. Yablon, A.D., Yan, M.F., Wisk, P., Dimarcello, F.V., Fleming, J.W., Reed, W.A., Monberg, E.M., Digiovanni, D.J., Lines, M.E.: Refractive index perturbations in optical fiber resulting from frozen-in viscoelasticity. Appl. Phys. Lett. 84(1), 19–21 (2004)
9. Yablon, A.D.: Optical and mechanical effects of frozen-in stresses and strains in optical fibers. IEEE J. Sel.Top. Quantum Electron 10(2), 300–311 (2004)
10. Liu, Y., Chiang, K.S.: CO_2 laser writing of long-period fiber gratings in optical fibers under tension. Opt. Lett. 33(17), 1933–1935 (2008)
11. Erdogan, T.: Fiber grating spectra. J. Lightw. Technol. 15(8), 1277–1297 (1997)

SAVI - A Model for Video Workload Generation Based on Scene Length*

Valter Klein Junior and Carlos Marcelo Pedroso

Federal University of Parana
Department of Electrical Engineering, Curitiba, Brazil
valter.klein@pucpr.br, pedroso@eletrica.ufpr.br

Abstract. The development of models for synthetic network traffic generation is essential for performance evaluation of transmission systems. The workload generation models are employed in network simulations, testing and performance predictions. This article presents a new model for workload generation of video encoded with MPEG, called SAVI (Scene Aware Video Workload Generation Model). This model provides an explanation for the short and long range dependence of video traffic, and was designed based on movie scene length. The resulting model presents good possibilities to support generalizations according to the movie style. Besides, SAVI is easier to parametrize if compared with the available models and presents low computational complexity. The model was developed by analyzing the traces of movies publicly available and has been tested through computer simulations. The synthetic traffic generated mimics properly the characteristics of real traffic, including the short and long range dependence.

1 Introduction

The performance evaluation of a system regards the analysis of certain measures of interest, through simulation or analytical tools, and demands the use of a model that properly represents the system under study. The development of a model is a process of creation and description, involving a certain degree of abstraction that, in most cases, involves a series of simplifications on the organization and operation of the real system. Usually this description takes the form of mathematical relationships, which together compose what is called a model [1]. A good model should represent the dynamic and stochastic behavior of the real system. Krunz and Makowski [2], Min Dai and Zhang [3], Manzoni et. al [4], among others, shown that video traffic often presents short and long range dependence: a good model for video workload generation must capture this time-dependent behavior.

The video traffic consists in a sequence of images generated at a constant rate, typically between 24-30 frames per second (FPS), each image represented

* This work was supported in part by CNPq (Conselho Nacional de Desenvolvimento Científico e Tecnológico) Foundation (Brazil), AEX8322/12-0.

V. Guyot (Ed.): ICAIT 2012, LNCS 7593, pp. 116–127, 2013.

by a frame consisting in a binary code representing the image pixels. The frames usually have spatial and temporal redundancy, these two features are exploited by encoding algorithms to reduce the frame size, resulting in a variable bit rate behavior.

The MPEG (*Moving Picture Experts Group*) [5] is a set of specifications for video and audio encoding. The MPEG-2/4 exploits the temporal redundancy in a frame, using this characteristic to reduce the frame size. The image is encoded using three types of frames identified by the letters I, P and B. The I-Frames (*Intra frames*) represent the information without the need of any other frame, the P-Frames (*Predictive frames*) require information from the last I or P-Frame and the B-Frames (*Bi-directional frame*) depend on information of previous I or P-Frame and also subsequent P-Frame. A Group of Pictures (GOP) starts with an I-Frame, which is followed by a sequence of B and P-Frames. To represent the structure of GOP, it is common to use the notation *(N, M)*, where N represents the number of frames per GOP and M represents the amount of B consecutive frames. For instance, *(12, 2)* denotes the sequence *IBBPBBPBBPBB*, repeated continuously along the length of video.

In this paper we propose a model for MPEG traffic generation, called SAVI (Scene Aware Video Workload Generation Model), which uses the scene length, the temporal dependence between the I-Frames of the same scene and the temporal dependence observed between I, P and B-Frames of the same GOP. By considering the scene length, it was possible to develop a model that captures the behavior of the system accurately and with good computational efficiency, if compared to existing models. The use of SAVI enables to perform a movie classification according to semantic characteristics of the movies, which facilitate the workload generation for a variety of scenarios. The existing approaches employ self similar series to generate the size of I-Frames, based on Hurst parameter (H) or use a sum of random variables to generate I, P and B-Frames. The SAVI model can be classified in this last category, but provides an explanation relating each random variable with observable movie characteristics, which is a novelty. Also, the SAVI provides an explanation to the short and long range dependence observed in video traffic.

This paper is organized as follows. Section 2 describes the main available models for MPEG workload generation. In Section 3 is shown the details of the SAVI model, and the Section 4 presents the algorithm for traffic generation and a comparison of real and synthetic traffic. Finally, the Section 5 presents the conclusions.

2 Traffic Models for MPEG Video

Garret and Willinger present in [6] a model that captures self-similar characteristics of the video traffic. The approach taken was to model the instantaneous transmission rate, which follows a heavy tail distribution. The authors suggest the use of a combination of Gamma and Pareto probability distribution functions (PDF). The authors also suggest an algorithm for traffic generation - however, the model does not contemplate the GOP structure or any correlation between the subsequent frames.

A model that consider the GOP structure for traffic generation was proposed by Krunz and Makowski in [2]. The authors identified that the the long range dependence of traffic is mainly influenced by the size of I, P and B-Frames. To model the size of the I-Frames, was used a sum of two random variables and the P and B-Frames, modeled with the Lognormal PDF.

O. Rose present in [7] a method for VBR video workload generation using the Memory Markov Chain (MMC) model. The idea is to observe the bandwidth usage and produce a state in the Markov chain for each level typically observed, with the bandwidth usage aggregated by an average process. While in a given state, the generator will produce traffic with an average rate. After a period of time, a state transition occurs and the system starts generating traffic with another average bandwidth. The author shows that it is possible to mimic the structure of auto-correlation observed in actual traffic. However, it is very difficult to find the number of states required. It was also presented an algorithm to configure the number of states of the MMC. The author recognizes that, at the end of the process, the number of states required approaches the number of scenes of the movie and the number of samples in the average process aproches the average scene length.

Min Dai and Zhang in [3] demonstrate that frames size of a GOP are strongly correlated. They analyzed several video traces encoded with MPEG-4 and the result indicates that there is a linear relationship between the size of P and B-Frames with the size of the I-Frame of a GOP. In order to generate the size of I-Frames was applied a self-similar model. The size of the first P-Frame of a GOP is estimated from the size of I-Frame and with the correlation between I and P-Frames. The size of the first B-Frame is calculated from the size of the first P-Frame and with the correlation between the P and B-Frames. The remaining P and B-Frames of the GOP is generated through the addition of a residue with Gamma PDF.

Fitzek and Reisslein encoded several videos with MPEG-4 and made available publicly [8]. The videos available are: Jurassic Park, The Silence of the Lambs, Star Wars Episode IV, Mr. Bean, Star Trek First Contact, The Firm, Formula 1, UEFA Champions League - Final 1996, German TV News, Sunday Night Program Auditorium and videos from a camera observing a person in front of a computer. All these videos were encoded in YUV format without data compression.

3 Scene Aware Video Workload Generation Model - SAVI

The models available in the literature do not explore the relationship between the size of I-Frames of a scene. Whereas the video content, a scene might be defined as *time interval in which a framework plan remained constant*. The structure of SAVI was design based on the observation that the scene length usually do not presents temporal dependence and can be modeled by a probability distribution function, besides the fact that the size of I-Frames tends to remain at same level for the entire scene and there is a strong temporal correlation between the sizes of the frames along the GOP.

In order to allow a comparison with existing models, three movies publicly available by [8] were analyzed. The movies are encoded with the GOP structure (12, 2), using the MPEG4 codec. The movies used in the study were *Star Wars Ep. IV*, *The Silence of the Lambs* and *Jurassic Park*.

3.1 Variables of the Model

The SAVI variables can be classified in two levels: (i) inner-scene, which represents the structure of frames inside the scene and (ii) outer-scene, which is characterized solely by the time duration of the scene, where s identifies a particular scene with the time length denoted by δ_s. Each scene s is comprised by one or more GOPs, and the sequence number of a GOP in the scene is denoted by g. The characterization of inner-scene uses the following variables:

- $\phi_I(s, g)$: Size of I-Frame the of GOP g and scene s.
- $\phi_P(s, g, i)$: Size of i_{th} P-Frame in GOP g and scene s.
- $\phi_B(s, g, j)$: Size of j_{th} B-Frame in GOP g and scene s.

For instance, $\phi_I(4, 10)$ represents the size of the tenth I-Frame of the fourth scene and $\phi_P(2, 7, 5)$ indicates the size of the fifth P-Frame belonging to the seventh GOP of the second scene. The structure of MPEG encoded video can be represented completely with this notation. Figure 1 illustrates three scenes for the movie *Jurassic Park*, each scene consisting of several GOPs, each GOP consists of various frames.

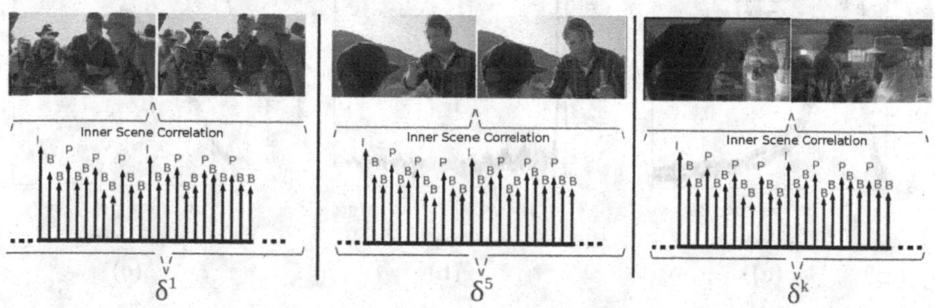

Fig. 1. SAVI scene splitting illustration

3.2 Modeling δ_s

The scene length has a fundamental role in SAVI. In order to model δ_s, the scene was identified using two approaches: the first one was the visual inspection, observing the time instant where there is a scene change. The procedure was repeated three times for each movie and calculating an average of observations. The second approach, as a complement, employs the algorithm proposed by [2], which suggests that a sudden change in the size of two successive I-Frames marks the beginning of a new scene. When the variation of size of two consecutive I-Frames are greater than a threshold, respectively of T_1 and T_2, this indicates the beginning of a new scene. Empirically by comparing the results of the algorithm with the practical observations, the values of T_1 and T_2 were respectively set at 15% and 20%, and the result was equivalent to the visual inspection.

After perform the scene identification, the autocorrelation function (ACF) of scene lengths was analyzed. Figure 2 (a) shows the empirical δ_s PDF for the three movies under consideration and Figure 2 (b) shows the ACF for the *Jurassic Park*. For all three movies, there is no significant temporal dependence between the scene lengths, i.e. the scene length is independent of previous scenes, as Figure 2 (b) illustrates. Thus, it is possible to characterize δ_s using a Lognormal PDF[1]. Figure 2 (c) shows the QQPlot graph comparing the theoretical Lognormal PDF with the empirical data. The QQPlot is a graphical goodness-of-fit test: if the two samples have the same distribution, the points should lie under a diagonal line at 45°, represented by the solid line in the figure. The points represent the quantiles observed in the video vs. same quantile of Lognormal theoretical PDF. The graph also shows the limits for a confidence level of 95% (dashed lines). Table I shows the parameters of Lognormal PDF for the movies under study. The result of Kolmogorv Smirnov goodness-of-fit test (KS-test) is also shown, and the calculated p-value indicates that the null hypothesis can not be rejected (occurs when p-value is greater than 0.05 [9]).

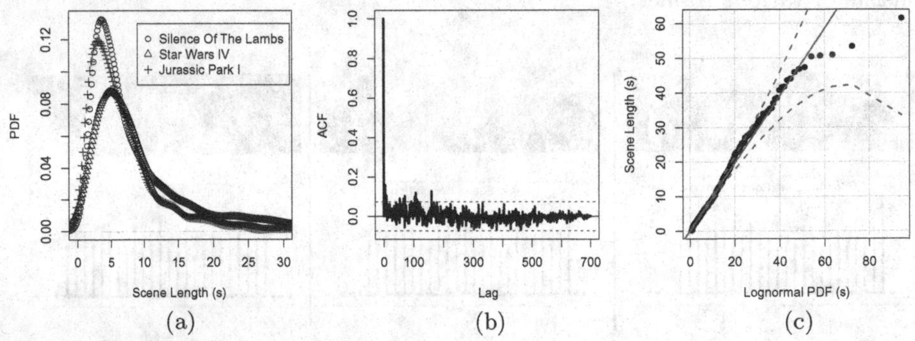

Fig. 2. Scene length: (a) empirical PDF for the three movies, (b) ACF of *Jurassic Park* and (c) QQPlot of *Jurassic Park*

[1] Probability density given by $f(x) = \frac{1}{x\sigma\sqrt{2\pi}} e^{-(lnx-\mu)^2/2\sigma^2}$, μ is the average and σ the standard deviation of $ln(x)$.

Table 1. Scene Length model

Title	Probability Distribution	Parameters	K-S test (p-value)
Jurassic Park	Lognormal	$\mu = 2.013$; $\sigma = 0.793$	0.36
Star Wars Episode IV	Lognormal	$\mu = 1.749$; $\sigma = 0.710$	0.40
The Silence of the Lambs	Lognormal	$\mu = 1.640$; $\sigma = 0.779$	0.66

3.3 Modeling $\phi_I(s, g)$

The size of I-Frames was modeled by considering the movie split in scenes. Within a scene, the time series formed by the size of successive I-Frames depend on the first I-Frame of the scene. However, the first I-Frame of each scene, $\phi_I(s, 1)$, has no time dependence with the I-Frames of previous scene. Thus, the approach taken was to model $\phi_I(s, 1)$ and, from its value, to obtain the size of the other I-Frames of the scene.

Modeling $\phi_I(s, 1)$. The $\phi_I(s, 1)$ was modeled with probability distributions. Figure 3 (a) shows the $\phi_I(s, 1)$ empirical PDF for *Star Wars Ep.IV*. The corresponding ACF is shown in Figure 3 (b), where can be seen that there is no significant correlation between $\phi_I(s, 1)$ of successive scenes. Figure 3 (c) presents the QQPlot, comparing the empirical $\phi_I(s, 1)$ with the Normal PDF. The procedure was repeated for the other three movies, with the distributions found and its parameters presented in Table II. This table also presents the p-value for KS-test, indicating the good adherence in all cases. For the movie *Jurassic Park* and *Star Wars Ep. IV* was used the Normal PDF and for *The Silence of the Lambs* was employed the Lognormal PDF.

Table 2. Modeling $\phi_I(s, 1)$

Title	Probability Distribution	Parameters	K-S test (p-value)
Jurassic Park	Normal	$\mu = 6170.5$; $\sigma = 2530.8$	0.31
Star Wars Ep.IV	Normal	$\mu = 3305.6$; $\sigma = 1106.5$	0.98
The Silence of the Lambs	Lognormal	$\mu = 8.47$; $\sigma = 0.53$	0.42

3.4 Modeling the Remaining I-Frames of the Scene

It was observed that, for a given scene, after the application of difference operator $\nabla^d Z_t = \phi_I(s, g) - \phi_I(s, g - d)$, $g \geq 2$, with $d = 1$, there was no significant temporal dependence between Z_t. Moreover, it is possible to use the Normal PDF to model Z_t within a scene. Figure 4 illustrates the empirical probability distribution of Z_t, with $d = 1$, compared with the theoretical Normal

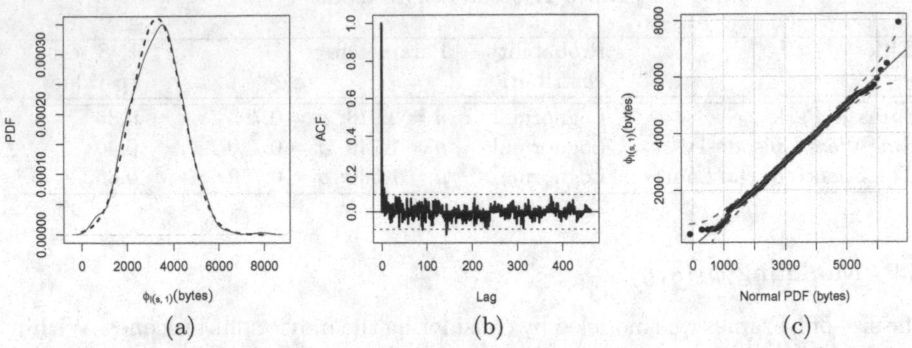

Fig. 3. $\phi_I(s,1)$: (a) Empirical PDF (solid lines), compared with the Normal PDF (dotted lines), (b) ACF and (c) QQPlot for Star Wars Episode IV

PDF of four scenes of *Jurassic Park*. Table III shows the result of KS-test for those scenes, where the *p*-value indicates the good similarity with the Normal PDF. A similar trend was observed in the other scenes of the movies under consideration.

Table 3. Modeling $\phi_I(s,g), g \geq 2$: four scenes of *Jurassic Park*

Scene Number	Probability Distribution	Parameters	KS-test (p-value)
59	Normal	$\mu_{sg} = 7.7$; $\sigma_{sg} = 170$	0.32
67	Normal	$\mu_{sg} = -5.1$; $\sigma_{sg} = 120$	0.31
131	Normal	$\mu_{sg} = -2.1$; $\sigma_{sg} = 150$	0.34
208	Normal	$\mu_{sg} = -6.7$; $\sigma_{sg} = 240$	0.75

Thus, the remaining I-Frames of a scene may be obtained from $\phi_I(s,1)$ using Equation 1, as follows:

$$\phi_I(s,g) = \phi_I(s,g-1) + N(0,\sigma_{sg}), g \geq 2 \tag{1}$$

where $N(0,\sigma_{sg})$ represents the standard normal distribution.

3.5 Modeling $\phi_P(s,g,i)$

The modeling of $\phi_P(s,g,i)$ is an adaptation of the idea originally presented by [3]. It was observed that the size of the first P-Frame of the GOP are correlated with the size of I-Frame which starts the GOP. The correlation is given by Equation 2, as follows:

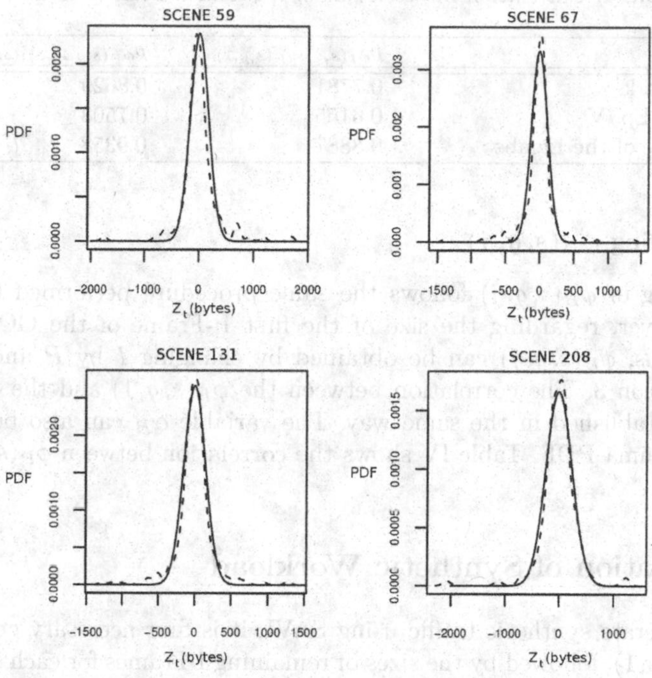

Fig. 4. Empirical PDF of the I-Frame size for several scenes of the movie Jurassic Park, after applying the ∇^1 operator (dotted lines), compared with the Normal PDF (solid lines)

$$\begin{aligned}\rho_{\phi_I(s,g),\phi_P(s,g,1)} =&(E[\phi_I(s,g)\cdot\phi_P(s,g,1)]-\\ &E[\phi_I(s,g)]\cdot E[\phi_P(s,g,1)])/\\ &\surd(E[\phi_I(s,g)^2]-E^2[\phi_I(s,g)]\cdot\\ &(E[\phi_P(s,g,1)]^2)-E^2[\phi_P(s,g,1)])\end{aligned} \tag{2}$$

The correlation value ρ is in the range from -1 to 1. The most significant correlation occur with $|\rho| = 1$, and $\rho = 0$ indicates no correlation between the variables. The movies under study were analyzed and the values obtained for ρ are shown in Table IV. The result indicates that there is a significant correlation between the size of the I-Frame and the first P-Frame of GOP.

The size of remaining P-Frames of GOP may be obtained using Equation 3, where α_P represents a random variable with Gamma PDF. Further details can be obtained in [3].

$$\phi_P(s,g,i) = \phi_I(s,g)\cdot\frac{\rho_{\phi_I(s,g),\phi_P(s,g,1)}\cdot\sigma_{\phi_P(s,g,1)}}{\sigma_{\phi_I(s,g)}} + \alpha_P \tag{3}$$

Table 4. Correlation between size of I, P and B-Frames of GOP

Title	$\rho_{\phi_I(s,g),\phi_P(s,g,1)}$	$\rho_{\phi_P(s,g,1),\phi_B(s,g,1)}$
Jurassic Park	0.7781	0.8629
Star Wars Ep.IV	0.6155	0.7508
The Silence of the Lambs	0.8887	0.9358

3.6 Modeling $\phi_B(s, g, j)$

The modeling of $\phi_B(s, g, j)$ follows the same procedure performed for the P-Frame, however, regarding the size of the first P-Frame of the GOP instead I-Frame. Thus, $\phi_B(s, g, j)$ can be obtained by changing I by P and B by P in the Equation 3. The correlation between the $\phi_B(s, g, 1)$ and the $\phi_P(s, g, 1)$ should be established in the same way. The variable α_B can also be modeled with the Gamma PDF. Table IV shows the correlation between $\phi_P(s, g, 1)$ and $\phi_B(s, g, 1)$.

4 Generation of Synthetic Workload

In order generate synthetic traffic using SAVI, it is first necessary generate δ_s, then the $\phi_I(s, 1)$, followed by the sizes of remaining I-Frames for each scene. The next step is to generate the P-Frames on the basis of I-Frames and B-Frames using as reference the first P-Frame of the GOP. The complete algorithm is shown in Figure 5. The total scene number of the movie is specified by $\mathrm{MAX_S}$, the number of P-Frames in a GOP is given by $\mathrm{MAX_P}$ and the number of B-Frames in a GOP is given by $\mathrm{MAX_B}$. Thus, the number of GOPs of a scene s can be calculated by Equation 4, as follows,

$$\mathrm{MAX_{GOP}}(s) = \left\lceil \frac{\mathrm{FRAME\_RATE} \cdot \delta_s}{1 + \mathrm{MAX_P} + \mathrm{MAX_B}} \right\rceil \tag{4}$$

The average for the movies studied were $\delta_s = 8.2$ seconds, $\mathrm{MAX_S} = 730$, $\mathrm{MAX_P} = 3$, $\mathrm{MAX_B} = 8$ and $\mathrm{MAX_{GOP}}(s) = 17$. Considering these constants and making $\mathrm{MAX_S} = n$, then the number of executions of the inner loops is limited by the constants $\mathrm{MAX_P}$, $\mathrm{MAX_B}$ and $\mathrm{MAX_{GOP}}(s)$, all these typically much smaller than $\mathrm{MAX_S}$, so that the worst case computational complexity is given by $O(n)$ [10].

The synthetic traffic generation was performed using the algorithm with the parameters extracted from three films studied. The synthetic traffic shows similar characteristics to real traffic in terms of mean and standard deviation of frames. Its important to verify if the temporal dependence structure of real traffic is present in the synthetic traffic. Figure 6 (a), (b) and (c) show the ACF of $\phi_I(s, g)$ generated by SAVI in comparison with the actual traces, for the three movies. It is observed that the model properly reproduce the characteristics of short and long range dependence.

```
for s ← 1 to MAX_S do
    Generate δ(s);
    Generate φ_I(s,1);
    Evaluate MAX_GOP(s) (Equation 4)
    for g ← 2 to MAX_GOP(s) do
        Generate φ_I(s,g);
        Generate φ_P(s,g,1);
        Generate φ_B(s,g,1);
        for i ← 2 to MAX_P do
            Generate φ_P(s,g,i);
        end
        for j ← 2 to MAX_B do
            Generate φ_B(s,g,j);
        end
    end
end
```

Fig. 5. SAVI algorithm for workload generation

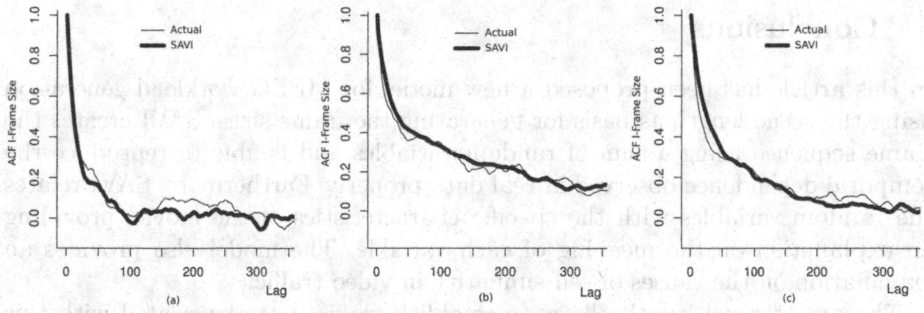

Fig. 6. ACF for $\phi_I(s,g)$ generated by SAVI compared with real traces for (a) Star Wars Ep.IV , (b) The Silence of the Lambs and (c) Jurassic Park

Figure 7(a), for comparison, shows the ACF of $\phi_I(s,g)$ generated by the model proposed in [3] (FARIMA), which uses a self-similar method to generate the size of I-Frames, without consider the scene structure, and also the model proposed by [2] (Krunz). One can observe that SAVI show a better performance if compared with those models. The scene length strongly affects the long range dependence. Figure 7(b) shows the autocorrelation function for three synthetic traces generated by SAVI with different scene length standard deviation. With the standard deviation of $ln(\delta_s)$ set at 1.4, the trace presents a strong short and long range dependence. With lower values for standard deviation the temporal dependence is attenuated, although it still present in trace.

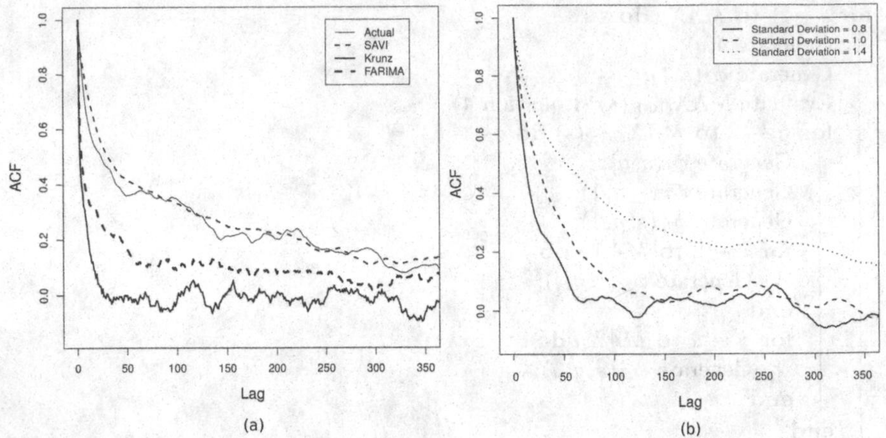

Fig. 7. (a) ACF for $\phi_I(s, g)$ generated by SAVI for the movie The Silence of the Lambs compared with several models and (b) Autocorrelation function of three synthetic traces generated by SAVI with several scene length standard deviation

5 Conclusions

In this article has been proposed a new model for MPEG workload generation using the scene length as basis for generating the frame sizes. SAVI creates the frame sequence using a sum of random variables and is able to reproduce the temporal dependence observed in real data properly. Furthermore, SAVI relates the random variables with the specific characteristics of the movie, providing an explanation on the meaning of each variable. The model also provides an explanation on the causes of self similarity in video traffic.

The use of scene length allows to establish traffic patterns related with this characteristic. This is difficult to achieve with existing models, which depend on parameters that can not be related so explicitly with the observable characteristics of the movie. Additionally, SAVI presents low computational complexity if compared to most of the available methods for video workload generation. As future work we are extending the analysis to other video traces.

References

1. Menascé, D.A., Almeida, V.A.F.: Capacity planning for Web performance. Prentice Hall (1998)
2. Krunz, M., Tripathi, S.K.: On the characterization of VBR MPEG streams. SIGMETRICS Performance Evaluation Rev. 25(1), 192–202 (1997)
3. Dai, M., Zhang, Y., Loguinov, D.: A unified traffic model for MPEG-4 and H.264 video traces. IEEE Transactions on Multimedia 11, 1010–1023 (2009)
4. Manzoni, P., Cremonesi, P., Serazzi, G.: Workload models of VBR video traffic and their use in resource allocation policies. IEEE/ACM Transactions on Networking 7(3), 387–397 (1999)

5. ISO: MPEG-4 part 14: MP4 file format; ISO/IEC 14496-14:2003, International Organization for Standardization (2003)
6. Garrett, M.W., Willinger, W.: Analysis, modeling and generation of self-similar vbr video traffic. In: SIGCOMM 1994: Proceedings of the Conference on Communications architectures, Protocols and Applications, pp. 269–280. ACM Press, New York (1994)
7. Rose, O.: A Memory Markov Chain for VBR traffic with strong positive correlations. In: 24th International Teletraffic Congress (ITC 16), Edinburgh, GB, pp. 827–836 (1999)
8. Fitzek, F., Reisslein, M.: MPEG-4 and H.263 video traces for network performance evaluation. IEEE Network 15(6), 40–54 (2001)
9. Jain, R.: The art of computer systems performance analysis: techniques for experimental design, measurement, simulation and modeling. John Wiley & Sons (1991)
10. Arora, S., Barak, B.: Computational Complexity: A Modern Approach, 1st edn. Cambridge University Press, New York (2009)

UNIVERSALLY: A Context-Aware Architecture for Multimedia Access in Digital Homes

Tayeb Lemlouma

IRISA Lab / University of Rennes I
IUT de Lannion, BP 30219, Rue Edouard Branly, 22302 Lannion Cedex, France
Tayeb.Lemlouma@irisa.fr

Abstract. The objective of this work is to improve the user's experience when using media resources in a digital home. We consider the use and access of media in any context and particularly in a resource-constrained context such as using mobile terminals through a wireless access. We focus our work on the *Digital Living Network Alliance* architecture since it knows a high penetration in homes but with only a small amount of users due to the complexity of the architecture. We propose *UNIVERSALLY* that aims to simplify the complexity of digital home architectures and optimize them. We consider limited terminals and users that are not always aware about setting up their devices. Unnecessary network resources and periodic traffic are avoided when no media resource is in use. The context awareness improves the user's experience by adapting media formats and avoiding the traffic of streaming resources that are not understood by the terminal.

Keywords: Digital home, context awareness, DLNA, UPnP, multimedia, Web, heterogeneous environments, context awareness, adaptation home network.

1 Introduction

The objective of a digital home is to offer an interoperable network that ensures using and sharing multimedia content in a seamless environment regardless: existing terminals and media sources (formats, location, delivery methods and protocols, etc.). Unfortunately, actual digital home networks do not meet this objective yet [21]. Indeed, users still unaware about the existence of some industrial technologies such as the Digital Living Network Alliance[1] (DLNA) already integrated in about 74 % of existing CEs but only with 6 % of real users [9]. Many reasons explain this situation. Mainly we cite the complexity of the proposed technologies inside the home network, the inter communication and cooperation between different industrial and norms, the heterogeneity of media formats and devices. Finally, the lack of intelligent components or services that help terminals and users to find, configure and connect their terminals in order to use the media content in the best possible and automatic way.

[1] The identification of some commercial standards, protocols or products is done only to describe the current research work and not for recommendation purposes.

V. Guyot (Ed.): ICAIT 2012, LNCS 7593, pp. 128–137, 2013.

Let us consider three concrete use cases: (1) a consumer who has DLNA enabled devices and do not realize they have this functionality; (2) a user, in an enabled DLNA home network, who wants to render a media item on its smart phone using a WiFi access and (3) a user, in an enabled DLNA home network, who wants to play a new added media item encoded in a format not compatible with its user agent (player). For the first use case, as mentioned previously, only a few number of users are able to use DLNA technology or are aware about its existence [9] due to the proper knowledge required for installation and setting operations. Hence the implicit network traffic and messages generated by DLNA and UPnP sources (Section 4) remains unnecessary if the user does not use any DLNA component or media item. In the use case (2), the user can not play the media item on its terminal because implicit DLNA protocols and norms (such as the multicast and SOAP) are not natively implemented by the device. Furthermore, periodic advertisements of services and the transmission of XML descriptions that have an important size are not adapted to the wireless access especially when it is shared by many users. The third use case highlights the lack of advanced adaptation techniques for existing and future media formats that are not supported by the end user agent. Indeed, in this use case, the transmission of the media item will consume the network bandwidth and the user agent cannot render the item correctly with the best adapted format.

The main motivation of our work is to enable the access to media content and services with heterogeneous terminals and without preliminary configurations and settings. Also, we aim to optimize the network traffic generated by DLNA components by allowing only necessary traffic when it is really needed. For the home network optimization, our proposition is to move toward a client-server model. Consequently, no traffic will be generated if the user does not ask the network for something. So, any transmitted data will be an answer of the user's request. Modern CEs and mobile terminals are an appealing platform for advanced functionalities and applications. However, many devices still not compatible with some protocols needed in a digital home architecture such as the multicast protocol [3]. This work proposes a complete and simple approach to solve this problem. To improve the accessibility of media servers and consider the existing heterogeneity of devices and formats, we propose to exclusively use the HTTP protocol and to generalize it to all the main components of the digital home. Indeed, HTTP is widely supported by the majority of limited terminals; it does not require advanced settings. HTTP does not make any restriction on the format of transmitted data, so it is easier to add media encoding and adaptation methods for limited devices. Devices' media capabilities can be described in specific profiles coupled with the available HTTP TCN negotiation [7]. Furthermore, the use of HTTP protocol needs only a web browser which is nowadays embedded in the majority of mobile and limited terminals. The user has only to know the Web address of the server without any advanced settings.

2 Related Work

In this section we discuss works related to the improvement of using media resources in a digital home architecture. Seen the complexity of this field and for a better understanding of the implied standards and technologies, the reader is invited to refer to the given references. In a digital home the dimensions to be considered are mainly:

the organization of the architecture itself, sharing media items inside the home, media services discovery using UPnP, services descriptions using XML related languages and the invocation of services using SOAP. In this section we study works related to these previous dimensions. We notice that there is only few number of works that consider the improvement or the modification of the digital home network architecture.

The use and the improvement of DLNA/UPnP within heterogeneous mobile devices has been explored in research work over the past few years. The work in [12] proposes UPnP based content sharing system for supporting multimedia devices in a digital home network. The work uses a server to which devices must be directly plugged in order to be integrated in the sharing system. This approach ignores other possible access network technologies (e.g. wireless access) that may be used by media servers or mobile terminals. In [10,20] a proxy's system is proposed for searching and streaming the media contents with the public IP network. Unfortunately, the proxy has not the functionality to adapt content discovery and formats for limited devices. Many works have been concerned by making easy the use and control of devices inside the home [1,11]. For instance, in [1], a Java-based automation system is designed in order to monitor, control, and interact with devices using a control and management engine (CAM). The devices are connected to an embedded system board (E-board), the control of devices does not include particular devices like media servers and renderers. The impact and the performance of DLNA in the home network has often been a concern. Most of the previous works have studied this impact either directly inside the digital home network or indirectly by evaluating the performances of related protocols such as UPnP and SOAP. These related works concern only a subset of the norms and technologies related to the complete DLNA architecture. We cite the work for Bluetooth (BT) Personal Area Network (PAN) inside the home [16] and in large home networks [17]. In [16], Liong and Ye have shown the negative impact of SSDP advertisements in PAN such as for BT power cost -when advertisements are spread- and channel's bandwidth usage especially for large SOAP messages, transfer and media streaming. The work of [17] evaluated the UPnP M-SEARCH messages (used to discover devices and services) by varying the jitter bound (MX field of M-SEARCH) and network size. The used simulated model [17] showed that when the number of root devices increases (generally above 50), the network knows negative performances regarding: the discovery effectiveness (percentage between announcement and real discovery), discovery latency and buffer overruns. Reasons are mainly the responses loss, the explosion of response at the level of control points (CPs) and collision periods in a large network. The work outlined new algorithms for adapting the MX field and an approach for replacing M-SEARCH queries in UPnP. Unfortunately, in DLNA heterogeneous and dynamic networks, we should expect several and different implementations of MX (that are compatible with the UPnP standard) and hence we must take them into consideration in a universal media access approach in order to coexist with existing digital home networks whatever their size. Hu et al. [8] considered the frequent notifications and designed an event mechanism that coexists with the original UPnP eventing method. The approach was to move from the TCP unicast eventing to a multicast scheme. It is based on an administratively scoped multicast delivery for service subscriptions and event notifications. This approach is not adapted to heterogeneous terminals that do not support mechanisms like the multicast.

Other related works have concerned the impact of using SOAP such as in [18] and [19] where an alternative of SOAP was proposed based on REST [6]. The adoption of such approach implies that existing DLNA components, in particular MSs, should be able to process the new REST URLs and to add a new mime-type in order to distinguish native SOAP POST and REST POST messages. Another consequence is that all the resources and data (even variables included in XML files) must follow a new addressing scheme that should be implemented by DLNA components. These modifications are hard to do on the existing architecture and cannot be interoperable with other architectures. Moreover, the description of resources and XML data access are already possible using standards such as the W3C POWDER, XPath and XQuery languages. In [13], Lee et al. propose to improve the UPnP QoS architecture for adaptive media streaming in home. They propose two new components, StatusMonitor and QoSAdapter for the network status and adaptation. The strong assumption for this work regarding a heterogeneous network is that the UPnP MS is assumed to support required streaming adaptation technique.

3 DLNA Framework

The objective of DLNA technology is to manage and distribute digital content from a source to all the compatible devices [4,5]. The key functions of DLNA are: connectivity and networking, device discovery and control, media management, media formats and media transport. Connectivity and networking use the existing network platform at home. Device discovery and control is based on the UPnP Device Architecture (UPnP DA) 1.0 [22]. Media management is based on the UPnP AV [23]. Media formats are defined as a set of required and optional format profiles. The media transport in DLNA is done over HTTP (Fig. 1). The RTP protocol is introduced recently and still optional [4,5].

Three entities are specified: devices, services and CPs. Services are functions provided by a device, found and invoked by a CP. The main functions of a UPnP device are: IP addressing, discovery (periodic advertisement of services), description of services and capabilities, control in response of CPs requests, eventing to notify registered CPs and presentation in HTML to possibly monitor the device. This depends on the specific capabilities of the presentation page and device and if the device has a presentation's URL. SSDP messages are sent over HTTPMU (HTTP Multicast over UDP) in order to discover resources in the network [22]. SOAP allows to specify available operations. In the audio video (AV) digital home, the three main entities are: the MS that offers media content, the media renderer that plays content and CPs that control what and how contents are played (Fig. 1). MS provides three services: Content Directory Service (CDS), Connection Manager Service (CMS) and AV Transport Service (AVT). A media renderer provides the Rendering Control Service (RCS), the CMS and AVT services. CDS provides actions for CPs in order to list media items and relative meta-data. RCS provides actions for a CP to control the rendering of a media resource. CMS handles connections with a device and AVT controls the player actions (play, seek, etc.). DLNA defines two main entities: Digital Media Server (DMS) and Digital Media Player (DMP). DMS is a UPnP/AV CDS device that provides media resources. DMP is a UPnP/AV CDS control point that can discover resources and render them.

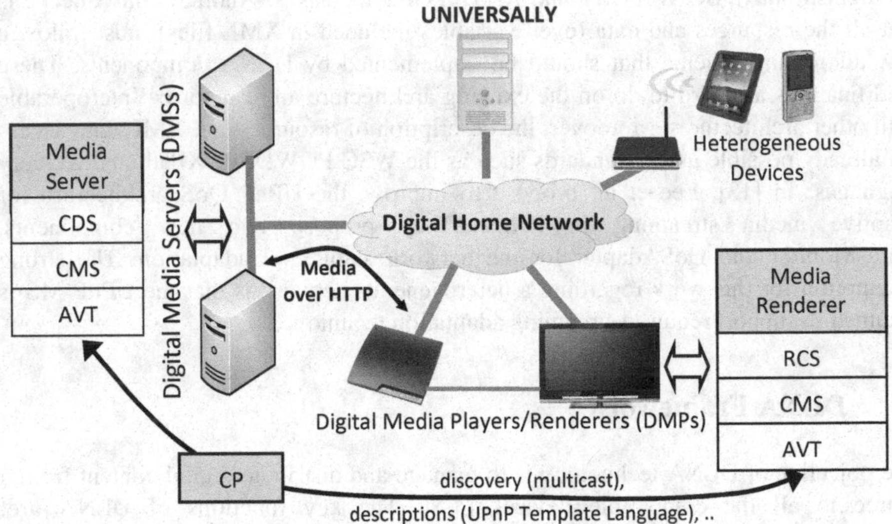

Fig. 1. The DLNA Framework. In order to render media items on heterogeneous devices, the UPnP main functions (such as the multicast and parsing long XML descriptions) must be supported. Furthermore, the device must be able to render correctly the original format. Periodic advertisements and long descriptions are transmitted over the same shared wireless network.

4 Proposed Architecture

The aim of our proposition is to enable and optimize the access and control of existing media resources in home for heterogeneous and mobile devices with limited access and rendering capabilities. The proposed system can easily integrate existing digital home architectures and optimize the way where the network resources are used and media resources are found and rendered (Fig. 1).

4.1 Considered Issues

In the DLNA architecture, based on the UPnP DA principles, when a device is added to the network it advertises services using multicast NOTIFY messages to

239.255.255.250:1900 IP address. Three discovery messages are specified for the root device, two for each embedded device and one message for each service type in each device. Consequently, at each announcement interval, $3+2d+k$ messages are sent (one root device, d embedded devices, and k distinct service types). The NOTIFY message uses a duration (CACHE-CONTROL which is at least 30 minutes) for which the advertisement is valid. Due to the unreliable nature of UDP, the *DLNA Interoperability Guidelines*, based on the UPnP DA 1.0, recommends that devices should send each of the above discovery messages more than once but not more than three times. Also, advertisements must be periodically re-sent prior to the CACHE-CONTROL value. The interval of sending the advertisement messages must be less than one-half of the CACHE-CONTROL value. Similarly, when a CP is added to the network, it searches for devices using multicast M-SEARCH messages sent more than once and periodically to guarantee that devices receive it. Each device answers with $3+2d+k$ messages for its root device, embedded devices and service types. In addition to the discovery advertisement and discovery search, the CP retrieves descriptions (using HTTP) of the discovered devices/services. It invokes actions on a device's services using SOAP. Device and service descriptions are written using the UPnP Template Language [22] based on XML and has usually an important size.

With DLNA/UPnP, the number, the nature (UDP and multicast) and the periodicity of UPnP advertisements can be inconvenient. Also, to be able to play one media resource, several messages and steps must be achieved. So, it is required for a mobile device that joins the digital home, to support the multicast, UPnP Template Language parsing, SOAP protocol and the unreliable nature of UDP especially over a wireless access. Moreover, there is no guarantee that the original format and profile of the requested media will be supported. This situation is not adapted for heterogeneous environments where rendering capabilities, access technology, bandwidth, congestion probability and power consumption are not the same for all the existing devices that can be connected through Ethernet, WLAN, Bluetooth, etc. The level of the control (provided by the UPnP presentation function) depends to the capabilities of each presentation page which is completely specified by the device's or service's vendor and not standardized in the UPnP DA.

4.2 UNIVERSALLY

We propose UNIVERSALLY: a new system that can be easily integrated into the digital home architecture and provide a universal access in a heterogeneous environment. In Fig. 1, we show that UNIVERSALLY component can be connected directly to the digital home network, the modular architecture of UNIVERSALLY is presented in Fig. 2. UNIVERSALLY is based on the client/server model, so a device aiming to discover media servers or playing a given media item will send one HTTP request to UNIVERSALLY in order to get the existing media servers or the media stream in the adapted format. The key idea is to provide an easy media access only when it is requested by the user's device. In addition to the adoption of the client/server model, all the proposed modules are new to the DLNA framework except the implemented main UPnP functions that exist on any control point.

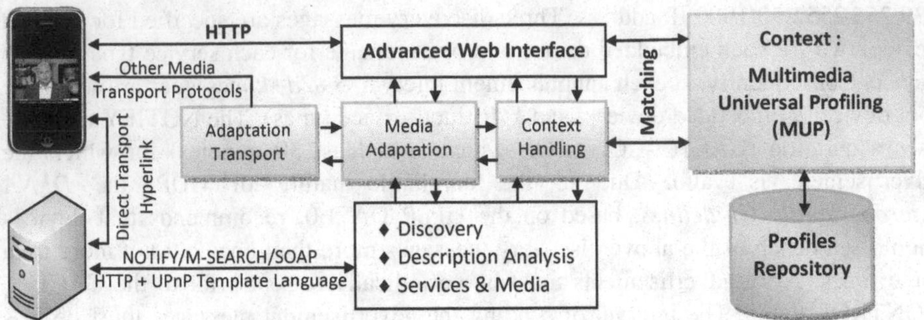

Fig. 2. Modular Architecture of *UNIVERSALLY*

Advanced Web Interface (AWI) Module. This module ensures a Web interface that devices can use to browse available DMSs and resources since it is done over HTTP. Once a media server or resource is found and displayed on the AWI, the user can use it directly thanks to hyperlinks. To perform DLNA media controls and actions (e.g. stream seek) over HTTP, a web server is implemented with a full support of the RANGE header as specified in the HTTP specification. AWI is dynamically adapted to the terminal's profile as we will discuss it later.

Adaptation Transport. In order to improve the media transfer, we extend the DLNA media transport protocol from HTTP to any transport protocol by including appropriate and supported transport methods using hyperlinks. For example, the HTML link of AWI can use RTP instead of HTTP if the context of the user agent supports RTP. In this case, the source of the link will not be the media server that stores the media item but another one that receives the stream in HTTP (from the media server) and deliver it in RTP.

UPnP Main Functions. UNIVERSALLY delegates the UPnP main functions (discovery, control, etc.) to a specific module that ensures the access for limited devices such as those which do not support the multicast natively or are not compatible with DLNA. The main functions are ensured by the mean of M-SEARCH messages sent when it is needed (i.e. as a consequence of the user's request). Since devices with advances capabilities can also use the proposed AWI, UPnP periodic advertisements of media services are stopped: only the responses to the UNIVERSALLY's M-SEARCH requests are authorized (i.e. when the "destination address" field of the answer's IP packet is the UNIVERSALLY's IP address). Unnecessary traffic is so avoided.

Media Adaptation and Context Handling. The context module is used to describe the hardware and software capabilities of devices that aim to play a media resource. We use the Multimedia Universal Profiling (MUP) schema based on the W3C RDF language and proposed in [14]. MUP allows the context manager of UNIVERSALLY to describe the profiles that are stored in a profiles repository and specify the displaying and rendering capabilities of a device. Near to 14000 different user agents are stored [15]. If the original format of a media is requested by a terminal but is not supported, it will be adapted then transferred to the device. Based on the device's profile, the Web interface is also dynamically adapted by performing a pagination of discovery results when the device explores media resources of available DMSs. The HTML pagination allows the dynamic generation of small HTML pages with next and previous links and so only small parts of the content is sent to the user [24]. The pagination is based on the number of direct resources (*child* XML element of a device or a directory [22]) which is extracted from the SOAP answer (*childCount* attribute of the XML element *DIDL-Lite/container* [22]) of a Browse/BrowseMetadata action sent from UNIVERSALLY.

We have experimented UNIVERSALLY (Fig. 3) with two MSs: *Java PS3 Media Server* 1.11.369 on two root devices and *TVersity Media Server* 1.9.2 on one root device. We used three kinds of renderers: a game box (a Play Station 3), a DLNA enabled TV (BRAVIA KDL-46Z5500 TV) and a mobile phone (a 3G iPhone, Fig. 3). These devices are connected through Ethernet except the mobile phone which is connected through a WiFi access point. In our experimentation, the AWI interface is accessible from the 192.168.1.11 IP address (port 1977). In a general case, UNIVERSALLY should be reached from a simple and local preconfigured DNS name for the users of the digital home. The context handling module has identified the three terminals based on the headers: *User-Agent*, *X-AV-Physical-Unit-Info* and *X-AV-Client-Info*. The TV and game box devices support natively the DLNA framework (user-agent="UPnP/1.0" with specific *X-AV* headers) which is not the case of the mobile phone. UNIVERSALLY has provided the access to all the existing MSs and media content in a paginated interface. Searching MSs are done only once when the user accesses the AWI interface. The AWI's home page is a simple page with an HTML *refresh* duration, after what the user is redirected to a new page where the result of services discovery is displayed. At any moment, the user can manually trigger a new services discovery. UNIVERSALLY has allowed to: avoid unnecessary traffic (NOTIFY and M-SEARCH), unify the eventual available presentations of MSs and devices, make the browsing of resources possible and optimal and avoid SOAP and XML UPnP handling and parsing for limited heterogeneous devices.

5 Conclusion

In this paper we discussed the universal access of media resources in a digital home for heterogeneous limited devices. With UNIVERSALLY we consider the accessibility and context awareness of media resources using the HTTP protocol and a client/server model. We introduced an approach that delegates the service discovery, descriptions analysis media control and context handling to a separate component. The component interacts with devices through the AWI interface which has enabled the use of MSs for non compatible devices. By avoiding the unnecessary traffic, the network's bandwidth usage is saved but it is necessary to put more effort into the definition and implementation of an intelligent strategy about Web caching and SOAP requests especially for services and XML descriptions that are relatively stables. Also, due to the repository size, the context handling should be optimized and the adaptation methods will be evaluated and enriched by new static and real-time transcoding methods to consider a large amount of devices media capabilities. Finally, we have to dynamically optimize the value of the HTML *refresh* attribute based on the MX value of the M-SEARCH request [22] and the adaptive jitter control for M-Search messages [17].

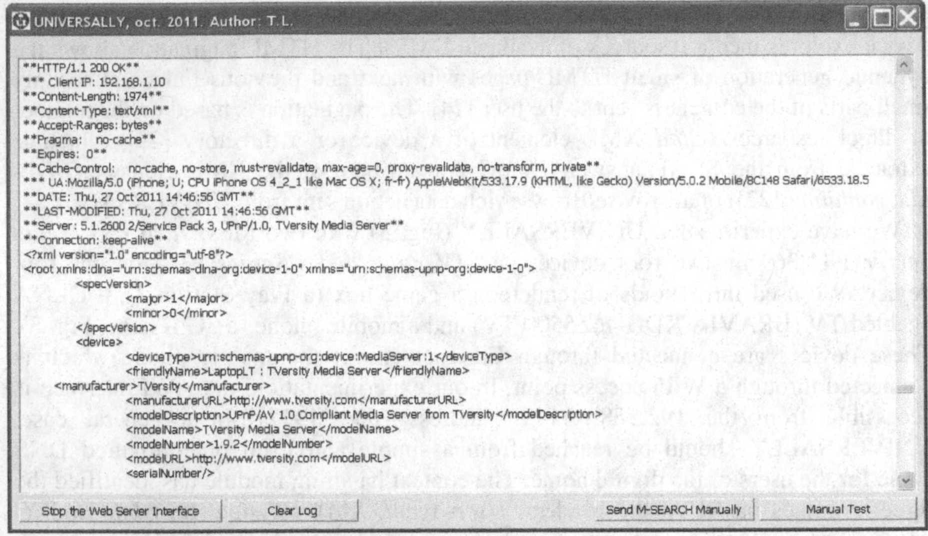

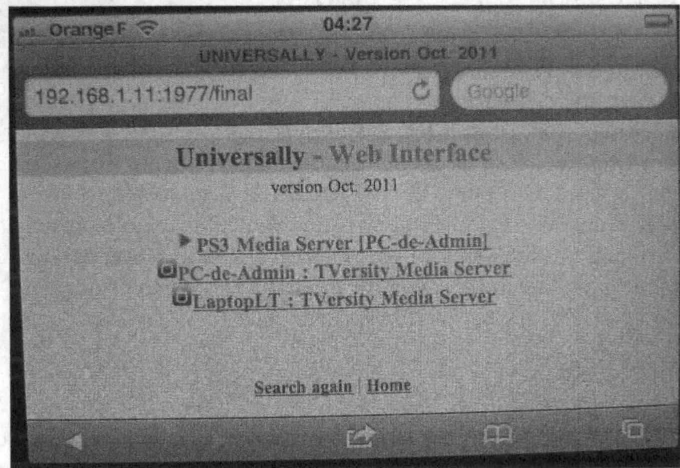

Fig. 3. UNIVERSALLY Interface and AWI Interface using a Mobile Terminal (iPhone)

References

1. Al-Ali, A.R., AL-Rousan, M.: Java-Based Home Automation System. IEEE Transactions on Consumer Electronics 50(2), 498–504 (2004)
2. Al-Mejibli, I., Colley, M.: Evaluating Transmission Time of Service Discovery Protocols by using NS2 Simulator. In: Proc. WiAD, pp. 1–6 (2010)
3. Deering, S.: Host Extensions for IP Multicasting, IETF, RFC 1112
4. Digital Living Network Alliances: DLNA Overview and Vision Whitepaper (2007), `http://www.dlna.org/`

5. Digital Living Network Alliance: DLNA Networked Device Interoperability Guidelines (October 2006), http://www.dlna.org/
6. Fielding, R.T.: Architectural styles and the design of network-based software architecture. In: Doctoral Dissertation. University of California, Irvine (2000), http://www.ics.uci.edu/fielding/pubs/dissertation/top.htm
7. Holtman, K., Mutz, A.: Transparent Content Negotiation in HTTP, IETF, RFC 2295
8. Hu, C.L., Huang, Y.J., Liao, W.S.: Multicast Complement for Efficient UPnP Eventing in Home Computing Network. In: Proc. POTABLE, pp. 1–5 (2007)
9. In-Stat: UPnP and DLNA—Standardizing the Networked Home. Research Information (2010)
10. Kim, J., Oh, Y.J., Lee, H.K., Paik, E.H., Park, K.R.: Implementation of the DLNA Proxy System for Sharing Home Media Contents. In: Proc. ICCE, pp. 1–2 (2007)
11. Kuriyama, H., Mineno, H., Seno, Y., Furumura, T., Mizuno, T.: Home Appliance Translator for Remote Control of Conventional Home Appliance. In: Proc. AINA, pp. 346–350 (2006)
12. Lai, C.F., Chang, S.Y., Huang, Y.M., Park, J.H., Chao, H.C.: A Portable UPnP-based High Performance Content Sharing System for Supporting Multimedia Devices. The Journal of Supercomputing (2010), doi:10.1007/s11227-010-0384-4
13. Lee, H.Y., Moon, S.T., Kim, J.W.: Enhanced UPnP QoS Architecture for Network-adaptive Streaming Service in Home Networks. IEEE Transactions on Consumer Electronics 53(3), 898–904 (2007)
14. Lemlouma, T.: Source of the Multimedia Universal Profiling (MUP) Schema (2012), http://people.irisa.fr/Tayeb.Lemlouma/mup/schema
15. Lemlouma, T.: An Overview of the MUP Repository's Identifiers (2012), http://people.irisa.fr/Tayeb.Lemlouma/mup/UNIVERSALLY_identifiers_repository_version_01_2012.txt
16. Liong, Y.L., Ye, Y.H.: Effect of UPnP Advertisements on User Experience and Power Consumption. In: Proc. CCNC, pp. 91–97 (2005)
17. Mills, K., Dabrowski, C.: Adaptive jitter control for UPnP M-Search. In: Proc. ICC, vol. 2, pp. 1008–1013 (2003)
18. Newmarch, J.: A Critique of Web Services. In: Proc. E-Commerce, pp. 391–398 (2004)
19. Newmarch, J.: A RESTful Approach: Clean UPnP without SOAP. In: Proc. CCNC, pp. 134–138 (2005)
20. Oh, Y.J., Lee, H.K., Kim, J.T., Paik, E.H., Park, K.R.: Design of an Extended Architecture for Sharing DLNA Compliant Home Media from Outside the Home. IEEE Transactions on Consumer Electronics 53(2), 542–547 (2007)
21. Socher, L.: The Digital Home: Highly Promising, Highly Complex. In: Annual Review of Communications, vol. 61. IEC Publications (2008)
22. UPnP Forum: UPnP Device Architecture 1.0. April 24 (2008), http://www.upnp.org
23. UPnP Forum: UPnP AV Architecture:1. September 30 (2008), http://www.upnp.org
24. Lemlouma, T.: Improving the User Experience by Web Technologies for Complex Multimedia Services. In: Proc. 8th International Conference on Web Information Systems and Technologies (WEBIST), pp. 444–451 (2012)

A User-Centric Network Architecture for Sustainable Rural Areas

Farnaz Farid, Seyed Shahrestani, and Chun Ruan

School of Computing, Engineering and Mathematics
University of Western Sydney
Sydney, Australia
{farnaz.farid,S.Shahrestani,C.Ruan}@uws.edu.au

Abstract. Heterogeneous networks offer interesting solutions to problems encountered in user-centric network architecture. Encompassing various communication technologies, they offer great potentials for addressing some of the challenges that ICT based remote services face. In this work, we focus on their deployment in rural areas and developing countries. More specifically, we examine how heterogeneous networks can be used in a user-centric architecture to improve application interactivity, interoperability, and network utilization. Restrictions of each constituent technology cause the architecture to have an upper limit in supporting simultaneous interactive applications. To investigate these limits, and to identify potential enhancements, we study an interactive education model. The considered interactivity, facilitated by heterogeneous networks, is between clients in rural areas and servers in an urban area. The underlying model architecture involves several communication technologies such as WiFi, Ethernet, WiMAX, and UMTS. Several scenarios relevant to this architecture are simulated and analyzed. For each scenario, videoconferencing sessions are initiated with variant number of users. The performance of the architecture in terms of capacity and key QoS parameters such as delay variation, end-to-end delay, and packet loss is evaluated. The results show that for most typical situations, WiFi-WiMAX combinations outperform other integrations.

Keywords: Heterogeneous network, Network architecture, UMTS, WiFi, WiMAX.

1 Introduction

Part of the millennium development goals set by the United Nations can be met by delivery of socioeconomic services based on heterogeneous network architecture. However, in general, provisions of such services through such networks are not widely common in developing countries. On the other hand, in industrialized world, heterogeneous networks play an important role in providing improved socioeconomic services. For instance, cluster of school concept *ICTPD* has been implemented in New Zealand utilizing network and communication technologies. Videoconferencing (VC) based distance education model has been successful in Alberta, Canada by

V. Guyot (Ed.): ICAIT 2012, LNCS 7593, pp. 138–150, 2013.

utilizing a high bandwidth broadband network, *Supernet* [1]. But for most developing countries, the benefits of similar types of projects are hard to be realized, as they lack the infrastructure needed for provision of fixed broadband technologies.

To resolve some of these issues, various solutions based on wireless technologies have been proposed and implemented for developing countries. For instance, *Daknet* is a WiFi-based system, which has introduced positive changes in rural areas [2]. It uses portable storage devices placed on vehicles as mobile access points to facilitate uploading, downloading, and synchronization of data. It focuses on providing Internet access and support for non real-time applications, such as e-mail, for rural areas. Only non real-time applications are supported as the project argues that in rural areas, people use non real-time network applications much more than real-time ones. While this may be true for some situations, to advance the quality of remote education, health and commerce services, interactivity is a requirement [3].

Another example is Long Distance WiFi based solution, *WiLD,* which has been deployed in India and Ghana to provide remote health and education services [3]. However, these networks experience highly variable delay and interference from external environment. Wireless mesh networks are able to extend the coverage area of developing regions [4]. But they face some fundamental issues when deployed in a larger area [3]. These include significant interference in overlapping cells due to a large number of access points. Another issue is the reduction in throughput as a result of increased hop length associated with an increasing number of low-gain omnidirectional antennas. Some studies have suggested the integration of WiFi-WiMAX for developing countries [5]. However, such approaches require custom-built radios and smart antennas.

Clearly, each solution has both positive and negative characteristics. As such, it does not seem feasible for any single communication technology to be able to provide an end-to-end sustainable solution that meets all of the interactivity and interoperability requirements. Each technology has its own pole capacity and QoS mechanisms, which make it appropriate for some particular applications and environments. To overcome the drawbacks of using one technology, heterogeneous networks offer promising solutions.

To discuss these ideas and potential solutions, the remainder of this paper is organized as follows. Section 2 discusses related work and establishes motivations for our work. Section 3 illustrates our proposed architecture. In Section 4 the simulation results for various scenarios used for examining and evaluating the proposed architecture are presented and analyzed. The last section concludes the paper and discusses our future works.

2 Related Work and Motivations

Related work to this study can be broadly divided in two categories. In one category, various network based solutions in context of rural area are discussed. The other one relates to provision of multimedia over heterogeneous networks. There is a growing interest from networking research community in utilizing different wireless and cellular technologies to provide education, health, and commerce based services in rural areas. Again, broadly speaking, these solutions can be classified into two main groups. The first one includes solutions based on 802.11 WLAN, 802.16 WiMAX and similar type technologies based solutions [2-5]. The second group consists of solutions based on cellular systems [6] and [7]. A third group of solutions can also be considered as the convergence these two types of technologies [8] and [9].

From a user point of view, the rising demand for multimedia traffic has opened up new interests in adaptive video streaming, videoconferencing and similar applications running over wireless and cellular networks. Delivery of on-demand video services in rural areas over 802.16 WiMAX networks has been studied in [10]. The study designs an extensive simulation model for H.264/AVC scalable video coding and investigates the system capacity and buffer-based congestion control algorithms. It also evaluates the performance of video streaming traffic in the context of WiMAX technology. The advantages of using 3G and particularly CDMA450 for rural areas have been discussed in [7].

Some of these studies have been expanded to design the necessary architecture to support video streaming [11]. However, the reported performance study only evaluates WiMAX networks through simulation. To complement that work, simulation analysis of video and voice traffic for different QoS classes in WiMAX is reported in [12]. Most of the published work in this area is concentrated on evaluating the performance of video streaming applications over heterogeneous networks. The majority of them then focus on WiMAX technology in the context of asymmetric multimedia applications such as video streaming. This paper expand on those works, in the sense that our research studies a heterogeneous network involving WiMAX, UMTS, WLAN, and Ethernet technologies. We also report on the performance analysis of some symmetric multimedia applications, such as VC.

VC is considered to be a highly effective tool in distance education [1]. Several VC based tele-education models for surgery have also been implemented in both industrialized and developing countries [13]. Essentially, four networking technologies are suggested for VC delivery. These include IP based networks, satellite communication systems, 3G systems, and other broadband technologies. Different VC applications use different architectures. Our work makes some novel contribution in understanding technological challenges in implementing VC over a heterogeneous network. This work also proposes an interactive education model over heterogeneous network and conducts the performance evaluation by studying behaviors of key network QoS parameters namely delay variation, end-to-end delay, and packet loss.

3 Proposed Architecture

Our proposed architecture is illustrated in Figure 1. In the proposed model, the conference participants of rural area are considered to be participating through 3G (UMTS),

WLAN, or Ethernet. The linkage between them and the urban area is through an IP-based network. The conference participants in urban area can be using WiMAX or Ethernet. A SIP-based proxy server sits between the urban area and the IP backbone. All video and audio data from both parties are transmitted via this server. The overall architecture of the Rural Area Network (RAN) can be considered in three network-technology based clusters. These are the UMTS/3G cluster, the WLAN cluster, and the Ethernet cluster. The Urban Area Network (UAN) may also be categorized in two of such clusters, namely the WiMAX and the Ethernet clusters.

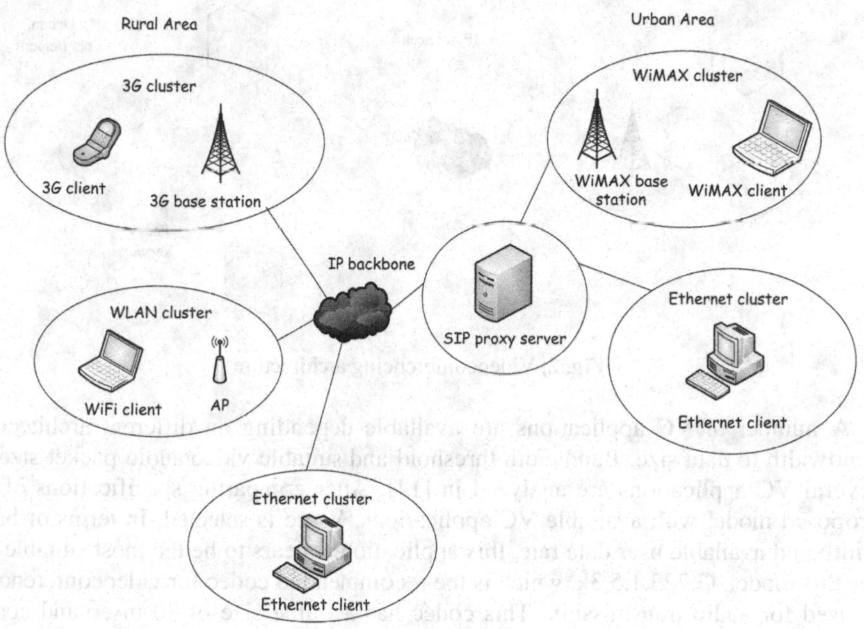

Fig. 1. Proposed model

Each RAN cluster has its own gateway that connects it to the IP backbone network, which in turn connects it to the proxy server of the UAN. The connection between the wireless access points and their wireless gateway nodes are considered to be provided by 45 Mbps Digital Signal 3 (DS3) links. The same links connect the wireless gateway nodes and the IP backbone network. A UMTS gateway node connects the UMTS GPRS support node (GGSN) to the IP-backbone network through a DS3 link. The gateway nodes connect UAN clusters to RAN through an IP backbone network.

Several architectures are suitable for VC applications. Peer-to-Peer (P2P) architecture can be used in a two-party VC session. In such architecture both participant can send data to each other directly. For a multi-party VC session, both P2P and server/client (S/C) based architecture are suitable. In a multipoint P2P VC session, users relay video to each other. On the other hand, in an S/C-based architecture, at first, the participants upload video to a server and then the server sends the video to the receiver. The proposed architecture is modeled over S/C based architecture. Figure 2 represents the architecture.

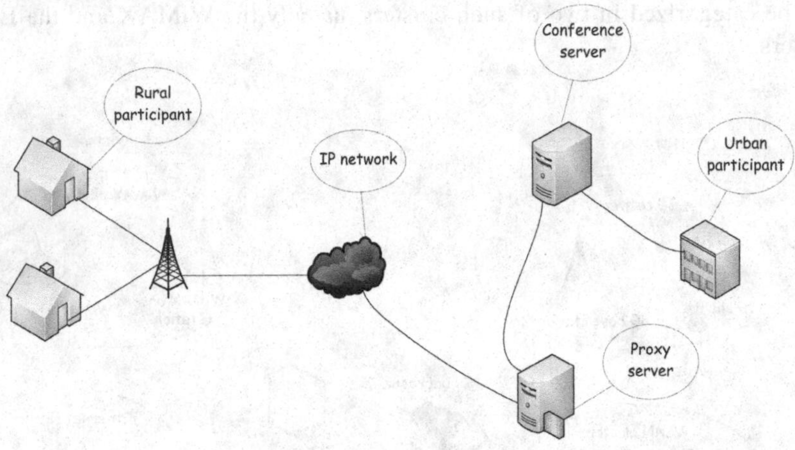

Fig. 2. Videoconferencing architecture

A number of VC applications are available depending on different architecture, bandwidth to data size. Bandwidth threshold and suitable video/audio packet size for several VC applications are analyzed in [14]. After comparing specifications of our proposed model with available VC applications, V see is selected. In terms of bandwidth and available user data rate, this application appears to be the most suitable one for this model. G.723.1.5.3k, which is the recommended codec for videoconferencing, is used for audio transmission. This codec has a frame size of 30 msec and coding rate of 5.3Kbps, with a payload size (*PL*) of 159 bytes. Table 1 summarizes the VC specifications.

Table 1. Videoconferencing specifications

Attributes	Values
Video frame rate per second	30
Video frame size (byte)	600
Video type of service	Differentiated service for Interactive multimedia (EF)
Audio codec	G.723.1.5.3k
Audio payload size (byte)	159
Bandwidth threshold (Kbit/s)	50

4 Result Analysis and Discussions

Multiple iterations of simulation were carried out to analyze the behavior of designed model from different perspectives. The system capacity is assessed for different types of traffic, the quality of video and voice transmissions are investigated ranging from a few to a large number of simultaneous participants. The analyses are discussed in detail in the following subsections.

4.1 Designed Scenarios

In the first scenario, two participants join the conference from each cluster of RAN. For instance, there are two participants in the UMTS cluster, one of them is in a conference with an urban participant located in the Ethernet cluster, and another participant of the same cluster is in a conference with an urban participant from the WiMAX cluster. In the same manner, participants from the Ethernet and the WLAN cluster join the conference with an urban participant.

Several other scenarios are designed with a variant number of simultaneous participants. In the second scenario, the number of participants is increased to twenty in each RAN cluster. For example, in the UMTS cluster, altogether, there are twenty participants. Ten of them are in a conference with an urban participant from the Ethernet cluster and ten other participants are in a conference with an urban participant from the WiMAX cluster. Both WLAN and Ethernet cluster support same number and type of conference. To elaborate, the urban participant located in the WiMAX cluster in UAN initiates a VC session with ten participants from the Ethernet cluster, ten participants from the WLAN cluster, and ten participants from the UMTS cluster of RAN.

In the third scenario, the number of participants is reduced to ten resulting in an equal number of participants in each RAN cluster for each urban user. In the fourth and the fifth scenario, the number of participants are reduced to eight and six respectively. Each VC session follows a specific naming convention, which is the name of RAN cluster of the participant followed by the name of the UAN cluster of the participant. For instance, the conference between a participant from the UMTS cluster of RAN and an urban participant from the WiMAX cluster is termed as UMTS-WiMAX pair/conference/transmission.

4.2 Performance Analysis

Performances for both video and voice transmissions of all VC sessions are tested against each scenario in terms of delay variation, end-to-end delay, and packet loss. Delay variation is the variance among end-to-end delay for all packets. End-to-end delay is calculated based on network delay, encoding delay, decoding delay, compression delay, and decompression delay. The acceptable performance values for these parameters are taken from [15]. Table 2 represents these values.

Table 2. Acceptable performance values for QoS metrics

Application	Metrics	Acceptable performance level
	Packet end-to-end delay	< =150 msec
Video transmission	Delay variation	<= 30 msec
	Packet loss	<=1%
	Packet end-to-end delay	<= 150 msec
Voice transmission	Delay variation	<=1%
	Packet loss	<=30 msec

Video traffic: In the first scenario, with three participants in each conference cluster, two in RAN side and one in UAN side the model achieves the acceptable performance level. Table 3 illustrates the values of each performance metrics received from the conference between three separate clusters of RAN and the Ethernet cluster of UAN. The conference between WiFi-Ethernet cluster show better performance than other cluster conference in terms of packet loss.

In case of conference between RAN clusters and the WiMAX cluster in UAN, the WiFi-WiMAX and the Ethernet-WiMAX conference experience insignificant packet loss. Other performance parameters such as end-to-end delay and delay variation also show a value within acceptance level. However, the participants in UMTS-WiMAX conference experience a higher packet loss than the former two. Similarly, end-to-end delay and delay variation exhibits a much higher value, which are 120 -220 msec and 1-14 msec.

In the next scenario, the number of participants in each conference cluster is increased to ten. Therefore, each urban participant is in a conference with thirty other simultaneous participants residing in different technologies. The model capacity is investigated in this stage of simulation. In case of UMTS-Ethernet conference, only one out of ten is able to join the conference. Although, all participants under the WiFi and the Ethernet cluster are able to join the conference and receive video data, the quality of received transmission varies. In case of conference with the urban user in the WiMAX cluster, seven out of ten participants in the Ethernet cluster are able to receive video transmission data. In case of participants in the WiFi cluster, only six out of ten are able to receive data successfully and two out of ten transmissions are successful in case of users in the UMTS cluster. However, the quality of received data for all users degrades drastically.

In terms of transmission quality, delay variation and end-to-end delay show insignificant difference from the previous scenario. However, users experience significant packet loss. Most of the users in the Ethernet cluster in RAN experience 6.67% to 13.3% packet losses. In case of WiFi-Ethernet conference, packet loss varies between 13% and 26%. Similarly, UMTS-Ethernet conference experience huge packet losses. Likewise, all conferences with the participant from the WiMAX cluster experience a significant amount of packet loss.

Table 3. Simulation results for RAN clusters – UAN cluster (Ethernet) conference

Conference type	Metrics	Resulting value
Ethernet-Ethernet	End-to-end delay	1.3 msec
	Delay variation	1.5*10-4 μs
	Packet loss	0.1 to 0.2%
WiFi-Ethernet	End-to-end delay	5.7 to 5.8 msec
	Delay variation	0.15 to 0.2 μs
	Packet loss	0%
UMTS-Ethernet	End-to-end delay	110 to 120 msec
	Delay variation	1 to 3 msec
	Packet loss	0%

To explore the capacity of the network further, in the third scenario, the participant number is reduced to five in each conference cluster. Therefore, each urban user from the WiMAX and the Ethernet cluster are in conference with 15 simultaneous users respectively. This time the successful connection ratio and packet loss improves significantly. Packet losses for all Ethernet-Ethernet video transmissions reduce to 3.3% and 6.67%. Few users of WiFi-WiMAX conference experience no packet loss and others experience 3.33% packet loss. However, the Ethernet-WiMAX and the UMTS-WiMAX cluster still experience significant packet losses.

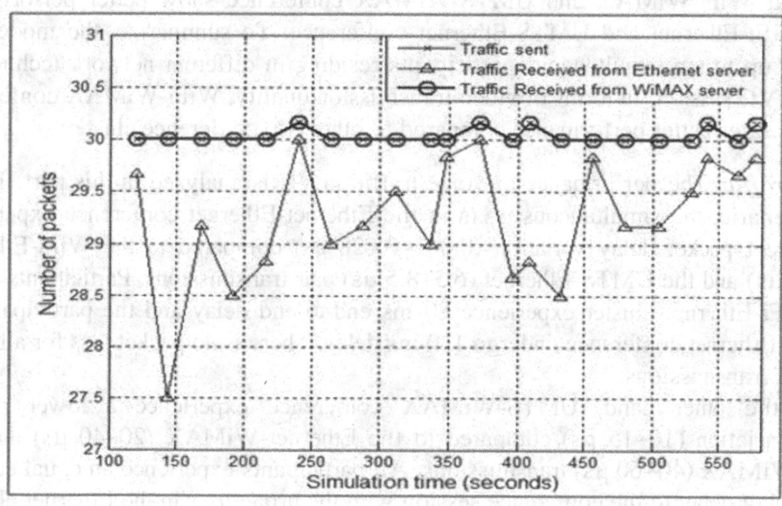

Fig. 3. Packet loss for WiFi clients

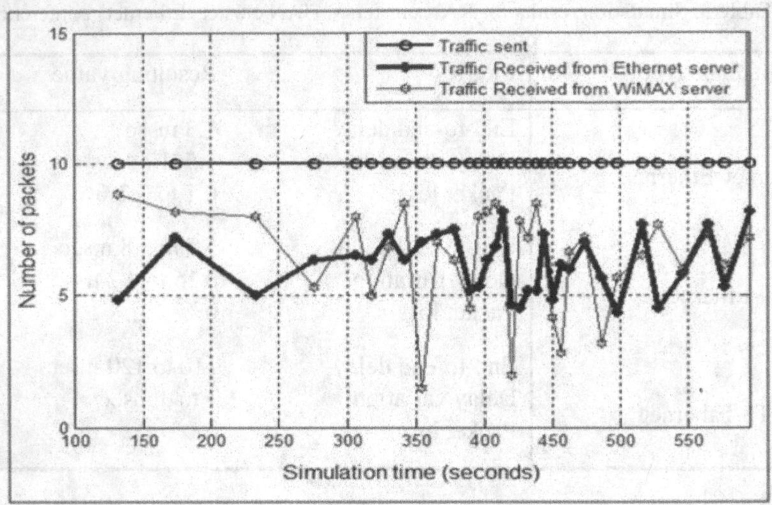

Fig. 4. Packet loss for UMTS clients

In the next scenario, the simulation is carried out with three simultaneous users in each conference cluster resulting in nine simultaneous RAN participants with one urban participant. As expected, the video transmission exhibits better results in terms of both capacity and quality. Two out of three participants from the WiFi-WiMAX cluster experience no packet loss. Participants in UMTS-WiMAX and Ethernet-WiMAX conference also exhibit better performance. Figure 3 and 4 show packet loss for the video transmissions in the third conference scenario. The figures clearly indicate that WiFi-WiMAX and UMTS-WiMAX conference show better performance than WiFi-Ethernet and UMTS-Ethernet conference. To summarize, the model can support up to ten simultaneous participants residing in different network technology in each VC session. In terms of video transmission quality, WiFi-WiMAX conference demonstrates better performance compared to other two conference clusters.

Voice traffic: The performance of voice traffic in VC is analyzed in this part. In the first scenario, the simultaneous users in the Ethernet-Ethernet conference experience the lowest packet delay variation (0.002~0.028 μs) compared to the WiFi-Ethernet (1.8~2 μs) and the UMTS-Ethernet (6.5~8.5 μs) pair transmissions. Participants under the WiFi-Ethernet cluster experience 80 ms end-to-end delay and the participants in UMTS-Ethernet conference undergo 130 ms delay. There is no packet loss for all three types of transmissions.

On the other hand, UMTS-WiMAX conference experience a lower packet delay variation (10~15 μs) compared to the Ethernet-WiMAX (20~40 μs) and the WiFi-WiMAX (40~60 μs) transmissions. All participants experience an equal end-to-end packet delay to the conference session with the urban user in the Ethernet cluster. There was no packet loss for all type of transmissions.

In the second scenario, likewise video transmissions not all participants are able to receive voice data successfully. In case of UMTS-Ethernet pair communication, only two out of ten users are able to receive data. All participants under Ethernet-Ethernet and WiFi-Ethernet conference are able to receive data. However, the quality does not meet the expected level. Similarly, all users under the Ethernet and the WiFi cluster are able to receive transmission from the urban user in the WiMAX cluster. However, some of the participants experience poor quality. Only two out of ten users from the UMTS cluster are able to receive data successfully.

After decreasing the number of participants, Ethernet-Ethernet and WiFi-Ethernet pair voice transmissions experience insignificant packet losses. UMTS-Ethernet conference experience more packet loss in comparison with the former two types of conferences. The conferences with the urban user in the Ethernet cluster show a higher degree of packet loss than the conferences with the user in the WiMAX cluster. Figure 5 shows the number of successful received packets for participants from the WiFi cluster. It is clearly visible from the figure that the WiFi-WiMAX conferences show less packet loss. Figure 6 shows a comparison between the number of successful packets received for UMTS-Ethernet and UMTS-WiMAX conferences. UMTS-WiMAX conference show less packet loss compared to the UMTS-Ethernet conference.

The values of end-to-end delay do not vary much in presence of large and few numbers of simultaneous participants. However, in terms of packet loss, voice transmissions from different pair conferences show different behaviors. When the simulation is carried out with twenty different simultaneous users, the conferences, which take place with the urban user in the Ethernet cluster, experience the highest amount of packet loss.

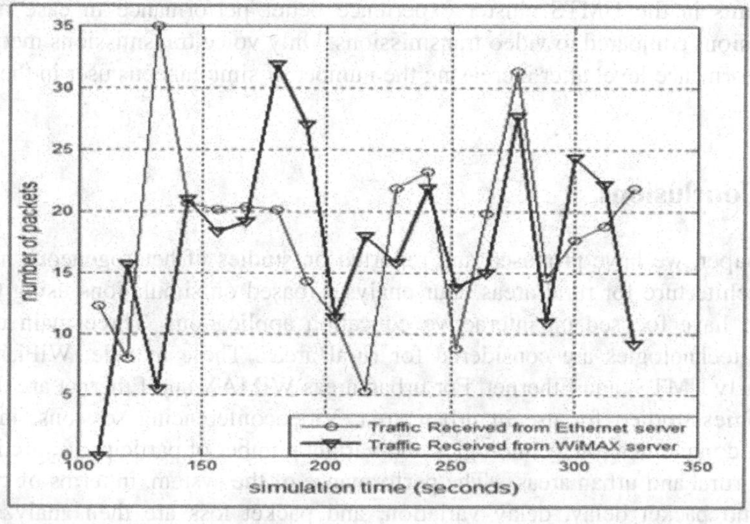

Fig. 5. Successful received packets for WiFi clients in voice transmissions

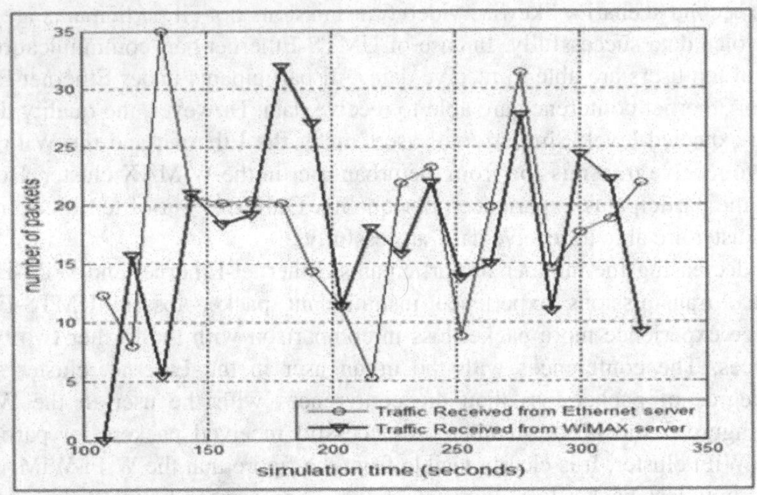

Fig. 6. Successful received packets for WiFi clients in voice transmissions

On the other hand, the conference which takes place between the WiFi and the WiMAX cluster, regardless of the number of simultaneous users, voice transmissions experience no packet loss. However, conference between the Ethernet and the WiMAX cluster and the UMTS and the WiMAX cluster experience some degree of packet loss.

To summarize, with ten simultaneous participants in each VC session the voice transmission experience better performance. Conference with the user in the WiMAX cluster exhibits better transmission quality. Voice transmissions in the conference with the user in the Ethernet cluster experience some amount of packet loss. Participants in the UMTS cluster experience better performance in case of voice transmissions compared to video transmissions. Only voice transmissions met acceptable performance level after increasing the number of simultaneous user in the UMTS cluster.

5 Conclusions

In this paper, we have proposed and reported on studies of heterogeneous network-based architecture for rural areas. Our analyses, based on simulations using OPNET Modeler, have focused on interactive education applications. Three main types of network technologies are considered for rural areas. These include, WiFi, 3G and particularly UMTS, and Ethernet. For urban areas WiMAX and Ethernet are the main technologies studied for use in urban area. Videoconferencing sessions, involving different communication technologies and variant number of participants, are initiated between rural and urban areas. The performance of the system, in terms of capacity, end-to-end packet delay, delay variation, and packet loss are then analyzed. The simulation results show that, the architecture can support up to ten simultaneous participants in each session. The results also show that the conference sessions exhibit higher levels of performance when the combination of WiMAX in urban areas and WiFi in rural areas are utilized. In our future works, we intend to evaluate the performance of this architecture for other symmetric and non-symmetric real-time and non real-time applications. We also intend to investigate how different admission control and adaptive videoconferencing algorithms can be used to improve the overall system performance.

Acknowledgment. We would like to thank OPNET for providing us with Modeler software license.

References

1. Anastasiades, P.S.: Interactive Videoconferencing and Collaborative Learning for K-12 Students and Teachers: Theory and Practice. Nova Science, New York (2009)
2. Pentland, A., Fletcher, R., Hasson, A.: DakNet: Rethinking Connectivity in Developing Nations. Computer 37, 78–83 (2004)
3. Lakshminarayanan, S., Sonesh, S., Rabin, P., Melissa, H., Anmol, S., Eric, B.: Rethinking Wireless for the Developing World. In: 5th Workshop on Hot Topics in Network (Hotnets), California (2006)
4. Seibel, R., Klann, N.-H., Waage, T., Hogrefe, D.: Wireless Mesh Networks for Infrastructure Deficient Areas. In: Pont, A., Pujolle, G., Raghavan, S.V. (eds.) WCITD 2010. IFIP AICT, vol. 327, pp. 26–38. Springer, Heidelberg (2010)
5. Singh, B., Mani, N., Kadyan, S., Shukla, R.K., Singh, A.: A High Performance Point-to-Point Rural Wi-Fi and Wi-Max Access Networks in Developing Regions. In: Second International Conference on Network Applications Protocols and Services (NETAPPS), pp. 203–208. IEEE Computer Society, Malaysia (2010)
6. Parikh, T.S., Lazowska, E.D.: Designing an Architecture for Delivering Mobile Information Services to the Rural Developing World. In: 15th International Conference on World Wide Web, pp. 791–800. ACM, Edinburgh (2006)
7. Sergiu, N., Sonesh, S., Bowei, D., Rabin, P., Eric, B., Victor, S., Zapp, T.: Potential of CDMA450 for Rural Network Connectivity. IEEE Communications Magazine 45, 128–135 (2007)
8. Badombena-Wanta, S., Sheybani, E.O.: Mobile Communications for Development: Enabling Strategic and Low-cost e-applications for Rural and Remote Areas. In: 9th Conference on Wireless Telecommunications Symposium (WTS), pp. 267–273. IEEE Press, Florida (2010)
9. Yan, Z., Ansari, N., Tsunoda, H.: Wireless Telemedicine Services over Integrated IEEE 802.11/WLAN and IEEE 802.16/WiMAX networks. IEEE Wireless Communications 17, 30–36 (2010)
10. Hillestad, O.I., Perkis, A., Genc, V., Murphy, S., Murphy, J.: Delivery of on-demand Video Services in Rural areas via IEEE 802.16 Broadband Wireless Access Networks. In: 2nd ACM International Workshop on Wireless Multimedia Networking and Performance Modeling, pp. 43–52. ACM, Spain (2006)
11. Djamal, A.A., Meddour, E., Ahmed, T., Rasheed, T.: Cross layer Design for Optimized Video Streaming over Heterogeneous Networks. In: 6th International Conference on Wireless Communications and Mobile Computing Conference, pp. 933–938. ACM, France (2010)

12. Kaarthick, B., Yeshwenth, V.J., Nagarajan, N.: Rajeev: Performance analysis of Video Conferencing and Multimedia Application Services over WiMAX. In: Advance Computing Conference (IACC), pp. 1109–1113. IEEE International, India (2009)
13. Augestad, K., Lindsetmo, R.: Overcoming Distance: Video-Conferencing as a Clinical and Educational Tool among Surgeons. World Journal of Surgery 33, 1356–1365 (2009)
14. Lu, Y., Zhao, Y., Kuipers, F., Van Mieghem, P.: Measurement Study of Multi-party Video Conferencing. In: Crovella, M., Feeney, L.M., Rubenstein, D., Raghavan, S.V. (eds.) NETWORKING 2010. LNCS, vol. 6091, pp. 96–108. Springer, Heidelberg (2010)
15. Cisco Systems, Inc., Enterprise QoS Solution Reference Network Design Guide, USA (2005)

A Relative Delay Measurement Method for Wideband Array with LFM Waveform

Yue-bin Chen, Fei Gao, Ji-hua Feng, and Wu-bang Hao

The Lab of Wireless Sensor Network Yunnan University of Nationalities, Kunming, China
cybuestc@sina.com

Abstract. A relative delay measurement system for digital wideband array radar using linear frequency modulation (LFM) waveform is put forward. Based on stretch processing technique and applying digital decimation method, the proposed measurement system can work at low processing rates, thus effectively reducing the computation and lowering hardware complexity. Moreover, by means of reasonable parameter setting and unique design construction, relative delay values among multiple digital transmit/receive (T/R) modules can be measured at one single measurement process. Specific conclusions are testified by simulations.

Keywords: Relative delay measurement system, Digital wideband array radar, LFM waveform, Measurement error, Stretch processing, FFT.

1 Introduction

A number of the modern electronic system applications require generation, processing, amplification, and emission of wideband waveforms. For example, to achieve high range resolution, radars must transmit and receive wide bandwidth waveforms [1]. Often, such radars are used for non-cooperative target identification [2], wherein high resolution is essential to good images of targets. At the same time, many radar applications also require high resolution in angle and flexible beam formation (i.e., scanning of beams in arbitrary direction) as well as range resolution. So, the array combining wide bandwidth waveforms more and more attracts people's attention.

These wide bandwidth waveforms are typically encoded, therefore lowering the peak transmitting power. Among the various coding schemes that have been proposed, linear frequency modulation (LFM) is the most popular choice [3].

When array antennas are used, the encoded pulses are radiated and received at each single T/R module. To maximize target gain in a direction of interest, the radiated or received signals must be coherent across the array. For wideband array radar, such coherence can be usually implemented by employing time delay technique, i.e. by delaying the wideband pulse (transmitting or receiving) different delay values across T/R modules of the array, therefore, the maximum signal gain in a direction of interest can be obtained [4][5].

V. Guyot (Ed.): ICAIT 2012, LNCS 7593, pp. 151–159, 2013.

Traditional time delay estimation techniques base themselves on the identification of the maximum value of the cross correlation function between the reference and delayed signal. Moreover, these estimators can use some form of interpolation between the points on the correlation function to obtain a better resolution than the sample period and thus are computationally expensive. Generally speaking, these methods require that all digital components operate at a rate proportional to the measured waveform bandwidth. Supposing the bandwidth of wideband array radar is very large, suitable components may not be available to implement real-time measurement, especially when the digital T/R modules employ band-pass sampling technique].

Based on the Dechirping theory, a new method is proposed in this paper. By using simple components and FFT algorithm, this method can measure multiple relative delays among wideband LFM pulses in a measuring process and to some extent, satisfy the requirement in real-time and precision. The effectiveness and efficiency of the method are confirmed by simulations

2 The Block Diagram and Steps of Measurement System

Assume that there are N modules to be measured and the whole measurement procedure entails these steps as follows:

Each output LFM pulse from N modules is delayed for a different setting value, and then is added by an addition with which a new sequence is obtained. For example, the output LFM pulse from the nth module is delayed $(n-N/2)\tau_c$. Without loss of generality, here we assume that N is an even number.

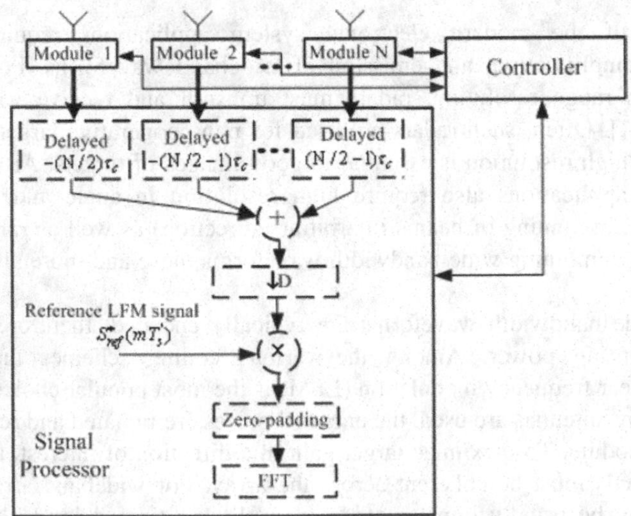

Fig. 1. Block Diagram of Proposed Delay Measurement System

After down-sampled by a factor of D, and then mixed by reference LFM waveform (namely, stretch processing), this new sequence is transformed into a band-pass signal consisting of N complex sinusoid sequences.

By means of analyzing the frequency contents of this band-pass signal (e.g. FFT), N relative delay estimates between modules' LFMs and reference LFM waveform can be obtained. In this process, zero-padding processing can be employed as a frequency interpolation form to lower the adverse effect of the discrete frequency sample noise.

The relative delay estimate between any two modules can be obtained by the difference between the two modules' measured delay values in Step 3.

Next, we will analyze the measurement process in detail. Assume that the controller in Figure.1 gives an output command to all N modules at the same time, and then the digitized output sequence from the nth module is expressed as follow:

$$X_n(mT_s) = S_n(mT_s) + n_n(mT_s) \tag{1}$$

where

$$S_n(mT_s) = \frac{a_n}{\sqrt{T_p}} rect(\frac{mT_s - \tau_n}{T_p}) \exp[j2\pi f_I(mT_s - \tau_n)] \text{ and}$$

$$\exp[j\pi u(mT_s - \tau_n)^2] \text{ and}$$

$$rect(t) = \begin{cases} 1 & -\frac{T_p}{2} \le t \le \frac{T_p}{2} \\ 0 & \text{otherwise} \end{cases}$$

where a_n and T_s represent the complex amplitude and sampling period respectively while f_I denotes the intermediate frequency (IF). The frequency modulation slope is determined by u and $u = B/T_p$, where T_p and B denote LFM pulse's duration and bandwidth respectively. $n_n(mT_s)$ represents the nth module's thermal noise and is usually considered as white Gaussian random process with zero-mean and variance σ_0^2. τ_n is the delay value relative to the LFM reference signal.

In general, for a wideband array, it is more practical to acquire the relative delay values between any two modules. In this paper, these estimate values of relative delay can be obtained by $\hat{\tau}_{nm} = \hat{\tau}_n - \hat{\tau}_m$, where $\hat{\tau}_n$ and $\hat{\tau}_m$ represent the estimate of the true time delay τ_n and τ_m respectively, with $\hat{\tau}_{nm}$ as the estimate value of the true relative delay τ_{nm} between the nth module and the mth module.

As stated previously, a set of output LFM pulses from N modules are delayed by the different setting values and then added, whose sum can be expressed as:

$$X(mT_s) = \sum_{n=0}^{N-1} \frac{a_n}{\sqrt{T_p}} rect(\frac{mT_s - (n - N/2)\tau_c - \tau_n}{T_p}) \exp\{j2\pi f_I[mT_s - (n - N/2)\tau_c - \tau_n]\} \exp\{j\pi u[mT_s - (n - N/2)\tau_c - \tau_n]^2\} + n_n(mT_s) \tag{2}$$

where τ_c is a constant delay whose value will be discussed in detail in Section 3 . In practice, for the sake of convenience we usually select τ_c to satisfy the condition: $\tau_c = CT_s$, where C is an integer. In this case the above-mentioned delay setting processing of LFM pulses can be easily implemented by making use of time-shifting operation.

After down-sampled by factor D , the $X(mT_s)$ in (2) can be transformed into the following expression:

$$X(mT_s^{'}) = \sum_{n=0}^{N\text{-}1} \frac{a_n}{\sqrt{T_p}} rect(\frac{mT_s^{'} - (n-N/2)\tau_c - \tau_n}{T_p}) \exp\{j2\pi$$

$$f_1[mT_s^{'} - (n-N/2)\tau_c - \tau_n]\}\exp\{j\pi u[mT_s^{'} - (n-N/2)\tau_c - \tau_n]^2\} + n_a(mT_s^{'}) \qquad (3)$$

where $T_s^{'} = \mathrm{D}T_s$ and the value of D will be determined in Section 3. Assume that the noise process on each module, mutually uncorrelated, have the same statistical properties, then $n_a(mT_s^{'}) = \sum_{n=1}^{N} n_n(mT_s^{'})$ remains white Gaussian noise process with zero-mean and variance $N\sigma_0^2$.

The LFM reference pulse is defined to be

$$S_{ref}(mT_s^{'}) = rect(\frac{mT_s^{'}}{T_{ref}}) \exp(j2\pi f_1 mT_s^{'}) \exp[j\pi u(mT_s^{'})^2] \qquad (4)$$

where T_{ref} is the duration of LFM reference sequence.

The stretch processing, i.e., $X(mT_s^{'})$ in (3) is mixed by the complex conjugate of the LFM reference sequence, can be expressed as

$$X_{or}(mT_s^{'}) = X(mT_s^{'})S_{ref}^{*}(mT_s^{'}) = S_{or}(mT_s^{'}) + n_{ar}(mT_s^{'}) \qquad (5)$$

where

$$S_{or}(mT_s^{'}) = \sum_{n=0}^{N\text{-}1} \frac{a_n}{\sqrt{T_p}} rect[\frac{mT_s^{'} - (n-N/2)\tau_c - \tau_n}{T_p}] \exp\{$$

$$-j2\pi f_1[(n-N/2)\tau_c + \tau_n]\}\exp\{-\mathrm{j}2\pi u[(n-N/2)\tau_c + \tau_n]\, mT_s^{'} + \mathrm{j}\pi u[(n-N/2)\tau_c + \tau_n]^2\} \qquad (6)$$

and $n_{ar}(mT_s^{'}) = n_a(mT_s^{'})S_{ref}^{*}(mT_s^{'})$ .It is easy to prove that $n_{ar}(mT_s^{'})$ is still a white Gaussian noise process with zero-mean and variance $N\sigma_0^2$.

For simplification, setting $\varphi_{rn} = -2\pi f_1[(n-N/2)\tau_c + \tau_n] + \pi u[(n-N/2)\tau_c + \tau_n]^2$, then (6) can be reduced to be

$$S_{or}(mT_s^{'}) = \sum_{n=0}^{N-1} \frac{a_n \exp(j\varphi_{rn})}{\sqrt{T_p}} rect[\frac{mT_s^{'} - (n-N/2)\tau_c - \tau_n}{T_p}]$$
$$\exp\{-j2\pi u[(n-N/2)\tau_c + \tau_n]mT_s^{'}\} \tag{7}$$

from (7), we can find out that, $S_{or}(mT_s^{'})$ is the sum of N complex sinusoid signals. In this case, the Fourier transform of $S_{or}(mT_s^{'})$ consists of the N sinc-like narrow pulse with the pulse width $1/T_p$ and frequency positions $-u[(n-N/2)\tau_c + \tau_n]$, $n = 0 \sim N-1$:

$$S_{or}(f) = T_p \sum_{n=0}^{N-1} \frac{a_n \exp(j\varphi_{rn})}{\sqrt{T_p}} \text{sinc}\{T_p[f + u[(n-N/2)\tau_c +$$
$$\tau_n]]\} \exp\{-j2\pi f[(n-N/2)\tau_c + \tau_n]\} \tag{8}$$

where $\text{sinc}(a) = \sin(\pi a)/\pi a$. If the estimate of the center frequency f_n of the nth complex sinusoid signal is obtained and hereby denoted by $\widehat{f_n}$, the delay estimate τ_n of the true time delay τ_n can be calculated by

$$\hat{\tau}_n = -\frac{\widehat{f_n} + u[(n-N/2)\tau_c]}{u} = -\left\{\frac{\widehat{f_n}}{u} + [(n-N/2)\tau_c]\right\} \tag{9}$$

In practical application, N frequency estimates ($\widehat{f_n}$, n=0~N-1) are very easy to obtain within one single fast Fourier transform (FFT) process during duration T_{ref}. In this case, the relative delay estimate $\hat{\tau}_{nm}$ between any two modules is obtained by

$$\hat{\tau}_{nm} = \hat{\tau}_n - \hat{\tau}_m = -[\frac{1}{u}(\widehat{f_n} - \widehat{f_m}) + (n-m)\tau_c] \tag{10}$$

where $\hat{\tau}_n$ and $\hat{\tau}_m$ represent the delay estimate of the nth and the mth modules respectively.

3 Measurement System Performance Analysis and Parameters Optimization

1. Carrying out differential operation in (10), then relative delay measurement error can be expressed as follows:

$$\Delta\tau_{nm} = -\frac{1}{u}(\Delta f_n - \Delta f_m) \tag{11}$$

where Δf_n and Δf_m are both the frequency measurement errors. From (11), we can see that, relative delay measurement error depends on the frequency measurement error and frequency modulation slope. Under certain frequency measurement accuracy, the frequency modulation slope u affects the accuracy of the relative delay measurement. The larger the frequency modulation slope becomes, the smaller the measurement error $\Delta\tau_{nm}$ is. This implies that the proposed measurement system is more suitable for the array employing the larger-bandwidth LFM waveform.

2. In (2), the constant delay τ_c has two roles. One is to separate the N sinc-like narrow pulses from each other with frequency spacing $u\tau_c$ after stretch processing. Then as long as τ_c satisfies the condition: $\tau_c \geq 2|\Delta\tau_{\max}|$ (where $\Delta\tau_{\max}$ is the possible maximum delay value among all modules), the N sinc-like narrow pulses will appear in frequency domain according to corresponding modules' numbering sequence. In such case when N frequency estimates are obtained, their corresponding module number is easy to determine. In practice, $\Delta\tau_{\max}$ only depends on the module hardware, and is usually considered as a known value.

The other role of τ_c is to ensure that the frequency spacing among sinc-like narrow pulses are wide enough to eliminate the adverse effect on measurement results caused by their interaction when measure process is performed.

3. In order to measure N LFM pulses simultaneously, LFM reference pulse duration must satisfy the following condition: $T_{ref} \geq (N-1)\tau_c + T_p$. In addition, considering the effect of the possible maximum delay value, a more reasonable condition that T_{ref} must satisfy is,

$$T_{ref} \geq (N-1)\tau_c + T_p + 2|\Delta\tau_{\max}| \tag{15}$$

4. After stretch processing, we can find that, $S_{or}(mT_s^{'})$ in (7) is a band-pass complex signal covering frequency domain: $[-u(\frac{N}{2}\tau_c - \tau_c + \tau_{N\text{-}1}),\ \ u(\frac{N}{2}\tau_c - \tau_0)]$, Moreover, considering the effect of the possible maximum delay value, the maximum frequency range that it can cover is $[-u(\frac{N}{2}\tau_c - \tau_c + |\Delta\tau_{\max}|), u(\frac{N}{2}\tau_c + |\Delta\tau_{\max}|)]$, and the corresponding bandwidth is equal to $u[(N-1)\tau_c + 2|\Delta\tau_{\max}|]$. In this case, in order to satisfy the requirement of the sampling theorem, the sampling frequency after down-sampling process must satisfy the condition:

$$f_s^{'} \geq u[(N-1)\tau_c + 2|\Delta\tau_{\max}|] \tag{16}$$

Therefore, when τ_c and $\Delta\tau_{\max}$ is known, the range of down-sampling factor D is determined: $\mathrm{D} \leq \left[f_s / f_s^{'} \right]$, where f_s is original sampling frequency and $[\cdots]$ denotes round-off operation.

5. From the analysis above, we conclude that, the intermediate frequency (IF) has no effect on the measured results.

6. In practice, in order to further simplify the system and satisfy the real-time requirement, the delayers in Figure.1 can be canceled, and these setting delay values of multiple LFM pulses can be implemented by controller's control command.

4 Simulation Results

In our experimental system, a digital radar array consisting of 16 modules is developed. The radar system parameters are determined as follows, LFM pulse bandwidth and duration are $B = 250\text{MHz}$ and $T_p = 20\mu s$ respectively, while the frequency modulation slope is calculated to be $u = 1.25\times10^{13}$. IF $f_1 = 796.875\text{MHz}$, original sampling frequency $f_s = 1/T_s = 637.5\text{MHz}$. The possible maximum delay value is known to be $\Delta\tau_{\max} = 0.5\mu s$. According to the analysis above, τ_c can be determined: $\tau_c = 2\Delta\tau_{\max} = 1\mu s$ and the LFM reference signal duration is $T_{ref} = N\tau_c + T_p + 2\Delta\tau_{\max} = 37\mu s$. In this case, from (16), the sampling frequency after down-sampling processing can be calculated by $f_s^{'} = u\{(N-1)\tau_c + 2\Delta\tau_{\max}\} = 212.5\text{MHz}$, and the down-sampling factor is determined as $\text{D} = 3$. All LFM signal have unit complex amplitude.

Here first assume that the relative delays between modules are zeros, and in this case these frequency positions of sinc-like narrow pulses only depend on setting delay values. With the module SNR 50dB, the result after stretch processing is shown in Figure.2 The solid lines in the figure represent the 16 modules' LFM pulses with the equal frequency spacing $u\tau_c = 12.5\text{MHz}$. The first solid line on the right-hand side represents the module 1 while the most-left one module 16. As discussed above, as long as the condition is satisfied: , such a corresponding relationship remains unchanged. For example, assume that there are delays existing in modules 3, 6 and 12, and their delay values (relative to the LFM reference pulse) are set to be $\tau_3 = 0.29872\mu s$, $\tau_6 = -1.5096\mu s$, and $\tau_{12} = 0.5\mu s$ respectively. After being delayed separately according to different setting values, the actual delay values are $-5\tau_c + \tau_3 = -4.7013\mu s$, $-2\tau_c + \tau_6 = -3.5096\mu s$, $4\tau_c + \tau_{12} = 4.5\mu s$, with their corresponding sinc-like narrow pulse frequency positions 58.76625MHz, 43.87MHz and -56.25MHz respectively, as shown with dashed lines in Figure.3 Note that the dashed line representing module 6 "jump to" the location between the modules 4 and 5 because its delay value $|\tau_6| = 1.5096\mu s$ is larger than $\tau_c = 1\mu s$, thus breaking the corresponding relationship between the sinc-like narrow pulse frequency positions and modules' numbering sequence. For this reason, in practical application the value of τ_c must be reasonably selected to satisfy the condition: $\tau_c \geq 2|\Delta\tau_{\max}|$.

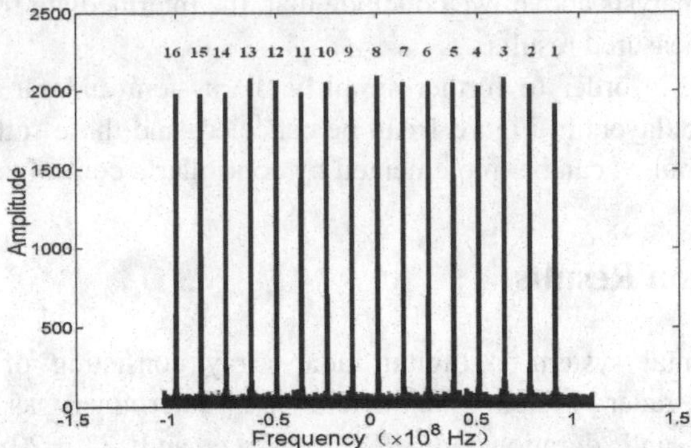

Fig. 2. The result of one single measurement process (no delays)

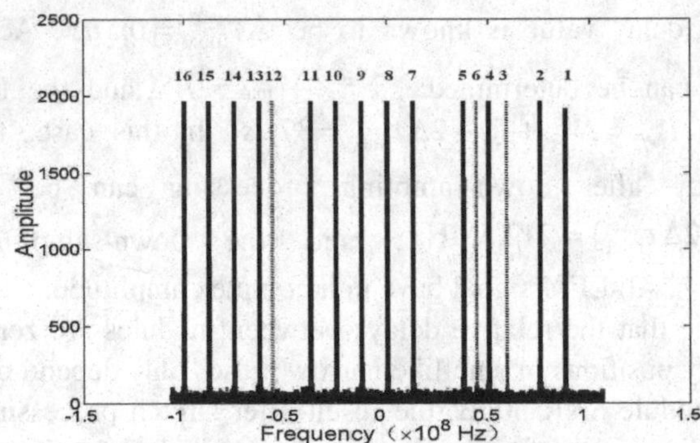

Fig. 3. The result of one single measurement process (existing delays)

5 Conclusion

In this paper, a relative delay measurement system suitable for digital wideband array radar employing wideband LFM waveform is developed. Based on stretch processing technique and digital decimation method, a measurement system is proposed to reduce the processing rates as well as lower the computational complexity. Moreover, measurement system performances are analyzed in detail and some related mathematical expressions are derived by which the measurement system parameters can be well optimized in theory. The validity of the proposed measurement system has been demonstrated by simulations. This measurement system has been successfully used in a wideband digital array experimental system.

Acknowledgment. This research is sponsored jointly by the Special Project of Yunnan Education Administration (2011ED09) and the National Natural Science Foundation of China under Grant No.31160234.

References

1. Linde, G.: Use of wideband waveforms for target recognition with surveillance radars. In: IEEE 2000 International Radar Conference, Alexandria, VA, USA, May 07-12, pp. 128–133 (2000)
2. Wehner, D.R.: High-Resolution Radar, 3rd edn. Artech House INC., Norwood (1995)
3. Day, R.H., Germon, R., O'Neill, B.C.: Pulse compression radar signal processor. In: Proceedings of the 1997 IEE Colloquium on DSP Chips in Real Time Instrumentation and Display Systems, pp. 1–5 (1997)
4. Corbin, J., Howard, R.L.: TDU quantization error impact on wideband phased-array performance. In: IEEE International Symposium on Phased Array Systems and Technology, pp. 457–460 (2000)
5. Hartman, N.F., Corey, L.E.: New integrated optic technique for time delays in wideband phased arrays. In: Seventh International Conference on Antennas and Propagation (ICAP 1991), pp. 918–921 (1991)

Signal Detection Based on Maximum-Minimum Eigenvalue in Rician Fading Channel

Sai-sai Feng, Yue-bin Chen, and Fei Gao

The Lab of Wireless Sensor Network, Yunnan University of Nationalities, Kunming, China
saisai19851108@163.com

Abstract. Signal detection is an essential section of Cognitive Radio. In this paper, a method is adopted based on the eigenvalue of the autocorrelation matrix of the received signal. This method is based on the random matrix theory, using the ratio from the maximum eigenvalue to the minimum eigenvalue as the test statistic to detect the existence of primary users, so as to improve the spectrum efficiency. Simulation based on the signal detection in the Rician fading channel, the results show that the performance of the adopted method is better than energy detection in the same fading environment.

Keywords: Signal detection, eigenvalue, Rician fading channel, detection performance.

1 Introduction

With the rapid development of wireless technology, people make the higher requests on the wireless broadband application, especially the utilization of spectrum is increasing tension under fading environment. Cognitive Radio [1] is an intelligent communication technology, whose first step is to detect whether the interested frequency band is free. It can dynamically choose and reuse these idle spectrum resources without impaction on the primary users. It is a solution for the low utilization rate of spectrum. Thus, signal detection is the key technology of Cognitive Radio.

Energy detection is a fundamental method in the several detect algorithms. It does not need any information of the detected signal and it robust to unknown dispersive channel. However, energy detection depends on the accurate power [2]. In the practical detection environment, it is difficult to obtain the reliable results for the influence of noise power uncertainty. In order to overcome the shortage, some researchers proposed a new method based on the eigenvalues of the received signal (called Maximum Minimum Eigenvalue detection- MME) in the reference [3]. Based on the random matrix theory, it obtained the eigenvalues of sample autocorrelation matrix of the received signal to detect the existence of primary users. This method can be used for kinds signal detection applications without information of the user's signal, the communication channel and the noise power. In this paper, we focus on the algorithms in fading environment and discuss its detection performance.

V. Guyot (Ed.): ICAIT 2012, LNCS 7593, pp. 160–168, 2013.

Especially Rician fading channel [4] mainly used to describe the wireless channel in the remote rural and town. It is an important channel model of outdoor wireless communication. Researching the performance of this method in Rician fading channel has a major practical significance.

2 The Sensing Reference Model and Algorithm

2.1 The Sensing Reference Model

The purpose of signal detection is to test the existence of primary user's signal in receiver. For the signal detection, there are two kinds of hypothesis: H_0, which means primary user's signal does not exist; H_1, which means primary user's signal exists. The two hypothesis are given respectively by formula as follows:

$$\begin{aligned} H_0: &\quad y(k) = n(k) \\ H_1: &\quad y(k) = he(k) + n(k) \end{aligned} \tag{1}$$

Where $y(k)$ is the received signal, $e(k)$ is the primary user's signal, $n(k)$ is the white Gaussian noise of the receiver, h is a gain factor of channel amplitude. Since $e(k)$ is transmitted through a wireless channel including the effect of multipath fading, $he(k)$ is expressed by $s(k)$, i.e. $s(k) = he(k)$.

Let P_d be the probability of detection which having detected the primary user's signal at hypothesis H_1. Let P_{fa} be the probability of false alarm which having detected the primary user's signal at hypothesis H_0.

2.2 Theoretical Analysis for MME Algorithm

Let us choose a factor L and define the vectors as follows:

$$\mathbf{y(k)} = \left[y(k) \quad y(k-1) \quad \cdots \quad y(k-L+1) \right]^T, \tag{2}$$

$$\mathbf{s(k)} = \left[s(k) \quad s(k-1) \quad \cdots \quad s(k-L+1) \right]^T, \tag{3}$$

$$\mathbf{n(k)} = \left[n(k) \quad n(k-1) \quad \cdots \quad n(k-L+1) \right]^T, \tag{4}$$

where $k = 0,1,\ldots,N-1$. $[\cdot]^T$ stands for transpose, L is matrix length. $\mathbf{y(k)}$ is the receiving signals after sampling, $\mathbf{s(k)}$ is primary user's signals after sampling and $\mathbf{n(k)}$ is the Gaussian white noise after sampling. Defining the autocorrelation matrices of the signals and noise as

$$R_y = E[\mathbf{y(k)}\mathbf{y}^\dagger\mathbf{(k)}], \tag{5}$$

$$R_s = E[\mathbf{s(k)}\mathbf{s}^\dagger\mathbf{(k)}], \tag{6}$$

$$R_n = E[\mathbf{n}(\mathbf{k})\mathbf{n}^{\dagger}(\mathbf{k})], \tag{7}$$

where superscripts $\dagger$ stand for transpose-conjugate, According to the nature of the matrix, we have

$$R_y = R_s + R_n.$$

Assume that H is a matrix about filter parameters as follow:

$$H = \begin{bmatrix} f(0) & f(1) & \cdots & f(N) & 0 & \cdots & 0 \\ 0 & f(0) & \cdots & f(N-1) & f(N) & \cdots & 0 \\ & & \ddots & & & \ddots & \\ 0 & 0 & \cdots & f(0) & f(1) & \cdots & f(N) \end{bmatrix} \tag{8}$$

where $\sum_{i=0}^{N} |f(i)|^2 = 1,\ i = 0,1,...,N$. According to (4) and (5), we have

$$R_n = E[\mathbf{n}(\mathbf{k})\mathbf{n}^{\dagger}(\mathbf{k})] = \sigma_n^2 HH^H. \tag{9}$$

Let $G = HH^H$, (9) can transform into $R_n = \sigma_n^2 G$, where σ_n^2 is variance of the white noise. Note that G is a positive definite Hermitian matrix. According to its characteristics, it can be decomposed to $G = Q^2$, where Q is also a positive definite Hermitian matrix. Let $\tilde{R}_y = Q^{-1}R_yQ^{-1}$ and $\tilde{R}_s = Q^{-1}R_sQ^{-1}$, hence, $\tilde{R}_y = \tilde{R}_s + \sigma_n^2 I_L$, where I_L is the unit matrix of order L .

Define the sample autocorrelations of the received signal as

$$\lambda(l) = \frac{1}{N_s} \sum_{m=0}^{N_s-1} y(m)y(m-l), l = 0,1,...,L-1. \tag{10}$$

where N_s is the number of samples.

In practice, we can only calculate the statistical auto-correlation matrix $R_y(N_s)$ by using a limited number of signal samples, and then approximately equal to be the sample auto-correlation matrix R_y , then

$$R_y \approx R_y(N_s) = \begin{bmatrix} \lambda(0) & \lambda(1) & \cdots & \lambda(L-1) \\ \lambda(1) & \lambda(0) & \cdots & \lambda(L-2) \\ \vdots & \vdots & \vdots & \vdots \\ \lambda(L-1) & \lambda(L-2) & \cdots & \lambda(0) \end{bmatrix}_{L \times L}. \tag{11}$$

Let $\lambda_{\max}$ and $\lambda_{\min}$ be the maximum and minimum eigenvalue of R_y , and $\rho_{\max}$ and $\rho_{\min}$ be the maximum and minimum eigenvalue of R_s . Thus, we obtain

$$\begin{cases} \lambda_{\max} = \rho_{\max} + \sigma_n^2 \\ \lambda_{\min} = \rho_{\min} + \sigma_n^2 \end{cases}.$$

Obviously, if $s(k)$ does not exit, $R_s = 0$, then $\rho_{\max} = \rho_{\min} = 0$, so $\lambda_{\max}/\lambda_{\min} = 1$; If $s(k)$ exits, $R_s \neq 0$, then $\lambda_{\max} > \lambda_{\min}$, i.e. $\lambda_{\max}/\lambda_{\min} > 1$. Hence, we can use the ratio of the maximum and minimum eigenvalue to detect the primary user's signal.

2.3 TheDetermination of Threshold

The threshold is sensitive to the performance of detect algorithms in low SNR. Due to we have no information on the signal, it is difficult to set the threshold based on the P_d. Thus we generally choose the threshold based on the P_{fa}. In recent years, some scholars have found the distribution of the largest eigenvalue by researching random matrix theory, and given by the theorem 1 as follow [5].

Theorem 1. Assume that the noise is real. Let $A(N_s) = \frac{N_s}{\sigma_n^2} R_n(N_s)$, $\mu = \left(\sqrt{N_s - 1} + \sqrt{L}\right)^2$, and $\upsilon = \left(\sqrt{N_s - 1} + \sqrt{L}\right) \cdot \left(\frac{1}{\sqrt{N_s - 1}} + \frac{1}{\sqrt{L}}\right)^{1/3}$. Assume that $\lim_{N_s \to \infty} \frac{L}{N_s} = y \ (0 < y < 1)$, then $\frac{\lambda_{max}(A(N_s)) - \mu}{\upsilon}$ converge with probability one to the Tracy-Widom distribution of order 1 (W_1), where $R_n(N_s)$ is the sample autocorrelation matrix of noise at no signal, $\lambda_{max}(A(N_s))$ is the largest eigenvalue of $A(N_s)$.

Bai and Yin found the limit of the smallest eigenvalue [6], and given by the theorem 2 as follow.

Theorem 2. Assume that $\lim_{N_s \to \infty} \frac{L}{N_s} = \xi (0 < \xi < 1)$, then $\lim_{N_s \to \infty} \lambda_{min} = \sigma_n^2 (1 - \sqrt{\xi})^2$.

According to the above theorems, we have

$$\begin{cases} \lambda_{max} \approx \frac{\sigma_n^2}{N_s} \left(\sqrt{N_s} + \sqrt{L}\right)^2 \\ \lambda_{min} \approx \frac{\sigma_n^2}{N_s} \left(\sqrt{N_s} - \sqrt{L}\right)^2 \end{cases}.$$

Because the cumulative distribution function F_1 of the Tracy-Widom distribution of order 1 have no accurate form expression at present, we generally calculate $F_1^{-1}(y)$ at certain points by the Table 1. For instance, $F_1^{-1}(0.10) = -2.78$, $F_1^{-1}(0.90) = 0.45$. Using the theorems, for the real signal, the probability of false alarm of the MME detection algorithm is

$$P_{fa} = P(\lambda_{max} > \gamma\lambda_{min}) = P\left(\frac{\sigma_\eta^2}{N_s}\lambda_{max}(\mathrm{A}(N_s)) > \gamma\lambda_{min}\right)$$
$$\approx P\left(\lambda_{max}(\mathrm{A}(N_s)) > \gamma\left(\sqrt{N_s}-\sqrt{L}\right)^2\right)$$
$$= P\left(\frac{\lambda_{max}(\mathrm{A}(N_s))-\mu}{\upsilon} > \frac{\gamma\left(\sqrt{N_s}-\sqrt{L}\right)^2-\mu}{\upsilon}\right)$$
$$= 1 - F_1\left(\frac{\gamma\left(\sqrt{N_s}-\sqrt{L}\right)^2-\mu}{\upsilon}\right).$$

From the definitions of μ and υ, we can obtain the threshold

$$\gamma = \frac{\left(\sqrt{N_s}+\sqrt{L}\right)^2}{\left(\sqrt{N_s}-\sqrt{L}\right)^2}\cdot\left(1+\frac{\left(\sqrt{N_s}+\sqrt{L}\right)^{-2/3}}{(N_s L)^{1/6}}F_1^{-1}(1-P_{fa})\right). \tag{12}$$

3 Rician Fading Channel

In mobile communication, due to the obstacles obstruct the line of sight, the strength of the received signals obey the Rician distribution when there are reflected signal, diffracted signal, scattered signal, etc, and a line of sight signal, we call this channel to be Rician fading channel. In the process of information transmission, Rician fading channel is considered to be a discrete-time memoryless channel where neither the receiver nor the transmitter knows the fading coefficients. The characteristics of this channel mainly rely on its amplitude distribution, the fading amplitude h_i at the ith time instant can be described as

$$h_i = \sqrt{(x_i+\rho)^2 + y_i^2}, \tag{13}$$

where ρ is the amplitude of line of sight component, x_i and y_i are two Gaussian random variables with mean zero and variance σ_0^2.

Defining $K = \frac{\rho^2}{2\sigma_0^2}$ as the Rician factor, it describes the ratio of the power of line of sight to all scattered waves. The probability density function of Rician fading channel $p(h)$ is given by

$$p(h) = \frac{h}{\sigma_0^2}\exp[-(h^2+\rho^2)/2\sigma_0^2]I_0[\frac{h\rho}{\sigma_0^2}], h \geq 0 \tag{14}$$

where $I_0(\cdot)$ is the zero-order modified Bessel function of the first kind.

In the experimental simulation of this Rician fading channel, we need to generate the uncorrelated fading sequences of the Rician distribution in MATLAB [7]. The mean- squared value of the Rician distribution is known to be $2\sigma_0^2(K+1)$. In order to make the signal power and SNR correspond, we usually required the Rician distribution with unit mean- squared value, i.e. $E\{h^2\}=1$. Thus (13) can be transformed as follow

$$h_i=\sqrt{\frac{(x_i+\sqrt{2K})^2+y_i^2}{2(K+1)}}, \tag{15}$$

where x_i and y_i are two Gaussian random variables with mean zero and variance $\sigma_0^2=1$.

4 Flow Chart and The Simulation Analysis

4.1 Flow Chart

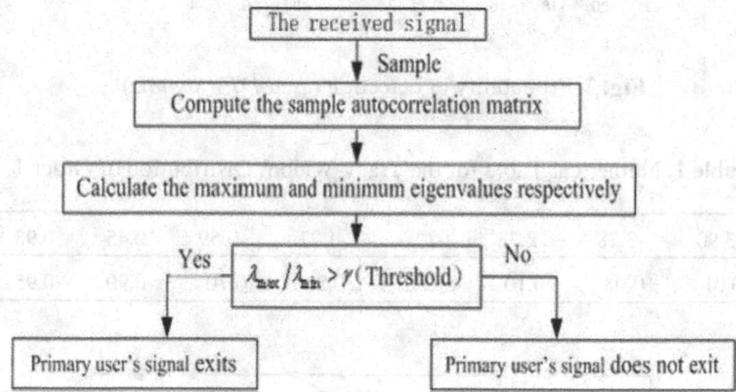

Fig. 1. MME Sensing Algorithm

4.2 The Simulation Analysis

In the following, we use the captured DTV signals [8] and the randomly generated BPSK as the primary signals respectively through Rician fading channel, and then simulate it in MATLAB. We compare and analysis the simulation results with energy detection. $EG-xdB$ respects the energy detection with $x-dB$ noise uncertainty in Fig.2 and Fig.3. We set the matrix length as $L=14$, use the number of samples as $N_s=100000$ and simulate 1000 Monte Carlo realizations. Fig. 2 and Fig.3 show the probability of detection (P_d) results for the energy detection and MME detection in Rician fading channel. No matter whether there is noise uncertainty, the probability of

MME detection is better than the probability of energy detection. When the variance of noise is accurately known, the performance of energy detection is a little good. But the performance of energy detection is much worse than MME detection obviously when there is noise uncertainty.

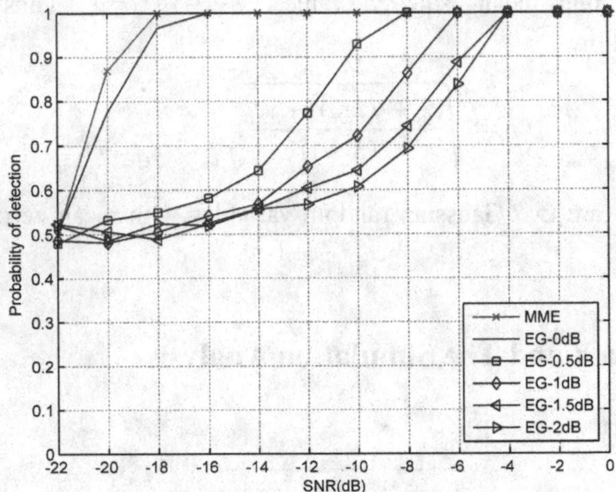

Fig. 2. Probability of detection (*used DTV signals*)

Table 1. Numerical Table for the Tracy-Widom Distribution of Order 1

t	-3.90	-3.18	-2.78	-1.91	-1.27	-0.59	0.45	0.98	2.02
$F_1(t)$	0.01	0.05	0.10	0.30	0.50	0.70	0.90	0.95	0.99

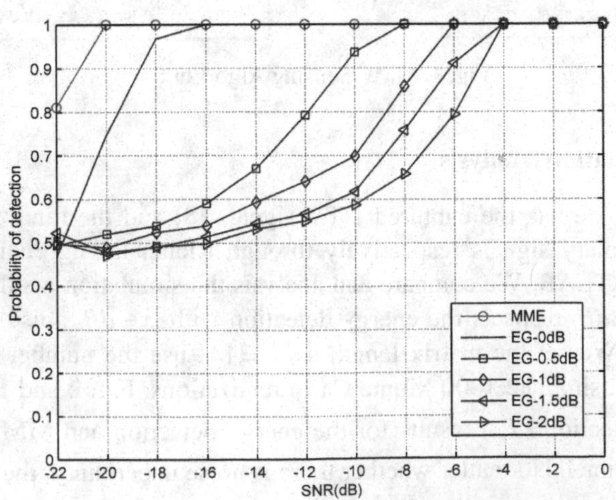

Fig. 3. Probability of detection (*used BPSK signals*)

To prove the impact of the number of samples, we choose the SNR at -18dB and vary the number of samples from 10000 to 80000. Fig.3 shows the P_d results. It is seen that the P_d of the energy detection without noise uncertainty and MME detection increases with number of samples. However, the P_d of the energy detection with noise uncertainty has no change. That is to say, increasing the number of samples cannot solve the problem of noise uncertainty.

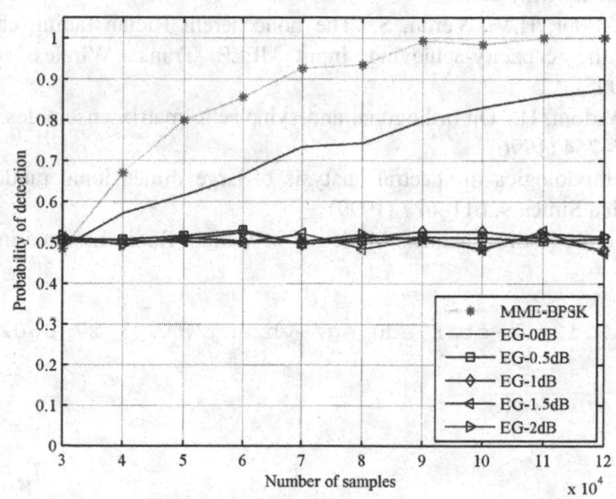

Fig. 4. Probability of detection (*used BPSK signals,* $SNR = -18dB$)

5 Conclusion

In Rician fading channel, the advantage of the MME algorithm is that its performance is much better than energy detection, whether noise uncertainty exits without information of the signal. The simulation of random generated BPSK and captured DTV show that the algorithm of MME can be used for kinds of signal detection applications, it has a good applicability and actionability.

Acknowledgment. This research is sponsored jointly by the Special Project of Yunnan Education Administration (2011ED09) and the National Natural Science Foundation of China under Grant No.31160234.

References

1. Mitola, J., Maguire, G.Q.: Cognitive Radio.Making Software Radios More Personal. IEEE Pcrsonal Communications 6(4), 13–18 (1999)
2. Sahai, A., Cabric, D.: Spectrum sensing: fundamental limits and practical challenges. In: Proc. IEEE International Symposium on New Frontiers in Dynamic Spectrum Access Networks (DySPAN), Baltimore, MD (November 2005)
3. Zeng, Y., Liang, Y.-C.: Maximum-Minimum Eigenvalue Detection for Cognitive Radio. In: IEEE ICC 2008 (May 2008)
4. Gursoy, M.C., Poor, H.V., Verdú, S.: The noncoherent Rician fading channel—Part I: Structure of the capacity-achieving input. IEEE Trans. Wireless Commun. 4(5), 2193–2206 (2005)
5. Tracy, C.A., Widom, H.: On orthogonal and symplectic matrix ensembles. Comm. Math. Phys. 177, 727–754 (1996)
6. Bai, Z.D.: Methodologies in spectral analysis of large dimensional random matrices, a review. Statistica Sinica 9, 611–677 (1999)
7. Kostov, N.: Mobile Radio Channels Modeling in Matlab. Radio Engineering 12(4), 12–16 (2003)
8. Zeng, Y.: `http://www1.i2r.a-star.edu.sg/~yhzeng/WAS_3_27_06022000_REF`

Collective Intelligence Based Place Recommendation System

Jehwan Oh[1], Ok-Ran Jeong[2], and Eunseok Lee[3]

[1] Department of Computer Science and Engineering,
University of Minnesota, Minneapolis, MN, USA
ohxxx245@umn.edu

[2] Department of Software Design and Management,
Gachon University, Republic of Korea
orjeong@gachon.ac.kr

[3] Department of Electrical and Computer Engineering,
Sungkyunkwan University, Republic of Korea
leees@skku.edu

Abstract. Recently, various place recommendation systems are being used by users under social network environment. As the place service gets composed of only the limited categories in case of being made up of the expert knowledge, it has a factor of lacking the information desired by users. In this study, a collective intelligence based QnA information in which many of users participate in was used in order to supplement the details lacking in the place information that was being built up through the existing expert knowledge. Based on these, this paper proposes a place recommendation service using the collective intelligence and heterogeneous information source convergence. Also, the fact that the method we have proposed is able to provide the place recommendation service in a useful way under the location based social network environment was shown through the experiment.

Keywords: Collective Intelligence, Location Based Services, Heterogeneous Information Source Convergence.

1 Introduction

Collective intelligence stands for the collective ability shown as many objects that belong to a group cooperate or compete with their own intellectual ability. This can solve the problems that require a great deal of effort or is impossible for one object to solve. The research of looking for an example of similar collective intelligence is being continued in various domains. In the web service domains, Wikipedia is representing the collective intelligence since the appearance of Web 2.0. Recently, various forms of collective intelligence service can be found[1] [2] [3] [4] [5][6][14].

Many services exist in a same domain and some of them provide similar services. Each service may have small scale of collective intelligence features. The users normally do not use the similar services at the same time and have tendency of using

V. Guyot (Ed.): ICAIT 2012, LNCS 7593, pp. 169–176, 2013.

the services that are suitable for their own taste. As a result, the users show an appearance of being dispersed according to the service they are using. It is necessary to integrate these services or their information in order to create a large scale of collective intelligence in the perspective of domain. But the current services are only considering their inner collective intelligence. The problems created from the various information and forms of each service must be solved during the mutual integration between many services.

A lot of people have been getting a great deal of interest especially in the place recommendation service[11][13]. Recently, various place recommendation services [7][8][9][10] exist on the web and many users are participating in them. These can be considered as the service using collective intelligence because they continue to raise the quality of information as many people participate to share the information on the place. But these are unable to use collective intelligence effectively in building up the information on the place that becomes the base of the services of same domains. They build up the information on the place directly through an expert knowledge. Although such method guarantees the quality of information to a certain extent, it requires a lot of cost and effort. Using the collective intelligence of other similar domains, the place information that becomes the base of place recommendation services can be built up without the knowledge of expert. In this paper, a case study which substitutes the existing place information that has been built up using expert knowledge as the place information built up using collective information by the use of location based services information. Through this study, the necessity of mutual integration of the services having the characteristics of collective information is verified and the issues created during the integration will be investigated. Also, the facts on having a design, which is difficult for each service to become integrated are verified to discuss on the factors that must be considered while designing the services for utilizing as a collective intelligence of large scale.

The remainder of this paper is organized as follows. In Section 2, we explain the proposed convergence process of heterogeneous information source. In Section 3, 4 and 5, we describe the integration process, tagging process and categorizing process in detail. In Section 6, we conclude the paper.

2 The Convergence Process of Heterogeneous Information Source

Figure 1 shows an overall view on the process of the case study proposed in this paper. It integrates by gathering the information provided from various location based social network services. As the place information of location based social network services include noise by itself and include different detailed information from each other, many exceptions must be considered while integrating these. Through the mechanism for supplementing the flaws after the integration, the problems to be created while using the integrated information can be prevented in advance. In this study, the tag and the category that are the most widely used related information have been selected as the supplementation targeted information. Our supplementation process is mainly composed of the process to create a tag and the process to create a category.

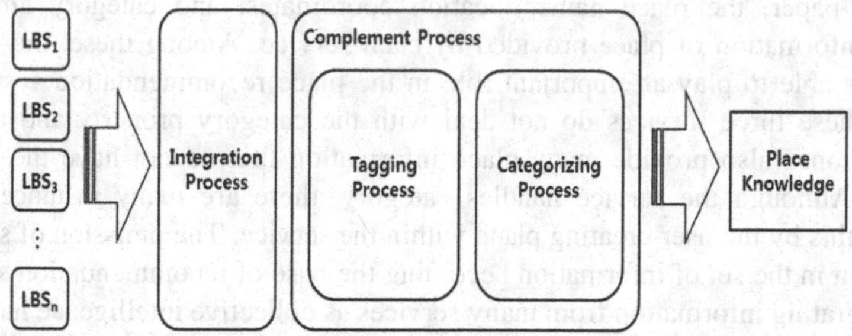

Fig. 1. The Convergence Process of Heterogeneous Information Source

The tagging process uses a heterogeneous information source in order to create a tag. It can use the test of web document search result or QnA search result by having the name of place as the query. These are also the details created by many users on that place. This is the special feature of collective intelligence. We extract the terms that can represent the place as tags by analyzing these results. The categorizing process learns the relationship between the tag and the category of place information that have categories. We determine the category of places that could not have category using a learned classifier. The place information that could not be used in the recommendation service because of not having categories will get to have categories through the supplementation process. The flaw of integrated place information gets reduced through our supplementation process. The supplemented integrated place information can be used as the place knowledge for the place recommendation service. But this information still has the problem to be solved in quality although it is abundant in quantity. These problems have been started from the problem on the design of location-based services that have provided the place information we used as the source of information. These services have not considered the collective intelligence between services when they were designed. The decline of collective intelligence efficiency caused by such design will be discussed at the end of this paper.

3 Integration Process

During the integration process, we gather place information from various location based social networks. Recently, many location-based services are appearing and more services are gradually providing the API for providing the information created from their own system. Using this API, the service providers are able to use the information provided by various services as the base knowledge for their own service. The place information was gained from three location based social network services called Brightkite, Foursquare and Gowalla in this study. These are top three location based social network services with most number of users worldwide. These services commonly deal with the place information in their own system. But they handle different property information from each other on the place.

In this paper, the place name, location coordinates, and category among the property information of place provided by each service. Among these, the category property is able to play an important role in the place recommendation system. But some of these three services do not deal with the category property and a part of remaining ones also provide many place information that do not have the category property. Although the service handles category, there are many instances of not assigning this by the user-creating place within the service. The omission of such core information in the set of information becoming the base of recommendation service is fatal. Integrating information from many services as collective intelligence has a lot of omitted information due to its nature. In our case, the property information called category falls under this (Table 1). Although only the information that has not omitted the target property information can be utilized, the integrated information can be quantitatively insufficient in this case. In order to supplement the category property omitted from such integrated information, we have applied a special process on the proposed case study. The next section explains this process in details.

Table 1. Example of Integrated Place Information

ID	Name	Latitude	Longitude	Category	Visits
37	Yum Yum Donuts	34.028237	-118.201088	Food	20
55	76 Gas Station	34.032977	-118.183792	-	37

4 Tagging Process

We have integrated the information of the services dealing with the place. Their partial omission of information makes the information set imperfect. The omitted information can be supplemented from other information sources. As the information such as name, latitude and longitude of the place exists even if the category information is omitted, the related information can be found using these as keywords. Also, many web services provide the function to conveniently use their information. The place information built up by an expert on the web is not used. This contradicts with our research objective. The accumulated information created little by little for a long period of time by many users has been used. But as there is so much information on the web, an effort is required even in verifying whether they are appropriate information. The two types of methods that can minimize such effort have been designed. The first candidate is the crawling by searching the websites such as Google. The web search services have the function of providing the information with greatest relationship with the keyword as priority. The text information of these can be imported and used by accessing the web page through the link of search results. The second candidate is to use the QnA services implementing the collective intelligence as the users ask and answer questions among each other. Although the quantity of information that can be gained from the services such as Ask.com or Yahoo Answers is little compared to the quantity of information through the web search, it has very little noise compared to the web search information. The common contents exist regardless of the characteristics of the information provided on the web page. The web page structures such as the contents related to log-in, navigation, company information or copyright and the programming contents such as html or JavaScript fall under these contents. The QnA services [12] provide questions and answers that are purely composed of the natural language. In fact, they have less unnecessary noise. Therefore, we will supplement the omitted information of the integrated place information using the information of Yahoo Answers. Just like the three locations based social network services providing the place information, Yahoo Answers provides the API to easily use one's own information. All questions are managed as ID while both the texts of selected answers and other answers on each question are provided[5].

We have gained the related questions from the QnA service using the name of place as the keyword. The search results on the related question of Yahoo Answers provide everything including the title of question, contents, selected reply and other replies. We can extract the keywords related to the corresponding place by analyzing these contents. We have eliminated the insignificant terms such as "a", "the" and "I'm" or the constructions commonly used in various situations of colloquial style. There are various parts of speech on the remaining terms. We have determined that the category will be useful in verifying the category. The most frequently appeared top 20 terms becomes the tags of the corresponding place. The number of tags is influence by the quantity of related search results on the question. A famous and popular place gets to have many keywords. The number of tags is different depending on the quantity of QnA texts. The verified tags may seem unrelated to the place by intuition. But some are clearly the terms that also intuitively express the place. Also, it is possible to infer the specific information of the place through the tags because the remaining terms may mechanically show a pattern related to the place itself or the one related to the features of the place.

5 Categorizing Process

In a recommendation service, the category is even more necessary in order to provide the information, which is suitable for the preference of user. For this reason, we have selected the category as a target for supplementation among many imperfect properties created while using the place information by integration in this study. In order to use the integrated place information as the base knowledge of recommendation service, the category property becoming the most basic property must not be omitted.

The tags related to the place verified from the former process may express the place or play the role of connecting the place and the category although not intuitively. The proposed process has used the Naive Bayesian Inference that was widely used in the past as it is one cast study substituting the existing expert knowledge of place recommendation service by integrating the place information of location based social network as collective intelligence. Although the tags may appear by being related to a specific category, it may also appear by different degree on all categories. The Bayesian network is effective in dealing with such uncertainty. While the classification method using Naive Bayesian sets the precondition as unrealistic strong independences assumption, it is effective for supervised learning. The spam mail filter through Naive Bayesian classifier is a famous example.

While importing the information on the place from the location based social network services, the ones that do not omit the category property have been used as training sets. The training sets that can learn the relationship between the tags and the category are created after verifying through the tagging process of their tags. Each tag term verified from the place information of training set has different relative appearance frequency depending on the category of the related place. Through such characteristics, we can verify the tag of place information without the category property to determine the category. Figure 2 shows the Naive Bayesian network used in the categorizing process. Each tag works independently have influence on determining the category.

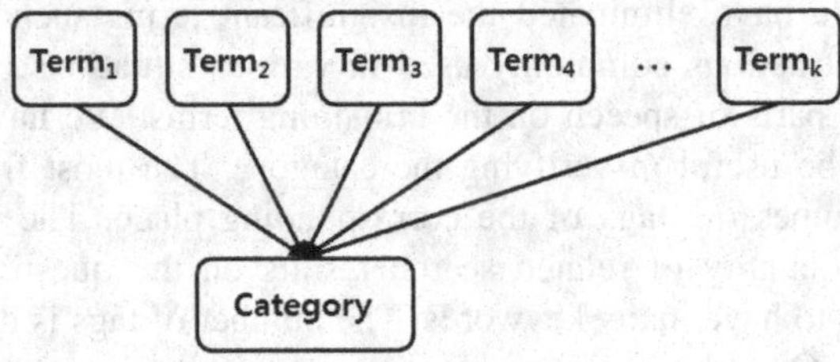

Fig. 2. Naive Bayesian Network Determining the Category from the Tags

The category having the highest posterior determines the category of the corresponding place. The posterior is calculated by the following formula.

$$p(C|T_1, \dots, T_n) = \frac{p(C)\prod_{i=1}^{n} p(T_i|C)}{p(T_1, \dots, T_n)} \quad (1)$$

C indicates each category and T indicates each term. The $p(T_i \mid C)$ multiplied at the numerator of above formula stands for the appeared frequency of each term on the total number of training cases that was classified as the corresponding category. One problem gets created while calculating the posterior in a special case where the evidence variable increases depending on the quantity of training sets just like this study. (a) We have considered 20 tags on one place. A great number of terms are appeared on each category while learning the tags and categories related to many places. This makes the number of appearances on the frequently appeared terms very few compared to the sum of appeared frequency on all words considered in learning. In this case, a very small value gets multiplied to the Formula (1) even if the word appeared while learning appears during the test. (b) In addition, the related terms between categories are appeared by relatively clear classification in this study. Therefore, the number of terms with appeared frequency of 0 gets increased on each category as we keep on learning more cases. If these terms not appeared while learning gets appeared during the test, 0 gets multiplied to Formula (1). Although a very small number which is not 0 can be applied by adjusting this number, many very small numbers are calculated whether the term appeared during the test appears during the training or not. In result, the posterior calculated on the category becomes a very small number to have difficulty in calculating and comparing. Therefore, 1 instead of 0 was multiplied to have prevent having influence on the posterior in case of (b).

Thus, the category on the place not including the category information among the place within the integrated information can be determined by solving the posterior calculation problem of Naive Bayesian network in a form which there is a vast number of evidence nodes. As the posterior gets reduced only in case where the term appeared during the training appears during the test, the category of a case in which the posterior is the smallest has been selected.

The purpose of study was to substitute the base place knowledge built up using expert knowledge in the recommendation service by integrating the information created by each of many users. The category property, which is the important information must not be omitted in order to be used for the recommendation. But the integrated place information was imperfect. Using the proposed process, the first imperfect integrated place information has been supplemented.

6 Conclusion

People have been sharing the place they know well from long time ago. As the computer has appeared and the web has developed, such action was changed into a service of providing place information or recommending the place. As the mobile devices that can verify the location information became widely spread, the services that had not utilized the concepts of location and place in the past have started utilizing them. Especially, the location based social networks are being changed into a form of sharing the location and the place information with the existing text using the location information of user. For the future studies, there would be better information source other than the method of getting information through QnA service and web crawling. The necessary related information could be supplemented even on the places that are not relatively famous existing only in specific areas. Also, the quantitative effect as well as the qualitative effect could be gained using collective intelligence.

Acknowledgments. This work was supported by Gachon University Research Fund in 2012, and by Basic Science Research Program through the National Research Foundation of Korea (NRF) funded by the Ministry of Education, Science and Technology (2012-0004177). This work was supported by National Research Foundation of Korea Grant funded by the Korean Government (Ministry of Education, Science and Technology.(NRF-2011–D00201).

References

1. Furtado, V., Ayres, L., Oliveira, M., Vasconcelos, E., Caminha, C., D'Orleans, J., Belchior, M.: Collective intelligence in law enforcement – The WikiCrimes system. Information Sciences 180(2), 4–17 (2010)
2. Yu, Y.H., Kim, J.H., Shin, K., Jo, G.S.: Recommendation system using location-based ontology on wireless internet: An example of collective intelligence by using 'mashup' applications. Expert Systems with Applications 36(9), 11675–11681 (2009)
3. Lykourentzou, I., et al.: CorpWiki: A self-regulating wiki to promote corporate collective intelligence through expert peer matching. Information Sciences 180(1), 18–38 (2010)
4. Gregg, D.: Developing a collective intelligence application for special education. Decision Support Systems 47, 455–465 (2009)
5. Oh, J.H., Jeong, O.R., Lee, E.S., Kim, W.: A framework for collective intelligence from internet Q&A documents. IJWGS 7(2), 134–146 (2011)
6. Agarwal, N., Galan, M., Liu, H., Subramanya, S.: WisColl: Collective wisdom based blog clustering. Journal of Information Sciences 180, 39–61 (2010)
7. Huang, Y., Bian, L.: A Bayesian network and analytic hierarchy process based personalized recommendations for tourist attractions over the Internet. Expert Systems with Applications 36(1), 933–943 (2009)
8. Kapetanios, E.: Quo Vadis computer science: From Turing to personal computer, personal content and collective intelligence. Data & Knowledge Engineering 67(2), 286–292 (2008)
9. Schiaffino, S., Amandi, A.: Building an expert travel agent as a software agent. Expert Systems with Applications 36(2), 1291–1299 (2009)
10. Yim, H.S., Ahn, H.J., Kim, J.W., Park, S.J.: Agent-based adaptive travel planning system in peak seasons. Expert Systems with Applications 27(4), 211–222 (2004)
11. Foursquare, https://foursquare.com/
12. Yahoo Answer, http://answers.yahoo.com/
13. Gowalla, http://gowalla.com/
14. Jeong, O.R., Oh, J.H.: Social Community Based Blog Search Framework. In: Third International Workshop on Social Networks and Social Web Mining, pp. 130–141 (2012)

Providing Reliability for Transactional Mobile Agents

Linda Zeghache, Michel Hurfin, Izabela Moise, and Nadjib Badache

CERIST - INRIA
l.zeghache@dtri.cerist.dz
{michel.hurfin,izabela.moise}@inria.fr
badache@wissal.dz
http://www.cerist.dz, http://www.inria.fr

Abstract. A transactional agent is a mobile agent that migrates from a site to another one in order to execute a distributed transaction assigned by a user. Works on transactional mobile agents have identified two problems that can not be solved by the agent alone. The first one is related to the reliability. The lack of a fault tolerant infrastructure and methodologies that address fault tolerant execution of mobile agents highlights a major drawback of this technology. The second problem for which the agent needs assistance is related to the atomic validation of the transaction. In this paper we address the mobile agent fault tolerance and the transactional support.

Keywords: Mobile agent, Fault tolerance, Distributed transaction, Atomic commitment, Commit at destination.

1 Introduction

The mobile agent technology aims at moving the code where the data are produced. Consequently, this technology seems appropriate for distributed transactions. A mobile agent is a computer program that can migrate autonomously from node to node, in order to perform some computation on behalf of the code's owner[7]. In our context, the code's owner is the customer who issues a transaction and expects a firm commitment of n traders about its n requests. A transaction can be used to organize the future walk of a customer: executing the transaction leads to identify n shops that can satisfy the client's requirements and make the necessary bookings of items. To illustrate this point, let us consider the following booking scenario.

When his car arrives at a mall, a client may launch a transaction denoted P;R;M;T which expresses his following booking requirements. Just before lunchtime, this client wants to find a shady place in the parking lot of the shopping center (request P, for Parking). Then, he wants to have breakfast on the terrace of a crowded but quiet restaurant, if a table protected from wind and sun is available (request R, for Restaurant). Today is the birthday of his girlfriend Christina. After lunch, he wishes to purchase an album from any metal band

V. Guyot (Ed.): ICAIT 2012, LNCS 7593, pp. 177–190, 2013.

among the top ten best-selling albums of the week but only if this album appears on the play-list of at least one customer who has about the same age as Christina (request M, for Music). Furthermore, he wants to offer her a black T-shirt on which the band name is printed (request T, for T-shirt).

The agent is in charge of exploring a geographical area (i.e. the mall). In order to move within this area, it relies on both fixed and ad-hoc networks. Indeed, an agent is a proven solution to cope with the dynamic changes that continually modify the topology (connections and disconnections, node's movings). Herein, for each of the n stages of the transaction, the agent must identify a node (called a place) able to satisfy the corresponding request. A node is defined as either a static or a mobile device owned by a trader. By definition, a node is a computing unit that provides an appropriate infrastructure to support a mobile agent migrating to and from that location. For a given request, a node is able, first, to test if it may satisfy the request and, second, to execute the corresponding work if needed. During both the test and the request's execution, a node may interact with its surrounding environment and in particular with available devices located nearby. As sensor-generated data fluctuate both with time and with the location of a device, the values taken into account are those available at the time of the visit of the agent. Regarding its communication capabilities, during the visit of an agent, a node can provide an IP address which can be used later to contact this node directly.

The concept of transactional mobile agent has been introduced as a mix between the agent technology and the transactional model. During its move, the agent discovers and visits n places that satisfy the n requests. During the agent's visit, a node records enough information so that it can subsequently either commit or abort the transaction.

Different works on transactional mobile agents [1][2][3][4][5] have identified two problems that can not be solved by the agent alone. The first one is related to the reliability. Any software or hardware component in a distributed system can be subject to failures : Agents and nodes may fail. After a certain time, the agent owner finds that the agent has not returned yet. In an asynchronous system such as the Internet it is impossible to detect correctly whether the agent has failed or is merely slow. Therefore, the agent owner has to wait for the agent to return. However, the agent execution can only proceed if the failed machine and the agent recover. In the meantime, the agent execution is blocked. Blocking is thus undesirable in a mobile agent execution and mechanisms that prevent blocking are needed. The problem of blocking is a fundamental issue in fault tolerance and can be addressed by masking the occurrence of failures in a computing system to the user. The mechanism suggested for this is replication. Although replication prevents blocking, it may lead to a violation of the exactly-once execution property. For instance, sending another agent if the first does not return after a certain time is a form of replication and may lead to multiple executions. Failure detection and recovery procedures that prevent blocking and ensure that the agent is executed exactly-once have to be defined.

The second problem for which the agent needs assistance is related to the atomic validation of the transaction. In the later example, there exists a dependence between the actions of the mobile agent, in that they all need to succeed or none at all. It is an additional property, called *execution atomicity*, that must be ensured. This property is crucial for any mobile agents performing dependent operations. Execution atomicity, however, is not sufficient. Rather, the mobile agent execution needs to run as a transaction ensuring the ACID properties (i.e., atomicity, consistency, isolation, durability)[8].

The rest of the paper is organized as follows. Section 2 defines our system model. Section 3 describes the proposed protocol. Section 4 gives the performance of our protocol implementation. Finally, Section 5 puts our contribution in perspective through some final remarks.

2 System Model

We assume an asynchronous distributed system in which there is no bound on message delay or process relative speed. Communication takes place exclusively through message exchange.

2.1 Agents, Places and Itinerary

We distinguish two types of agents, see Figure 1. When a client launches a transaction T_α, a *mobile agent* a is created. This agent is able to migrate autonomously throughout a defined geographical area. Within this region any node that offers services must also provide an execution environment that allows the agent to reach the node and to execute its code. Thus codes related to the n different stages of the transaction can be transferred and executed on remote sites. A second type of agent is used to detect and recover the mobile agent. We call it a *watch agent*. A watch agent is in charge of executing a monitoring code on behalf of its creator once this one has left the node. According to the usual terminology, a visited node is called a place as it corresponds to a context in which the agent executes. The node where the agent a is initially created corresponds to the place p_0. Starting from this initial place, the agent will move to discover a path (called an itinerary). Each place implements a service called the *Lookup directory* which allows to store information about the agent that has visited this place.

The notation T_α refers to a transaction uniquely identified by α. We assume that a client generates a different identifier for each new transaction. Let us assume that the transaction T_α consists of n successive requests: $T_\alpha \equiv R^1_\alpha; R^2_\alpha; ...; R^i_\alpha; ...; R^n_\alpha$. The integer value x is called the stage of the request R^x_α while n represents the length of the transaction.

Places that provide a similar service such as selling T-Shirts are called *alternative places*. However, the places are provided by different shops, they are not replicas of each other. For each stage x, the number of alternative nodes that may satisfy a request R^x_α depends on the demand of the client. Obviously, a

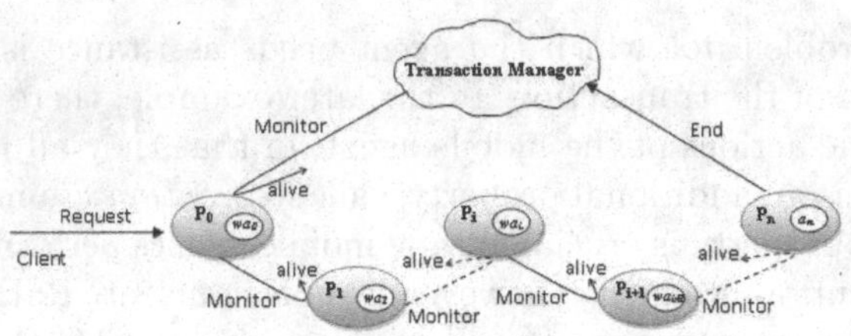

Fig. 1. Agent System Model

client that is looking for a place to eat is less difficult to please than a client looking only for a pizzeria.

The sequence of places between the agent source and destination (i.e., $p_0, p_1, ..., p_n$) is called the *itinerary* of the mobile agent. An itinerary must satisfy the following property: if a place p_k is listed in the itinerary, the associated node has confirmed that it was able to execute the request R_α^k at the time of the visit of the agent. We assume that each place provides an interface to allow the agents to compute and commit the service requests. The method Execute() computes the request Ri of the transaction T and returns the result. This result can be null if the service is not available and can't be satisfied. We assume that the resources required to provide the service are booked for a limited period of time. A booking can be canceled at any time and for any reason (timeout expired, reallocation of the resources to another request,...). We define an entity called a Transaction Manager to manage the execution of the distributed transaction.

2.2 Fault Model

Machines, places, or agents can fail. A failing place causes all agents running on it to fail as well. Similarly, a failing machine causes all places and agents on this machine to fail as well. A link failure causes the loss of the messages or agents currently in transmission on this link. The failures mentioned above are called infrastructure failures. As we deal with transactional agents we consider the failure of the request execution (unfavorable outcome). If the requirements expressed by a request can not be fullfilled, the outcome is unfavorable: we consider that a semantic failure has occured during the execution of this request[6].

3 Proposed Protocol

The proposed solution is based on temporal replication and recovery to ensure the fault tolerance of the agent. This agent executes a distributed transaction composed of n requests. Each request is executed on a place of the network. The agent ensures the atomicity of the transaction relying on a commit at destination approach. In this case an atomic commitment protocol is applied at the end of the execution of the n requests. Our protocol in based on the behaviour of the Mobile agent (ma), Watch Agent (wa) and the TM:

3.1 Mobile Agent Behaviour

Service Execution and Path Discovery. When a client launches a transaction T_α, a mobile agent Aa is created. This agent moves to n different places to execute the requests of the transaction. At each place p_i the agent identifies the alternative places that may satisfy the request of the next stage S_{i+1}. As the identities of the n nodes are not specified in the transaction itself, a mechanism for discovering sites that are likely to participate in the transaction is required. In order to be selected to execute a request, a node has usually to be registered in public repositories as a possible alternative for this type of request. In a commercial context, such a registration is natural and is part of the promotion process and business development: it helps to inform potential customers about the services and products offered. The discovery process may rely on various mechanisms. The fact that a node is considered as an alternative node does not imply that it can currently satisfy the client's needs. For example, a registered restaurant is perhaps already full or its noise level is too high compared to the wishes of the client. For a given request, once different alternative nodes have been discovered, their ability to execute the request is evaluated in an order that is usually not left to chance. For example, minimizing the physical distance between any two consecutive nodes involved in the transaction can be an extra wish of the client. To take into account such an additional requirement, a greedy strategy is often chosen. The different stages of the request are analyzed in sequence: looking for a solution at stage $x+1$ begins only once a node N_i that satisfies the request R_α^x has been found. The alternative nodes that may execute the request R_α^{x+1} are considered one after another from the nearest to farthest from N_i till one of them is able to satisfy the request. This greedy strategy often, but not always, yields an optimal solution where the physical path that connects all the selected nodes is minimal. In commercial applications, the execution of a request typically results in the booking of some resources. As a consequence, reservations made during the visit of an agent can be cancelled very late (when the transaction is aborted). In general, a long-lasting booking of resources is not desirable. It can be detrimental to the trader's interest. Indeed, while a resource is blocked, the seller may refuse to satisfy other requests that require the same resource. If the transaction (for which the trader was prepared to satisfy a request) aborts, he may miss many sales. Consequently, we suppose that the trader keeps control over its resources for as long as possible. When an alternative node N_i is contacted to execute a request R_α^x , it has to assess whether it can satisfy the request and run it once. If the node can not satisfy the request, the outcome is negative and the node keeps no information about its failed attempt to execute the request. Otherwise, if enough resources are available and all the operations are successful, the outcome is positive. In that case, the required local resources are booked on a temporary basis and the result of the execution, as well as how this computation may later affect the local state of the node are logged in a versatile memory. At this point, the node has made no firm commitment. A booking can be cancelled at any time and for any reason (timeout expired, reallocation of the resources to another request,...). In a trading context, a request often refers to local resources that are for sale (articles, deliveries, ...). If they are not available, the request can not be satisfied by the node. If the transaction commits, they are purchased and consumed by the client. As mentioned before, the resource allocation system has to be as flexible as possible. In particular, firm booking have to be done as late as possible. In our example, a shopkeeper can set aside an item (a parking space, a table, a disk, or a T-shirt). During a limited period of time, this product will be considered already sold or assigned. Yet, the node can revoke this temporary commitment.

Fault Detection and Recovery. In the above description, nothing complicates and delays the progress of the agent. Yet as mentioned before, two phenomena disrupt the creation of an itinerary. First, the node selected to be the next place is not always able to satisfy the request's requirements. Second, crash failures may affect the agent and the node currently visited. To cope with crash failure, monitoring mechanisms have to be created and activated by the agent itself all along its itinerary. More precisely, before leaving the place p_k to migrate to p_{k+1}, the agent creates a fixed agent called a watch agent which observes the agent during its attempt to move. A watch agent is in charge of executing a monitoring code on behalf of its creator once this one has leaved the place. In favorable circumstances, the agent will create a path of length n and will leave behind n watch agents (one per site visited). Failures are detected using classical detection mechanisms: to prove that it is still alive an agent sends periodically messages to the last created watch agent. Before starting its execution, the mobile agent registers in the lookup directory of the current place. This service allow to give information about each agent that have visited the corresponding place. An entry in the LD contains the following information:

- *Tid* : Transaction Identifier.
- Tag : The tag associated to the mobile agent execution stage. It is presented in the next section.
- Stage : The current stage.
- State : The agent execution state, it takes four possible values : Computing (the agent is executing the request), Satisfied (the agent finished the execution of the request which is satisfied), Unsatisfied (the agent finished the execution of the request but it is not satisfied), Crashed (abnormal termination of the agent execution because of a failure).

The directory service allows to get the state of the agent execution in the local place. When a watch agent receives no messages, it suspects that a crash has occurred on the next place. It sends a replica of the mobile agent to the suspected place. The replica Consults the directory service (LD) to check the state of the suspected agent and acts according to that state. When the state is *crashed*, it tries to restart the execution of the request. However, if the state is *computing* it sends a message *alivema* to the watch agent at the previous place and dies. When the state is *unsatisfied* it sends the message *failed* to the watch agent and dies. Finally, if the state is *satisfied* it sends the message *alivewa* to previous and dies. Of course, as the monitoring of the agent is performed by a single watch agent which may fail, this watch agent has also to be monitored. To solve this problem, all the watch agents form a chain of control that maps the last itinerary discovered by the agent. The watch agent of the visited place p_k is monitored by the watch agent of the previous place p_{k-1}. Of course, such a solution relies on the assumption that the first element in the chain (i.e. the place p_0) is either safe or under the control of another external entity that is reliable. Once this germ of reliability is established, the simple monitoring mechanism allows to detect failures (crash of a visited node, crash of the agent) and to create a new copy of the agent.

3.2 Watch Agent Behaviour

The watch agent is created at each stage to monitor the mobile agent execution. It waits for the periodic heartbeats (alivema messages) sent by the mobile agent. The watch agent itself must be fault tolerant. This is ensured by using a chain dependency consisting of all the watch agents created along the itinerary of an agent. Every watch agent wa_i monitors its successor wa_{i+1} and the most recent one added to the chain, monitors the mobile agent :

$$wa_0 \rightarrow wa_1 \rightarrow \ldots wa_{i-1} \rightarrow wa_i \rightarrow ma$$

Each watch agent sends *alivewa* messages to its previous in the chain. When the watch agent receives this message for the first time it switches from the monitoring of the mobile agent to the monitoring of the watch agent. The head of the chain must be monitored to preserve the dependency. In this article this task is delegated to the service of the availability of the Source (denoted AS) provided by the support network; the dependency becomes as follows:

$$AS \rightarrow wa_0 \rightarrow wa_1 \rightarrow \ldots wa_{i-1} \rightarrow wa_i \rightarrow ma$$

The pseudo code of the watch agent is depicted in the Figure 2. It is composed of three tasks:

- Task 1(the delegation): When the watch agent is created for the first time, it is responsible of sending the heartbeats of the mobile agent. This means that the watch agent checks periodically the state of the mobile agent and sends the *alivema* messages to the previous in the chain dependency. When the mobile agent moves to the next place, the watch agent skips this task.
- Task 2 (the watching): After the migration of the mobile, the watch agent starts the watching task. It waits for the messages sent by the agent at the next place. If it does not receive a message within a timeout period, it suspects a failure of either the agent or the place where the agent is running. So it sends a new copy of the agent to the suspected place. When the new copy reaches that place, it verifies the state of the suspected agent and reports the state to the watch agent by sending a corresponding message:

```
Class Watch Agent {
Control=false;
Dependency ={previous, next};
Task 1:
1. Periodically do {
2. getAgentState() ;
3. if state =running send alivema to previous
4. if state = moved  Control=true;
5. if state=crashed  LookDir.state='crashed'; die();
}
6. While true {
Task 2:
If (Control) {
1.  || wait receive alivema
2.     Reset (timeout);
3.  || wait receive alivewa
4.     Reset (timeout);
5.  || wait receive failed
6.     Send ma to an alternative place
7. || wait receive double
8.     Send double to previous; control=false;
9.  || wait receive end
10.  Send end to previous; control=false;
11.|| wait Timeout
12.      Restore  ma from the checkpoint
13.|| wait receive Canceled
14.     Send failed to previous
15.|| wait receive End
16.     send end to previous, control=false
17.     Periodically send (alivewa) to previous;
 }

Task 3:
18.|| wait receive prepare
19.     Send vote (Tid, R_i, Tag);
20.|| wait receive decide (outcome)
21.     Send decide (Tid, R_i, Tag, outcome); Die;
21. ||wait receive terminate
22.     decide (Tid, R_i, Tag, 'abort'); Die();
    } //end while
}// end class
```

Fig. 2. The Watch Agent Pseudo Code

– If the state is *computing*: it means that the agent is still running on the current place and the alivema message is lost, so it sends *alivema* to its previous and dies;
– If the state is *unsatisfied*: this means that the agent finished the computation of the request with no satisfaction. So it sends *failed* to its previous and dies;
– If the state is *satisfied*: this means that the agent finished its computation and moved to another place. So it checks if the watch agent still exists otherwise it creates it and sends *alivewa* to its previous and dies;
– If the state is *crashed*: this means that the agent disappears and its computation is undone, so it sets the state to *computing* and tries to execute the request again. Whenever, the mobile agent can't reach the suspected place, it tries to discover an alternative place. If this research fails, the agent informs its watch agent by sending a failed message.

The watch agent detects a semantic failure when the service is not delivered for the following causes: 1) the request is not satisfied (service not available) and the mobile agent sends a failed message to the watch agent, 2) There is no alternative place for the next stage (no place offers the service) , 3) The service provider cancelled the booking for some reason according to its booking strategy (the service is no more available, the booking timeout period is reached, etc.) so the service provider sends a cancelled message to the watch agent. In case of semantic failure the watch agent starts a new copy of the mobile agent on an alternative place if any. Otherwise it sends failed message to its previous in the chain dependency.
- Task 3 (The commit): Besides the controlling behavior (Task2), the watch agent has another role (Task3) which consists of the participation in the commitment of the global transaction. In this task the watch agent expects three types of messages: 1) Prepare (Tid, Tag): Upon the arrival of this message from the AC service, the watch agent invokes the vote method which checks the state of request if it is still *Booked*, it sets this state at *PrepareYes* and returns *yes.* If the state is *Cancelled* the vote method returns *NO* and sets the state at *PrepareNo.* The watch agent sends the returned value to the AC service. 2) Decide (Tid, Tag, outcome): Upon the arrival of this message, the watch agent invokes the decide() primitive which acts according to the outcome value: if the outcome is *Commit*: the transaction is committed and the state is set to *Commit.* If the outcome is *Abort*: the transaction is aborted. After committing or aborting the transaction the watch agent dies. If the outcome is Release: the prepared transaction is released which means the resources are unlocked without committing or aborting the transaction. And the state *PrepareYes* is changed to *Booked.* If the state is *PrepareNo*, it doesn't change. 3) Terminate (Tid,Tag): upon the arrival of this message, the watch agent aborts the transaction in the current place by invoking decide (Tid, R_x, Tag, *Abort*) and dies.

3.3 The Exactly-Once Execution

Perfect failure detectors, which eventually detect all failures, are unrealistic in the Internet. Hence, we assume unreliable failure detectors that can make false suspicions. A correct agent can be erroneously suspected to be crashed by an watch agent located on the previous place. In that case, a new agent is generated and moves towards an alternative node while the former continues its way in the network. Both agents follow different paths but can later visit the same node regarding the same request. In that case, we define a strategy presented bellow, that authorizes only one agent to progress the others are stopped to ensure exactly-once execution. Any node visited by two agents regarding the same request of the same transaction, can easily determine (at the time of the second visit) in which order it has received the two agents (the oldest and then the newest or the newest and then the oldest). A node authorizes an agent to progress only if its visit is the first one related to this request or if all the previous visits have been done by older agents and that the transaction is not committed. When a agent is not authorized to continue, it stops its execution and sends a Double message to the external entities. This message contains the prefix of an itinerary that can not be completed.

Note that a node keeps track of all the visits already made by other agents in the Lookup directory (LD). To test if the new visit is allowed or not the node use a *Tag* to date the visits of the agents at each stage. For a visit corresponding to stage S_i of the transaction, the Tag is a sequence of i integers $t_1 t_2 ... t_i$ where each t_j with $1 \leq j \leq i$ is the number of agents that have left the place $p_j - 1$: this includes the first agent that has visited the place $p_j - 1$ and the possible $t_j - 1$ replicas generated by the watch agent located in the place $p_j - 1$. In Figure 3, we illustrate a possible scenario in the case of the transaction P;R;M;T. False suspicions are depicted by dotted crossed lines while real crash are represented by continuous crossed lines. There are two End messages including two full itineraries with two different tags. The first tag equal to 1121 and the second equal to 2211. The Double message contains a partial itinerary and a tag equal to 211. In the next section, we will show that the atomic commitment protocol take advantages of the full itineraries but also of the partial ones.

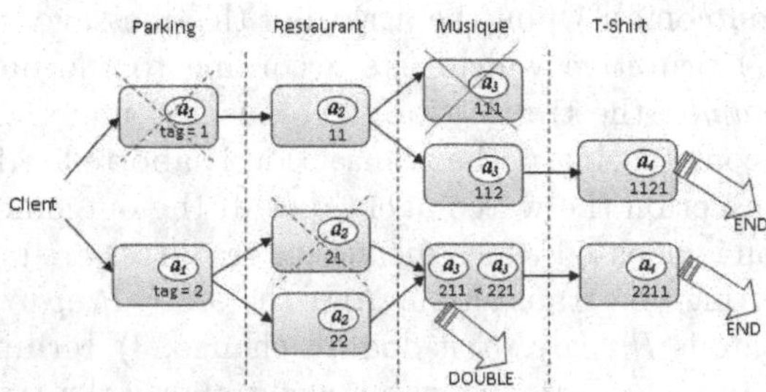

Fig. 3. False suspicions and multiple itineraries

If two agents regarding the same transaction meet at the destination, only one is committed.

3.4 The Transaction Manager

As explained earlier, ensuring the availability of a first place (also called a source, herein) cannot be ensured by an agent alone. A centralized and reliable entity can be defined to assist all the agents in their monitoring, validation and logging tasks. This entity is called *Transaction Manager* (denoted TM). Two services are provided by the TM: Availability of the Sources (denoted AS) and Atomic Commit (denoted AC) see Figure 4.

Whenever it wants to start a new transaction T_α, a client activates the AS service by sending a ReqAS message. The client does not have to remain connected while waiting for the outcome. The AC service is activated when the TM receives a ReqAC message from an agent (or from the AS service).

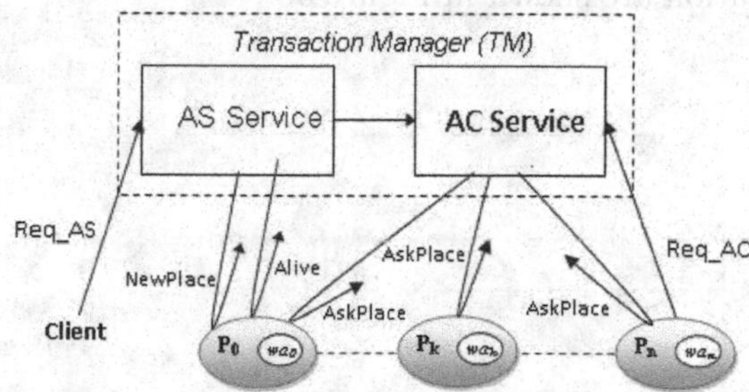

Fig. 4. The Transaction Manager services

Any ReqAC message contains the identities of the visited places. This information denotes either a complete itinerary (composed of one place per stage) or just a prefix of an itinerary. During the migration of an agent, a visited place only confirms that its current state allows to satisfy the request corresponding to the current stage. The AC service constructs possible itineraries and validates one of them when this is possible. The AS service and the monitoring tasks performed by each visited place ensure that at least one message will be received. Thus, AC does not require a timeout mechanism, as it can be sure that at least one agent will contact it. The AC service is activated when a first message related to a given transaction is received. After the receipt of a ReqAC message, AC builds an itinerary (or at least the highest prefix) and tries to test it. All the places on this itinerary participate to the distributed atomic transaction. The AC service sends an *AskPlace* query to all the places and waits for their replies (Yes or No). A place that replies Yes must take the necessary steps for committing or aborting the transaction: it executes the transaction up to the point where it will be asked to commit or to abort. Based on the gathered votes, AC decides whether to commit (only if all votes are Yes) or to wait for alternative places that may substitute a place that voted No or has not yet replied. When the timeout Δ expires, the AC service aborts the transaction. A single reliable machine can act as a stable coordinator and provide both services. To cope with failures that may occur, replicas have to be defined and a leader has to be elected among them.

4 Performance Results

In this section we present some performance result. We implement the proposed protocol on top of an existing mobile agent platform, without modifying existing code. We use JADE[9] as the Java mobile agent platform. The mobile agent classes are not locally available on the places. Our performance tests are run on six machines (Pentium IV 3.00 GHz PCs, 1 Go of RAM). The machines are connected by 100 Mbps Ethernet. The jade platform is running under JDK1.5 Virtual Machine. To measure the performance of the protocol, we use a simple service running on every place. The agent has a small computation to do. The tests are made using the simple agent (not reliable) and the FT-agent (reliable due to all the mechanisms described within this paper). The results of the performance evaluation are shown in Figure 5.

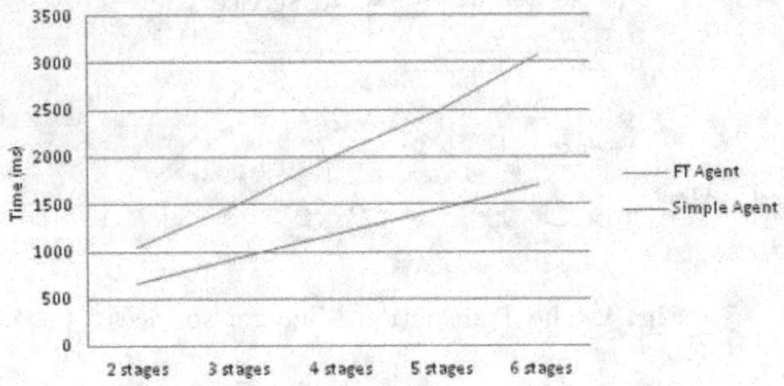

Fig. 5. The costs of Simple Agent and Fault Tolerant Agent execution with increasing number of stages

The FT-Agent introduces a performance overhead of about 160 when compared with the execution time of the simple agent, without fault-tolerance. The protocol offers two advantages. Firstly, temporal replication provides fault tolerance during the mobile agent trip. Secondly, the transactional scheme copes with the long running transaction where the booking can be cancelled before the end of the mobile agent trip. In this case the whole transaction will not be committed. Our protocol anticipates the detection of this semantic failure by launching another agent on another path before the end of the transaction. Failures of places caused by the failures of the physical node or failures of the runtime environment (e. g. the agent system) will be tolerated. After such a failure, the mobile agent will be recovered and sent to another place to create another path. During this recovery time a second failure can happen. In our protocol this second failure could be tolerated. The cost becomes higher when we want to achieve a higher level of fault-tolerance.

Figure 6 depicts the case of catastrophic failure (cascading failure) where each place fails when recovering the agent on the next one, the failed agent is always

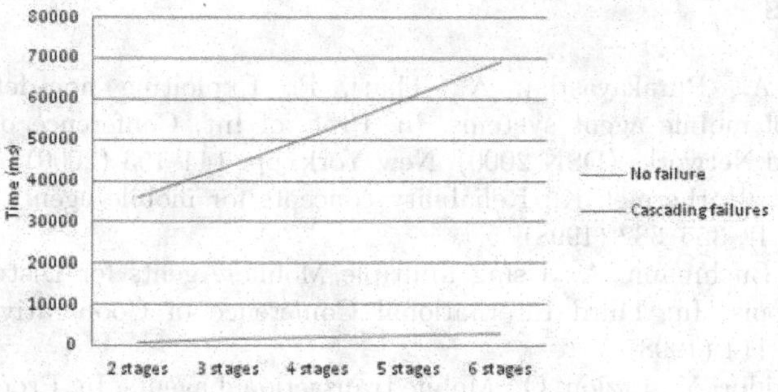

Fig. 6. Round trip time [ms] of a FTAgent in case of Cascading failures

recovered, i.e., we have a 100 recovery. But the time of the round trip of the mobile agent becomes higher because at each place the watch agent waits for the timeout expiration to detect a failure and looks for an alternative place to launch a new agent.

5 Conclusion and Future Works

The main contribution of this work is adding transactional semantics at the execution model of mobile agents and ensuring their reliability. We propose a commit at destination fault-tolerant approach to detect and recover infrastructure failures. This approach prevents blocking and ensures that the agent is executed exactly-once. We present the mobile agent as an adequate technology to implement the concept of transactions, recognized as a powerful approach to model distributed applications. We define a flexible booking strategy that permits to the trader to keep control over its resources for as long as possible and allows to avoid resources locking in case of long running transaction. In the proposed solution, an agent may identify different sets of n nodes that satisfy the requirements expressed in the transaction. Rather than just checking the first one, the commitment phase is revisited to increase the chance of reaching a positive outcome (Commit) by increasing the number of trials. For a given transaction, the atomic commitment protocol can be run multiple times till a significant decision (Abort or Commit) is adopted. A single reliable machine can act as a stable TM and provide both services. To cope with failures that may occur, replicas have to be defined.

References

1. Mohindra, A., Purakayastha, A., Thati, P.: Exploiting non-determinism for reliability of mobile agent systems. In: Proc. of Int. Conference on Dependable Systems and Networks (DSN 2000), New York, pp. 144–153 (2000)
2. Strasser, M., Rothermel, K.: Reliability concepts for mobile agents. Int. J. Coop. Inf. Syst. 7(4), 355–382 (1998)
3. Vogler, H., Buchmann, A.: Using Multiple Mobile Agents for Distributed Transactions, coopis. In: Third International Conference of Cooperative Information Systems, p. 114 (1998)
4. Sher, R., Aridor, Y., Etzion, O.: Mobile transactional agents. In: Proc. of 21st IEEE Int. Conference on Distributed Computing Systems (ICDCS 2001), Phoenix, AZ, pp. 73–80 (2001)
5. Pleisch, S., Sciper, A.: Execution atomicity for non-blocking transactional mobile agents. In: Proc. of Int. Conference on Parallel and Distributed Computing and Systems (PDCS 2003), Marina del Rey, CA (2003)
6. Pleisch, S., Schiper, A.: Approaches to fault-tolerant and transactional mobile agent executionan algorithmic view. ACM Comput. Surv. 36, 219–262 (2004)
7. Object Management Group. Mobile Agent System Interoperability Facilities Specification, OMG TC Document orbos/97-10-05 (November 1997), http://www.omg.org
8. Gray, J., Reuter, A.: Transaction Processing: Concepts and Techniques. Morgan Kaufmann, San Mateo (1993)
9. The Java Agent DEvelopement framework, http://jade.tilab.com/

On the Security of Lv et al.'s Three-Party Authenticated Key Exchange Protocol Using One-Time Key

Eun-Jun Yoon

Department of Cyber Security, Kyungil University,
33 Buho-Ri, Hayang-Ub, Kyungsan-Si, Kyungsangpuk-Do 712-701, Republic of Korea
ejyoon@kiu.ac.kr

Abstract. In 2012, Lv et al. proposed a new three-party authenticated key exchange (3PAKE) protocol using one-time key which aims to achieve more efficiency with the same security level of other existing 3PAKE protocols. Lv et al. claimed that their proposed 3PAKE protocol is secure against various known attacks. However, this paper points out Lv et al.'s 3PAKE protocol is still vulnerable to off-line dictionary attacks unlike their claim.

Keywords: Authentication, 3PAKE, Dictionary attacks, One-time key, Network security, Cryptography.

1 Introduction

Three-party authenticated key exchange protocol (3PAKE) is an important cryptographic technique for secure communication. 3PAKE allows two communication parties to securely agree a fresh session key with the help of a trusted server [1]. Password-based 3PAKE protocol has attracted a lot of attention due to its simplicity and convenience in key agreement. It allow users to communicate securely over public networks simply by using easy-to-remember passwords. Many password-based 3PAKE protocols have been proposed [2–18] in recent years. A good design of the password-based 3PAKE protocol should be secure under various attacks which include common protocol attacks (man-in-the-middle attacks and replay attacks) and cryptanalysis attacks (off-line dictionary attacks, undetectable on-line dictionary attacks, and detectable on-line dictionary attacks)[15–18].

In 2007, Lu and Cao [3] proposed a simple 3PAKE protocol (in short, S-3PAKE) built upon the earlier two-party PAKE protocol due to Abdalla and Pointcheval [4]. However, it is founded out that S-3PAKE is vulnerable to various attacks according to recent works in [5–10, 14]. In 2009, Huang [11] proposed a 3PAKE protocol in five steps without using server's public key. In 2012, Lv et al. [18] proposed a low cost three-party authenticated key exchange protocol with one-time key in order to further improve the security functionality of the scheme claimed in [11]. Lv et al. claimed that their proposed 3PAKE protocol

V. Guyot (Ed.): ICAIT 2012, LNCS 7593, pp. 191–198, 2013.

is more efficient with less time consuming compared with other existing 3PAKE protocols. Moreover, their proposed 3PAKE protocol has been formally verified using AVISPA tools with a systematic security analysis. However, this paper points out Lv et al.'s 3PAKE protocol is still vulnerable to off-line dictionary attacks unlike their claim in which an attacker exhaustively enumerates all possible passwords in an off-line manner to determine the correct one [15–17].

The remainder of this paper is organized as follows. We subsequently review Lv et al.'s 3PAKE protocol in Section 2. The off-line dictionary attacks on Lv et al.'s 3PAKE protocol are presented in Section 3. Finally, we draw conclusions in Section 4.

Table 1. Notation used in Lv et al.'s 3PAKE protocol

A, B	Two clients which also represent their own identities.
S	A trusted server.
pw_a	The symmetric key shared between A and S.
pw_b	The symmetric key shared between B and S.
G, q, g	A finite cyclic group G generated by an element g of a prime order p.
N_b	Nonce chosen by B.
$H(M)$	Secure one-way hash function.
$\{M\}_k$	Ciphertext which symmetric encrypt M with k.

2 Review of Lv et al.'s 3PAKE Protocol

This section reviews the Lv et al.'s 3PAKE [18]. Throughout the paper, notations are employed in Table 1.

Suppose that two participants A and B want to share a new secret session key K with the assistance of the server S for their further communication in Lv et al.'s protocol. Both communication parties cannot authenticate each other directly and have to resort to the trusted server S for a session key agreement based on the Diffie-Hellman key exchange. Fig. 1 depicts the Lv et al.'s 3PAKE protocol, which works as follows.

1. $A \rightarrow B$: $RQ_A = \underbrace{A, g^x, \{A, g^x\}_{H(A,g^x,pw_a)}}$

   A chooses a random number $x \in Z_p$, computes g^x and one-time key $H(A, g^x, pw_a)$, gets $RQ_A = A, g^x, \{A, g^x\}_{H(A,g^x,pw_a)}$ then sends RQ_A to B.
2. $B \rightarrow S$: $RQ_B = \underbrace{B, g^y, \{B, g^y\}_{H(B,g^y,pw_b)}}, RQ_A$

   Upon receiving message from A, B first checks the freshness of g^x, then B chooses a random number $y \in Z_p$ and a nonce N_b, computes g^y and one-time key $H(B, g^y, pw_b)$, gets $RQ_B = B, g^y, \{B, g^y\}_{H(B,g^y,pw_b)}$ then sends RQ_B, RQ_A to S.

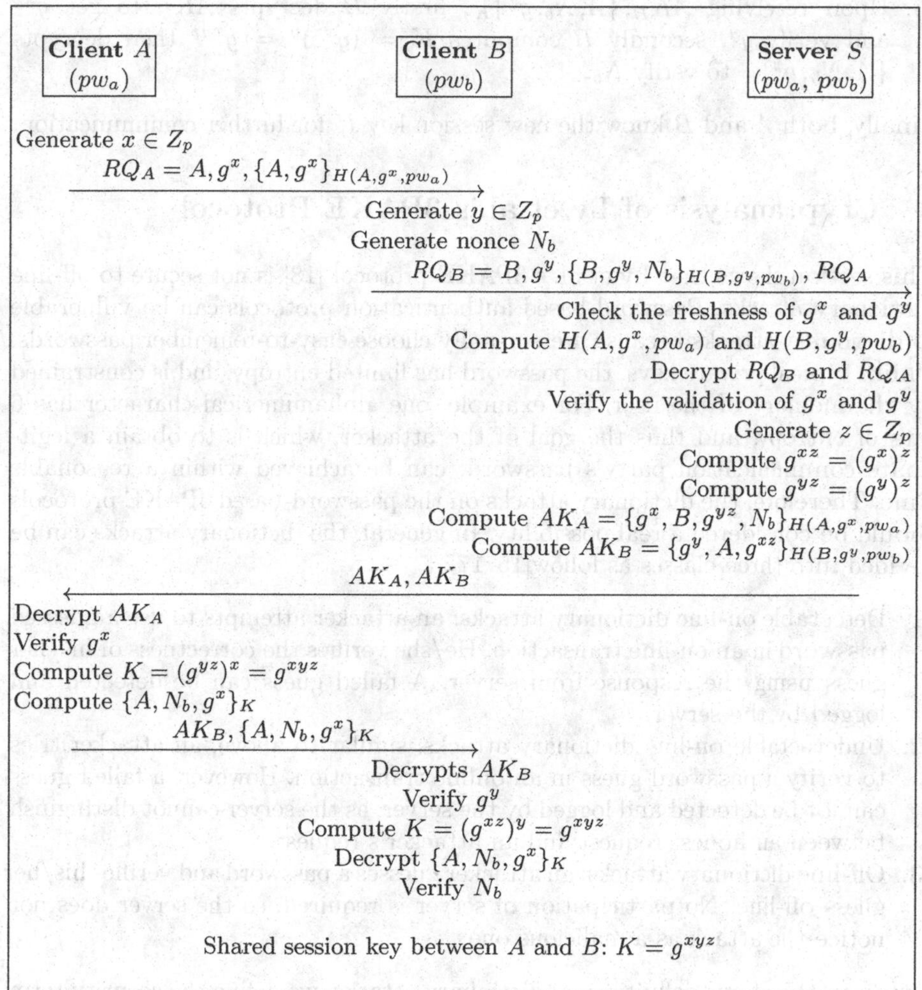

Fig. 1. Lv et al.'s 3PAKE protocol

3. $S \rightarrow A$: $AK_A = \underbrace{\{g^x, B, g^{yz}, N_b\}_{H(A,g^x,pw_a)}}$, $AK_B = \underbrace{\{g^y, A, g^{xz}\}_{H(B,g^y,pw_b)}}$

   Upon receiving RQ_B, RQ_A, the authentication server S first checks the freshness of g^x and g^y, then S uses received g^x, g^y to compute $H(A, g^x, pw_a)$, $H(B, g^y, pw_b)$ respectively then decrypts RQ_B, RQ_A for verification the validation of g^x and g^y. If the verification is failed then stop this session, otherwise S chooses a random number $z \in Z_p$, computes $g^{xz} = (g^x)^z$, $g^{yz} = (g^y)^z$ and gets $AK_A = \{g^x, B, g^{yz}, N_b\}_{H(A,g^x,pw_a)}$, $AK_B = \{g^y, A, g^{xz}\}_{H(B,g^y,pw_b)}$, at last sends AK_A, AK_B to A.
4. $A \rightarrow B$: $AK_B, \{A, N_b, g^x\}_K$

   A decrypts AK_A, verifies g^x, gets g^{yz} and N_b, computes $K = (g^{yz})^x = g^{xyz}$, then gets $\{A, N_b, g^x\}_K$ and sends $AK_B, \{A, N_b, g^x\}_K$ to B.

5. Upon receiving $AK_B, \{A, N_b, g^x\}_K$, firstly B decrypts AK_B to get g^{xz} and verify g^y, secondly B computes $K = (g^{xz})^y = g^{xyz}$ then decrypts $\{A, N_b, g^x\}_K$ to verify N_b.

Finally, both A and B know the new session key K for further communication.

3 Cryptanalysis of Lv et al.'s 3PAKE Protocol

This section shows that Lv et al.'s 3PAKE protocol [18] is not secure to off-line dictionary attacks. Password-based authentication protocols can be vulnerable to dictionary attacks because users usually choose easy-to-remember passwords. Unlike typical private keys, the password has limited entropy, and is constrained by the memory of the user. For example, one alphanumerical character has 6 bits of entropy, and thus the goal of the attacker, which is to obtain a legitimate communication party's password, can be achieved within a reasonable time. Therefore, the dictionary attacks on the password-based 3PAKE protocols should be considered a real possibility. In general, the dictionary attacks can be divided into three classes as follow[15–17]:

1. Detectable on-line dictionary attacks: an attacker attempts to use a guessed password in an on-line transaction. He/she verifies the correctness of his/her guess using the response from server. A failed guess can be detected and logged by the server.
2. Undetectable on-line dictionary attacks: similar to above, an attacker tries to verify a password guess in an online transaction. However, a failed guess cannot be detected and logged by the server, as the server cannot distinguish between an honest request and an attacker's request.
3. Off-line dictionary attacks: an attacker guesses a password and verifies his/her guess off-line. No participation of server is required, so the server does not notice the attack as a malicious one.

Based on the above definitions of dictionary attacks, we define the security term needed for security problem analysis of the Lv et al.'s 3PAKE protocol as follows:

Definition 1. *A weak secret (password pw_i) is a value of low entropy Weak(k), which can be guessed in polynomial time.*

3.1 Off-line Dictionary Attack 1

An adversary can perform the following "off-line dictionary attack 1". Let us assume that an adversary *Eve* has intercepted one of the A's past login request messages, i.e., $RQ_A = \underbrace{A, g^x, \{A, g^x\}_{H(A,g^x,pw_a)}}$. Then *Eve* can perform an off-line dictionary attack to obtain pw_a as follows:

1. *Eve* generates a candidate password pw_a^* from password dictionary which called D.
2. *Eve* computes $H(A, g^x, pw_a^*)$.
3. *Eve* decrypts $\{A, g^x\}_{H(A,g^x,pw_a)}$ with $H(A, g^x, pw_a^*)$ and then obtains (A^*, g^{x^*}).
4. *Eve* compares (A^*, g^{x^*}) with the intercepted (A, g^x).
5. If (A^*, g^{x^*}) is equal to (A, g^x), then *Eve* has guessed the correct password pw_a^* , otherwise, *Eve* performs steps 1-4 repeatedly until $(A^*, g^{x^*}) \equiv (A, g^x)$ by choosing another password pw_a^{**} .

The algorithm of the off-line dictionary attacks for getting the password pw_a is as follows:

Off-line Dictionary Attacks$(A, g^x, \{A, g^x\}_{H(A,g^x,pw_a)}, D)$

```
{
  for i := 0 to |D|
  {
    pw_a* ← D;
    H(A, g^x, pw_a*);
    (A*, g^x*) = {A, g^x}_{H(A,g^x,pw_a)·H(A,g^x,pw_a*)};
    if (A*, g^x*) =? (A, g^x) then
      return pw_a*
  }
}
```

After the adversary *Eve* has obtained the user A's password pw_a^* using the above off-line dictionary attack method, the adversary *Eve* can impersonate A by forging A's sending message $RQ_A^* = \underbrace{A, g^e, \{A, g^e\}_{H(A,g^e,pw_a^*)}}$, where e is a random number $\in Z_p$. Therefore, Lv et al.'s 3PAKE protocol is vulnerable to off-line dictionary attack 1.

3.2 Off-Line Dictionary Attack 2

An adversary can perform the following "off-line dictionary attack 2". Let us assume that an adversary *Eve* has intercepted one of the B's past login request messages, i.e., $RQ_B = B, g^y, \{B, g^y, N_b\}_{H(B,g^y,pw_b)}, RQ_A$. Then *Eve* can perform an off-line dictionary attack to obtain pw_b as follows:

1. *Eve* generates a candidate password pw_b^* from password dictionary which called D.
2. *Eve* computes $H(B, g^y, pw_b^*)$.
3. *Eve* decrypts $\{B, g^y, N_b\}_{H(B,g^y,pw_b)}$ with $H(B, g^y, pw_b^*)$ and then obtains (B^*, g^{y^*}, N_b^*).
4. *Eve* compares (B^*, g^{y^*}) with the intercepted (B, g^y).
5. If (B^*, g^{y^*}) is equal to (B, g^y), then *Eve* has guessed the correct password pw_b^* , otherwise, *Eve* performs steps 1-4 repeatedly until $(B^*, g^{y^*}) \equiv (B, g^y)$ by choosing another password pw_b^{**} .

The algorithm of the off-line dictionary attacks for getting the password pw_b is as follows:

Off-line Dictionary Attacks$(B, g^y, \{B, g^y, N_b\}_{H(B,g^y,pw_b)}, D)$
{
  for $i := 0$ to $|D|$
  {
    $pw_b^* \leftarrow D$;
    $H(B, g^y, pw_b^*)$;
    $(B*, g^{y*}, N_b^*) = \{B, g^y, N_b\}_{H(B,g^y,pw_b) \cdot H(B,g^y,pw_b^*)}$;
    if $(B^*, g^{y^*}) \stackrel{?}{=} (B, g^y)$ **then**
      return pw_b^*
  }
}

After the adversary *Eve* has obtained the password pw_b^* using the above off-line dictionary attack method, the adversary *Eve* can impersonate B by forging B's sending message $RQ_B^* = \underbrace{B, g^e, \{B, g^e, N_e\}_{H(B,g^e,pw_b^*)}}, RQ_A$, where e is a random number $\in Z_p$ and N_e is a nonce. Therefore, Lv et al.'s 3PAKE protocol is vulnerable to off-line dictionary attack 2.

3.3 Real Applications for the Proposed off-line Dictionary Attacks

Passwords are the most common methods of user authentication and key exchange on the Internet environment. For practical security applications, password-based authentication and key exchange protocols are required when making use of Internet network services like E-learning, on-line polls, on-line ticket-order systems, roll call systems, on-line games, etc. In real security applications, users offer the same password as above to access several application servers for their convenience [17]. Thus, an adversary *Eve* may try to use the guessed password pw_a to impersonate the legal user A to login to other systems that the user A has registered with outside this Lv et al.'s 3PAKE protocol-based server. If the targeted outside server adopts the normal authentication and key exchange protocol, it is possible that the adversary *Eve* can successfully impersonate the user A to login to it by using the guessed password pw_a. Therefore, the password breach cannot be revealed by the adversary's actions.

4 Conclusions

The 3PAKE technology has been widely deployed in various kinds of applications. This paper demonstrated that Lv et al.'s password-based 3PAKE protocol still insecure to off-line dictionary attacks. For this reason, Lv et al.'s 3PAKE protocol cannot use for practical application, especially in the resource-limited environments and real-time systems. Further works will be focused on improving the Lv et al.'s 3PAKE protocol which can be able to provide greater security and to be more efficient than the existing 3PAKE protocols by an accurate performance analysis.

Acknowledgements. We would like to thank the anonymous reviewers for their helpful comments. This work was supported by Basic Science Research Program through the National Research Foundation of Korea(NRF) funded by the Ministry of Education, Science and Technology(No. 2010-0010106) and partially supported by the MKE(The Ministry of Knowledge Economy), Korea, under the ITRC(Information Technology Research Center) support program (NIPA-2012- H0301-12-2004) supervised by the NIPA(National IT Industry Promotion Agency).

References

1. Lin, C.-L., Sun, H.-M., Steiner, M., Hwang, T.: Three-party encrypted key exchange without server public-keys. IEEE Communications Letters 5, 497–499 (2001)
2. Yeh, H.-T., Sun, H.-M., Hwang, T.: Efficient three-party authentication and key agreement protocols resistant to password guessing attacks. Journal of Information Science and Engineering 19, 1059–1070 (2003)
3. Lu, R., Cao, Z.: Simple three-party key exchange protocol. Computers & Security 26(1), 94–97 (2007)
4. Abdalla, M., Pointcheval, D.: Simple password-based encrypted key exchange protocols. In: Menezes, A. (ed.) CT-RSA 2005. LNCS, vol. 3376, pp. 191–208. Springer, Heidelberg (2005)
5. Chung, H.-R., Ku, W.-C.: Three weaknesses in a simple three-party key exchange protocol. Inform. Sciences 178(1), 220–229 (2008)
6. Guo, H., Li, Z., Mu, Y., Zhang, X.: Cryptanalysis of simple threeparty key exchange protocol. Computers & Security 27(1), 16–21 (2008)
7. Phan, R.C.-W., Yau, W.-C., Goi, B.-M.: Cryptanalysis of simple three-party key exchange protocol (S-3PAKE). Inform. Sciences 178(13), 2849–2856 (2008)
8. Chen, T., Lee, W.-B., Chen, H.-B.: A round-and computation-efficient three-party authenticated key exchange protocol. Journal of Systems and Software 81, 1581–1590 (2008)
9. Yoon, E.-J., Yoo, K.-Y.: Improving the novel three-party encrypted key exchange protocol. Computers Standards & Interfaces 30, 309–314 (2008)
10. Nam, J., Paik, J., Kang, H.-K., Kim, U.-M., Won, D.: An off-line dictionary attack on a simple three-party key exchange protocol. IEEE Commun. Lett. 13(3), 205–207 (2009)
11. Huang, H.-F.: A simple three-party password-based key exchange protocol. International Journal of Communication Systems 22, 857–862 (2009)
12. Lee, T.-F., Liu, J.-L., Sung, M.-J., Yang, S.-B., Chen, C.-M.: Communication-efficient three-party protocols for authentication and key agreement. Computers & Mathematics with Applications 58, 641–648 (2009)
13. Yang, J.-H., Chang, C.-C.: An efficient three-party authenticated key exchange protocol using elliptic curve cryptography for mobile-commerce environments. Journal of Systems and Software 82, 1497–1502 (2009)

14. Debiao, H., Jianhua, C., Jin, H.: Cryptanalysis of a simple three-party key exchange protocol. Informatica 34, 337–339 (2010)
15. Kim, H.-S., Choi, J.-Y.: Enhanced password-based simple three-party key exchange protocol. Computers & Electrical Engineering 35, 107–114 (2009)
16. Ding, Y., Horster, P.: Undetectable on-line password guessing attacks. ACM Operating Systems Review 29(4), 77–86 (1995)
17. Kim, H.-J., Yoon, E.-J.: Cryptanalysis of an enhanced simple three-party key exchange protocol. Communications in Computer and Information Science 259, 167–176 (2011)
18. Lv, C., Ma, M., Li, H., Ma, J., Zhang, Y.: An novel three-party authenticated key exchange protocol using one-time key. Journal of Network and Computer Applications (2012), http://dx.doi.org/10.1016/j.jnca.2012.04.006

Mechanisms to Locate Non-cooperative Transmitters in Wireless Networks

Éric Barthélémy[1,2] and Jean-Marc Robert[1]

[1] École de Technologie Supérieure (ETS), Montréal, Québec, Canada
jean-marc.robert@etsmtl.ca
[2] TELECOM Lille 1, Lille, France

Abstract. This paper proposes new mechanisms for locating a non-mobile transmitter in wireless communication or sensor networks. They rely on a set of trusted cooperative receivers that are able to measure the residual strengths of the received signals from the transmitter. These mechanisms cannot rely on the information provided by the transmitter since the latter can be malicious. Laurendeau and Barbeau [1] proposed such a localisation mechanism. Unfortunately, it uses an approximation algorithm which is too restrictive. The difficulty comes for the fact that no good approximation of the difference of two log-normal variables exists. Thus, we propose new algorithms that rely either on better approximations or a geometric interpretation of the problem.

Keywords: Localisation, Log-normal shadowing, Adversarial model.

1 Introduction

Wireless technologies are now ubiquitous in communication and sensor networks. However, this comes with an increase in the number of attacks exploiting their weaknesses. Hence, it is important to find methods to detect these attacks effectively and successfully identify their originator. Laurendeau and Barbeau [1] described many advantages of using the physical position of an attacker rather than simply its logical network identifier which can be easily spoofed. Unfortunately, their solution has some problems and is based on a strong hypothesis. It assumes that the effective isotropic radiated power (EIRP) used by any transmitter to send its signals is within a given confidence interval.

Our goal is to design mechanisms allowing a set of trusted cooperative receivers to locate a non-mobile transmitter. These receivers collaborate with each other without any attempt to alter the process. This task is challenging since transmitting entities may seek to thwart the localisation mechanisms. The proposed solutions are based on receivers that can measure the residual strengths of the received signals (RSS) from a transmitter. From these values, it would be possible to find the exact position of the transmitter in an ideal environment. However, the strength of a signal fluctuates during its propagation. It depends on the environment in which it propagates. Thus, it is difficult to find precisely the position of a transmitter from only the strength of its received signals.

V. Guyot (Ed.): ICAIT 2012, LNCS 7593, pp. 199–212, 2013.

In this paper, we first revisit the HPB algorithm [1]. The algorithm uses an approximation of the difference of two log-normal random variables, which discards too many legitimate solutions. Unfortunately, once the algorithm is corrected, it does not give very good results any more.

We then propose new mechanisms to locate a non-mobile transmitter. The first one is based on Monte Carlo methods approximating the difference of two log-normal random variables. The second one is based on a geometric interpretation of the received signals. It intersects a set of annuli representing the possible positions of the transmitter. Both solutions rely on the same EIRP hypothesis than the HPB algorithm. A third mechanism is given that avoids to use any hypothesis. This is interesting when the confidence interval of the EIRP hypothesis is not very tight.

Finally, all the proposed mechanisms are evaluated and compared to each other. Some mechanisms give better performance when the transmitter is close to the receivers and other ones when the transmitter is far from them.

2 Radio Propagation Model

To estimate the *path loss* of the strength of a signal during its propagation, the *Log-Normal Shadowing* model is often used [2]. It defines the loss over a distance d as follows:

$$L(d) \triangleq \overline{L}(d_0) + 10n\log(\frac{d}{d_0}) + X \tag{1}$$

This is based on three parameters linked to the environment in which the signal propagates: $\overline{L}(d_0)$, n and X. The parameter $\overline{L}(d_0)$ represents the average strength loss incurred over a reference distance d_0. The Friis transmission equation describing the ideal propagation of a signal into space at a frequency of 2.4Ghz (see [3,1]) can be used to determine this value for $d_0 = 1m$:

$$\overline{L}(d_0) = 10\log(\frac{4\pi f d_0}{c})^2 = 40 \text{ dB}.$$

The loss exponent n and the Gaussian random variable X with parameters $(0, \sigma^2)$ depend on the environment in which the signal propagates. Their values can be measured empirically or set up to typical values as shown in Table 1:

Table 1. Typical values of n and σ for some environments [4]

Environment	n	σ (in dB)
Free Space	2	0
Urban Area Cellular Radio	2.7 - 3.5	10 - 14
In building line-of-sight	1.6 - 1.8	4 - 7
Obstructed in building	4 - 6	5 - 12

Based on the Log-Normal Shadowing model, the distance between a transmitter and a receiver can be derived from (1). Hence, this distance is given by the following equation:

$$d = d_0 \times 10^{\frac{L(d)-\overline{L}(d_0)-X}{10n}} \tag{2}$$

The propagation loss $L(d)$ of a signal corresponds to the difference between the EIRP used by the transmitter (P) and the residual strength of the received signal (RSS). Thus, (2) can be rewritten as follows:

$$d = d_0 \times 10^{\frac{P-RSS-\overline{L}(d_0)-X}{10n}} \tag{3}$$

However, without the cooperation of the transmitter, it is impossible to know the EIRP value and estimate this last equation.

3 Related Work

Bahl and Padmanabhan [5] proposed RADAR, a mechanism to locate a non-mobile transmitter in a building. In the first step, a transmitter sends signals from each possible position in the building. The RSS values of these signals are measured by each trusted receiver. These values are kept in a reference grid. In the second step, each receiver measures the RSS value of the signal received from the transmitter. A centralized system compares these values with those of the reference grid to find the possible positions. They also proposed to use a model close to the *Log-Normal Shadowing* model to derive the grid measurements analytically instead of experimentally.

Bahl *et al.* [6] improved RADAR and considered the movements of the transmitter and the changes in the environment.

Laurendeau and Barbeau [1] considered the same problem in some adversarial set-up. In such a context, the transmitter does not cooperate with the receivers. Any information provided by the transmitter should not be considered as truthful. The *Hyperbolic Position Bounding* (HPB) algorithm first recovers securely the RSS values measured by each trusted receiver. Thus, the distance d_i between the transmitter and receiver R_i lies probably between the following bounds derived from (3):

$$d_i^-(P) = d_0 \times 10^{\frac{P-RSS_i-\overline{L}(d_0)-z_\rho\sigma}{10n}} \tag{4}$$

$$d_i^+(P) = d_0 \times 10^{\frac{P-RSS_i-\overline{L}(d_0)+z_\rho\sigma}{10n}} \tag{5}$$

Since X_i is a Gaussian random variable with parameters $(0, \sigma^2)$, there is a constant z_ρ s.t. $|X_i| < z_\rho\sigma$ with probability ρ [7]. Typically, the confidence level parameter of the algorithm ρ is set to 95%.

The next step is to estimate the value of $d_i - d_j$, for any pair of receivers R_i and R_j. To do this, the HPB algorithm assumes that the EIRP used by the transmitter (P) lies in some confidence interval $[P^- \dots P^+]$. This hypothesis is referred as the *EIRP hypothesis.* Based on this hypothesis, the HPB algorithm derives the following bounds:

$$\delta^-_{i,j} \triangleq d^-_i(P^-) - d^+_j(P^-) \quad (6)$$
$$\delta^+_{i,j} \triangleq d^+_i(P^+) - d^-_j(P^+). \quad (7)$$

These equations define two hyperbolas delimiting the region where the transmitter is likely to be. This region corresponds to the locus of points p s.t.

$$\delta^-_{i,j} \leq d_{\mathrm{E}}(p, p_i) - d_{\mathrm{E}}(p, p_j) \leq \delta^+_{i,j} \quad (8)$$

where $d_{\mathrm{E}}(p, q)$ is the Euclidean distance between p and q.

Symmetrically, it is possible to obtain the inequality:

$$-\delta^+_{j,i} \leq d_{\mathrm{E}}(p, p_i) - d_{\mathrm{E}}(p, p_j) \leq -\delta^-_{j,i} \quad (9)$$

By combining (8) and (9), the HPB algorithm can obtain a relatively strict region representing the most likely positions of the transmitter. This region is defined by the lower bound $\max\{\delta^-_{i,j}, -\delta^+_{j,i}\}$ and the upper bound $\min\{\delta^+_{i,j}, -\delta^-_{j,i}\}$.

When more than two receivers are available, simply repeat for each pair of receivers and intersect all the resulting regions. The accuracy of the HPB algorithm increases with the number of pairs used. However, the chances of success diminish with this number since only one of these pairs can exclude a position. In fact, the probability that the transmitter is in the intersection of k regions could be as bad as ρ^k. It would be exactly ρ^k if the observations are independent. However, they are not. The probability should be higher but can be hardly estimated. It is therefore necessary to find a minimum set of pairs that offers the best chances of success.

Bhatia [8] proposed to use *four-square* antennas to improve the HPB algorithm. This type of antenna is able to determine from which direction a signal originates. In this way, if the antenna determines that the transmitter is in the Northeast quadrant, this quadrant region is simply intersected with the region obtained with the HPB algorithm.

Finally, *HPB Learning Ability* [9] is another technique based on the HPB algorithm. It goes through a learning stage during which it finds the most effective pairs of receivers. The choice of these pairs plays a crucial role since it has an impact on the likelihood of a successful localisation.

4 Analysis of the HPB Algorithm

Unfortunately, the HPB algorithm [1] is based on an inaccurate approximation of the difference of two log-normal random variables. Let P denote the EIRP used by a transmitter and let RSS_i and RSS_j denote the residual strength of the signals received by R_i and R_j, respectively.

Equations (4) and (5) can be used to derive the following inequalities:

$$d_i^-(P) - d_j^+(P) < \begin{matrix} d_i^-(P) - d_j^-(P) \\ d_i^+(P) - d_j^+(P) \end{matrix} < d_i^+(P) - d_j^-(P)$$

This forms a lattice whose supremum $\Delta_{i,j}^+(P) \triangleq d_i^+(P) - d_j^-(P)$ and infimum $\Delta_{i,j}^-(P) \triangleq d_i^-(P) - d_j^+(P)$.

Knowing that $P \in [P^- \cdots P^+]$ (the EIRP hypothesis), it is possible to find the maximal supremum and the minimal infimum on this interval:

$$\Delta_{i,j}^+ \triangleq \max_{P \in [P^- \cdots P^+]} \Delta_{i,j}^+(P) \tag{10}$$

$$\Delta_{i,j}^- \triangleq \min_{P \in [P^- \cdots P^+]} \Delta_{i,j}^-(P). \tag{11}$$

These values are defined differently in the original HPB algorithm – see (6) and (7). Unfortunately, the infimum $\Delta_{i,j}^-(P)$ does not always reach its minimum value at P^-. By definition,

$$\Delta_{i,j}^-(P) = d_0 \times 10^{\frac{P}{10n}} \left[10^{\frac{-RSS_i - \overline{L}(d_0) - z_\rho \sigma}{10n}} - 10^{\frac{-RSS_j - \overline{L}(d_0) + z_\rho \sigma}{10n}} \right].$$

If $RSS_j - 2z_\rho\sigma < RSS_i$, this value is negative. Thus, the function $\Delta_{i,j}^-(P)$ is decreasing on the interval $[P^- \cdots P^+]$ and reaches its minimum value at P^+.

Similarly, if $RSS_j + 2z_\rho\sigma < RSS_i$, the function $\Delta_{i,j}^+(P)$ is decreasing on the interval $[P^- \cdots P^+]$ and reaches its maximal value at P^-.

Table 2. The endpoints of the confidence interval for $d_i - d_j$.

Case	Condition	$\Delta_{i,j}^-$	$\Delta_{i,j}^+$
I	$RSS_i < RSS_j - 2z_\rho\sigma$	$\Delta_{i,j}^-(P^-)$	$\Delta_{i,j}^+(P^+)$
II	$RSS_j - 2z_\rho\sigma \leq RSS_i \leq RSS_j + 2z_\rho\sigma$	$\Delta_{i,j}^-(P^+)$	$\Delta_{i,j}^+(P^+)$
III	$RSS_j + 2z_\rho\sigma < RSS_i$	$\Delta_{i,j}^-(P^+)$	$\Delta_{i,j}^+(P^-)$

This table summarizes the different cases that the corrected HPB algorithm would have to deal with. Notice that these cases are totally symmetric. Contrary to what Laurendeau and Barbeau [1] claim, there is no advantage to consider the confidence intervals of $d_i - d_j$ and $d_j - d_i$.

Consider Case I where $RSS_i < RSS_j - 2z_\rho\sigma$. Then,

$$\Delta_{i,j}^-(P^-) < d_{\mathrm{E}}(p, p_i) - d_{\mathrm{E}}(p, p_j) < \Delta_{i,j}^+(P^+).$$

On the other hand, since $RSS_i + 2z_\rho\sigma < RSS_j$,

$$\Delta_{j,i}^-(P^+) < d_{\mathrm{E}}(p, p_j) - d_{\mathrm{E}}(p, p_i) < \Delta_{j,i}^+(P^-)$$
$$-\Delta_{j,i}^+(P^-) < d_{\mathrm{E}}(p, p_i) - d_{\mathrm{E}}(p, p_j) < -\Delta_{j,i}^-(P^+).$$

But, by definition

$$-\Delta_{j,i}^{-}(P^{+}) = -(d_j^{-}(P^{+}) - d_i^{+}(P^{+})) = \Delta_{i,j}^{+}(P^{+})$$
$$-\Delta_{j,i}^{+}(P^{-}) = -(d_j^{+}(P^{-}) - d_i^{-}(P^{-})) = \Delta_{i,j}^{-}(P^{-}).$$

Therefore, this first case is symmetric. The symmetry of the other cases can be shown similarly.

The HPB algorithm must be modified as shown in Table 2. The hyperbolas delimiting the region where the transmitter should lie have to be defined with these new bounds. Unfortunately, the corrected HPB algorithm does not give very good results any more. In Table 3, the values were obtained by simulating the propagation of a single signal with an EIRP of 30 dBm towards two receivers in an environment with parameters $n = 2.76$ and $\sigma = 5.62$ dB. The confidence interval for the EIRP is $[15 \cdots 40]$ dBm and the confidence level parameter of the algorithm ρ is set to 95%.

Table 3. Simulating the propagation of a signal towards two receivers located at $(350, 500)$ and $(650, 500)$.

Example	Bounds	Transmitter position	$d_1 - d_2$	$d_1 - d_2$ HPB [1]		$d_1 - d_2$ Corrected HPB	
1	Case II	(675,600)	237	−102	119	−822	965
2	Case II	(675,550)	273	−8	131	−68	1059
3	Case I	(660,510)	296	188.7	187.7	23	1511
4	Case II	(500,550)	0	−70	175	−571	1406

By the triangle inequality, the value of $d_1 - d_2$ should be truncated to -300 or 300. While the corrected HPB algorithm gives useless bounds in Ex. 1 and 4 and loose bounds corresponding to half-planes in Ex. 2 and 3, the original HPB algorithm gives incoherent bounds which do not contain the value of $d_1 - d_2$.

The examples in Table 3 represent the various cases that the HPB algorithm has to deal with. It is possible to show that it gives erroneous results in many cases. As seen in the upper part of Fig. 1, the original HPB algorithm gives erroneous bounds most of the time when the transmitter is very close to a receiver. In these cases, the estimated upper bound is lower or the estimated lower bound is higher than the actual value. On the other hand, as seen in the lower part of the figure, the corrected algorithm gives bounds which are very loose.

Further analysis of the problem can show that the number of incoherent bounds derived by the original HPB algorithm depends on the transmitter location. Two other experimentations were made. In the first case, the transmitter was located at $(550, 600)$ and the original HPB algorithm gave incoherent bounds in 17% of the simulations. In the second case, the transmitter was moved relatively far from the two receivers at $(550, 800)$ and the number of incoherent bounds was reduced to 2%.

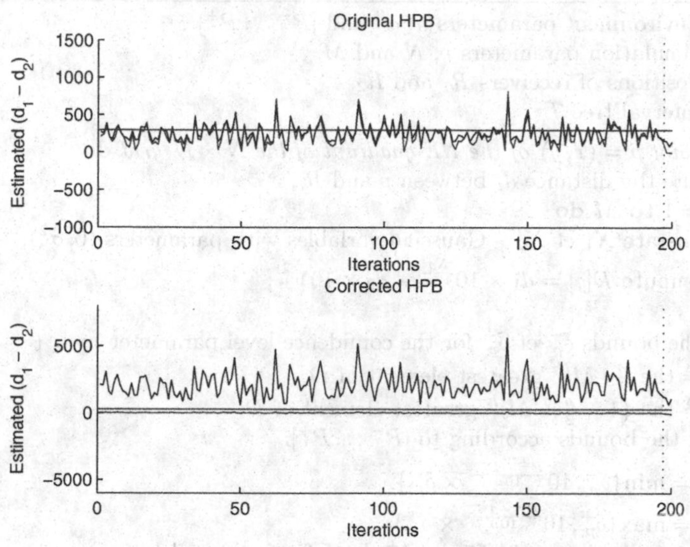

Fig. 1. Simulations of a signal issued by a transmitter located at $(660, 510)$ and sent towards two receivers at $(350, 500)$ and $(650, 500)$. The estimated upper and lower bounds for $d_1 - d_2$ are shown for both versions of the HPB algorithm. The horizontal line at $y \simeq 290$ indicates the difference of the distances.

5 Monte Carlo Methods

The HPB algorithm tries to approximate the difference of two log-normal random variables. However, the distribution of such a variable is hard to estimate. Usually, approximations and Monte Carlo methods are used to deal with these variables (e.g., [10,11]).

The localisation mechanism proposed in this section is based on Monte Carlo methods. It is divided into two steps. The first one is the preprocessing step which determines by simulation confidence intervals for $d(p, R_1) - d(p, R_2)$, for each possible position p of the transmitter. The second one is the localisation step finding the possible positions of the transmitter coherent with the observations. This approach is very similar to RADAR [5].

Consider a $N \times N$ grid centered on the midpoint between receivers R_1 and R_2. For each point p of this grid, simulate the propagation of M signals using (1). If the EIRP of these signals is known, it is possible to find a confidence interval containing $d(p, R_1) - d(p, R_2)$ with a probability of at least ρ. It is sufficient to estimate the distribution of $d(p, R_1) \times 10^{\frac{X_1}{10n}} - d(p, R_2) \times 10^{\frac{X_2}{10n}}$ and find a maximal lower bound δ_p^- and a minimal upper bound δ_p^+ such that the proportion of the M values smaller than δ_p^- or greater than δ_p^+ is at most $\frac{\varrho}{2}$. This last step can be done in linear time by using the algorithm proposed by Blum et al. [12].

input : Environment parameters n, σ^2 and $[P^- \dots P^+]$
input : Simulation parameters ρ, N and M
input : Positions of receivers R_1 and R_2
output: Interval tree $\mathcal{T}$
for *each point* $p = (x, y)$ *of the NE quadrant of the* $N \times N$ *grid* **do**
  Compute the distance d_i between p and R_i;
  for $j = 1$ **to** M **do**
    Generate X_1 et X_2 – Gaussian variables with parameters $(0, \sigma^2)$;
    Compute $D[j] = d_1 \times 10^{\frac{X_1}{10n}} - d_2 \times 10^{\frac{X_2}{10n}}$;
  end
  Find the bounds δ_p^- et δ_p^+ for the confidence level parameter ρ:
    $\delta_p^- \triangleq$ the $\frac{\rho}{2} \cdot M^{th}$ greatest element of D
    $\delta_p^+ \triangleq$ the $\left(1 - \frac{\rho}{2}\right) \cdot M^{th}$ greatest element of D;
  Adjust the bounds according to $[P^- \dots P^+]$:
    $\delta_p^{*-} \triangleq \min\{\delta_p^-, 10^{\frac{P^+ - P^-}{10n}} \times \delta_p^-\}$
    $\delta_p^{*+} \triangleq \max\{\delta_p^+, 10^{\frac{P^+ - P^-}{10n}} \times \delta_p^+\}$;
  Add the 1-dim interval $[\delta_p^{*-} \cdots \delta_p^{*+}]$ in $\mathcal{T}$ for (x, y) and $(x, -y)$;
  Add the 1-dim interval $[-\delta_p^{*+} \cdots -\delta_p^{*-}]$ in $\mathcal{T}$ for $(-x, y)$ and $(-x, -y)$;
end

Algorithm 1. Reference grid and Interval tree

Once the bounds δ_p^- and δ_p^+ are determined, they should be scaled up according to the EIRP confidence interval $[P^- \cdots P^+]$. In the worst case, a transmitter uses the minimum value P^- and the receivers use the maximum value P^+ to estimate the difference of the two distances with the following equation:

$$d_0 \times 10^{\frac{P^+ - RSS_1 - \overline{L}(d_0)}{10n}} - d_0 \times 10^{\frac{P^+ - RSS_2 - \overline{L}(d_0)}{10n}}. \qquad (12)$$

In such a case, the receivers overestimate the distance by a factor of $10^{\frac{P^+ - P^-}{10n}}$. Therefore, the bounds should be scaled up accordingly as follows:

$$\delta_p^{*-} \triangleq \min\{\delta_p^-, 10^{\frac{P^+ - P^-}{10n}} \times \delta_p^-\} \quad \text{and}$$
$$\delta_p^{*+} \triangleq \max\{\delta_p^+, 10^{\frac{P^+ - P^-}{10n}} \times \delta_p^+\}.$$

The approximation of the distribution of $d_1 - d_2$ is shown in Algorithm 1. Based on the symmetry of the problem, it is sufficient to simulate only the points in one of the four quadrants of the grid. This step has to be done only once for each pair of receivers, since it does not depend on the position of the transmitter to be located.

Once the interval tree $\mathcal{T}$ has been built, the measurement of residual strengths of the received signals can be used to estimate the possible positions of the transmitter. It is sufficient to find the confidence intervals in $\mathcal{T}$ containing the query value derived from (12) as shown in Algorithm 2.

input : Environmental parameters n, d_0, $\overline{L}(d_0)$ and $[P^- \ldots P^+]$
input : Interval tree $\mathcal{T}$
input : Measured strengths RSS_1 et RSS_2
output: The possible positions

1 Compute
$$d = d_0 \times 10^{\frac{P^+ - RSS_1 - \overline{L}(d_0)}{10n}} - d_0 \times 10^{\frac{P^+ - RSS_2 - \overline{L}(d_0)}{10n}};$$
2 Enumerate all the k intervals in $\mathcal{T}$ containing d;
3 Determine the grid points associated to these intervals;

Algorithm 2. Localisation step

The construction of the 1-dim interval tree $\mathcal{T}$ supporting point queries is a classic problem in computational geometry [13]. The data structure $\mathcal{T}$ containing the $O(N^2)$ intervals and allowing to find rapidly all the intervals containing a point can be built in $O(N^2 \log N)$ time and $O(N^2)$ space. Hence, the preprocessing step described in Algorithm 1 can be done in $O(N^2M + N^2 \log N)$ time and $O(N^2)$ space. Once the data structure is built, the k intervals containing the query point can be listed in only $O(k + \log N)$ time.

6 New York Style Bagel Algorithm

The residual strength of a signal measured by a receiver can be interpreted as a geometric object. From (3), the minimum d_{min} and maximum d_{max} distances between a receiver and a transmitter can be determined – with respect to the confidence level parameter of the algorithm ρ. Indeed, d_{min} can be obtained if the minimal EIRP and the maximal noise values are used:

$$d_{min} \triangleq d_0 \times 10^{\frac{P^- - RSS - \overline{L}(d_0) - z_\rho \sigma}{10n}}$$

On the other hand, d_{max} can be obtained if the maximal EIRP and the minimal noise values are used:

$$d_{max} \triangleq d_0 \times 10^{\frac{P^+ - RSS - \overline{L}(d_0) - (-z_\rho \sigma)}{10n}}$$

Thus, this new localisation mechanism relies on the same EIRP hypothesis as the two previous mechanisms.

These two bounds can be used to define an annulus centered at the receiver, which corresponds to the most likely positions of the transmitter. Unfortunately, this annulus is very fat – hence its name *New York style bagel* algorithm. As seen in Fig. 2(a), only the annulus centered at $(350, 650)$ is clearly visible. For the other annuli, only the interior circles are apparent. These interior circles delimitate the regions to discard. In this figure, the possible positions lie therefore inside the large circle and outside the small ones.

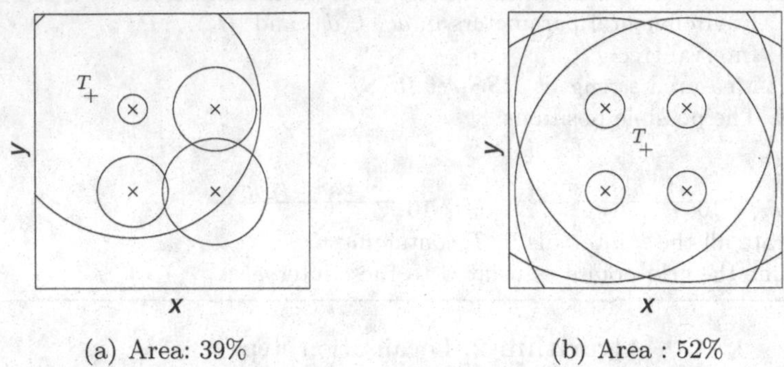

(a) Area: 39%   (b) Area : 52%

Fig. 2. The region containing the possible locations of the transmitter T corresponds to the intersection of four fat annuli

Figures 2(a) and 2(b) illustrate the results obtained with four receivers. Monte Carlo methods are used to evaluate the areas of the regions representing the possible positions of the transmitter. This localisation mechanism requires a strict EIRP hypothesis. Otherwise, the annuli would be too fat and their intersection would cover almost the entire space. In the examples presented in these figures, the EIRP interval is $[28 \cdots 32]$ dBm and the confidence level parameter of the algorithm ρ is set to 95%, giving an overall confidence level of at least 81%.

7 Circle Algorithm

The solutions presented so far have the same drawback as the original HPB algorithm. They all rely on the EIRP hypothesis. The New York style bagel algorithm is particularly impacted by a loose hypothesis. Fortunately, it is possible to overcome this problem by determining the position of a transmitter directly from the difference of the residual strengths of the received signals.

The residual strength of the signal received by R_i can be derived from (1):

$$RSS_i = P - \overline{L}(d_0) - 10n \log(\frac{d_i}{d_0}) + X_i.$$

Therefore, it is possible to eliminate the EIRP hypothesis directly by calculating the difference of the residual strengths of the received signals:

$$RSS_1 - RSS_2 = 10n \log(\frac{d_2}{d_1}) + (X_1 - X_2). \quad (13)$$

As X_1 and X_2 are Gaussian random variables with parameters $(0, \sigma^2)$, their difference Y is a Gaussian random variable with parameters $(0, 2\sigma^2)$ [7]. So, (13) can be rewritten as follows:

$$\frac{d_2}{d_1} = 10^{\frac{(RSS_1 - RSS_2)}{10n}} \times 10^{\frac{Y}{10n}} \quad (14)$$

The variable Y can be bounded by the following values:

$$-\sqrt{2}z_\rho\sigma < Y < \sqrt{2}z_\rho\sigma \tag{15}$$

where z_ρ depends on the confidence level parameter of the algorithm ρ.

By combining (14) and (15), it is possible to bound the ratio of the distances as follows:

$$\delta_{1,2}^{-} \triangleq 10^{\frac{(RSS_1-RSS_2)-\sqrt{2}z_\rho\sigma}{10n}} \leq \frac{d_2}{d_1} \leq 10^{\frac{(RSS_1-RSS_2)+\sqrt{2}z_\rho\sigma}{10n}} \triangleq \delta_{1,2}^{+}$$

Hence, a transmitter should be found at position p iff p is such that:

$$\delta_{1,2}^{-} \leq \frac{d_{\mathrm{E}}(p,p_1)}{d_{\mathrm{E}}(p,p_2)} \leq \delta_{1,2}^{+} \tag{16}$$

where p_i corresponds to the position of receiver R_i.

When $RSS_1 - RSS_2 \geq \sqrt{2}z_\rho\sigma$ (similar to Case I in Table 2), the lower bound $\delta_{1,2}^{-}$ is greater than 1. In this case, the transmitter can only be found outside the smaller circle (defined by $\delta_{1,2}^{+}$) and inside the larger one (defined by $\delta_{1,2}^{-}$). Note that the smaller circle is necessarily included in the large one. This case is illustrated in Fig. 3(a).

On the other hand, when $0 \leq RSS_1 - RSS_2 < \sqrt{2}z_\rho\sigma$ (similar to Case II in Table 2), the lower bound $\delta_{1,2}^{-}$ is smaller than 1 and the upper bound $\delta_{1,2}^{+}$ is greater than 1. In this case, the transmitter can only be found outside of two distinct circles. The right circle corresponds to the lower bound while the left one corresponds to the upper bound. This case is illustrated in Fig. 3(b).

Finally, the other two cases are symmetric to the first two cases.

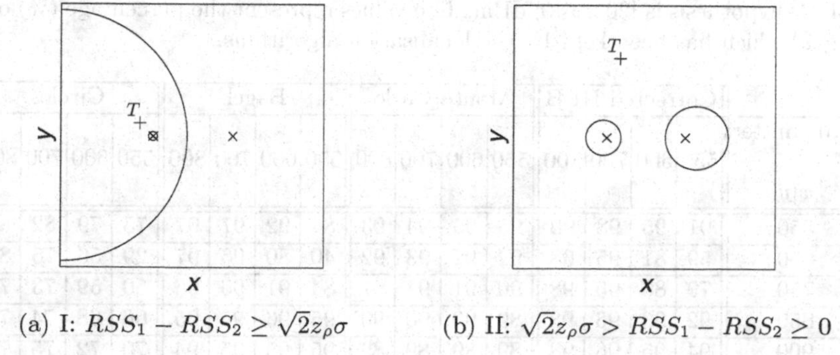

(a) I: $RSS_1 - RSS_2 \geq \sqrt{2}z_\rho\sigma$ (b) II: $\sqrt{2}z_\rho\sigma > RSS_1 - RSS_2 \geq 0$

Fig. 3. The region containing the possible locations of the transmitter T

8 Experimentation and Comparison

Four different localisation mechanisms have been proposed in this paper: a corrected version of the HPB algorithm, a Monte Carlo algorithm using the same principle as the HPB algorithm, an algorithm using a simple geometric interpretation of the information and, finally, an algorithm making no assumptions whatsoever on the EIRP used by the transmitter. In this section, we compare these algorithms and find which algorithm should be used in a given situation.

To compare the effectiveness of our mechanisms, we rely on the areas of the regions computed by these algorithms and the confidence interval associated with these areas. The confidence interval can be obtained analytically, while the area has to be approximated using Monte Carlo methods. The area is expressed as a percentage of the total grid. Smaller is the region, better is the algorithm.

The New York style bagel algorithm intersects two regions (one per receiver). To obtain a confidence level of at least 95%, as the other algorithms, a confidence level parameter ρ close to 97.5% must be used for each of the two regions.

The simulations are carried out on a grid of $1000m \times 1000m$. To compute the area of a region obtained by a localisation algorithm, we divide the grid in N^2 squares of area $(\frac{1000m}{N})^2$. They are represented by their central point. If one of them lies in the region, we consider that all its corresponding square lies in the region. As the value of N increases, the accuracy of the evaluation increases – as well as the simulation time. For example, if $N = 50$, the area of a circle with a radius of $300m$ can be approximated with an error of less than 0.3%.

In this section, the tables show the area of the grid which contains the possible positions of the transmitter as computed by a pair of trusted receivers. To produce these tables, 2700 signals have been simulated with (3) for each mentioned position. Thus, each area is the average of these experimentations.

Table 4. Comparison of the localisation mechanisms with two receivers assuming that the EIRP hypothesis is [20 . . . 40] dBm. The values represent the percentage (%) of the total grid which has been kept by the localisation algorithms.

	Corrected HPB				Monte Carlo				Bagel				Circles			
Transmitter $x\|y$	550	600	700	800	550	600	700	800	550	600	700	800	550	600	700	800
550	91	95	98	99	95	95	94	93	84	92	97	97	75	79	82	83
650	59	81	95	98	92	92	93	92	40	80	96	97	29	56	75	80
750	79	86	95	98	90	91	91	91	84	91	96	96	50	59	73	79
850	92	93	96	98	89	90	90	90	95	96	95	95	66	68	74	79
900	94	95	96	98	89	89	89	89	95	95	95	94	70	72	75	78

Table 4 shows clearly that the Circle algorithm is quite advantageous compared to any other algorithm having a very bad estimation of the EIRP used by a transmitter. On the other hand, among the algorithms using the EIRP hypothesis, the Monte Carlo algorithm is slightly more accurate than the other ones when the transmitter is far (e.g., last two rows or columns of each subtable). The New York style bagel algorithm is slightly more accurate when the transmitter is close (e.g., first three rows and first two columns of each subtable). Nevertheless, these algorithms are rather ineffective.

Table 5. Comparison of the localisation mechanisms with two receivers assuming that the EIRP hypothesis is [28 . . . 32] dBm. The values represent the percentage (%) of the total grid which has been kept by the localisation algorithms.

Transmitter	Corrected HPB				Monte Carlo				Bagel				Circles			
$x \mid y$	550	600	700	800	550	600	700	800	550	600	700	800	550	600	700	800
550	78	85	93	97	92	92	90	88	40	53	76	84	75	79	82	83
650	52	70	90	96	84	86	87	86	13	39	73	83	29	56	76	81
750	69	77	90	95	80	82	83	82	44	57	76	81	51	59	73	78
850	86	88	93	96	78	79	79	79	72	74	79	79	66	68	74	79
900	90	92	94	96	77	78	78	77	76	77	78	77	70	72	75	78

The analysis is different if the receivers have a good evaluation of the EIRP used by a transmitter. In Table 5, the New York Style Bagel algorithm is better than any other mechanism when the transmitter is close to the receivers (e.g., the first three rows and first two columns of the subtables). In the other cases (e.g., the last two rows or the last column of the subtables), the Monte Carlo, the New York Style Bagel and the Circle algorithms all perform equally badly. It is interesting to remark that the corrected HPB algorithm is even worst in those cases. Most likely, the overly conservative approximation of the two log-normal variables difference may explain this.

Finally, we should remark that two algorithms performed exceptionally well if the transmitter is an extreme position very close to one of the receivers. These results are presented in the last table of this section.

Table 6. Comparison of the localisation mechanisms with two receivers when the transmitter in an extreme position. The values represent the percentage (%) of the total grid which has been kept by the localisation algorithms.

Extreme position (660, 510)				
EIRP	Corrected HPB	Monte Carlo	Bagel	Circles
[20..40] dBm	46	91	4.1	2.92
[28..32] dBm	41	81	1.09	2.88

9 Conclusion

The objective of this paper was to present new mechanisms to locate non-cooperative transmitters in wireless networks. The HPB algorithm proposed by Laurendeau and Barbeau [1] relies on an approximation of the difference of two log-normal variables which has some flaws. Once corrected, this algorithm is not very discriminative any more. Fortunately, we were able to present better solutions. One of them does not rely on any assumption on the transmitters.

The comparison of the proposed mechanisms is restricted to the simple case where two receivers try to locate a transmitter. The next question to address is to see how to deploy few receivers in a restricted area in order to improve the accuracy of these algorithms. Obviously, the deployment of trusted receivers is costly. We should avoid deploying redundant receivers. On the other hand, when a transmitter is close to a receiver, this receiver is more accurate in its evaluation. The question is therefore to find the best trade-off possible.

References

1. Laurendeau, C., Barbeau, M.: Insider attack attribution using signal strength-based hyperbolic location estimation. Security and Communication Networks 1(4), 337–349 (2008)
2. Rappaport, T.S.: Wireless Communications Principles and Practice, 2nd edn. Prentice-Hall, Englewood Cliffs (2002)
3. Friis, H.T.: A note on a simple transmission formula. Proceedings of the I.R.E and Waves and Electrons 34(5), 254–256 (1946)
4. Carrington, M.: Detecting the evil twin attack in a single hop wireless network using four-square antennas. Master of computer science, Ottawa (2011)
5. Bahl, P., Padmanabhan, V.: Radar: An in-building RF-based user location and tracking system. In: Proc. of the Nineteenth IEEE INFOCOM Conference, vol. 2, pp. 775–784. Tel Aviv, Israel (2000)
6. Bahl, P., Padmanabhan, V., Balachandran, A.: Enhancements to the radar user location and tracking system. Microsoft Research, 1–13 (2000)
7. Grinstead, C.M., Snell, J.L.: Introduction to probability, 2nd edn. American Mathematical Society (1998)
8. Bhatia, P.: Strategy for detection and localization of evil-twin transmitters in wireless networks. Master of computer science, Ottawa (2010)
9. El Sayr, E.: Learning based hyperbolic position bounding in wireless networks. Master of science, Ottawa (2009)
10. Beaulieu, N.C., Xie, Q.: An optimal lognormal approximation to lognormal sum distributions. IEEE Transactions on vehicular technology 53(2), 479–489 (2004)
11. Beaulieu, N.C., Rajwani, F.: Hightly accurate simple closed-form approximations to lognormal sum distributions and densities. IEEE Communications letters 8(12), 709–711 (2004)
12. Blum, M., Floyd, R.W., Pratt, V.R., Rivest, R.L., Tarjan, R.E.: Time bounds for selection. J. Comput. Syst. Sci. 7(4), 448–461 (1973)
13. De Berg, M., Cheong, O., Van Kreveld, M., Overmars, M.: Computational Geometry: Algorithms and Applications, 3rd edn. Springer (2008)

Mantle: A Novel DOSN Leveraging Free Storage and Local Software

Antonino Famulari and Artur Hecker

Télécom ParisTech, France

famulari@telecom-paristech.fr, artur@enst.fr

Abstract. We present Mantle, a novel framework for decentralized Online Social Networks (OSN). Mantle defines a privacy-preserving OSN kernel and can leverage any storage facilities for storing user data. Mantle is designed to execute all OSN specific logic on user devices. It supports the development of third-party applications and mediates all actions of the latter to protect user data, metadata and interactions. In this work, we focus on Mantle's interaction and notification mechanisms, which use publish/subscribe model.

1 Introduction

The logically centralized structure of most of popular OSNs raises the issue of dependence on one single authority, in particular the Service Provider (SP), with full access to both data (such as shared content) and metadata (for example related to interactions, statistics) of its users. This raises the additional question of possible user profiling performed by the OSN provider also outside the borders of the actual OSN platform. Meanwhile, the operations and maintenance of the OSN platform (consumed bandwidth and storage, dedicated code and platform development, etc.) represent a huge cost for OSN providers, leading SPs to put users' privacy in the background. Furthermore, the presence per se of a unique SP as Central Authority implies the possibility of some form of censorship: how would an OSN react if their users started promoting a rival OSN? As another example, Facebook, Google and Twitter, have recently announced the possibility of performing country-specific censorship so as to become compliant to legal requirements in different countries.

Modern OSN providers explicitly put users in a condition of dependence on the platform itself in that: i) users can only interact with the members of the same platform, ii) migration from one platform to another, to the best of our knowledge, is not supported by any current mechanism and finally, iii) deleting your own profile from a platform currently only renders the content inaccessible, without any guarantee of actual deletion of the content. Thus, in a futuristic view of a Social Web, in which a substantial part of interactions are performed via social platforms, being bound to one single platform bears substantial risks.

As an alternative to logically centralized architectures for Online Social Networks (OSNs), several decentralized approaches have been proposed [1, 2, 3]. Such architectures (called DOSN) aim to preserve user privacy while offering a service analogous

V. Guyot (Ed.): ICAIT 2012, LNCS 7593, pp. 213–224, 2013.

to the centralized counterparts, including analogous perspectives for new possible functionalities. With a prudent implementation, the requirements in terms of privacy and control on the own data can be better fulfilled by decentralizing storage of both user's data and metadata as well as user-to-user interaction facilities. Existing architectures, however, have several limitations in that they either have strong requirements in terms of necessary resources (e.g. users need to store their data on Virtual Machines (VM)), or the service is not equivalent to the one provided by centralized counterparts (e.g. limited availability of user data).

1.1 Our Contribution

In this paper, we propose Mantle, a privacy-preserving DOSN that relies on two functional components: storage servers and a *kernel* implemented on user clients. Mantle stores all data on general-purpose online storage. This permits to leverage existing online storage facilities as OSN storage and to reduce OSN-specific extra costs. To protect user data on such storage, Mantle uses cryptographic mechanisms. All logic of the OSN service resides on user clients, and relies on a publish/subscribe model for handling user-to-user interactions. Mantle features efficient rekeying with support for user-transparent key revocation.

2 Related Work

It is possible to identify two main classes of approaches to the decentralization of OSNs: i) Approaches that rely on a P2P overlay between main nodes (spanning from full P2P approaches to approaches that rely on some services in addition to the main usage of the P2P overlay) and ii) approaches that decentralize service on functionally different entities, usually employing specific servers for different functions and relatively thin clients. One important drawback of P2P OSNs is data availability, which is due to nodes going offline. P2P OSNs try to mitigate the problem using replication techniques. However, at the best of our knowledge none, among the proposed architectures for P2P OSNs, can guarantee same levels of availability as centralized counterparts.

For this reason, we focused on the second category. Such works use permanent external servers so as to achieve a better level of data availability. The used storage and computation facilities largely differ in the related proposals but share a common trait of providing a Personal Container for user data. An important difference between the previous works access control policy enforcement: while some proposals rely on active reference monitors [10], others rely on key management for encryption and integrity protection.

Vis-à-Vis [4] and PrPl [5] use user-specific VMs as entry point to users' data. In particular, they both rely on Amazon EC2 running VMs. Such VMs play the role of reference monitors for performing access control. Diaspora[1] uses so-called "hubs" for user data storage, which also play the role of reference monitors. Contrary to centralized OSN, there can be many hubs run by different authorities: Diaspora therefore

[1] http://www.joindiaspora.com

decentralizes OSNs. However, such approaches result in high deployment and maintenance efforts and may translate into costs for the end users, since either the discussed proposals rely on paid resources, or users must possess their own online resources.

In Persona [1], attribute-based encryption (ABE) is used to implement group-based access control. The logic of the service is based on external applications that treat data and handle related metadata. While Persona can assure protection of content, the need for exposing ABE attributes, such as "friends" or "family", projects *transparent relationships* violating user's privacy. In contrast, in Facebook or Google+ users do not know *lists* and *circles* of their friends. Also, the implementation of Persona either relies on servers running Apache/MySQL and PHP or the applications provide their own resources for storing users' data.

Generally, previous works cannot guarantee user privacy in terms of *anonymity* of the requester or the *untraceability* of interactions: for example, similarly to Facebook, Vis-à-Vis or PrPl's VMs, as well as Diaspora's hubs, are aware about who is requesting data of a specific user (and need to store user authentication credentials).

3 Motivation of Our Work

Based on limitations of previous work discussed above, we defined a new set of requirements (REQ) that can be summarized as follows:

1 - Decentralize content storage and interaction facilities, yet provide functionalities common to existing OSNs.

2 – Protect users' data, metadata, interactions and social graph from any principal except for involved parties (e.g. users taking part to a private conversation, recipient of a given shared content etc.), from any storage facility that might be used for storing users' data and from third party applications.

3 – Be independent from any central authority; especially at the OSN system level (e.g. a service provider).

4 - Allow account suppression yielding unavailability of all data of the concerned user account, at least for any central authority.

5 – Easy deployment in terms of necessary resources, so as to make DOSN deployments more realistic.

6 - Allow efficient revocation of rights transparently to the (concerned) users, since a transparent mechanism allows more general usage (e.g. in common OSNs, when a user removes one friend, notifying the removed user is in general not notified).

REQ 2 is particularly important since it includes two crucial concepts for Mantle. Firstly, we believe that group memberships and, de facto, the corresponding trust levels, assigned by a user should not be visible for the concerned users: e.g. a *contact* of a user should not be aware whether he is member of user's *neighbors* or *friends* groups. Secondly, as it happens in most centralized OSNs, we believe that users should not be aware of who, among their contacts, browses their content. While the decision what a person shares should only belong to this person, preserving user privacy cannot leave aside the untraceability of user-to-user interactions.

Finally, the proposed solution should be also suitable for a use on mobile devices (smartphones, tablets etc.): direct interactions, which characterize most P2P solutions [2] [3], are hard to achieve on mobile devices with the typical 2G-3G connectivity.

Table 1. Previous work comparison

Work\REQ	2	3	5	6
Vis-à-Vis [4]	N	Y	N	Y
PrPl [5]	N	Y	N	Y
Persona [1]	(only data)	N	N	N
Sun [6]	?	Y	N	(only efficient)
Diaspora	N	Y	N	Y

REQ 1 is fulfilled by each DOSN, while none of discussed works fulfill REQ 4. Table 1 presents how previous work fulfills remaining requirements. In Sun [6], no interaction mechanism is proposed, so that it is not possible to evaluate requirements 1 and 2.

4 Mantle

4.1 Overview

To fill the existing gap, in this paper we propose Mantle, a framework that provides primitives for Decentralized OSNs (REQ 1), in which all service-related logic is implemented in user-owned user clients. Differently from other works, which focus on Access Control (i.e. [1]) or right revocation (i.e. [6]), we focus on the definition of a new interaction mechanism. In particular, interactions leverage the publish-subscribe model and are handled locally, with no mediation by any centralized authority (REQ 2 and REQ 3). Besides, for some types of interactions, Mantle can use existing messaging services, e.g. email, as signaling mechanisms. Mantle leverages general-purpose storage facilities for an OSN service and can use any HTTP or WebDAV [7] share, including free storage provided by commercial services like DropBox[2], skydrive[3], box.net[4], etc (REQ 5). This assures further control on shared data (REQ 2 and REQ 4). The specific interaction model allows for efficient right assignment and revocation. Finally, users whose rights have been revoked are not notified (REQ 6).

4.2 Interaction Model

Users in Mantle may establish relationships and share different content with other principals and entire groups of contacts on the basis of locally defined *lists* of principals (with a local scope), similar to Facebook's *lists of friends* and Google+'s *circles*.

---

[2] `http://www.dropbox.com`
[3] `http://www.skydrive.live.com`
[4] `http://www.box.net`

For the sake of generality, in this paper, we refer to one-hop relationships as "*contacts*". Besides, Mantle provides facilities for handling *communities*. The latter are managed by one or more principals and, differently from *lists*, well-known to all members. As such, some communities can be publicly advertised. Each entity (user, community or list) has an *entity_id*: For the users it needs to be unique and can be calculated as a hash of the email address, while for communities and lists each manager can issue any *ID*, provided he assures local coherence of *ID*s. Similarly to centralized OSNs, Mantle must allow to notify each user of each action/interaction in which they are involved. In Mantle, content can only be shared by uploading the corresponding protected data to the own personal area. This area is available at the selected storage service, as preconfigured by the user in the user client. To retrieve the data of some other user, a user needs to know the URL of the corresponding storage service. To access the content, a user also needs the corresponding cryptographic key.

4.3 Trust and Security

Undesirable Events

In accordance with [11], we consider violating security and privacy of users in the OSN context consisting of one of the following actions: 1) Unduly accessing users' data/metadata, 2) Tracing social graph/user-to-user interactions, 3) Sybil attacks 4) Impersonation of other users.

4.4 Trust and Security Model

Storage facilities- Storage services are trusted to correctly store Mantle's data without modifying or deleting any content. They are also expected to provide a sufficient availability. However, they are not generally trusted: servers and their operators might try to read any stored data and to trace user-to-user interactions (Threat 1). To counter this threat, unauthorized observation of users' data and related metadata is forbidden via encryption functions together with a key management/distribution mechanism. Besides, the storage entity could track IP addresses for public access and possible storage account for private access to storage areas (Threat 2). However, since in Mantle anybody can download a file from a given URL without authentication, doing so does not permit the storage entity to track OSN identities of users, generally considered more critical since closer to user's real identity.

Other users- Users get in contact mainly following real-life based meetings (or via other communication means such as IM or email) and mutually exchange the addresses of their storage servers. When a user establishes a relationship with another principal, he authorizes the latter to access a portion of his content from his storage space. Any user needs to trust his contacts to not distribute/copy the content to which they have access. In Mantle, this means that a user trusts his contacts for not exposing the assigned keys (with the related privileges) to third parties. Besides, we consider Sibyl and impersonation attacks against social networks (threats 3 and 4). To counter these, in Mantle, trust relationships may be used in the establishment of new relationships, e.g. two users can get in contact with each other via a common, trusted, friend. Since users can only get in contact based on real-life meetings, via other trusted mechanisms or via a common friend, Sibyl and impersonation attacks are prevented.

Applications- The *kernel* in Mantle could trace the interactions of the local user; users trust their kernel not to collect and store such data on any external entity and not to perform profiling. On the top of the kernel, third-party applications are executed. The latter are considered in general *untrusted* and could access user data or expose user activity in an unauthorized manner. To counter that, the applications do not have direct access to user data. In Mantle, we use the local kernel as reference monitor. The applications have to rely on the basic primitives of the kernel, acting as a sandbox for each operation on user data.

5 Implementation

5.1 Storage Services

The only requirement for Storage Services is that they provide a public space accessible via the Internet, thus supporting a basic *get()* function for retrieving pieces of content. Only the owner of the space is authorized to post content on it (*post()* function).

5.2 User Client – The Kernel

The Kernel is the only entity in Mantle that can access user data and handle metadata and interactions. The main functionalities of the Kernel are: 1) Provide an API with basic OSN functionalities (e.g. interactions, comments etc.); 2) Support several alternatives for storing data; 3) Handle keys for protecting content.

Functionalities – The kernel allows the user sharing content with all the entities and handles notifications relying on the publish/subscribe model. This is achieved reporting each activity in the context of the OSN in stream-files called *activity streams*. Several *activity streams* are maintained, one for each different list of contacts/community. So as to get notified about other principal's activities, users subscribe to *Activity streams* maintained by the latter. Such activity streams are encrypted so as to be only available to specific groups of users; they are then stored on the public section of the storage service. Each piece of content is independently encrypted, stored on the storage service and shared in this way.

6 Access Control

Mantle only supports two access types: some user can write or read data to the storage space.

Write access control to the storage space is implemented by the storage service. It is only allowed under an OSN-independent storage account of the *owner* of the storage space. In contrast, read access is public from the perspective of the storage service.

The read access control follows the definitions of the owning user regarding the objects (content) and the roles of the accessing subjects in his social network. Only the owning user is authorized to grant read access to (i.e. share) some content to other OSN entities (i.e., in Mantle, to users, groups or communities). The owner is also allowed to revoke such read access right at any time[5]. The read access control is implemented as a combination of key management and encryption mechanisms.

In Mantle, we use Group Encryption (GE) [8]. *Lists* and *communities* are provided with cryptographic keys. Concretely, this means that all members of the entity share these cryptographic keys. In the following, procedures are described for sharing content with specific Mantle entities.

1) *Settings-* Each user U generates an asymmetric key-pair PKu/SKu. Other principals use PKu of U for encrypting content for U. 2) *Sharing with all the contacts-* Each user additionally shares one Unique Symmetric Key (USK) with all his contacts. USK is used for encrypting any personal information meant for all the contacts of a user. 3) *Lists of friends-* For each local list, a symmetric List Key (LK) is generated and distributed to other list members. Such key is used for normal sharing operations with contacts within the list. 4) *Communities-* For each community, members use a symmetric Community Key (CK) for sharing content within the community. In addition to CK, an asymmetric key-pair is defined (CPK/CSK). The CSK is distributed to all the members of the community, while the CPK is publicly available. This allows: i) Non-members to encrypt for the community (using CPK)/members to decrypt (CKS) and ii) Members of the community to share publicly readable content signed as "member of a given community" (CSK)/non-members to verify a signature (CPK).

Table 2. Different kinds of keys in Mantle

SK_u	PK_u,CPK_i	LK_i, CK_i	CSK_i
Private	Public	Shared within lists/communities	Shared within communities
Symm	Asymm	Symm	Asymm

In Table 2 we show all keys that a user U might issue and whether such keys are private, public or shared and with whom. LK, CPK/CSK and CK have an index *i* since they are specific to one community/list *i* managed by the specific user U. Each user will thus own all the keys he issued and all the keys that he needs for interactions that he is allowed to perform.

6.1 Hierarchical Groups

In Mantle, groups have a hierarchical structure inspired by [8]. Each group is composed of several *subgroups*, and each *subgroup* is assigned a subgroup key. Members of a generic group are aware of belonging to the group as well as to all the subgroups

[5] Content is not re-encrypted following to a revocation. That means thatm until the content is not changed, revoked users can still access it.

of the hierarchy, and own the decryption keys for the group and all the subgroups they belong to. This allows the issuer of the group to address content to the entire group as well as to specific subgroups.

7 Interaction Mechanism

7.1 Basics

Mantle's interaction model follows the publish-subscribe principle. Each user reports any action in the context of the OSN in stream-files, namely *activity streams.* Each user *subscribes (in the sense of actively polling)* to a number of *activity streams* of his contacts. *Activity streams* are composed of one entry (row) for each action in the context of the OSNs. Each entry has a well-known format that we can abstract as: <date:time>; <description>. *Activity streams*, are used so as to announce activities (*notify* operation): reading such files users are informed of the last activities, performed by the owner of the specific activity stream, which concern them (for example if contacts shared a picture with them). However, a complete description (*describe* operation) of the activity is only accessible to recipient users. We now show how such *activity streams* are used for different typical activities in the OSN context.

Public activity Stream - Microblogging
A first activity stream is publicly accessible by any principal within (and possibly also outside) the OSN. Such file is thus stored in an unencrypted form on the storage space at a well-known URL. It is used for implementing Twitter-like *following* interactions.

Main Activity Stream
All the contacts of a user have access to the *main activity stream.* This means that such file is encrypted with the Unique Symmetric Key shared with all the contacts, USK. This activity stream: *Notifies* and *describes* (according with above definitions of such operations) interactions for *all* contacts; *Notifies* but does *NOT describe* interactions for specific contacts (this means that details of the activity are not reported in the entry, which points to an activity descriptor that is only accessible to the recipient user)*; Notifies* but does *NOT describe* interactions for specific lists of contacts. It also *Notifies* but does *NOT describe* interactions for subgroups (in the sense of section 6.1) of friends. Each entry is explicitly addressed to one specific contact, list of contacts or subgroup with the notation: *To: <entity_id>*. So as to further preserve privacy, the entity_id can be substituted by a nonce on which interacting parties agree time by time. Note that: (i) all contacts of a user, independently of the *lists* in which they have been inserted, download such file and look within the latter for content addressed to them; ii) Contacts need to know the *ID*s of all the lists and subgroups (of the hierarchy) of which they are members, but do not need to know the trust relationship assigned to them nor other contacts within the same lists. Although contacts of a user can see with whom the latter is interacting, the mechanism can be extended so as to reach further anonymity of interactions by using pseudonyms and relying on relationship-specific *activity streams* for some specific contacts.

List Activity Streams
Finally, an activity stream is defined for each list. Each activity for a specific list is thus *described* there. Contacts within each list know how to retrieve such content.

Using the *main activity stream* for all notifications permits to limit the number of *subscription/downloads* of *activity streams* per first-hop relationship. Each user subscribes only to the *main activity stream* of his contacts, and only if he is notified of a new action, e.g. for a given list he downloads the *list activity streams* containing the description.

7.2 Basic Interactions

Creating and Handling a Profile
So as to create a profile, a user must download Mantle application on his device. The user configures the kernel providing his storage account credentials of the selected storage server. The user can then create his profile. Profile-related data are only stored on the chosen storage space. The user profile is composed of a public part, publicly accessible by everybody, and a private part characterized with restricted accessibility. The profile page contains "pointers" (URLs) to several pieces of content: the profile picture, status, PK_u of the user etc. When visiting another user's profile, the application will aggregate all the data pointed within the profile of the visited user so as to show a user profile page as we are used to see in common OSNs.

Adding a User
So as to get in contact, two users must agree offline to establish a relationship and must exchange with each other the address of their storage server (hosting their public profile, public key etc.). This exchange can be real-life based or can be performed via other means, e.g. email, IM, etc. Since users get in contact and exchange the address of their storage server via real-life meetings (or similar), no further authentication mechanism is necessary. In fact, each user is the only responsible for what he stores on his storage server. Generic user A and user B, subscribe (actively polling) each to the public activity stream of the other. Within their own stream they will thus enter a message, addressed to the other user, pointing to relationship descriptions and related keys. For example, user A will address a message to user B attesting that the latter is now a member of one or more groups (without however revealing the relationship of such groups, e.g. friends or coworkers). This message will also contain a pointer to the corresponding group keys, encrypted with user B's PK; user A can obtain this public key from the public profile of user B). The message content itself is encrypted with user B's PK. Once user B has read the message, he will subscribe to user A's main activity stream and will look for possible actions in groups he is now member of.

Removing a User from a Group
The *main activity stream* is also used for revoking rights of specific users. Following the example in Figure 1, if we want to revoke user1, all the *subgroups* of the highest possible level in the hierarchy, which do not contain the revoked user, must be notified. The subgroup *IDs* are not secret, while members of groups and subgroups

must thus be kept secret. Members of each group will always look for content addressed to such group IDs in the *main activity stream*. The handler of the list could thus revoke one user by simply diffusing a new key to such subgroups and using a new list activity stream, while the revoked user would simply see no more activity.

Browsing the Activity List

So as to browse the list of activities of friends of a generic user A, user A needs to download and decrypt the main activity streams of friends of user A. By doing so, the application gets notified about all the actions of the several friends of the user A, related to the latter. The download of such main activity streams can be done at launch time, periodically and on demand. In the case of bad network conditions it is possible to limit such browsing to some "high priority" contacts (e.g. the ones with whom user A interacts the most), so as to reduce waiting times and network activity.

Sharing Content and Commenting on Comments

The sharing user uploads each shared piece of content on the own storage space. He thus notifies concerned contacts by reporting the new activity in the related activity streams. Since each user can only upload content on his own storage space, the mechanism for commenting on others' content will follow a similar approach as for posting content. In particular, if a user A wishes to post a comment on a user B's content, he shares a new piece of content addressed to user B containing the comment to a specific object shared by user B and a reference to the object itself. This approach implies that user B has to connect to the service so as to "see" the new comments to his content and add them to the related objects. Although this leads to a less interactive model, in which rapid comment proliferation is only possible if the owner of the object is online, this guarantees users more privacy and more control on their own data and directly related comments and metadata. In fact each user is aware and can approve/discard each comment on his content, included his wall.

8 Evaluation

The described mechanisms allow the required basic interactions yet preserve users' privacy in the discussed sense. Indeed i) users only write their data to their own storage space; ii) storage spaces do not allow any write access but from the owner, iii) data protection mechanisms enforce that read access control is as defined by the owner. In Mantle, there is no need to ever copy your data into the authority of somebody else, and therefore the suppression of a specific account or a specific piece of content assures inaccessibility to other users within the context of Mantle, while the service hosting users' data never obtains access to the content (due to encryption). The local handling of all interactions by the trusted kernel, based on the publish-subscribe principle, and the resulting distribution and asynchrony of connections renders the traceability more difficult. The possibility of addressing content to specific subgroups assures a transparent and a relatively efficient revocation. Yet, using several sets of keys results in no further complexity, since for basic sharing operations only one key per list or community (GK) is used. On the other hand, in [9] authors show that a user with 300 friends and 2000 defined groups (there referred as *attributes*) would have a overhead of 15 MB for storing all the keys, which however represents not a big problem whether the user relies on services like DropBox as storage.

To estimate the performance of the basic architecture, we do not consider user profile sizes or profile content, but concentrate on the added overhead of Mantle (due to distribution of files and the applied encryption). We here consider the case of a Mantle application launch. On launch, Mantle client has to download several activity streams (one per contact/community) and decrypt their content. From here on, the procedure is in principle the same as for any other OSN. We therefore conducted tests in a scenario of a user with 130 contacts (average user), who downloads and decrypts 130 main activity streams. Here, all contacts use DropBox service for storing personal data. The size of activity streams is about 2KB, the used encryption mechanism is AES (128 bits). We measured the download time over university Ethernet, home Wi-Fi and public 3G connections, and the decryption performance with a typical PC (2.2 GHz core with 2 GB of RAM). We measured average combined download times of 3.5, 6.9 and 11.4 seconds respectively for all the 130 files, while all the decryption operations of the 130 files take an average of 0.511 seconds. Note that the decryption can start in parallel to downloads as file downloads are completed. Using a PC, the bottleneck is therefore in the download of the activity stream files. However, in absolute, the measured figures are encouraging: it should not be a problem to use Mantle, including on less powerful devices such as tablets or smartphones (average factor 10 for decryption, thus about 5 seconds for all the 130 files, but comparable network performance).

Table 3. Performance

	Univ. Eth.	WiFi	3G
PC	3.5 sec	6.9 sec	11.4 sec
Smartphones	5.1 sec	6.9 sec	11.4 sec

Table 3 resumes necessary time for browsing the activity list in the case of a user with 130 friends both for PC and Smartphone. Since the decryption and the download can be executed in parallel, the bottleneck is the highest among download and decryption time.

Note that the performance can be further enhanced by following a limited set of contacts in degraded network conditions or by specifying orders and preferred contacts.

Basic interactions, such as sharing a piece of content, need for 1) the upload of the new content, and the 2) download, decryption, modification (adding the new activity) and new upload of the related activity streams. However the total amount of time is relatively low and comparable to analogue activities in common OSNs.

9 Conclusions and Fure Works

Mantle proposes a new privacy preserving approach to online social networking. We are working on a complete implementation for evaluating further functionalities as well as performance on several devices. We are also working on a mechanism allowing several managers for a community and partially anonymous interaction within the latter, so as to participate to some communities by only revealing limited personal information. Finally, we work on proper handling of *activity streams* so as to reduce their size to the benefit of performance.

References

1. Baden, R., Bender, A., Spring, N., Bhattacharjee, B., Starin, D.: Persona: an online social network with user-defined privacy. ACM SIGCOMM (2009)
2. Buchegger, S., Schioberg, D., Vu, L., Datta, A.: PeerSoN: P2P Social Networking - Early Experiences and Insights. In: SNS (2009)
3. Cutillo, A., Molva, R., Strufe, T.: Safebook: a Privacy Preserving Online Social Network Leveraging on Real-Life Trust. IEEE Communication Magazine (2009)
4. Shakimov, A., et al.: Privacy, Cost, and Availability Tradeoffs in Decentralized OSNs. In: WOSN (2009)
5. Seong, S., et al.: PrPl A Decentralized Social Networking Infrastructure. In: MCS (2010)
6. Sun, J., Zhu, X., Fang, Y.: A Privacy-Preserving Scheme for Online Social Networks with Efficient Revocation. In: 2010 Proceedings IEEE INFOCOM (2010)
7. Dusseault, L. (ed.): HTTP Extensions for Web Distributed Authoring and Versioning (WebDAV), INTERNET RFC 4918 (June 2007)
8. Wong, C.K., Gouda, M., Lam, S.S.: Secure Group Communication using key graphs. IEEE/ACM Transactions on Networking 8(1) (2000)
9. Gunther, F., Manulis, M., Strufe, T.: Cryptographic Treatment of Private User Profiles (2011), `http://eprint.iacr.org/2011/064` (last checked March 14, 2012)
10. Lampson, B.: Protection. Proc. 5th Princeton Conf. on Information Sciences and Systems, Princeton (1971); Reprinted in ACM Operating Systems Rev. 8(1) (January 1974)
11. Bilge, L., Strufe, T., Balzarotti, D.: All Your Contacts are Belong to Us: Automated Identity Theft Attacks on Social Networks. In: WWW (2011)

Descriptional Entropy: Application to Security Software Analysis

Anthony Desnos[1] and Robert Erra[2]

[1] Virustotal
[2] ESIEA, CVO lab
adesnos@virustotal.com, erra@esiea.fr

Abstract. We propose here a tool we call *descriptional entropy*, that generalizes the classical Shannon Entropy. The tool is interesting *per se* and truly generic, *i.e.* it can be used with any files, it allows to define the "complexity" of a sequence, whatever is this sequence, it could be anything, from pictures to numerical data files or genetic sequences or *softwares*. It can be used for example to index, to sort or compare a set of files (or fragments of files).

The classical Shannon entropy is used in the current version of the software Androguard, with other algorithms like Normalized Compression Distance. But the next release of Androguard will use the descriptional entropy in place of the Shannon entropy. One of the main problem with Android applications is the plagiarism due to the facilities to modify and spread an application. Another problem is to detect malicious parts in an Android application, which is not so obvious. Androguard, written in Python and easy to use, can greatly help to analyse and compare Android applications.

Keywords: Shannon and Descriptional Entropy, Normalized Compression Distance, Malware, Android Application, Complexity Sequence.

1 Introduction

How complex is a string sequence ? There are a lot of situations where we need a tool to answer. We want to compare DNA sequences [10, 13], music files, pictures [4] or softwares [1–3, 6, 12, 16].

More exactly, we need a computable measure of the complexity of a sequence, for example to index, to sort or compare a set of files. The sequence can be whatever can be stored in a file. In this paper, we will say sequence, for any sequence of ascii characters. We are interestd in softwares, a software can be malicious or not, we will say *goodware* for a software that is not a malware.

So, can we define the "complexity" of a sequence? Let us give a simple example, we consider the four sequences:

- $S_1 =$ "*aaabbb*"
- $S_2 =$ "*ababab*"
- $S_3 =$ "*bbbaaa*"
- $S_4 =$ "*abbaab*"

V. Guyot (Ed.): ICAIT 2012, LNCS 7593, pp. 225–230, 2013.

It is easy to see that S_1 is the reverse of S_3, so it could be interesting for any function $Comp()$ defined as a measure of the complexity of a sequence to verify $Comp(S_1) = Comp(S_3)$.

The intuition tells us that S_1 and S_3 are more "close" than S_1 and S_2 or S_2 and S_3; S_2 is more "complex" than S_1; and S_4 is more "complex" than S_1, S_2 and S_3.

Let S be a sequence of characters, with an "alphabet" of n different symbols (generally characters). Let p_i be the computed probability of occurence of each of the n character in S, we will call the histogram vector $Hist = \{p_1, ...p_n\}$ and then the classical Shannon entropy of the sequence S is defined by:

$$\mathcal{H}(C) = -\sum_{i=1}^{n} p_i \log(p_i).$$

Let us see the simple example with S_1, S_2 and S_3, the alphabet is $\{"a", "b"\}$ they will have the same histogram vector entropy: $Hist(S_1) = Hist(S2) = Hist(S3) = \{1/2, 1/2\}$ which will give the same entropy: $\mathcal{H}(S_1) = \mathcal{H}(S2) = \mathcal{H}(S3) = 1$.

So, we have $\mathcal{H}(S_1) = \mathcal{H}(S3)$, however we also have $\mathcal{H}(S_1) = \mathcal{H}(S2)$ which contradicts S_2 *is more complex than* S_1, so the function is not suitable.

Let us give another problem with the classical Shannon entropy, if S is a sequence of characters, S...S, a concatenation of S and $\mathcal{H}$ the Shannon entropy, then we have $\mathcal{H}(S) = \mathcal{H}(SS) = \mathcal{H}(SSS) = \mathcal{H}(S...S)$, this is not really good !

We will see than we can do better with the a generalization of the Shannon entropy that we will call the *descriptional Entropy.*

2 From the Classical Shannon Entropy towards the Descriptional Entropy

A lot of measure of the complexity of a sequence have been proposed. For example, the Lempel-Ziv complexity [5, 8] is defined as the number of different subsequences (patterns) in a sequence when we apply the LZ algorithm. The sequence complexity, or the complexity index, of a sequence $S = s_1...s_n$ is defined as the number of different subsequences in S [7, 14].

In all cases we obtain a number which is difficult to use, or we have to take the histogram vector. But to compare two histogram vectors of unequal size is not easy. We propose here a new approach.

Given a complexity measure based on the count of different subsequences, we can compute the histogram vector $Hist(S) = \{P_1, ...P_N\}$ (which means we have N different subsequences) for this set, so now we can compute the entropy of this histogram vector. We propose to call this entropy the *Descriptional Entropy* of a sequence:

$$H_d(Hist(S)) = -\sum_{i=1}^{N} P_i \log_2(P_i). \tag{1}$$

To simplify we will write $H_d(S)$ for $H_d(Hist(S))$.

3 The Simple Example

Let us show it with the simple example. To simplify we neglect the "empty" sequence which is used sometimes:

1. For $S_1 =$ "*aaabbb*": the subsequence set is (in alphabetical order)

$$\{a, aa, aaa, aaab, aaabb, aaabbb, aab, aabb, aabbb, ab, abb, abbb, b, bb, bbb\}$$

so the histogram vector will be

$$Hist(S_1) = \left\{\frac{1}{7}, \frac{2}{21}, \frac{1}{21}, \frac{1}{21}, \frac{1}{21}, \frac{1}{21}, \frac{1}{21}, \frac{1}{21}, \frac{1}{21}, \frac{1}{21}, \frac{1}{21}, \frac{1}{21}, \frac{1}{7}, \frac{2}{21}, \frac{1}{21}\right\}$$

and the descriptional entropy will be (if we use the base 2 log function):

$$H_d(S_1) = 2\log(7)/(7\log(2)) + 4\log(21/2)/(21\log(2)) + 11\log(21)/(21\log(2))$$

which gives: $H_d(S_1) = 3.74899$.

2. For $S_2 =$ "*ababab*" the descriptional entropy will be:

$$H_d(S_2) = 3\log(7)/(7\log(2)) + 8\log(21/2)/(21\log(2)) + 4\log(21)/(21\log(2))$$

which gives $H_d(S2) = 3.3321$.

3. For $S_3 =$ "*bbbaaa*" the descriptional entropy will be:

$$H_d(S_3) = H_d(S_1)$$

which gives $H_d(S3) = 3.74899$.

4. For $S_4 =$ "*abbaab*" the descriptional entropy will be:

$$H_d(S4) = 2\log(7)/(7\log(2)) + 2\log(21/2)/(21\log(2)) + 13\log(21)/(21\log(2))$$

which gives: $H_d(S4) = 3.84423$.

So, we have: $H_d(S2) = 3.3321 < H_d(S_1) = H_d(S3) = 3.74899 < H_d(S4) = 3.84423$: we can *sort* the sequences! The result $H_d(S_1) = H_d(S3) = 3.74899$ is classical, the result $H_d(S2) = 3.3321 < H_d(S_1)$ is a little bit surprising but the whole set of inequalities is a good new; and we have S_4 is more "complex" than S_1, S_2 and $S3$.

Let us give another simple example, if we choose $S_5 =$ "*bbbbbaaaaa*" and $S_6 = S_5S_5 =$ "*bbbbbaaaaabbbbbaaaaa*" : we will have $H_d(S_5) = 4.82265$ and $H_d(S_6) = 6.68825$. It is not so difficult to verify experimentally that: for any sequence S: $H_d(S) < H_d(SS) < H_d(SSS) < H_d(S......S)$ but, despite it seems an easy result, the authors have been unable to prove it. It could be interesting to have a proof. Of course, for a very long sequence S the (practical) computational complexity of the computation of $H_d(S)$ is not cheap. We could probably find a fast(er) algorithm, based for example on some variation of the Aho-Corasick, Boyer-Moore or Knuth-Morris-Pratt algorithms. But we can also say: we just consider only subsequence of length bounded by a suitable integer k.

4 Application to the Real World: Androguard

How can we verify that two numerical objects are identical? It's easy, you just have to compare all characters, one by one, of the two files. But how can we say that two numerical objects are "similar" but not identical? Can we define a measure of "similarity" [4], which will give ipso facto a measure of "dissimilarity" [9]? The Normalized Compression Distance (NCD) [4, 9] is a possible answer but we think it is an interesting problem to define such a similarity measure using only the descriptional entropy of two sequences. It is still an open problem.

But what are these numerical files we want to analyse or to compare ? It could be anything, from pictures to numerical data files. The most interesting objects from a security point of view are goodwares or malwares, (remind: a goodware is not a malware). It can be Android applications or anything that you would like to identify, to analyse or to compare: firewall rules, log files etc.

While the tool we present here is truly generic, *i.e.* it can be used with any files, it has been applied, with other algorithms like NCD [4, 9], to a real subject: the analysis and comparison of Android applications. One of the main problem with Android applications is the plagiarism due to the facilities to modify and spread an application. Another problem is to detect malicious parts in an Android application.

The first author of this paper has developed a tool, Androguard [1], with the help of G. Gueguen, that helps to solve pratically these two problems; he also maintained an *Open Source Database of Android Malware* [11] where you can find analysis links and few signatures for Android malware. The main difficulty is to create a signature because you must choose carefully which method/class you would like to add in the database, in order to avoid as much as possible false positives.

But you can also use Androguard to check if your Android application has not been stolen by someone else by analysing multiples files. Imagine that you created an open source algorithm and you wish to know if your algorithm has been rip off by a proprietary software. Of course, it is possible to have others databases of any "things" if you wish, from a cryptographic functions database to a DNA database ...

The other problem, how to detect malicious parts in an Android application, can be simply defined as : how can we choose quickly, from a set $\mathcal{M}$ of known software files $\{m_1, ...m_n\}$, with $n \geq 1$, the subset of the files of $\mathcal{M}$ the "most similar" to a target A ? And how can we find quickly interesting differences without using a direct approach like graph isomorphism [6, 12, 2, 3] between 2 similar but different applications ?

Androguard follows the ideas presented in [2, 3] : we can change the *granularity* (or the resolution) of the analysis. For example, we can use any tactics not on full files but on different (smaller) objects : the functions and methods/classes.

Using the entropy, classical or descriptional, we can select the most interesting elements more quickly. We can use a filtering tactic to select the better files of the malware set $\mathcal{M}$, the current version of Androguard uses two different but similar tactics [2, 16]:

1. the NCD [2, 3] for a first filtering tactic to filter the set of candidates;
2. the classical entropy for a second filtering tactic the set $\mathcal{M}$, which gives a *set of candidates*.

The next release of Androguard will use the descriptional entropy. Tests on real Android applications and malware show that it gives better results than the classical entropy.

The algorithm (1) [2] describes formally the idea of the filtering tactic using the entropy (classical or descriptional). We suppose to have the "file"of a new application A and a database of M known functions $\mathcal{F} = \{f_1, \cdots f_M\}$, we suppose also that we can find all functions of A.

For each function $f_{A,i}$ of A, the algorithm (1) outputs a set of candidates: $\mathcal{F}_H = \{f_i\}_{i=1}^{i=K}$ is the set of already known functions such that the entropy of each file in $\mathcal{F}_H = \{f_i\}_{i=1}^{i=K}$ has an entropy very close to the function $f_{A,i}$ of A, *i.e.* such that for all $i = 1, \cdots K$ we have the following inequality:

$$|\mathcal{H}(f_{A,i}) - \mathcal{H}(f_j)| < \delta_H \tag{2}$$

The parameter ϵ_H is another threshold parameter, the *entropy* threshold parameter, a real number to be chosen by the user.

Algorithm 1. Filtering by Entropy of functions

Input:
  – a new file A ;
  – a database of M known functions $\mathcal{F} = \{f_1, \cdots f_M\}$;
  – a real $\delta_H > 0$: the threshold real ;
Output: – a set of functions $\mathcal{F}_H = \{f_i\}_{i=1}^{i=K}$;
Begin:
  $\mathcal{F}_H = \{\}$;
  Find all the functions $f_{A,1}, \cdots f_{A,N}$ of the file A ;
  For i=1 **To** M **Do** ;
    For j=1 **To** N **Do** ;
    If $|\mathcal{H}(f_{A,i}) - \mathcal{H}(f_j)| < \delta_H$;
  Then $\mathcal{F}_H = \mathit{Append}(\mathcal{F}_H, f_j)$;
    EndFor ;
  EndFor ;
  Return $\mathcal{F}_{\mathcal{H}}$;
End.

Due to lack of space, we refer to [16] where a lot of practical examples are given that show how to use the *descriptional or classical* entropy and the NCD on real Android applications and malwares.

5 Conclusion

We have presented here the *descriptional entropy*, that generalizes the classical Shannon Entropy. The tool is interesting *per se* and truly generic, it allows to define the "complexity" of a sequence, whatever is this sequence, it could be anything, from pictures to numerical data files or genetic sequences or *softwares*. So, it can be used to index, to *sort* or to compare a set of files, goodwares or malwares, or fragments of such files.

The descriptional entropy has been used in the next release of the software Androguard, to detect plagiarism and malicious parts in an Android application.

The authors would like to thank the (anonymous) reviewers, their valuable comments and suggestions have given to the authors the opportunity to make a more clear paper.

References

1. Androguard, `http://code.google.com/p/androguard/`
2. Darcel, R., Erra, R., Payet, P.: Exact and Approximate Graph Matching Algorithms for Binary Malware Analysis via Entropy and Normalized Compression Distance between Nodes. In: EICAR 2011 (2011)
3. Caillat, B., Desnos, A., Erra, R.: BinThavro: Towards a useful and fast tool for Goodware and Malware Analysis. In: ECIW 2010 (2010)
4. Cilibrasi, R., Vitanyi, P.: Clustering by compression. IEEE Transactions on Information Theory 51(4), 1523–1545 (2005)
5. Danaksok, A.D., Gaoglu, F.G.: On Lempel-Ziv Complexity of Sequences
6. Dullien, T., Rolles, R.: Graph-based comparison of executable objects. In: SSTIC 2005, Rennes (2005)
7. Janson, S., Lonardi, S., Szpankowski, W.: On average sequence complexity, `http://www.cs.ucr.edu/~stelo/papers/tcs04.pdf`
8. Lempel, A., Ziv, J.: On the complexity of finite sequences. IEEE Transactions on Information Theory IT 22, 75–81 (1976)
9. Li, M., Vitanyi, P.: An introduction to Kolmogorov Complexity and Its Applications. Springer (1997)
10. Needleman, S.B., Wunsch, C.D.: A general method applicable to the search for similarities in the amino acid sequence of two proteins. J. of Molecular Biology 48(3), 443–453 (1970)
11. Opensource Database of Android Malware, `http://code.google.com/p/androguard/wiki/DatabaseAndroidMalwares`
12. Sabin, T.: Comparing binaries with graph isomorphisms, `http://razor.bindview.com/publish/papers/comparingbinaries.html`
13. Shallit, J., Wang, M.-W.: Automatic Complexity of Strings. NCSE Reports 21 (1-2), 4–5 (2001)
14. Shallit, J.: On the maximum number of distinct factors in a binary string. Graphs Combin. 9, 197–200 (1993)
15. `http://www.c-sharpcorner.com/uploadfile/acinonyx72/calculating-the-normalized-compression-distance-between-two-strings/`
16. Similarities for Fun & Profit. Phrack Magazine issue #68, `http://www.phrack.org/issues.html?issue=68&id=15#article`

Adaptative Delay Aware Data Gathering Strategy for Wireless Sensor Networks

Nour Brinis[2], Leila Azouz Saidane[2], and Pascale Minet[1]

[1] INRIA Rocquencourt, 78153 Le Chesnay cedex, France
[2] National School of Computer Science, University of Manouba, 2010 Tunisia
rinis.nour@gmail.com, pascale.minet@inria.fr, leila.saidane@ensi.rnu.tn

Abstract. Extending the network lifetime is a challenging problem in wireless sensor networks. Using additional mobile agents called data collectors in order to gather data from sensor nodes and carry them to the sink, reveals a convenient solution. Intuitively, a great sensor nodes energy conservation can be achieved by single hop data gathering strategies. However, these strategies may lead to significantly increase the data latency in the network. Previous studies propose to introduce local relay transmissions in order to reduce the data gathering time. Most of these strategies rely on a static parameter in order to choose the data collector trajectory. In this paper, we focus on a novel data gathering strategy that aims at dynamically selecting the data collector trajectory according to the required data delivery delay deadline. In other words, the data collector may change its trajectory according to the urgency of the gathered data. For this purpose, we propose an algorithm for coloring the network area into red and green disks, according to the delay deadline required by the sensor nodes. Only the red disks must be visited during a tour of the data collector. Simulation results demonstrate that the proposed scheme significantly outperforms static cluster based gathering strategies by efficiently adapting the tolerated data latency to the consumed energy rate.

Keywords: Wireless sensor network, data gathering, delay, energy, data collector.

1 Introduction

Wireless Sensor Networks (WSNs) is involved in many fields of scientific applications, such as environment monitoring, health treatment, space exploration and others [1]. Each application has specific characteristics in terms of data accuracy, delivery delay... A WSN is usually composed of a large number of battery-operated sensor nodes having sensing, wireless communication and computation capabilities. Many researches relay on exploiting the application tolerability parameters in order to extend the network lifetime. One of the proposed solutions consists of using additional mobile data collectors in order to gather data and carry them to the sink, while conserving the energy of the static sensor nodes. These solutions are especially relevant for delay tolerant sensor applications.

V. Guyot (Ed.): ICAIT 2012, LNCS 7593, pp. 231–242, 2013.

In this paper, we focus on the problem of delivering data to the sink while conserving sensor nodes energy, in a WSN not necessarily fully connected. Our proposed strategy is based on the use of a mobile data collector, denoted DC, for gathering data from sensor nodes that are assumed to be static. We target especially delay tolerant applications. Our goal consists of carrying the sensed data to the sink before the delivery delay deadline expiration while minimizing the static sensor nodes energy consumption. Therefore, we propose a gathering strategy that adapts the data gathering strategy according to the required delivery delay. For this purpose, the DC colors the network area into red and green disks according to the required delivery delay deadline. Each red-green coloring corresponds to a maximal hop count local transmission. The network coloring may change during a tour of the DC according to the required delivery delay deadline of the collected data. Only the red disks must be visited by the DC. We evaluate our solution in terms of rate of delivered data meeting the required delivery delay and the corresponding rate of energy consumption.

The paper is organized as follows. In Section 2, we briefly present the state of the art related to data gathering strategies. Afterwards, we define our data collection scheme by presenting the algorithms describing the network coloring in Section 3. In Section 4, we evaluate the proposed solution and present the simulation results. Finally, we conclude the paper and give some directions for our future works in Section 5.

2 Related Work

Data gathering is one of the important issues addressed in many sensor applications in order to minimize the energy consumption. In spite of their great benefit in terms of energy conservation, visiting each node in order to collect data may be an infeasible solution especially in a very dense senor network. This is due to the exponential increase of the data latency while the nodes density increases. So, one of the alternative solutions consists of visiting the transmission range of each node in order to perform the data gathering by single hop transmission. This solution has been studied in [2] focusing on the Single Hop Data Gathering SHDG strategy. It was shown that the above-mentioned direct contact data gathering strategies have better benefit when the DC trajectory is controllable. Indeed, the static sensor nodes can in that case predict the data collector arrivals and therefore, they turn on their radio component only during the appropriate time corresponding to the data collector arrivals, in order to transmit their sensed data. Otherwise, static sensor nodes will deplete energy for detecting the data collector presence by listening to the polling messages. Therefore, the shorter is the data gathering transmission range and the more accurate are the predictable data collectors arrivals, the fewer is the network energy depletion. However, shortening the transmission range is only acceptable for delay tolerant application deployed on a sparsely sensor network. For this purpose, studies in [3], [4] and [5] propose to perform a cluster based gathering strategy. The data collector has to travel around the selected cluster heads in order retrieve data previously aggregated in these nodes. These studies differ on the criteria of constructing the clusters. In [5], two algorithms have been proposed in order to select the cluster heads that will aggregate data from static nodes by at most d hops bound. The centralized algorithm SPT-DCA is based on the construction of the minimum spanning tree. This tree will be explored node by node starting from the farthest one, in order to select the cluster head nodes that will aggregate the data from neighboring nodes at a given d hops bound. A decentralized version of the algorithm, called PB-PSA, is proposed. It relays on exchanging probing messages for the selection of the appropriate cluster heads. Studies in [6] propose a cluster definition according to the detection of the connectivity islands (partitions) of the network. Then, the cluster head is chosen in the middle of the partition and having the maximum residual energy. Rao and Biswas [7] presented a generic framework assuring a k-hop data collection without using nodes locations. They proposed a distributed algorithm which identifies a subset of nodes as navigation agents (NAs), then it computes a sink navigation path using ANT based distributed TSP solution which stops at the immediate neighbors of each NA, called designated gateways (DGs), to collect data.

Most of the previous data gathering studies deal with extending the network lifetime in a sparsely sensor network. For cluster based strategies, solution depends mostly on a static parameter such as the number of served nodes, the remaining energy, or a fixed bound of relay hops. This paper deals with improving the network lifetime via an Adaptive Delay Aware Data Gathering strategy, called ADA-DG. Our strategy aims at adapting the hops bounded gathering strategies according the delivery delay deadline given by the sender sensor node. In the following sections, we detail our proposal.

3 Data Collection Scheme

As discussed above, a direct contact data collection strategy contributes to maximize the network lifetime, by single hop data transmissions and predictable DC arrivals. However, this strategy may lead to an unacceptable data delivery delay, due to the lengthy tour of the DC. So, our data gathering strategy ADA-DG aims at finding a tradeoff between the data delivery delay and the energy consumption. For this strategy, the following assumptions were considered:

- All sensor nodes have the same communication range, denoted r_c and assume to maintain symmetric data links between neighboring nodes.
- Each sensor node has two independent components: sensing and communication units. Both units are powered from the same limited source of power (battery).
- The mobile data collector, denoted DC, has a large computational capacities.
- Each sensor node is able to compute their residual energy.
- Each sensor node and the DC have a memory sufficient to store the collected data.
- All the sensor nodes have to be visited in each tour of the DC.

3.1 Principle of the Solution

The key idea of ADA-DG consists of finding the suitable trajectory of the DC for each required data delivery delay deadline. In other words, each static sensor node sends their collected data to the DC with incorporating the tolerated data delivery delay deadline, denoted DDD. Knowing the DDD, the DC selects the suitable trajectory that allows to carry data to the sink at the appropriate time while minimizing as much as possible the static nodes energy consumption. The suitable trajectory is selected according to a suitable selection of a relay hops bound, denoted Hmax. Initially, the DC must discover the network. For this purpose, it visits the transmission range of each nodes, by stopping in the break points defined in [8]. [8] defines these break points as the tops of equilateral triangles of edge length $\sqrt{3}.r_c$. By this way, we ensure the exploration of all static sensor nodes by visiting a break point in their transmission range. The number of Break points is denoted nbp. At the end of this step, the DC records for each Break point BPi:

- *Ngh(BPi)*: the set of nodes attached to the concerned Breakpoint.
- the connectivity links between all nodes.

Hence, after this phase, the DC maintains an undirected graph $G(S, E)$ modeling the underligned network, where S is the set of sensor nodes $S = \{1, 2, ..., Ns\}$ and E is the set of edges between neighboring sensor nodes. the set of edges between neighboring sensor nodes. These information are used in order to plan an optimal tour for the DC. The basic idea consists of selecting a subset of the whole break points, which will be colored Red, denoted $RBPs$. Only the $RBPs$ must be visited by the DC. The remaining nodes attached to the remaining break points will be affiliated to one of the $RBPs$. So, our solution aims at coloring the graph G into red-green disks. Each graph coloring is performed according to a fixed value of the number of relay hops to reach the DC. Initially, Hmax is fixed to one, When the DC receives an urgent data, it selects another value of Hmax such that the sensed data arrives at time to the sink. Each Hmax-bounded colored graph remains the same until the occurrence of any network topology change or the energy attenuation of a node affiliated to a green disk into a minimal threshold, denoted Eth. In that case, the DC will be notified of these changes and a computation of a novel Hmax colored graphs will be performed. When the DC arrives into a RBP , it stops for a period, denoted break period, in order to gather data. Upon receiving the DC polling message, the affiliated sensors upload sensed data to the DC within at most Hmax hops. The local data collection is further presented in Section 3.3. The mobile collector starts its tour from the static data sink, which is located necessarily in a red Break point, collects data packets at the $RBPs$ and then turns back to the data sink. In the section 3.2, we explain the network coloring algorithm.

3.2 Centralized Algorithm for Network Coloring

After the network discovery step, the DC maintains the following variables:

- The initial set of Break points $BP = \{BP_1, BP_2, ..., BP_{nbp}\}$.
- For each BP_i, the DC maintains the list of static nodes associated to it, called $Ngh(BP_i)$.

Given, a value of $Hmax$, we aim to find a subset of BP that have to be colored red. The network coloring problem is divided into two steps. The first step consists of translating our problem into a logical satisfiability problem, which is the goal of Algorithm 1. The output of this Algorithm is a set of logical constraints representing the logical clauses. These clauses define the different possibilities to construct red-green network.

Algorithm 1. Graph coloring problem formulation

Require: a sensor network $G(S, E)$, the relay hop bound $Hmax$, a sink S, a set of nbp BPs : $\{BP_1, BP_2, ..., BP_{nbp}\}$, Ngh: the set of $Ngh(BP_i)$, $1 <= i <= nbp$.
Ensure: : A set of logical clauses $C_1, C_2, ..., C_{nbp}$

```
for i = 1 to nbp do
    if S ∈ Ngh(BP_i) then
        Color(BPi) ← red; C_i ← true; Break
    end if
    if Ngh(BP_i) is empty then
        Color(BPi) ← Green; C_i ← true; Break
    end if
    C_i ← true;
    for each n ∈ Ngh(BP_i) do
        if Er(n) <= E_th then        ▷ Er(n) is the residual energy of node n
            Color(BP_i) ← red; C_i ← true; Break
        end if
        D is set false
        for h = 1 to Hmax do
            for each node m/(n, m) ∈ E do
                if m ∈ Ngh(BP_j)/j ≠ i then
                    D ← D ∨ BP_j
                end if
            end for
            n ← m
        end for
        if D is false then
            Color(BPi) ← red; C_i ← true; Break;
        else
            C_i ← C_i ∧ D
        end if
    end for
end for
```

Let χ be the set of propositionnel variables $\{BP_1, BP_2, ..., BP_{nbp}\}$, a variable of χ is set truth means that the corresponding BP is red, otherwise, it is green. The output of Algorithm 1 is a set of logical clause $\{C_1, ..., C_{nbp}\}$. For example, let C_i the clause corresponding to the break point BP_i is:
$C_i = BP_j$ *or* $(BP_k$ *and* $BP_l)$
this constraint means that:
"BP_i is Green" $\Rightarrow$ *"BP_j is red" or "BP_k and BP_l are red"* (1).
With the aforementioned definition, (1) can be written as:
$\neg BP_i \Rightarrow BP_j \vee (BP_k \wedge BP_l)$
Our goal is to satisfy all the C_i clauses. So, we define the clause $C = \bigwedge\limits_i C_i$. The number of possible words is $N = 2^{nbp}$ We denote by $\chi = \{x^{(1)}, x^{(2)}, ..., x^{(N)}\}$ the set of possible words. A truth assignment defines a corresponding truth value of C, $C \in \{true, false\}$. Using the Truth table Generator, we calculate the corresponding truth table. We hold the truth vectors for which C is *true*. Our goal is to find the trajectory visiting the minimum number of red break points, this means that the required solutions is that having the minimum number of truth values in their truth statement. We may have many solutions, so, we denote $\chi_{MinR} = \{x^{(1)}, x^{(2)}, ..., x^{(l)}\}$ the set of words generating a truth value with minimum number of truth variables. The second criteria for selecting the RBP consists of minimizing the cost of the selected trajectory, in terms of number of relay hops. Algorithm 2 calculates this cost for each truth solution of χ_{MinR}. Then, the word offering the minimal cost will be chosen to select the $RBPs$. This selection is performed using the Algorithm 2, besides to the definition of the new set of neighbor nodes affiliated to each $RBP_i : Ngh$. Once the red break points are selected, the DC calculates the shortest possible route that visits each RBP exactly once and returns to the origin RBP containing the sink. This route is calculated using the heuristics for the Traveling Salesman Problem TSP. Figures 1, 2 and 3 illustrate respectively the network configuration, the result of our network coloring algorithm and the result of SPT-DCA algorithm, on a network of 36 sensors scattered over a 100m x 100m square area. The connectivity is represented by a solid link between any two neighboring sensors. The static data sink is located in the Disk of the BreakPoint 7. $Hmax$ is set 2.

A comparison of these two gathering schemes is performed in Section 4.

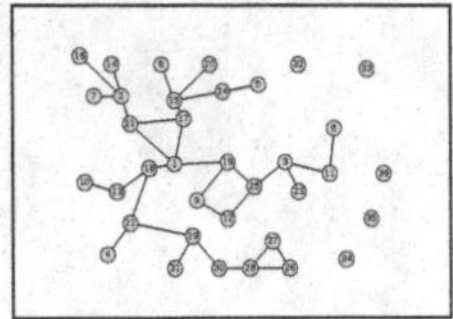

Fig. 1. Network configuration

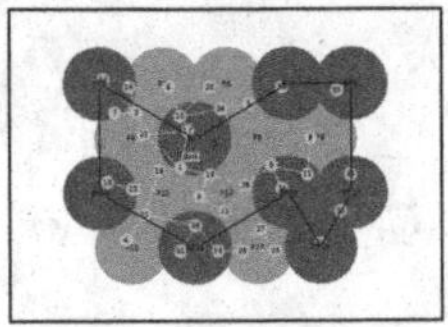

Fig. 2. DG Hmax=2

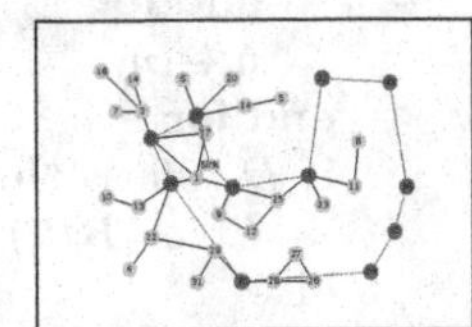

Fig. 3. SPT-DCA Hmax=2

Algorithm 2. *RBPs* selection and *Ngh* update

$knet \leftarrow 0$
$Ngh_i \leftarrow Ngh$
$Cnet \leftarrow Hmax * N$
for each $x^{(k)} \in \chi_{MinR}$ **do**
  for i/BP_i is green in $x^{(k)}$ **do**
    $Cmin \leftarrow (Hmax * card(Ngh(BP_i)))$ ▷ $card(Ngh(BP_i))$ is the cardinality of $Ngh(BP_i)$
    for each k/C_{ik} is true in C_i **do** ▷ $C_{ik} = \underset{l}{\wedge} BP_l$
      $C(C_{ik}) \leftarrow 0$
      for each node in $Ngh(BP_i)$ **do**
        for $h = 1$ to $Hmax$ **do**
          if $\exists(n, m) \in E/m$ in BP_l of C_{ik} **then**
            $C(n) \leftarrow h$;
            $Ngh(BP_l) \leftarrow Ngh(BP_l) \cup \{n\}$; Break;
          end if
        end for
        $C(C_{ik}) \leftarrow C(C_{ik}) + C(n)$
      end for
      if $C(C_{ik}) < Cmin$ **then**
        $Cmin \leftarrow C(C_{ik})$
      end if
    end for
    $C(x^{(k)}) \leftarrow C(x^{(k)}) + Cmin$
  end for
  if $C(x^{(k)}) < Cnet$ **then**
    $knet \leftarrow k$
    $Ngh_{knet} \leftarrow Ngh_k$
  end if
  $Ngh = Ngh_i$
end for
$RBP = RBP(x^{(knet)})$
$Ngh = Ngh_{knet}$

3.3 Delay-Aware Data Gathering Strategy

The goal of our strategy is to adapt the trajectory length to the application requirements in terms of delivery delay deadline. Using this strategy provides strong probabilistic guarantees on data delivery time to do not exceed the deadline fixed by the sender node. Two principles issues must be resolved in order to take benefit of the hops bound adaptability to the delivery delay deadline. The first issue consists of predicting the time of the DC arrivals. Due to the variability of the hops bound during the same tour of the mobile, the arrivals of the DC can not be predicted accurately. By contraries, sensor nodes can predict the period during that the DC must arrive: this period is $[DelayWaitMin, DelayWaitMax]$.

The $DelayWaitMin$ is that provided if the following used hops bound is fixed to the absolute value of $Hmax$, denoted $AHmax$, which refers to the shortest possible DC trajectory. The $DelayWaitMax$ is that provided if the following considered hop bounds is fixed to the minimal value of $Hmax$. Knowing that the value of $Hmax$ would not decrease starting from the current Break Point position to the sink and assuming that its minimal value from the sink to the current break point is 1, DC computes the $DelayWaitMax$.

The $DelayWaitMin$ and $DelayWaitMax$ are illustrated in the Figure 4. The red trajectory represents the shortest possible trajectory, the blue one represented the effectively pursued trajectory and the green one represents the longest possible trajectory.

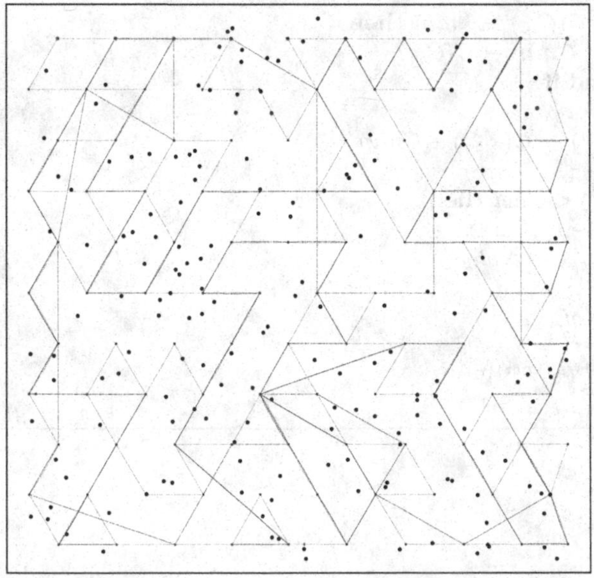

Fig. 4. Longest, shortest and effective DC tour

Besides, the delay between the DC stops is at least the time delayed for moving between two adjacent Break point: $\sqrt{3}.r_c$, denoted TBP. So, each sensor node begins listening the radio channel each TBP period, otherwise, it remains sleeping.
Once the DC stops at a break point, it knows the number and location of static sensor nodes to poll. In order to avoid the collision between the sender nodes data, DC implements the spatial-division multiple access $SDMA$ technique[9] by mounting multiple antennas. this technique aims at detecting the equivalents nodes for which the data may not interfere. These equivalent nodes will send their data in a same slot set by the DC.

Algorithm 3. Delay aware data gathering strategy

Hmax=1
DC stops at the first BP, to which the sink is affiliated, called BP_{sink}
DC determines the next RBP, $Hmax = 1$
for each RBP_i **do**
  DC determines the minimal required DDD, called DDD_{min}.
  DC calculates the delivery delay $DD(BP_i, BP_{sink})$, with the current $Hmax$ value
  if $DD(BP_i, BP_{sink}) > DDD_{min}$ **then**
    choose $Hmax$ generating an acceptable DDD.
    DC performs the network coloring ▷ if the corresponding colored graph is not yet calculated.
    DC moves to the next RBP
  end if
end for

---

4 Performance Evaluation

In this section, we evaluate the performance of the proposed ADA-DG strategy and compare it with the fixed relay hop count gathering strategies, denoted DG with specifying the $Hmax$ bound in the following results. Our solution is also compared with the centralized SPT-DCA solution and with the direct contact data gathering strategies: SHDG and the solution for which each node of the network is visited by the data collector, denoted ENDG in Figures 5 and 6. Each presented performance evaluation result is the average of 50 simulation experiments on a square simulation area of side length 600m. we depicts in Figure 5 and 6 respectively the average hops count and the obtained tour length for each gathering scheme when the total number of nodes varies from 60 to 500 to represent different node densities. We consider that each new measurement is performed by deploying randomly the appropriate number of nodes on those already deployed. Figure 5 shows that the average relay hop count increases as the network is denser. This is reasonable because when the density increases, the connectivity between nodes increases and so the number of red disks decreases. That is why, the relay hop count increases with the limit of the $Hmax$ bound.

For the same reason, we notice that using our strategy the tour length decreases when the network density increases. Otherwise, with a low network density, sensors will be more sparsely deployed in the simulation zone. Therefore, the probability to have nodes previously affiliated to a given break point polled from a farther break point decreases. The impact of introducing new connected nodes by randomly deploying new nodes has less effect on the tour length when the number of nodes is sufficiently large because of the rely hop count limitation.

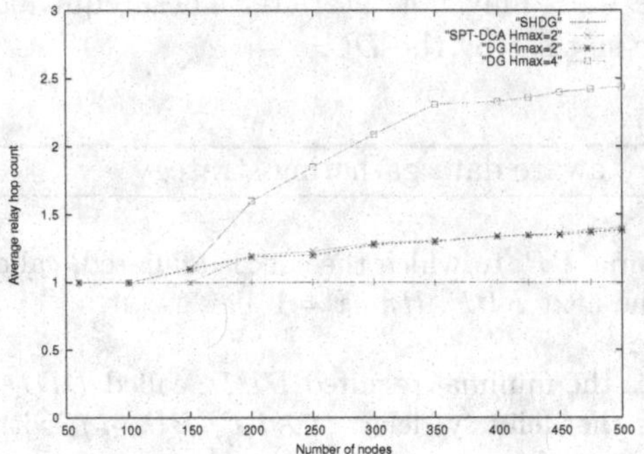

Fig. 5. Average hops count

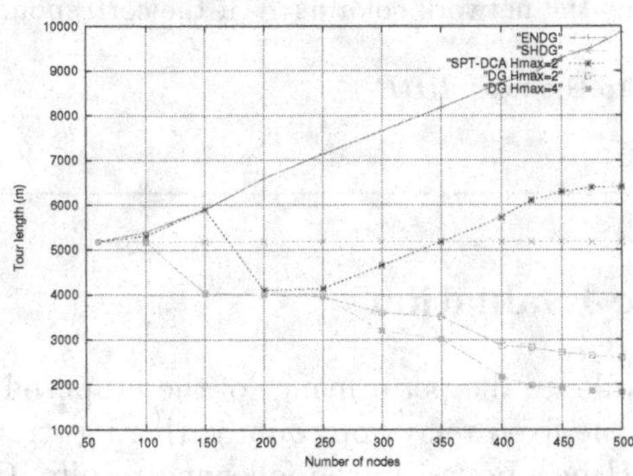

Fig. 6. Tour length

In contrast, the tour length, using SPT-DCA and ENDG strategies, increases when the number of deployed nodes increases. This is due to the acute dependency of these solutions of the sensor locations. SPT-DCA shows that the tour length stabilizes starting from a sufficiently large number of nodes. This is reasonable because the newly deployed nodes have higher probability to be affiliated with a previously selected cluster head. In order to evaluate our adaptative delay aware data gathering solution, we evaluate the probability of meeting the delay mentioned by the sender node. We suppose that the required delay is randomly chosen in the interval [2000, 3000] second. Due the randomness of the delay deadline choice, each following result is the average of 100 experiments.
Table 1 summarizes the simulation Networking parameters:

Table 1. Simulation parameters

Network configuration	Network area	(600m X 600m)
	r_c	50m
	Bandwidth	2Mbps
	Mac protocol	802.11
	DC speed	1m/s
	Break period	15s
Energy model	Type	Battery
	Initial Energy	15 Joules
	Transmit power	0.36 Watt
	Receive power	0.24 Watt
	Sensing power	0.015 Watt

Figure 7 plots the probability of respecting the required delay in the cases of fixed and variable relay hop count. this probability is defined as:

$$\frac{Received\_Pkts\_Meeting\_DDD}{Total\_Received\_Pkts} \tag{1}$$

It was shown that when the number of deployed nodes is sufficient to construct a short trajectory while respecting the $Hmax$ bound, ADA-DG guarantees to carry data to the sink before deadline expiration. The corresponding average consumed energy by DC tour, denoted $Avg - energy$, is depicted in Table 2, for different data gathering schemes. In this table, we present also the average delivery delay and the average relay hop count, denoted respectively $Avg - delay$ and $Avg - RHop$ the consumed energy rate for a given DC tour is defined as :

$$\frac{Energy_{beforeTour} - Energy_{afterTour}}{Energy_{beforeTour}} * 100 \tag{2}$$

Table 2 shows that ADA-DG outperforms other considered strategies but its energy depletion is impacted by the $AHmax$ value. So, this value must be properly estimated.

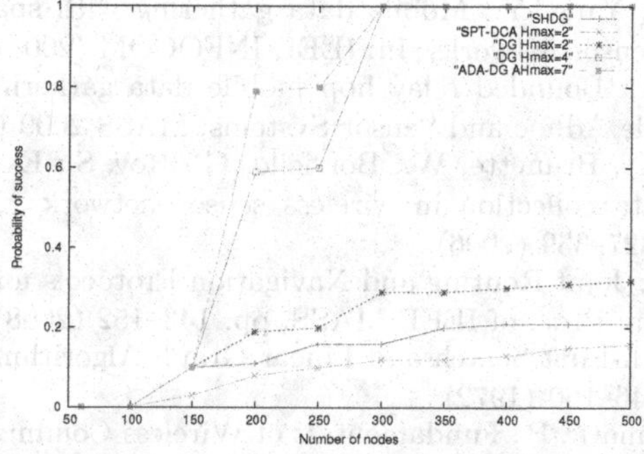

Fig. 7. Probability of meeting the required DDD

Table 2. Simulation results

Data gathering scheme	Avg-RHop	Avg-Energy	Avg-delay(s)
SPT-DCA (Hmax=2)	1.2	38%	4975.25
DG (Hmax=2)	1.1	32%	3625.21
DG (Hmax=4)	2.3	12%	2215.23
ADA-DG (AHmax=7)	1.9	41%	2316.12
ADA-DG (AHmax=5)	1.9	39%	2316.12
ADA-DG (AHmax=4)	1.78	38.2%	2316.29

5 Conclusion

In this paper, we proposed a data gathering strategy adapting the data collector trajectory to the delivery delay deadline. Indeed, only selected break points are visited by the data collector in order to carry the gathered data at time to the sink. To validate the proposed solution, we conducted extensive simulations and analyzed the probability of meeting the required delivery delay deadline and the corresponding rate of energy consumed for this purpose. We compare this solution with the fixed bounded relay hop solutions and the SPT-DCA one. It has been shown that ADA-DG outperforms SPT-DCA strategy especially for the dense networks. However, our strategy is affected by the unpredictable data collector arrivals. Our future work consists of modeling analytically the proposed ADA-DG solution and retrieving an analytical estimation of the appropriate absolute relay hop count.

References

1. Akyildiz, I.F., Su, W., Sankarasubramanian, Y., Cayirci, E.: Wireless sensor networks: A survey. Computer Networks 38(4) (March 2002)
2. Ma, M., Yang, Y.: Data gathering in wireless sensor networks with mobile collectors. IEEE IPDPS (2008)
3. Saad, E.M., Awadalla, M.H., Darwish, R.R.: Adaptive Energy-Aware Gathering Strategy for Wireless Sensor Networks. International Journal of Distributed Sensor Networks (2009)
4. Zhao, M., Ma, M., Yang, Y.: Mobile data gathering with space-division multiple access in wireless sensor networks. In: IEEE INFOCOM (2008)
5. Zhao, M., Yang, Y.: Bounded relay hop mobile data gathering in wireless sensor networks. In: Mobile Adhoc and Sensor Systems, MASS 2009 (2009)
6. Jain, S., Shah, R.C., Brunette, W., Borriello, G., Roy, S.: Exploiting mobility for energy efficient data collection in wireless sensor networks. Mobile Netw. Appl. (MONET) 11(3), 327–339 (2006)
7. Rao, J., Biswas, S.: Joint Routing and Navigation Protocols for Data Harvesting in Sensor Networks. In: Proc. of IEEE MASS, pp. 143–152 (2008)
8. Tarjan, R.E.: Depth-First Search and Linear Graph Algorithms. SIAM Journal on Computing 1(2), 146–160 (1972)
9. Tse, D.N.C., Viswanath, P.: Fundamentals of Wireless Communication. Cambridge University Press (May 2005)

Overcoming the Deficiencies of Collaborative Detection of Spatially-Correlated Events in WSN

Martin Peres, Romain Perier, and Francine Krief

Université de Bordeaux, LaBRI
{martin.peres,romain.perier,krief}@labri.fr

Abstract. Collaborative WSN are known to efficiently correlate sensors' events to detect spatially-correlated events with a low latency. However, because of the drastic reduction of messages sent to the network administrator, it is difficult for him/her to understand in what state the network is. In this paper, we propose a modality-agnostic collaborative detection of spatio-temporally correlated events that drastically lowers power consumption by both reducing and localising communication. This contribution can then be used to expose better auditing capabilities that overcome the problems usually found in collaborative networks. These capabilities can in turn be used by both the administrator and the network itself to, for instance, automatically react to faulty sensors. Experiments validate the interest of our proposal in an intrusion detection scenario.

Keywords: Wireless Sensor Networks, collaborative event-detection, low-latency, energy-efficient, autonomic-networking.

1 Introduction

As today's society expects the availability of information in real time on about anything, the problem of collecting and distributing information from remote or poorly-accessible places becomes more and more apparent.

The use of Wireless Sensor Networks (WSN) as a mean to lower deployment cost compared to a traditional wired sensor network is a widely accepted fact. WSN are already used in several fields such as monitoring air-quality, seismic activity, forest fires, structural integrity of a building and also area intrusion detection.

Sensor nodes are small wireless network nodes characterised by their very low processing power and storage capacity (both ROM and RAM). They are also characterised by very limited energy resources. Despite these constraints, sensors are usually expected to be secure and serve data with a relatively low latency and operate over a long period without swapping their batteries.

As the number of sensor networks grows, less and less human resources can be used to administrate them. This problem can be addressed by working towards autonomic and collaborative WSN that would not only lower maintenance but also improve the quality of service and increase power efficiency.

V. Guyot (Ed.): ICAIT 2012, LNCS 7593, pp. 243–257, 2013.

This research has been conducted during the DIAFORUS project [9]. The project's goal is to develop an energy-efficient framework for distributed applications and functions over redundant unattended sensors. As a demonstration of the framework, an intrusion detection application was written using redundant and heterogeneous sensors.

In Sect. 2, we introduce the state of the art concerning distributed and collaborative decision-making in Wireless Sensor Networks. Section 3 describes our proposal and how we believe it can not only reduce power consumption but also improve collaboration and error reporting. Then, Sect. 4 evaluates the proposal in an intrusion detection scenario and Sect. 5 introduces the future work. Section 6 concludes the paper.

2 State of the Art

According to [1], the energy cost of transmitting 1 KB over a distance of 100 m is approximately the same as the cost of executing 3 million instructions by a 100 million instructions per second (MIPS)/W processor. Moreover, with processors' efficiency doubling every 18 months (Koomsley's law [7]), it is clear that processor time is getting cheaper and cheaper while communications are bound by physical properties that limits efficiency improvements.

Based on these facts, it is clear that improving the lifespan of WSNs means diminishing both the number and the average length of communications.

The following describes common data-processing schemes and architectures for WSN and compares them from a number and average communication length point of view.

2.1 The Sink

Wireless Sensor Networks started as simple ad-hoc networks with the information flow going from all the sensors to the gateway. Indeed, each sensor node would collect data from the sensor, average/aggregate it and then send this data to the gateway. The gateway either processes the information itself, stores it or sends it through the Internet to another server. This gateway node is often refered as "the sink" as all the traffic ultimately is routed through him.

In this kind of WSN, sensors' readings are usually stored before being sent in batch to limit the number of packets at the expense of latency.

The average communication length on these architectures is the average route length that links every sensor node to the gateway. As all sensor nodes send data periodically, this kind of network's lifespan depends on how often the sensors' data is sent to the gateway.

2.2 Cluster-Based Data Aggregation

A way to lower the average length of communication is to let a data-aggregation cluster node gather data from his surrounding nodes, aggregate it into a single message and send it to the gateway.

This architecture introduces two kinds of communications:

- Short-distance: A one-hop communication
- Long-distance: A multi-hop communication to the sink

Long-distance communications should be avoided as much as possible to lower power consumption in the network. Indeed, they not only consume energy on both the emitter and gateway, but they also consume the energy of every routing node in-between. Moreover, nodes around the route are also consuming more energy because they need to receive and parse at least the MAC header in order to determine if they are the recipient or not. Finally, since the gateway is always the ultimate destination for every packet, the closer a node is to the gateway, the less likely the communication medium is to be available because of the ever-increasing traffic found when getting closer to the gateway. This further increases power consumption.

On the other hand, short-distance communications consume energy on a much more limited zone and more uniformly.

With the cluster-based data aggregation architecture, most communications are local and thus, spatially spread power consumption more evenly.

2.3 Local Event Detection

Instead of addressing the average communication length problem, local event detection addresses the problem of the number of messages.

Both the sink and the cluster-based data aggregation architectures rely on the outside of the network to process data. These architectures are data-oriented as they only acquire and forward sensors' data to the gateway.

If the WSN just feeds an application that is run outside the network, then it is possible to reduce the number of messages by only sending sensors' data conditionally [8].

For instance, in an intrusion detection application, it isn't necessary to constantly send the raw values read by the sensors. Instead, local processing of sensors' data avoids unnecessary transmissions by letting the sensor node detects whether the sensor detects something or not.

Local event detection may be challenging for sensor nodes because of their very tight CPU, ROM and RAM constraints, but it is possible to use digital signal processing units(DSP) [11] as these processors are getting more and more efficient [7].

Awareness of the WSN's application enables sensor nodes to limit the number of messages they emit by filtering the unneeded information [4][10].

2.4 Collaborative Detection

In spatially-correlated sensor networks, collaborative detection builds on the concepts of both local data aggregation and cluster-based data aggregation.

Sensors are first locally correlated to filter unneeded information and then, these information are collected in a cluster in order to correlate all the sensors of a given area [12][14].

This method further limits the message count by avoiding false positives induced by defective or ill-calibrated sensors. Less false positives also means reduced long-distance communications.

This method also works on heterogeneous sensor networks [6][2] and is also known to produce better results than value-fusion as found in cluster-based data aggregation when fault-tolerance is needed [3][13].

This architecture provides both a lower average communication distance and fewer messages in the network because of its aggressive filtering at both the node level and the cluster level.

However, to our knowledge, already-existing collaborative detection networks do not abstract the sensor modality. This severely limits the addition of new sensors at run time since the correlating node needs to be aware of all the sensor types and know how to correlate them.

Moreover, collaborative detection makes it more difficult for the network administrator to know if the network is operating correctly because of the low volume of messages. In case of a detection failure, it also makes it harder for her/him to debug what went wrong because no logs are available on her/his work computer.

Finally, because of the correlation found in collaborative detection, it is difficult for the network administrator to detect faulty sensors.

3 Our Proposal

To address the shortcomings of the state-of-the-art collaborative detection, we propose three different reasoning components:

- modality-agnostic collaborative detection of spatio-temporally correlated events
- offline logging capabilities
- sensors reputation management

3.1 Modality-Agnostic Collaborative Detection of Spatio-Temporally Correlated Events

Our proposal is based on the following assumptions:

1. an area defines a spatial zone where all sensors are correlated and can communicate with each other;
2. area's sensors should all detect an intrusion within a definite maximum time called maximum intrusion time;
3. sensors are noisy and randomly emit false positives;
4. sensors' may not be reachable at all time;
5. sensors are ill-calibrated.

Assumptions 1 and 2 have to be enforced when sensors are deployed. It also means network's lifespan can be improved by using collaborative detection to lower both the number of messages and the average distance of communications.

Assumptions 3 and 4 mean that the network should be fault-tolerant and thus, be using decision-fusion [3].

Assumption 5 raises the problem of sensors correlation. Since non-calibrated sensors' values cannot be averaged, it means that the values read by the sensor can only be interpreted by the sensor node that produced it. Indeed, the value can only be interpreted when put into its context, that is to say, the previous values/trends. Moreover, decision-fusion mandates the sensor to produce a decision whether it detects an event or not.

Thus, instead of reporting a given value, a sensor needs to locally correlate its values then decides if an event is going on or not. If an event is detected, a confidence rating ranging from 1 to 3 is attributed to the detection.

This proposal abstracts the sensor type and has many additional benefits such as:

- hiding away calibration errors from the correlation node;
- correlating sensors of arbitrary type.

Messages between the sensors and the reasoning node are sent using a Publish/Subscriber communication paradigm. This is done to ease the creation of topic of interests sensors can subscribe to. Moreover, publisher do not have to know which sensor nodes are interested in. This allows the creation of an highly-dynamic collaborative behaviour.

In our proposal, individual sensors are required to detect events by themselves and give a confidence rating ranging from 1 to 3. The algorithm that should be followed highly depends on the sensor modality and the event that should be captured. As an example, let's imagine we want to use a binary infrared optical barrier to detect a car driving down a street. The signal produced by the sensor will be a simple square whose length will depend on the speed of the car.

To detect such a square signal, the sensor node can poll the sensor's value periodically. The polling period depends on how wide the optical barrier is and how fast the car is. The maximum speed of the event to detect is one parameter of the area. As soon as the polled sensor detects something, a correlation timer is set. If the value sensor keeps on detecting something for, for instance, more than a tenth of the minimum detection time, then a message (hereinafter referred to as "alert") should be sent to the correlation node with the minimal confidence level. The confidence level should then be increased gradually to 3 as long as the sensor keeps on detecting the intruder.

When the correlation node receives an event from a sensor (alert), it stores both the current timestamp and the confidence level into memory for future reference. Then, it calculates the area criticality level by summing the contribution of all the sensors of the area.

A sensor's contribution to the criticality level is the confidence level of the alert times the age factor. The age factor linearly decreases from 1 to 0 in *correlation_time* seconds. The correlation time should be roughly the same as the maximum time it takes for an event to happen. In a intrusion detection scenario, it is the maximum time it takes for a pedestrian to cross the area.

The age factor is important because alerts should expire after some time. Moreover, older alerts shouldn't influence the correlation as much as fresh alerts do. The choice of a linearly decreasing function is motivated by the simplicity of implementation. It may however need to be adjusted depending on the kind of application you want to use this system in.

Computing the area's criticality level is done following (1).

$$age\_factor(a) = \begin{cases} 0 & \text{if alert\_age(a) > correlation\_time} \\ 1 - \dfrac{alert\_age(a)}{correlation\_time} & \text{otherwise} \end{cases}$$

$$\begin{aligned} alert\_age(a) &= current\_time() - alert\_timestamp(a) \\ contrib\_alert(a) &= confidence(a) * age\_factor(a) \\ criticality &= \sum_{a=0}^{alert\_count} contrib\_alert(a) \end{aligned} \quad (1)$$

When most sensors from an area simultaneously detect an event, the criticality level of the area should be higher than a threshold that depends on the number of sensors in the area and the minimal correlation factor we want to achieve.

When the criticality level goes over the threshold, the correlating node of the area publishes a message telling that an event has been detected by the area. This message, hereinafter referred to as alarm, can then be used by other nodes to trigger automatic actions such as lighting up a light-bulb or an alarm.

Being able to automatically trigger responses to an event enables fully autonomic collaborative WSN.

We also propose that the first node to be added to an area should be "elected" as the correlating node. However, this node may not be available during the whole lifespan of the network for the following reasons:

– energy source depletion;
– hardware malfunction;
– selective jamming on this node.

To overcome these challenges, the correlation node role should be split in two. Both correlation nodes would subscribe to the alerts sent in their area. The only difference between the two nodes would be that the master node (the first one elected) would emit an alarm as fast as possible. On the contrary, the slave correlation node (the second node to be added to the area) would wait for a few seconds before emitting an alarm unless the master node emits the alarm before the expiration of the delay.

This proposal increases reliability by avoiding the single point of failure that was the correlation node. However, a re-election should be made whenever the master correlation node's battery is running low or when the slave correlation node detects that the master isn't behaving correctly. In this case, the slave should elect himself as the master and query a list of potential candidates in order to select a suitable slave node to succeed him. If the slave node becomes unavailable, the master node should re-elect another slave node.

The election of a correlation node should be made according to these criteria:

– energy available (in Joules, not percentage);
– number of hops to the gateway;
– number of routes to the gateway.

Redundancy could then be further improved by electing n correlation nodes with an increasing delay between detection and the emission of an alarm. This works because every node of the area can communicate with each others (assumption 1).

However, redunding the correlation node comes at the expense of power consumption and thus, the network lifespan. Indeed, every correlating node is required to subscribe and receive every alert and alarm sent by the area and process them. As a result, the average power consumption of the correlating nodes is higher than other nodes in the area. This means there is trade-off between power consumption and redundancy.

3.2 Offline Logging Capabilities

Due to the drastic message reduction found at the gateway when using in-network reasoning, auditing the system becomes difficult. Auditing is needed by the network administrator to understand what is going wrong with the system in case of false positives or negative detections.

To address this problem, the correlating node should be required to store the history of what happened in an area in the past hours or days. Given the stringent constraints found on sensor nodes, it is impossible to store all the data. It is thus important to find an efficient way to only keep meaningful data.

The proposed solution stores events. An event is characterised by a local time stamp, a confidence level and the list of sensors contributing to this event and their relative contribution to it.

The system can only store a selected few events. When a new event needs to be stored, a usefulness score is attributed to each event in the history. The event with the lowest score gets replaced by the new event.

An important event is an event that both drove the confidence level close to the alarm threshold and was also a local maximum for a long time. However, when an event gets older, its importance tends to lower. This is why the scoring system (2) depends on the confidence level of the event, how long it was a local maximum and the age of the event.

$$score(e) = \frac{confidence(e) * local\_max\_time(e)}{1 - \frac{age(e)}{max\_storage\_time}} \tag{2}$$

The history can then be queried on-demand by a network administrator using a REST-like protocol such as CoAP [5].

3.3 Sensors Reputation Management

The history is not only useful to the network administrator, it is also useful to the WSN itself. An obvious usage of the history is to juge how useful a sensor usually is at detecting a certain type of event. We refer to this usefulness score as reputation.

We separate reputation in two scores:

- False positive: How often are the events emitted by a sensor not correlated with his surrounding nodes;
- False negative: How often is a sensor not participating in the correlation of real events.

Both reputations are represented by a value ranging from 0 to 1, 0 being the lowest possible reputation and 1 being the best.

$$reputation\_fp(a,s) = \frac{area\_detection\_count\_involving(a,s)}{sensor\_events\_count(s)} \quad (3)$$

False positive reputation is calculated when alerts are deleted from the history. When an alert is deleted, the detection count (sensor_events_count(s)) of the associated sensor is incremented. If the alert has been used to emit an alarm, then the alarm counter of the associated sensor (area_detection_count_involving(a,s)) is incremented. The false positive reputation is just the ratio of alerts that have been correlated over the total alert count for a given sensor. The equation is detailed in (3).

$$reputation\_fn(a,s) = \frac{sensor\_correlated\_count(s)}{area\_detection\_count(a)} \quad (4)$$

False negative reputation is calculated when an event is added to the history. If the event is an alarm, then the alarm count (area_detection_count(a)) is incremented. Then, all the sensors that participated to this alarm have their correlation count incremented (sensor_correlated_count(s)). False negative reputation is the ratio of how many times a sensor was involved in the emission of alarms over the total alarm count, the equation is detailed in (4).

Additionally, the reasoning node could alert the administrator when one sensor gets one of his reputations lower than a certain threshold. It can also be used during the correlation process to weight a sensor contribution according to its false positive reputation. A lower false positive reputation would result in a lower contribution during the event correlation.

4 Evaluation

For evaluating our proposal, we used a physical intrusion detection scenario. The latency of detection should be under 10 seconds and usually around 5 seconds. It was decided that sensor nodes shouldn't correlate values for more than 1 second before sending it to the network. This leaves up to 4 seconds for the network to carry the detection message and its acknowledgement(ACK). The event is re-emitted if no ACK is received by the sensor node that emitted the detection message.

It is however unnecessary to flood the network with alarms when an intrusion is detected. Two alarms can be separated by at least the area's minimum crossing time unless a new sensor has been correlated with an existing alarm. This amendum to the rule is made so as the administrator gets new meaningful information in the timeliest fashion. This proposal enables the administrator to be aware of the current situation while also limiting the number of messages.

The evaluation has been carried out in a custom-made simulated environment based on FreeRTOS. Each simulated sensor node is executed as a FreeRTOS Linux process. When a sensor sends a message, instead of sending it through the radio like it would be done on real nodes, the message is sent using TCP sockets to a program called dispatcher. The dispatcher emulates the communication medium. It forwards the message to the destination node if nodes are within reach of each other.

The dispatcher gets the sensor nodes' location from an XML deployment file. This file not only lists the sensor nodes, their positions and their radio range, it also contains all the sensor-specific configuration such as what sensors (modality) are connected to each sensor node and how (i2c address, gpio line, ...). This deployment file is used to generate the node configuration as C header files that are then compiled and linked with the node's firmware.

In simulation, the values read by the sensors are generated using a simulation environment called Diase. This environment, developed for the ANR DIAFORUS, enables:

- the deployment of a simulated network;
- the creation of intrusion scenarios;
- the monitoring of both sensor nodes and the network.

Monitoring gathers data from the network using a REST protocol for constrained applications called CoAP. It then displays the gathered data into a textual or a graph form.

Figure 1 is a screenshot of Diase running an intrusion scenario.

4.1 Modality-agnostic Collaborative Detection of Spatio-Temporally Correlated Events

Distributed and collaborative detection is meant to lower both the number and the average length of communications. We evaluate those metrics in this subsection.

Sensors are never perfect, if calibrated to detect the smallest event they will be prone to false positives. We choose to model the detection of an event by a sensor using a Bernoulli distribution. When no real intrusion is going on, sensors will have a probability p of wrongly detecting an intrusion and a probability of $1-p$ of not detecting one. The experience is repeated every second.

Fig. 1. Diase simulating an intrusion scenario

This means we have a probability p of getting a false positive. Knowing this, we evaluate how many messages are exchanged in different kinds of Wireless Sensor Networks. A distinction between short-distance (no hops) and long-distance (towards the gateway) communications is also introduced. The number of messages is then compared to the number of values read by the sensor. This comparative study is done for an area of 3 nodes, reading values every second for 30 minutes. The results can be found in Table 1.

Table 1. Comparing WSN data management on a 3-nodes area with a sensor noise probability (p=0.1, f=1Hz)

WSN type	readings	short-distance	long-distance
Sink	5400	0 (0%)	5400 (100%)
Cluster aggregation	5400	3600 (67%)	1800 (33%)
Local detection	5400	0 (0%)	540 (10%)
Collaborative detection	5400	$\leq$ 540 (10%)	< 180 (3.33%)

In the *sink* WSN, all sensors readings are forwarded to the gateway every second to fulfil the 1 second correlation time rule. This only generates long-distance traffic and is the worst possible case.

In the *cluster data aggregation* WSN, 2 of the 3 sensors send their values to the aggregation node. This node aggregates these 2 values with the value of his sensor in one message before sending it to the gateway. This means 67% of the traffic is local and 33% of the traffic is long-distance.

In the *local event detection*, sensors detect intrusions themselves. When they detect a suspicious event, they forward the acquired value to the gateway. As the sensor's probability to detect an event is 10%, then 10% of the values read are forwarded to the gateway and thus, be considered as long-distance communications. No short distance traffic is generated.

In the *collaborative detection* WSN, when sensors detect an event, it is sent to the correlation node. This node then correlates these events that expire after a certain amount of time that depends on the maximum time it takes to cross the area. This means up to 10% of the communications will be local. This value depends on the number of sensors connected to the correlation node. Telling how often a long-distance communication will happen is non-trivial because this highly depends on the algorithm used to correlate the local events. We now move on to testing the influence of the sensor noise and the correlation time on the number of short-distance and long-distance communications in our proposal. All these communications are false positives, so lower is better. We simulate the worst case scenario, when no sensors are connected to the correlation node.

Table 2. Message count in DIAFORUS with noisy sensors (f=1Hz, p=0.1) and a correlation time c. Experiment time of 30 minutes

Correlation	readings	short-distance	long-distance	$\frac{long}{short}$ ratio
c=10s	5400	545 (10%)	8 (0.15%)	1.5%
c=20s	5400	558 (10.3%)	23 (0.43%)	4.1%
c=40s	5400	541 (10%)	32 (0.59%)	6%
c=60s	5400	516 (9.5%)	33 (0.61%)	6.3%
c=90s	5400	525 (9.7%)	40 (0.74%)	7.7%
c=120s	5400	518 (9.5%)	41 (0.76%)	7.8%
c=150s	5400	552 (10.2%)	50 (0.93%)	9%
c=180s	5400	520 (9.6%)	56 (1.03%)	10.7%

In Table 2, we evaluate the influence of the correlation time over the number and length of communications. As expected, the number of local detections is around 10%, which is the sensor noise. Concerning the long-distance communications, the longer the correlation time, the higher the number of messages. This can be explained because the longer the correlation time, the higher the probability of correlation between sensors. Areas should then be as small as possible to limit the number of false positives.

In Table 3, we evaluate the influence of the sensor noise over the number and length of communications. As expected, the number of local detections is linear

Table 3. Message count in DIAFORUS with noisy sensors (f=1Hz, p) and a correlation time of 180s. Experiment time of 30 minutes

Sensor noise	readings	short-distance	long-distance
p=0	5400	0 (0%)	0 (0%)
p=0.002	5400	11 (0.2%)	0 (0%)
p=0.02	5400	94 (1.7%)	0 (0%)
p=0.1	5400	545 (10%)	56 (1.03%)
p=1	5400	5400 (100%)	210 (3.89%)

with the sensor noise. Long distance communications count is increasing with the sensor noise.

In tables 2 and 3, the number of long distance communications don't scale linearly with the correlation time and noise probability because of the no-alarm-re-emission policy that is meant to limit the number of messages. In the case of Table 3, when p=1, we got an average of an alarm every 8.5 seconds even though the minimum intrusion time was set to 10 seconds. The 15% difference is due to the amendum to the no-alarm-re-emission policy that states than an alarm could be re-emitted if a new sensor was correlated with the on-going alarm.

With a relatively small correlation time (60s) and a relative low probability of false positive (2%), no alarms has been emitted during these 30 minutes. In normal situations, both the number and the average length of communications were lowered compared to non-collaborative approaches. Sensors' average noise determining the minimum number of messages that will be sent. In the worst case scenario studied, the number of messages is increased by 3.9% compared to the "Sink WSN" architecture while the average communication distance tended towards 0 hops which is an considerable improvement on large scale networks for both latency and power consumption.

4.2 Sensors Reputation Management

In the previous subsection, we investigated the influence of the average sensor's noise and the maximum intrusion duration on the average communication length and the number of messages. We saw that most of the time, the reasoning node was able to filter false positives as long as sensors aren't too noisy. In the case of a single faulty sensor, it is likely that the administrator will never receive any information concerning this sensor.

We created one scenario to validate both false positives and negatives. It features 2 areas which can be seen in Fig. 2.

Area 1 is composed of sensors 1, 2 and 3 and is meant to test false negatives. An intruder is repeatedly detected by sensors 1 and 2 but is never detected by sensor 3. No sensor noise was added to ease validation. After some time, nodes 1 and 2 are expected to have both a perfect false negative and a perfect false positive reputation while node 3 is expected to have a perfect false positive reputation but the lowest false negative reputation because it never contributed to any alarms.

Area 2 is composed of sensors 4, 5 and 6 and is meant to test false positives. An intruder is repeatedly detected by sensors 5 but is never detected by sensors 4 and 6. Again, no sensor noise was added to ease validation. After some time, nodes 4 and 6 are expected to have both a perfect false negative and a perfect false positive reputation. However, node 5 is expected to have a perfect false negative reputation along with the lowest false positive reputation because none of the alerts it sent led to emission of an alarm.

Results found in Table 4 are perfectly matching the expected reputation values. These results demonstrate the ability of our proposal to detect both the false positive and the false negative cases.

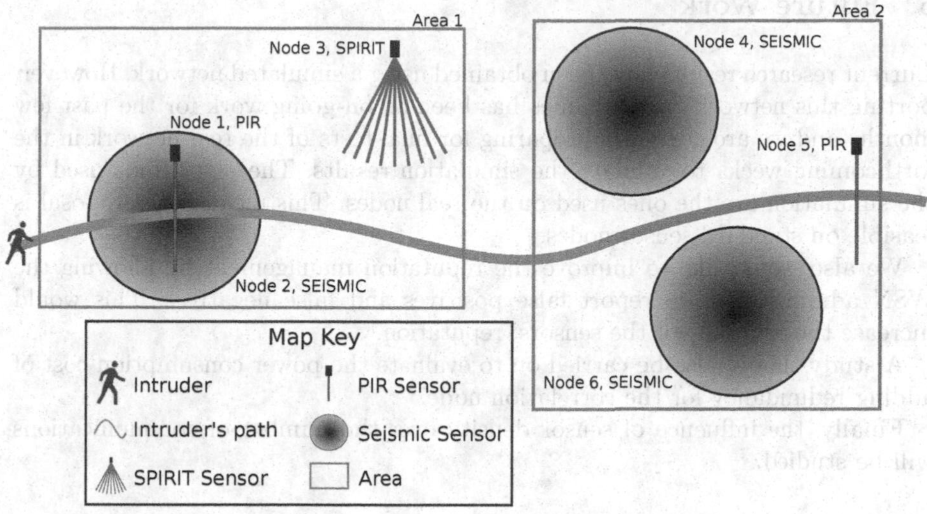

Fig. 2. Scenario validating the reputation. 2 areas, 6 sensors.

Table 4. Results of the reputation experiment found on Fig. 2

Node ID	False positive reputation	False negative reputation
1 & 2	1 (18/18)	1 (283/283)
3	NaN (0/0)	0 (0/283)
4 & 6	NaN (0/0)	NaN (0/0)
5	0 (0/9)	NaN (0/0)

The scenario has then been changed to simulate the impact of noise (p=0.1, f=1Hz) on the sensors' reputation. The results are shown in Table 5.

With a noise probability (p=0.1, f=1Hz), sensors apparently sent an alert every 10.7s in average. With a correlation time of 20 seconds, it was pretty likely for all sensors to be participating in all alarms that were sent during these 30 minutes. This explains the false negative reputation of 1 for all three nodes.

As expected, the false positive reputation of sensors 1, 2 and 3 is quite low. It would be even lower if not all sensors were faulty or if not all sensors were so noisy because less alarms would have been sent.

Table 5. Reputation of noisy sensors (p=0.1, f=1Hz) after 30 minutes and correlation time of 20 seconds

Node ID	False positive reputation	False negative reputation
1	0.34 (57/168)	1 (119/119)
2	0.34 (57/167)	1 (119/119)
3	0.34 (57/169)	1 (119/119)

5 Future Work

Current research results have been obtained using a simulated network. However, porting this network on real nodes has been an on-going work for the past few months and we are currently preparing for final tests of the real network in the forthcoming weeks to validate the simulation results. The algorithms used by the simulation are the ones used on the real nodes. This means our proposal is feasible on standard sensor nodes.

We also would like to improve the reputation management by allowing the WSN administrator to report false positives and false negatives. This would increase the accuracy of the sensors' reputation.

A study should also be carried on to evaluate the power consumption cost of adding redundancy for the correlation node.

Finally, the influence of sensor density over the number of communications will be studied.

6 Conclusion

In this paper, we demonstrated a modality-agnostic collaborative detection of spatio-temporally correlated events. Correlating sensors' values inside the network instead of forwarding data to the gateway achieves a drastically lower power consumption by both reducing and localising communication. Our contribution enhances the state-of-the-art collaborative networks by abstracting sensors which allows the reasoning node to correlate ill-calibrated heterogeneous sensors. This abstraction also eases the creation of better auditing capabilities that overcome the problems usually found in collaborative networks. These capabilities can be used by both the administrator and the network itself to, for instance, automatically react to faulty sensors.

Acknowledgements. This work is part of research project called DIstributed Applications and Functions Over Redundant Unattended Sensors (DIAFORUS) [9], funded by the French National Research Agency (ANR).

References

1. Akyildiz, I.F., Su, W., Sankarasubramaniam, Y., Cayirci, E.: Wireless sensor networks: a survey. Computer Networks 38, 393–422 (2002)
2. Andersson, D., Fong, M., Valdes, A.: Heterogeneous Sensor Correlation: A Case Study of Live Traffic Analysis (2002)
3. Clouqueur, T., Ramanathan, P., Saluja, K.K., Wang, K.C.: Value-fusion versus decision-fusion for fault-tolerance in collaborative target detection in sensor networks. In: Proceedings of Fourth International Conference on Information Fusion (2001), `http://citeseerx.ist.psu.edu/viewdoc/summary?doi=10.1.1.116.6587`

4. Croce, S., Marcelloni, F., Vecchio, M.: Reducing power consumption in wireless sensor networks using a novel approach to data aggregation. The Computer Journal 51(2), 227–239 (2008), http://comjnl.oxfordjournals.org/content/51/2/227
5. Frank, B., Shelby, Z., Hartke, K., Bormann, C.: Constrained application protocol (CoAP), https://tools.ietf.org/html/draft-ietf-core-coap-03
6. He, Y., Li, M., Liu, Y.: Collaborative query processing among heterogeneous sensor networks. In: Proceedings of the 1st ACM International Workshop on Heterogeneous Sensor and Actor Networks, HeterSanet 2008, pp. 25–30. ACM, New York (2008), http://doi.acm.org/10.1145/1374699.1374705
7. Koomey, J., Berard, S., Sanchez, M., Wong, H.: Implications of historical trends in the electrical efficiency of computing. IEEE Annals of the History of Computing 33(3), 46–54 (2011)
8. Krishnamachari, B., Estrin, D., Wicker, S.B.: The impact of data aggregation in wireless sensor networks. In: Proceedings of the 22nd International Conference on Distributed Computing Systems, ICDCSW 2002, pp. 575–578. IEEE Computer Society, Washington, DC (2002), http://dl.acm.org/citation.cfm?id=646854.708078
9. LaBRI: Diaforus (2010), https://diaforus.labri.fr/doku.php (accessed May 25, 2012)
10. Lazzerini, B., Marcelloni, F., Vecchio, M., Croce, S., Monaldi, E.: A fuzzy approach to data aggregation to reduce power consumption in wireless sensor networks. In: Annual Meeting of the North American Fuzzy Information Processing Society, NAFIPS 2006, pp. 436–441 (June 2006)
11. Letian, H., Guangjun, L.: A reconfigurable system for digital signal processing. In: 9th International Conference on Signal Processing, ICSP 2008, pp. 439–442 (October 2008)
12. Nasipuri, A.: Collaborative Detection of Spatially Correlated Signals in Sensor Networks. In: Proceedings of the 2005 International Conference on Telecommunication Systems Modeling and Analysis. Dallas, Texas (November 2005)
13. Ould-Ahmed-Vall, E., Heck Ferri, B., Riley, G.: Distributed Fault-Tolerance for event detection using heterogeneous wireless sensor networks. IEEE Transactions on Mobile Computing 11(12), 1994–2007 (2012), http://ieeexplore.ieee.org/xpl/articleDetails.jsp?reload=true&arnumber=6030876
14. Phani Kumar, A.V.U., Reddy, V.A.M., Janakiram, D.: Distributed collaboration for event detection in wireless sensor networks. In: Proceedings of the 3rd International Workshop on Middleware for Pervasive and Ad-Hoc Computing, MPAC 2005, pp. 1–8. ACM, New York (2005), http://doi.acm.org/10.1145/1101480.1101491

A Low-Complexity and High-Performance Beamforming Scheme for mmWave WPAN Systems*

Ying-Tsung Lin[1], Huan-Shun Yeh[1], and Sau-Gee Chen[2]

Department of Electronics Engineering & Institute of Electronics, National Chiao-Tung University, Hsinchu, Taiwan
{ytlin.ee97g,poly0529.ee98g}@nctu.edu.tw, 2sgchen@mail.nctu.edu.tw

Abstract. This work presents an efficient technique which significantly enhances the performance of current codebook-based beamforming scheme for mmWave WPAN communication systems. The proposed technique, named CB-AoDE, is firstly applied to the transmit side, and estimates the angle-of-departure (AoD) based on the feedback SNRs from the receive side during the beam-search process. The estimated AoD is then used to generate a more accurate transmit beam vector. The same procedure can be as well applied to estimate the angle-of-arrival (AoA) which helps generate the corresponding receive beam vector. Simulation results show that the proposed technique performs averagely 1.8dB, 1.4dB and 1dB better than the codebook-based scheme in AWGN, light-of-sight (LOS), and Non-LOS (NLOS) channels, respectively. Moreover, the proposed one only needs one DAC and ADC at transmit and receive sides, respectively. The hardware cost and computational complexity are thus tremendously reduced.

Keywords: beamforming, IEEE 802.15.3c, beam switching.

1 Introduction

Multiple-Gbps wireless communication systems for wireless personal area network (WPAN) have been actively developed since recent years, due to high demand in the applications of uncompressed video and data streaming applications. IEEE 802.15.3c [1] and IEEE 802.11.ad [2] standards, operating in the 60GHz (or mmWave) band, are major standards for these applications. However, the nature of the high propagation loss in the 60GHz band leads to less transmission coverage and lower the link quality. Techniques using multiple antennas are necessary in overcoming these problems. Particularly, in view of the hardware cost and available bandwidth, the technique of beamforming, instead of spatial multiplexing, are generally adopted. In existing literatures, several beamforming techniques have been proposed for mmWave WPAN systems. Firstly, the optimal beamforming [3] can achieve optimal performance but inherits the problem of high computational complexity, because a large number of antennas is defined and

---

* This work was supported by the NSC, Taiwan, under Contracts NSC 100-2219-E-009 -016 and NSC 100-2220-E-009 -026.

V. Guyot (Ed.): ICAIT 2012, LNCS 7593, pp. 258–263, 2013.

supported in both IEEE 802.15.3c and IEEE 802.11.ad standards. A lower-complexity hybrid beamforming [4] is proposed to enhance the antenna gain for WPAN systems but still requires the complicated optimal beamforming at the receive side.

In order to simplify the hardware implementation, mmWave systems adopt the codebook-based beamforming scheme which predefines simplified beam vectors in terms of the number of antennas, and best beam vectors for transmit and receive sides are obtained by a cross-layer beam-search process and determined in terms of the feedback SNR information [5]. However, it suffers performance degradations as compared to the optimal one. Therefore, in order to enhance the performance, this work presents a low-complexity and high-performance beamforming technique, codebook-based beamforming with angle-of-departure estimations (CB-AoDE), which estimates the AoD via the feedback SNR information available after the completion of the beam-search process. The estimated AoD is then utilized to generate a more accurate transmit beam vector. Its performance can very closely approach the optimal beamforming with higher phase resolutions but with much lower hardware costs. This work focuses on discussing the case of the IEEE 802.15.3c. However, the same technique can be applied to the 802.11.ad due to their high similarity.

2 System Model

Fig. 1 shows the system diagram of a system exploiting the codebook-based beamforming with M_t and M_r antennae at the transmitter TX (DEV1) and receiver RX (DEV2) sides, where w_i and c_j denote elements in $M_t \times 1$ vector $\boldsymbol{w}$ and $M_r \times 1$ vector $\boldsymbol{c}$ at the i-th and j-th antennae of TX and RX, respectively. Besides, the operator $\circ$ denotes entrywise multiplications.Note that 1-D antenna array with the wavelength λ is assumed in this work. The steering vector, $\mathbf{a}(\bullet)$, can be expressed as

$$\mathbf{a}(\theta) = [1 \quad e^{j\frac{2\pi}{\lambda}d\cos\theta} \quad \dots \quad e^{j\frac{2\pi}{\lambda}(M-1)d\cos\theta}]^{\mathrm{T}}, \tag{1}$$

where d denotes the distance between adjacent antennas and is equal to $\lambda/2$. Mathematical expressions of the system model are given as

$$\begin{aligned} z &= \mathbf{c}^H \left\{ \left[\left(\mathbf{a}(\theta_r)\mathbf{a}^T(\theta_t) \right) \circ \mathbf{H} \right] \mathbf{w} \frac{x}{\sqrt{M_t}} + \mathbf{n} \right\} \\ &= \mathbf{c}^H \left(\tilde{\mathbf{H}}\mathbf{w} \frac{x}{\sqrt{M_t}} + \mathbf{n} \right) \\ &= \left[\left(\mathbf{c}^* \circ \mathbf{a}(\theta_r) \right)^T \mathbf{H} \left(\mathbf{a}(\theta_t) \circ \mathbf{w} \right) \right] \frac{x}{\sqrt{M_t}} + \mathbf{c}^H \mathbf{n}, \end{aligned} \tag{2}$$

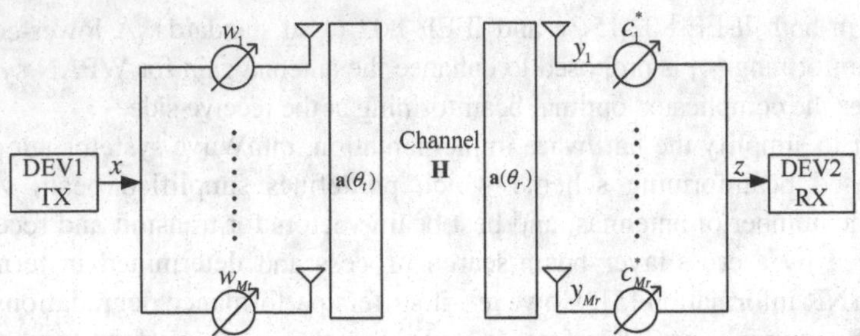

Fig. 1. A block diagram of an MIMO system using the codebook based beamforming

where $\mathbf{H}$ and $\mathbf{n}$ are the $M_r \times M_t$ channel matrix due to multipath effects and an $M_r \times 1$ AWGN vector with $\mathcal{CN}(0, \sigma_n^2 \mathbf{I}_{M_r})$, respectively. In addition, $\tilde{\mathbf{H}}$ denotes the channel matrix containing the steering vector information. Besides, θ_t, θ_r and $\mathbf{a}(\bullet)$ are angles of departure for the DEV1, DEV2, and the function of the steering vector, respectively. The mean and variance of the transmit signal x are also modeled as 0 and 1 for simplicity. Note that the $\sqrt{M_t}$ term in (2) is to normalize the transmit power. Next, consider that

$$E\left[\left|\mathbf{c}^H \mathbf{n}\right|^2\right] = M_r \sigma_n^2, \tag{3}$$

Then, the overall output SNR in Fig. 1 is

$$\gamma = \frac{\left|\mathbf{c}^H \tilde{\mathbf{H}} \mathbf{w}\right|^2}{M_t M_r \sigma_n^2} = \frac{\left|\left(\mathbf{c}^* \circ \mathbf{a}(\theta_r)\right)^T \mathbf{H}\left(\mathbf{a}(\theta_t) \circ \mathbf{w}\right)\right|^2}{M_t M_r \sigma_n^2}. \tag{4}$$

3 The Proposed Beamforming Scheme

This section introduces the proposed scheme, CB-AoDE, where the AoD information is estimated based on the information of feedback SNRs and selected beam vectors. Note that the proposed scheme is performed after the stage of the beam-search process is completed.

In this work, the SNR estimation and the average noise power are assumed perfect and static, respectively, during the beam-search process. Fig. 2(a) gives an example of the proposed technique. Beams i and j, whose corresponding beam vectors are $\mathbf{w}_i$ and $\mathbf{w}_j$, at DEV 1 are assumed to be associated with the highest and second highest feedback SNRs, respectively. The procedure to derive AoD θ_t is described in more details as follows.

Step 1: Select two beams with the highest two feedback SNRs, γ_i and γ_j based on the feedback information.

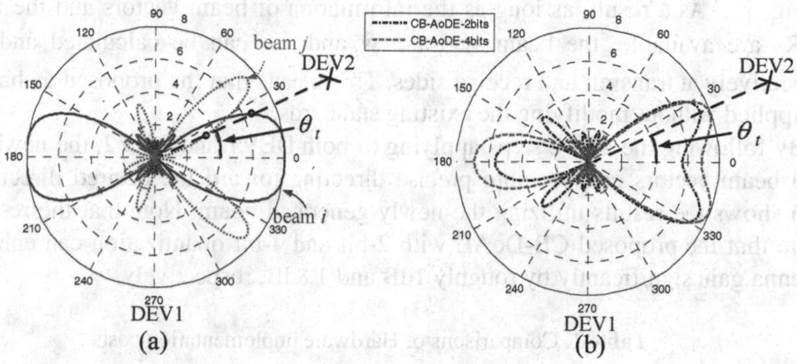

Fig. 2. Illustrations of the beamforming techniques with 8 antennas, θ_t = 25 degree, for (a) the IEEE 802.15.3c codebook beamforming (b) the CB-AoDE beamforming

Step 2: Take the ratio of γ_i and γ_j (in expanded form)

$$\frac{\gamma_i}{\gamma_j} = \frac{\left|\left(\mathbf{c}^* \circ \mathbf{a}(\theta_r)\right)^T \mathbf{H}\left(\mathbf{a}(\theta_t) \circ \mathbf{w}_i\right)\right|^2}{\left|\left(\mathbf{c}^* \circ \mathbf{a}(\theta_r)\right)^T \mathbf{H}\left(\mathbf{a}(\theta_t) \circ \mathbf{w}_j\right)\right|^2} = \frac{\left|\sum_{m=0}^{M_t} w_{i,m} e^{j2\pi\cdot(m-1)(\frac{d}{\lambda})\cos\theta_t}\right|^2}{\left|\sum_{n=0}^{M_t} w_{j,n} e^{j2\pi\cdot(n-1)(\frac{d}{\lambda})\cos\theta_t}\right|^2}, \tag{5}$$

where $w_{k,l}$ denotes the element of the k-th beam vector at the l-th antenna. Since γ_i, γ_j, and beam vectors, $\mathbf{w}_i$ and $\mathbf{w}_j$, are known, θ_t remains the only unknown variable. Hence, the estimated AoD, $\hat{\theta}_t$, can be obtained by solving the equality in (5). Finally, θ_t can be justified whether it is located in $[0,\pi]$ or $[\pi,2\pi]$ during the quasi-omni beam-search process.

Step 3: Generate and quantize the new beam vector according to the estimated AoD as

$$\hat{\mathbf{w}}_i = fix_B(\mathbf{a}^*(\hat{\theta}_t)), \tag{6}$$

where $fix_B(\bullet)$ quantize the argument to the closest 2^B phases equally dividing $[0,2\pi]$.

Step 4: Re-do steps 1 to 3 to obtain the newly generated beam vector $\hat{\mathbf{c}}_i$ for DEV 2 in Fig. 1. As a result, as long as the information of beam vectors and the feedback SNRs are available, the beam vectors, $\hat{\mathbf{w}}_i$ and $\hat{\mathbf{c}}_i$, can be calculated and applied respectively at transmit and receive sides. This means that the proposed technique can be applied without modifying the existing standards.

By following the above steps applying to both DEV1 and DEV2, the newly generated beam vectors can be more precise directing toward the desired direction. Fig. 2(b) shows the results utilizing the newly generated beam. Note that the results illustrate that the proposed CB-DoAE with 2-bit and 4-bit quantization can enhance the antenna gain significantly by roughly 1dB and 1.8dB, respectively.

Table 1. Comparisons of Hardware implementation costs

Schemes	# of DACs	# of ADCs
SVD[6]	M_t	M_r
IEEE 802.15.3c[1]	1	1
Hybrid[13]	1	M_r
CB-AoDE	1	1

4 Simulation Results

In this section, simulation results and comparisons with previous works are presented. Channel models, CM 1.1 and CM 2.1, defined in IEEE 802.15.3c [1] are adopted for the simulated LOS and NLOS cases. Perfect synchronization and SNR estimations are also assumed. In addition to the proposed technique, various existing beamforming schemes, SVD [3], Hybrid [4] and the codebook-based, are compared as well. Besides, the theoretical optimal bound is provided under various channel conditions. The number of beam patterns for the codebook-based one is equal to the number of antennas. Furthermore, in order to investigate the effect of the quantized phases, simulations for both 2-bit and 4-bit quantizations of the CB-AoDE scheme are also shown.

Fig. 3(a) and Fig. 3(b) show the simulated results under the LOS and NLOS channels, respectively. The performances of the proposed CB-AoDE with the 4-bit quantization are consistently close to the SVD ones. On the other hand, CB-AoDE with the 2-bit quantization outperforms the original codebook beamforming scheme by roughly 1.4dB and 1dB for both LOS and NLOS channels, respectively. Table I summarizes the hardware costs of various beamforming schemes. For SVD and Hybrid, both require M_r ADCs in order to calculate beamforming vectors digitally. This means that not only multiple ADCs and DACs are required, but extremely high costs to implement the digital circuit especially for mmWave WPAN systems. Although the codebook-based beamforming is already a comparatively low-cost solution, it undoubtedly suffers performance degradation due to its over-simplification. The hardware cost of the proposed CB-AoDE technique only requires the same amount as the codebook-based one, but its performance with the 2-bit phase quantization can approach the hybrid one and even closer to the SVD with the 4-bit phase quantization.

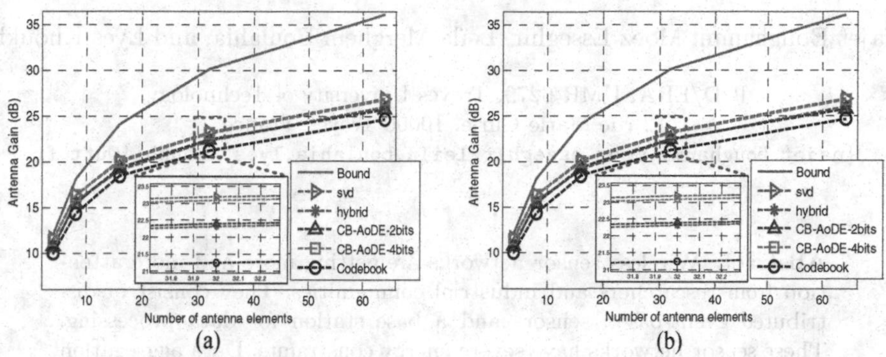

Fig. 3. Performance comparison for (a) the LOS channel and (b) the NLOS channel

5 Conclusion

In this work, the proposed CB-AoDE technique utilizes the information of the feedback SNRs and the knowledge of selected beam vectors to estimate the AoD, which is then used to generate the new beam vector. Comparisons for performance and hardware costs with various existing beamforming techniques, including SVD, hybrid beamforming and the IEEE 802.15.3c's codebook-based one, are conducted. The numerical results show that the proposed one can provide comparable performance of the hybrid beamforming, but at much lower implementation costs. In addition, the proposed one with the 4-bit phase quantization can achieve similar performance of the SVD's. This technique can also be directly applied to current WPAN systems.

References

1. IEEE Standards 802.15.3c, Part 15.3: Wireless Medium Access Control (MAC) and Physical Layer (PHY) Specifications for High Rate Wireless Personal Area Networks (WPANs), http://www.ieee802.org/15/pub/TG3c.html
2. IEEE 802.11ad PAR Document, http://www.ieee802.org/11/Reports/tgad_update.htm
3. Tiraspolsky, S., Jeon, B.J., Kim, J.H., Rubtsov, A., Flaksman, A., Ermolayev, V.: mmWave SVD-based beamformed MIMO communication systems. In: Proc. of IEEE Consumer Comm. and Networking Conf., pp. 1–5 (January 2010)
4. Yoon, S.H., Jeon, T.H., Lee, W.Y.: Hybrid beam-Forming and beam-switching for OFDM based wireless personal area networks. IEEE J. Select. Areas Commun. 27(8), 1425–1432 (2009)
5. Lin, Y.T., Kuo, C.H., Chen, S.G.: Efficient channel and SNR estimation schemes and their analysis for the mmWave signal carrier system. Int. Journal of Electrical Engineering 18(5), 245–253 (2011)

Energy Efficient Aggregation in Wireless Sensor Networks

Najet Boughanmi, Moez Esseghir, Leïla Merghem-Boulahia, and Lyes Khoukhi

ICD/ERA, UMR 6279, Troyes University of Technology,
12 rue Marie Curie, 10000 Troyes, France
{najet.boughanmi,moez.esseghir,leila.boulahia,lyes.khoukhi}@utt.fr

Abstract. Wireless sensor networks are getting more and more attention from researchers and industrial communities. They consist of distributed event-based sensors and a base station for data processing. These sensor networks have severe energy constraints. Data aggregation mechanisms are used to decrease the power consumption in these networks by combining several messages. In this paper, we present an energy efficient data aggregation mechanism. In this mechanism, the node which is aggregating and transmitting the message to the base station is chosen based on its energy and proximity to the base station. The nodes decide to participate in the aggregation process based on a participation relevance function. The efficiency of this aggregation mechanism is shown through simulation results in terms of network lifetime and reception rate.

Keywords: wireless sensor network, energy efficiency, data aggregation.

1 Introduction

The wireless sensor networks (WSNs) consist of a large number of inexpensive wireless nodes. Each node has computational power, sensing and communicating ability. The WSNs are getting an increasing interest from the researcher and the industrial communities due to their wide range of applications, as for example, vehicule tracking, environmental sensing and activity monotoring [1, 2].

Since the wireless nodes are powered by batteries that cannot be changed, the power issue is very important in the case of wireless sensor networks. Moreover, the amount of energy consumption for communication is far superior to the one used for processing. Thus, energy enhancement mechanisms focus on the optimization of the communication power consumption. The energy of these sensor nodes can be saved thanks to the data aggregation technology. Data aggregation consists in regrouping information gathered by several nodes in one message and transmitting this message to the base station. The data aggregation enhances the energy saving in wireless sensor networks as shown in [3, 4, 5].

In this paper, we focus on data aggregation mechanism for event-based structure free wireless sensor network for energy saving. We propose a data aggregation algorithm in which the energy consumption is enhanced through the choice

V. Guyot (Ed.): ICAIT 2012, LNCS 7593, pp. 264–273, 2013.

of the aggregator node (called aggregation head) and the participant nodes. Moreover, we propose an implementation of this aggregation protocol for the IEEE 802.15.4 standard.

The paper is organized as follows. The related work is presented in Section 2. In Section 3, we present our proposal. The simulation results are given in Section 4. The conclusion and the future work are given in Section 5.

2 Related Work

Several works deal with data aggregation in wireless sensor networks specially for the tree-based structure networks. The reliability of the communication in the WSN using an aggregation algorithm and message redundancy are addressed in [6, 7]. In [6], the authors presented an aggregation algorithm against malicious attacks done by any compromised or faulty node in the network. In the proposed algorithm, a node broadcasts its estimation of the global aggregated result to all its neighbors instead of broadcasting its sensed information. This algorithm constructs a tree for the aggregation and routing and it ensures security via the messages redundancy. Fauji et al. [7] presented an aggregation algorithm based on the spreading of information via gossip. In this algorithm, all the nodes are capable of selective message reception. The nodes can detect the convergence of the aggregation early. Thus, this aggregation algorithm is better than the pure version of gossip in energy consumption. Since we aim to enhance the lifetime of the sensor networks, the message redundancy is not the best alternative to be used since it leads to resources misuse.

Villas et al. [8] proposed to use a routing tree for data aggregation. The redundant data are aggregated at intermediate nodes in order to reduce the communication costs and energy consumption. This tree-based algorithm needs to build the tree and to update it periodically which consumes a lot of energy.

Wen et al. [9] proposed a cluster-based data aggregation routing to reduce the total energy consumption. The authors presented heuristics for cluster construction based on the average energy consumption and the maximum number of source nodes. Compared to cluster-based algorithm (Highest Degree [HD], Lowest-ID Algorithm [LID], Average Energy Consumption [AEC], Low Energy Adaptive Clustering Hierarchy [LEACH] [10], Low Energy Adaptive Clustering Hierarchy Centralized[LEACH-C][10]), this technique enhances the total energy consumption, but there is an energy cost to build the cluster based sensor network and update it.

Most of the data aggregation algorithms are proposed for tree-based structure. However, these structure-based algorithms suffer from high maintenance overhead. Thus, in this work, we are interested in structure-free sensor networks.

Chih-Min et al. [11] presented a structure-free and energy balanced data aggregation technique for wireless sensor networks. This algorithm consists in two parts. In the first part, some nodes are selected as aggregators depending on their positions and in the second part the aggregated data are sent to the sink. The authors assume the nodes are synchronized and that they know their own location.

In [12], the authors presented a partial data aggregation technique. This work discusses the tradeoffs between the data accuracy, transmission delay and energy consumption. The network model used in this study is a simple one, and the results are not proved to be the same for more complex networks.

Sardouk et al. proposed in [13, 14] a multi-agent data aggregation mechanism for structure-free event-driven wireless sensor networks. Each sensor network decides to participate or not in a data aggregation session depending on: the importance of the information, its density, the criticity of its position and its residual energy. These parameters are weighted and used in the decision function. This data aggregation mechanism enhances the energy consumption of the sensor network. However, the aggregator node is chosen depending on the event detection (the first node to detect an event is the aggregator node) and its residual energy is not taken into account.

We note that most of data aggregation mechanisms are proposed for the structure-based wireless sensor networks. Moreover, the data aggregation algorithms for structure-free sensor networks need to be improved to enhance the sensor network lifetime. In this work, we use the decision mechanism proposed in [15], we propose a head aggregation selection mechanism and we present an implementation of the data aggregation mechanism for the IEEE 802.15.4 standard.

3 Proposal

In this paper, we focus on the structure-free wireless sensor networks. We use the decision metric presented in [13] to let the nodes decide if they participate in the data aggregation session or not. This decision metric called the participation relevance R in a data aggregation session is computed as

$$R = \alpha * E + \beta * \frac{1}{D} + \theta * P + \omega * I$$

where

- α, β, θ and ω are weighting factors,
- E is the residual energy,
- D is the density,
- P is the criticity of the node's position,
- I is the importance of the information

We propose to choose the aggregation head depending on its residual energy and its distance from the sink. Moreover, we present an implementation of the data aggregation mechanism in the IEEE 802.15.4 standard.

3.1 Aggregation Mechanism

We study now the energy consumption. When the node i detects an event, it broadcasts a data aggregation request $AgRq$ to its neighbors (we consider it has N neighbors). Let E_{AgRq} be the power needed to broadcast the data aggregation request. If i has N neighbors, N nodes will receive the message sent by i and consume E_{AgRqR}. Each of these N node calculates its participation relevance metric to decide if it will participate to the current aggregation session. Each node accepting to participate sends an aggregation response *AgResp* message to the node i. Let x be the number of nodes participating in the aggregation session and E_{AgResp} the power consumed by the transmission of each aggregation response message. The energy used by the aggregation E_A is given by

$$E_A^i = E_{AgRq} + N * E_{AgRqR} + x * (E_{AgResp} + E_{AgRespR}). \tag{1}$$

with $E_{AgRespR}$ is the energy consumed by the node i when it receives a data aggregation response message.

The path separating the node i and the base station has N_{hop}^i hops. Let E_T and E_R be the energy needed to transmit and to receive a message. The energy used to transmit the message to the base station E_{TT} is equal to

$$E_{TT} = N_{hop}^i * (E_T + E_R).$$

The total energy consumption E using the aggregation mechanism is given by

$$E = \sum_{i \in path} (E_T + E_R + E_A^i). \tag{2}$$

The total energy consumption without using the aggregation mechanism is equal to

$$E = S * N_{hop} * (E_T + E_R). \tag{3}$$

with S is the number of nodes who will send a message to the sink concerning the same event, and N_{hop} is the number of nodes in the path to the sink.

Based on (2) and (3) we can notice that the energy consumed when aggregation is used can be highly lower if N_{hop}^i is large and if E_A^i corresponds to a reasonable amount.

3.2 Aggregation Head Selection

The aggregation head can be each node which detects the event and initiates the aggregation session. This node sends the aggregation request, receives the aggregation responses and transmits the message. Thus it consumes

$$E_{AgRq} + x * E_{AgRespR} + E_T.$$

Since the aggregation head consumes more energy than the other nodes participating in the aggregation session, it should be selected carefully to enhance the lifetime of the network and ensure better reception rate. The criteria used to select a node i as the aggregation head are:

1. Its residual energy E_{res}
2. Its proximity to the base station: number of hop separating this node i from the base station N^i_{hop} hops
3. Its identifier id

The aggregation algorithm is presented in Figure 1. The algorithm to select an aggregation head is as follows:

1. If a node i detects an event, i sets it to be the aggregation head ($AgHd = true$) and it sends an aggregation request message to its neighbors(N). The $AgRq$ message contains the residual energy E_{res}, the number of hops to the base station N^i_{hop} and the node identifier id.
2. When receiving an $AgRq$ message from a node j, the node i checks if he has detected the same event ($AgHd = true$). Then he decides if he is still the aggregation head by comparing first the residual energy, then the number of hops to reach the base station and and finally the identifiers. Identifiers will specifically be used when two or more nodes have the same residual amounts of energy and are at same number of hops of the sink. Note that the number of hops are calculated using AODV routing algorithm.

3.3 Aggregation Mechanism Implementation for IEEE 802.15.4 Standard

The IEEE 802.15.4 standard (IEEE 2006 [16]) is convenient to wireless communication constraints since it uses low-data-rate, low-power and low-complexity short-range radio frequency transmissions. The MAC protocol supports two operational modes that may be selected by the coordinator: beacon-enabled mode and non beacon-enabled mode. We propose to add our data aggregation algorithm to this standard.

In order to use the proposed aggregation mechanism with the IEEE 802.15.4 standard [16], we need to add two frames for the aggregation request message and the aggregation response message. Thus, we use the MAC command frame specified in the IEEE 802.15.4 as shown in Figure 2.

Since the aggregation request and the aggregation response messages are sent to the neighbors of a node i, we use the shortest address information (4 bytes). Moreover, the command type field uses the values from 0×00 to 0×09 whereas the values from $0 \times 0a$ to $0 \times ff$ are not used. We choose to use one byte to optimize at maximum the energy consumed by nodes. We propose to use the $0 \times 0a$ to indicate if the frame is an aggregation request or an aggregation response frame. Then, we use the command payload field to include the sent data. In the aggregation request case, the command payload field contains:

1. The aggregation session identifier,
2. The sender residual energy,
3. The number of hops separating the sender from the base station,
4. The sender identifier.

```
while true do
  AgHd ← false;
  if an event is detected then
    AgHd ← true;
    send_AgReq(E^i_res, N^i_hop, id^i);
    initiate(timeout);
  end if
  if receive(AgRq(E^j_res, N^j_hop, id^j)) then
    if AgHd = true then
      if E^j_res > E^i_res then
        AgHd ← false;
      else if N^j_hop > N^i_hop then
        AgHd ← false;
      else
        if id^j < id^i then
          AgHd ← false;
        end if
      end if
    end if
    if AgHd = false then
      ParticipationRelevance ← computeParticipationRelevance()
      if ParticipationRelevance > threshold then
        send_AgResp();
      end if
    end if
  end if
  if receive(AgResp) then
    extract data from AgResp and compute aggregated data (mean) ;
  end if
  if timeout = 0 then
    send_aggregated_data();
  end if
end while
```

Fig. 1. Data aggregation algorithm

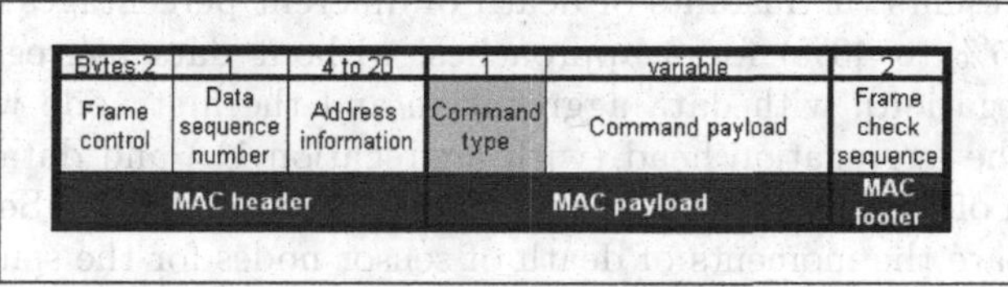

Fig. 2. Mac Command Frame

In the aggregation response case, the command payload field contains:

1. the aggregation session identifier,
2. the sensed data.

The MAC data frame is shown in Figure 3. The MAC header and footer varies from 9 to 25 octets. Moreover, the standard fixes the PHY header to 6 bytes and the maximum packet size to 127 bytes. Therefore, we can use from 96 to 112 bytes for the aggregated data. The aggregated data packet contains the data collected from the participating neighbors. The data payload is then the concatenation of the address and the sensed data collected from these nodes. We fix the address field to 4 bytes and the sensed data field to 1 byte. So each participating node needs 5 octets in the aggregated data packet. Since the total data payload varies from 96 to 112 bytes, the number of aggregated data in one packet varies from 19 to 22.

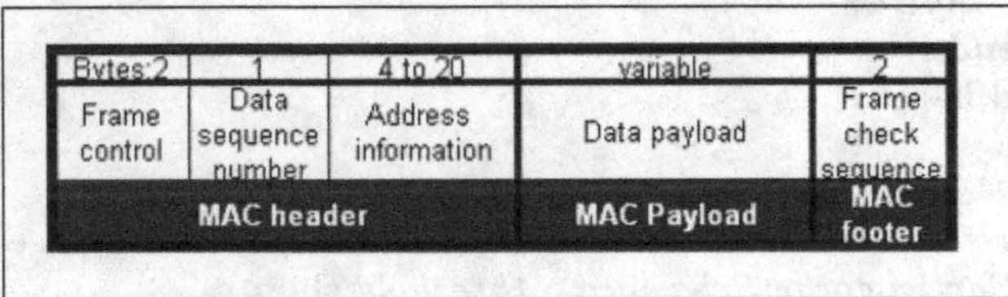

Fig. 3. Mac Data Frame

4 Simulation Results

We present in this section the simulation results obtained using the network simulator ns-2 [17].

4.1 Wireless Sensor Network Lifetime

In order to evaluate the performance of our proposal, we use the sensor network lifetime metric by focusing on the individual nodes time of failure. We consider that when more than 40% of the sensor nodes are dead, the wireless network looses its connectivity and the coverage of the sensed area.

Figure 4 presents the instants of death of different percentages of the sensor nodes (from 5% to 40%) for 3 approaches: without data aggregation (called without aggregation), with data aggregation and the first node which detects the event is the aggregation head (with aggregation 1) , and data aggregation with selection of the aggregation head (with aggregation 2) (see Section 3).

If we compare the moments of death of sensor nodes for the sensor networks with and without aggregation, we find that the sensor nodes not using the data aggregation loose their energy before the one aggregating their messages. As first conclusion and contribution, the data aggregation mechanism enhances the wireless sensor networks lifetime.

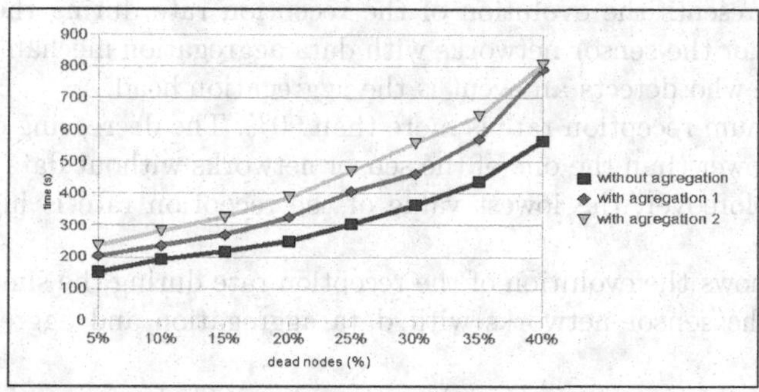

Fig. 4. Wireless sensor network lifetime

Moreover, the selection of the data aggregation head enhances the sensor network lifetime too. In fact, compared to the data aggregation without an aggregation head selection, our proposal which selects an aggregation head has longer lifetime. This proves the efficiency of our solution.

4.2 Reception Rate

The second parameter we use to evaluate the wireless network performances is the reception rate. The reception rate is the ratio of the total number of received messages by the total number of sent messages.

Figure 5 gives the evolution of the reception rate during the simulation time (1000s) for the sensor networks without data aggregation.

The maximum reception rate is less than 60%. Moreover, the reception rate is almost equal 0 at 600s.

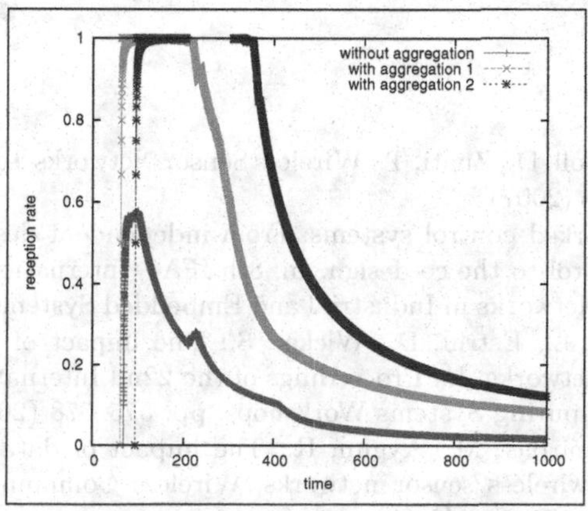

Fig. 5. Reception rate through time

Figure 5 presents the evolution of the reception rate during the simulation time (1000s) for the sensor networks with data aggregation mechanism in which the first node who detects an event is the aggregation head.

The maximum reception rate is more than 90%. The decreasing of the reception rate is slower than the one of the sensor networks without data aggregation (Figure 5). Moreover, the lowest value of the reception rate is higher than 0 (about 8%).

Figure 5 shows the evolution of the reception rate during the simulation time (1000s) for the sensor networks with data aggregation and aggregation head selection.

The maximum reception rate is almost equal to 100% for a period of 300s. The decreasing of the reception rate is slower than the one of the sensor networks with data aggregation and without aggregation head selection (Figure 5). Moreover, the lowest value of the reception rate is higher than 10%.

The data aggregation mechanism enhances the reception rate in the sensor networks and the selection of the data aggregation head improves the reception rate compared to the one obtained without any head selection mechanism. This enhancement of the reception rate is the result of the improvement of the energy saving

5 Conclusion

In this work, we propose a data aggregation mechanism with a selection of the aggregation head. The simulation results show that this mechanism leads to the enhancement of the sensor network performance : lifetime and reception rate. Moreover, we present an implementation of this mechanism for the IEEE 802.15.4 standard.

In our future works, we will try to implement our approach on a real test bed that uses wireless sensor nodes equipped with IEEE 802.15.4.

References

[1] Sohraby, K., Minoli, D., Znati, T.: Wireless Sensor Networks Technology, Protocols, and Applications (2007)

[2] Song, Y.: Networked control systems: From independent designs of the network qos and the control to the co-design. In: 8th IFAC International Conference on Fieldbuses and Networks in Industrial and Embedded Systems (FET 2009) (2009)

[3] Krishnamachari, L., Estrin, D., Wicker, S.: The impact of data aggregation in wireless sensor networks. In: Proceedings of the 22nd International Conference on Distributed Computing Systems Workshops, pp. 575–578 (2002)

[4] Akkaya, K., Demirbas, M., Aygun, R.: The impact of data aggregation on the performance of wireless sensor networks. Wireless Communications and Mobile Computing 8(2), 171–193 (2008)

[5] Boulis, A.: Aggregation in sensor networks: an energy-accuracy trade-off. Ad Hoc Networks 1(2-3), 317–331 (2003)

[6] Sen, J.: A robust and secure aggregation protocol for wireless sensor networks. In: Proceedings of the 2011 Sixth IEEE International Symposium on Electronic Design, Test and Application, DELTA 2011, pp. 222–227. IEEE Computer Society, Washington, DC (2011)

[7] Fauji, S., Kalpakis, K.: A gossip-based energy efficient protocol for robust in-network aggregation in wireless sensor networks. In: 2011 IEEE International Conference on Pervasive Computing and Communications Workshops (PERCOM Workshops), pp. 166–171 (March 2011)

[8] Villas, L., Boukerche, A., Filho, H.S.R., de Oliveira, H.A.B.F., Araujo, R., Loureiro, A.A.F.: DRINA: A Lightweight and Reliable Routing Approach for in-Network Aggregation in Wireless Sensor Networks. IEEE Transactions on Computers 99 (2012) (PrePrints)

[9] Wen, Y.F., Anderson, T.A.F., Powers, D.M.W.: On energy-efficient aggregation routing and scheduling in IEEE 802.15.4-based wireless sensor networks. Wireless Communications and Mobile Computing (2012)

[10] Heinzelman, W.B., Chandrakasan, A.P., Balakrishnan, H.: An application-specific protocol architecture for wireless microsensor networks. IEEE Transactions on Wireless Communications 1(4), 660–670 (2002)

[11] Chao, C.M., Hsiao, T.Y.: Design of structure-free and energy-balanced data aggregation in wireless sensor networks. In: 11th IEEE International Conference on High Performance Computing and Communications, HPCC 2009, pp. 222–229 (June 2009)

[12] Li, W., Bandai, M., Watanabe, T.: Tradeoffs among delay, energy and accuracy of partial data aggregation in wireless sensor networks. In: 2010 24th IEEE International Conference on Advanced Information Networking and Applications (AINA), pp. 917–924 (April 2010)

[13] Sardouk, A., Mansouri, M., Merghem-Boulahia, L., Gaiti, D., Rahim-Amoud, R.: Multi-Agent System Based Wireless Sensor Network for Crisis Management. In: 2010 IEEE Global Telecommunications Conference (GLOBECOM 2010), pp. 1–6 (December 2010)

[14] Sardouk, A.: Data aggregation in wireless sensor networks based on cooperative agents. PhD thesis, University of technology of Troyes (2010)

[15] Sardouk, A., Rahim-Amoud, R., Merghem-Boulahia, L., Gaiti, D.: A multi-criterion data aggregation scheme for wsn. In: IEEE International Conference on Wireless and Mobile Computing, Networking and Communications, WIMOB 2009, pp. 30–35 (October 2009)

[16] IEEE 802.15 WPAN Task Group 4 (TG4), `http://www.ieee802.org/15/pub/TG4.html`

[17] Network simulator NS-2, `http://www.isi.edu/nsnam/ns/`

Energy Optimization of Mesh Access Networks

Guy Pujolle[1,2] and Khaldoun Al Agha[3]

[1] ITCE, Postech, Pohang, Korea
Guy_Pujolle@postech.ac.kr
[2] UPMC, Paris, France
Guy.Pujolle@upmc.fr
[3] LRI, Orsay, France
Khaldoun.Alagha@lri.fr

Abstract. This paper deals with the minimization of energy consumption in mesh access networks. As proposed in 3GPP, future wireless access networks will be based in part on mesh technology. Indeed, as all access points cannot be connected by optic fibers to the core networks, we propose to realize a mesh network to connect altogether hotspots and femtocells. To optimize the energy consumption we have developed a Start-and-Stop mechanism permitting to turn-off all unused physical machines. Moreover, we developed a virtual environment to work with virtual machines instead physical machines. This permits to move virtual resources from one physical point to another one. Finally, we describe the piloting system based on the autonomic paradigm, and associated with a knowledge plane. This piloting system is able to minimize the energy consumption in future mesh access networks.

1 Introduction

The goal of this paper is to conceptualize, then to describe the work that was performed to realize a prototype for virtual mesh access networks with low energy consumption. The prototype is mainly based on virtual networking with a piloting system able to manage resource allocation of each virtual network, and with the urbanization of virtual machines implemented on the physical network equipment.

The energy consumption is much more important at the periphery of a network than in the core: this is due to the number of communication links that have to be deployed without sharing with other customers. On the contrary the core network is multiplexed into all the customers.

The way we decided to explore the problem is stopping a maximum number of network equipment by multiplexing all the routes on a small number of paths. This permits to stop all the other machines. So during the nights, 80 to 99% of the machines can be stopped. To reach this solution, we are using several elements:

1- First of all, we developed a technology called Start and Stop permitting network elements to be stopped when no job is available.
2- We achieved a totally virtualized environment where all network equipment are virtualized.

V. Guyot (Ed.): ICAIT 2012, LNCS 7593, pp. 274–282, 2013.

3- We operated a knowledge plane to retrieve all information necessary to pilot the algorithms necessary to multiplex all routes on few paths. This has been achieved using virtualization and moving virtual resources on common paths.

An example of a piloting system is an automatic system which can create a virtual network with specific resource requirements, like minimum bandwidth, processing capacity or even virtualized network infrastructure equipment, such as routers, label-switched routers, home gateways, firewalls, network devices, and wireless access points. To achieve this goal, an autonomic-oriented architecture is proposed to support self-organized, self-controlled, and self-managed processes. This architecture is based on a piloting plane that will help to choose the best parameters in order to optimize the behavior of the virtual mesh networks. Specifically, the autonomic-oriented architecture will associate a situated view to each virtual network equipment. The situated view is used to determine the context and to optimize the urbanization of all virtual machines. A situated view is the knowledge of the adjacent physical or virtual resources (one or more steps away) that a physical or virtual machine requires in order to make a decision by itself.

In this paper, we create, delete, and manage virtual networks on the fly. A GUI will provide the facility to deploy instantaneously a mesh network and to remove it if necessary. However, the real difficulty when deploying a new network is to be able to prove that the resources that are allocated to the new network are sufficient so that the necessary quality of service (QoS) is guaranteed. This is where urbanization of the virtual resources is used. By urbanization we mean how to place the different virtual resources in the physical network.

This paper describes 1) a virtual mesh network, 2) an interface to set up and delete a virtual network on the fly, 3) an automatic piloting system for controlling the virtualisation environment in order to fulfill all requirements, and 4) a piloting system with its control algorithm, which will be able to minimize energy consumption. For minimizing energy consumption, out of peak hours (say 5 hours a day) the routes will be multiplexed on common paths to be able to turn off a large number of physical machines that are no longer useful for traffic forwarding.

In the paper, self-piloting is used to place new virtual networks, and facilitate continuous tuning of the slices, adaptation to unpredictable conditions, prevention and recovery from failures and provision of a dependable network environment. The self-piloting scheme is realized by using urbanization control algorithms with the best available knowledge. The goal of the piloting plane is to collect in a concerted way the knowledge necessary to optimize dynamic creation and destruction of slices and the distribution of the physical resources to optimize both quality of service and energy consumption. It is clear enough that these two improvement schemes are contradictory. One of the objectives of this proposal is to maintain the quality of service while turning off a maximum number of physical devices.

This paper aims at providing an optimized network and service layer solution, which guarantees built-in, automated piloted QoS, and self-optimization of energy consumption.

This paper will provide a start and stop mechanism described in section 2. Then section 3 will be devoted to the question: how virtual resources are positioned automatically on the physical machines. This is the urbanization of the network. Indeed, we defined algorithms for controlling the urbanization of virtual resources so that Service Level Agreements (SLAs) are maximized and energy consumption is minimized. Then, in section 4, we conceptualize, and design the piloting system for controlling all the virtual resources. This system will be associated with the virtualisation paradigm to control the utilization of the physical resources used by the different mesh virtual networks. This piloting system is based on an autonomic platform with autonomous and real time properties. Finally section 5 describes the piloting algorithm, the evaluation of the performance of the solution concerning energy consumption, and the improvements that could be achieved.

1.1 Start and Stop

The Start and Stop procedure consists in switching off/on the power of a node according to its usefulness for the network. An usefulness could be measured according to several metrics. In our study the usefulness is fixed to the combination of three different states: (i) the node is not routing the traffic of other nodes, (ii) the node does not have applications in progress and (iii) the node after switching off its power is not going to interrupt connectivity of other nodes. If those conditions are valid then the node makes a SAVE-TO-RAM or a SAVE-TO-DISK to reduce its energy consumption.

The node then switches on its power on the demand with an external device (WAKE on LAN for example) or if this feature is not available, a timer is programmed to switch on the node periodically and it again re-measures its usefulness to switch off or to stay alive.

In the example of Figure 1, we see that node D could be turned off because it will not disturb interconnection of node A to the network. However, nodes G, E and F should stay on to continue their role of relays for the other nodes.

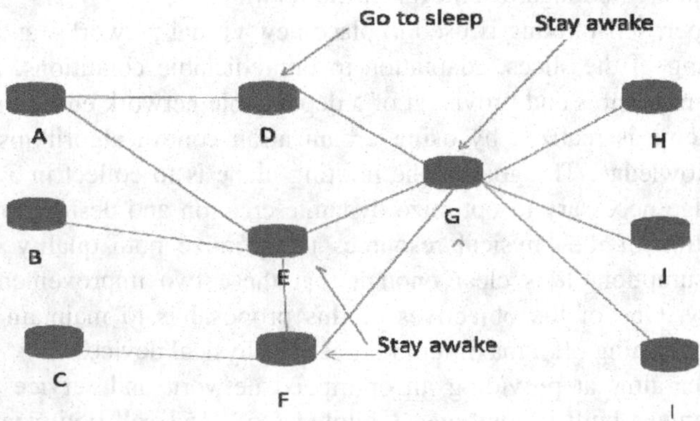

Fig. 1. Example of network topology

Mesh networks are using TCP/IP stack and provides routes according to some protocols such as OLSR, AODV, etc. In proactive protocols like OLSR [1], each node contains a partial view of the topology and could improve the energy consumption of the network by using this topology information. The idea is to use in a distributed manner this information locally in a node in order that the node could decide if it has to go to sleep or to stay awake.

When a node possesses locally the topology of the network, it could deduct its utility for the remaining nodes. The algorithm that we use is for the node to:

- drop itself from the topology,
- select randomly one of its neighbor,
- apply a Depth First Search [2] algorithm of this neighbor.

If the neighbor could reach all the remaining nodes of the network then the node turns off its power. On the contrary, the node keeps its power on.

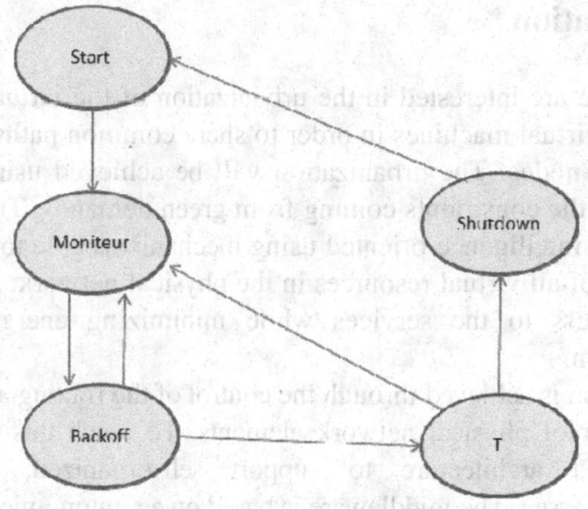

Fig. 2. The process of the S&S

The S&S is a process with four states as shown in Figure 2:

1) Start (delay): This state waits during "delay" seconds, and then starts the activity of the node (daemon). Once the daemon is running, the S&S goes to the state Monitor.

2) Monitor (delay): In this state the process checks the status of the node and the status of the network traffic every "delay" milliseconds. If the test estimates that the node must go to sleep, the process goes to the Backoff state (backoff_min, backoff_max).

3) Backoff (min, max): This state waits for a random time of at least "min" milliseconds and no more than "max" milliseconds. After this period, a new check (the same as Monitor) is performed. If the situation has not changed (the node must go to sleep) then the S&S transit to the state T (delay). Otherwise, it returns to the State Monitor. If, during the backoff state, the node receives a message indicating the extinction of another node, it returns to the State Monitor.

4) T (delay): this state is made to compensate for the propagation time of messages in the network. If during delay, the node gets an extinction message from another node, it goes back in the state Monitor.

5) Shutdown (delay): This state sends an extinction message to all other nodes in the network, and then stops the daemon and put the node to sleep for "delay" seconds.

At start-up, the S&S is in the start state (0). Here is an example of values that can be given for the operation of the S&S:

update_period: 10000 ms
backoff_min: 5000 ms
backoff_max: 15000 ms
restart_delay: 2 s
wakeup_delay: 40 s

2 Urbanization

In this section, we are interested in the urbanization of the virtual resources to allow the migration of virtual machines in order to share common paths and turn off a maximum number of nodes. The urbanization will be achieved using a piloting system able to cope with the constraints coming from green demands. The architecture of the piloting system is intelligence-oriented using mechanisms able to control automatically the placement of all virtual resources in the physical network. This placement must improve the access to the services while minimizing energy consumption and resource utilization.

The urbanization is achieved through the control of the routing algorithm to turn off a maximum number of physical network elements. To reach this goal, we propose an autonomic-oriented architecture to support self-organized, self-controlled, and self-managed processes. The middleware is based on an autonomic platform. This architecture provides a piloting plane (different names could be provided to this plane as orchestration, governing, etc.) that will help to choose the best parameters to optimize the behavior of the network. Indeed, the autonomic-oriented architecture will associate to each physical resource a situated view that will be used to determine the context and to choose and optimize control algorithms for the urbanization and energy consumption of all the virtual resources.

Creation and destruction of virtual networks on the fly are available. This permits to create new virtual mesh networks with customized virtual resources. A GUI provides the facility to deploy easily mesh networks and to remove it when necessary. However, the real difficulty when deploying a new virtual network is to be able to prove that the resources affected to this network are sufficient to provide the quality of service (QoS) necessary to guarantee the different service level agreements (SLAs). This is why an urbanization algorithm has been developed to place the virtual resources necessary to realize the requirement of the users and minimize the energy consumption. For energy consumption, we turn off a maximum number of network elements by multiplexing flows on the same paths and to allocate virtual resources on common physical network elements. For this purpose, the piloting system distributes physical resources to optimize network urbanization. Customized virtual networks can be created and dropped when necessary. The piloting system and the virtualization scheme allow a much better use of physical resources of the network bringing customized networks to the client. Moreover, the piloting system is able to optimize the energy consumption of the network.

3 The Piloting System

The knowledge and piloting planes imply an intelligence-oriented architecture using mechanisms able to control automatically the placement of all virtual machines into the physical network. The approach is a particularly attractive solution through the development of an automatic piloting system with intrinsic properties as autonomy, proactivity, adaptability, cooperation, and mobility.

The piloting system is definitely a new paradigm. Indeed, this system includes two sub planes that are aggregated into the piloting system. The two sub-planes form the autonomic plane. So, within the piloting system some mechanisms have to be integrated to drive the control algorithms. Indeed, the partition of the piloting system into two sub-planes has the advantage of simplifying the presentation but indeed these two sub-planes are strongly related: the knowledge and the configuration planes are developed in an integrated way. This piloting system has to drive the network through the control plane. For this purpose, the piloting system has to choose the best algorithms available within the control plane to reach the goal decided by the system. Due to the emergence in network environments of virtual control algorithms the choice of the best control algorithm is crucial. The second action of the piloting system is to decide about values to be given to the parameters of the different algorithms. As a summary, the piloting system has to configure the control plane which itself configures the data plane.

Currently, in traditional networks the control algorithms are not chosen and the values of the parameters are selected through information collected directly by the algorithms themselves. The advantage of the piloting system is to react in real time on the behavior of the control algorithms. This piloting process aims to adapt the network to new conditions and to take advantage of the piloting agent to alleviate the global system. We argue that a distributed intelligent agents system could achieve a quasi-optimal adaptive control process because of the following two points: (1) each agent holds different processes (behavior, dynamic planner and situated view) allowing to take the most relevant decisions at every moment; (2) the agents are implicitly cooperative in the sense that they use a situated view taking into account the state of the neighbors.

This architecture has several advantages. First there is a simplification for recovering knowledge necessary for feeding the piloting system. Indeed, in current systems, every control algorithm has to retrieve by itself all the knowledge necessary to execute the algorithm. This behavior is shown in Figure 3.

In this situation, all the control algorithms (routing, CAC, flow control, quality of service, security, availability, mobility management, etc.) have the obligation to look for their own information to decide what is the best routing algorithm, what is the best flow control scheme, what is the best parameters for security control, etc. Indeed, all these algorithms need the same information or knowledge with a strong probability. Thus, in parallel, these algorithms have specific signaling packets to retrieve the same information.

Moreover, the different algorithms are not correlated and could decide somewhat contradictory decisions. In the piloting architecture, the decision process is definitely different. This process is outlined in Figure 4. We see in this figure that the control algorithms are fed by the distributed Piloting System encapsulating the Knowledge plane where all the knowledge is. Moreover, this process permits to add new knowledge to pilot the control algorithms. For example, for a routing algorithm in a wireless mesh network, it is possible to add some knowledge on the electromagnetic field if available. This could be crucial in a real time or critical control process.

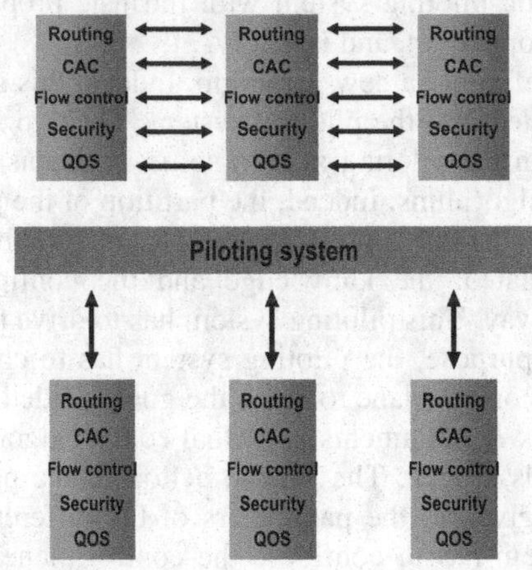

Fig. 3. Advantage of the knowledge plane

More precisely, the platform can be built on a multi-agent system to offer some intelligence. The multi-agent system is formed with agents situated in all network equipment (common to all virtual instances). The architecture is shown in Figure 4.

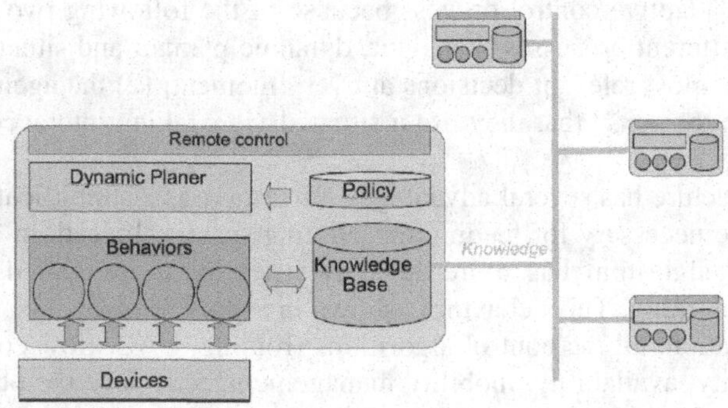

Fig. 4. The agent architecture

The different entities of the agent architecture are as follows. Each agent maintains its own view of the network on the basis of information obtained through the knowledge plane. This agent-centric view of the network is called the situated view, and is focusing on the agent's close network environment. This produces the knowledge basis that forms the knowledge plane.

The behaviors are autonomic software components permanently adapting themselves to the environment changes. Each of these behaviors can be considered as a specialized function with some expert capabilities. Each behavior is essentially a sense->decide->act loop. Typical categories of behaviors are as follows:

• Producing knowledge for the situated view in cooperation with other agents.

• Reasoning individually or collectively to evaluate the situation and decide to apply an appropriate action, e.g. a behavior can simply be in charge of computing bandwidth availability on the network equipment (NE). It can also regularly perform a complex diagnostic scenario or it can be dedicated to automatic recognition of specific network conditions.

• Acting onto the NE parameters, e.g. behavior can tune QoS parameters.

Behaviours have access to the situated view which operates within each agent as a whiteboard shared among thc agent's behaviors. Moreover, some behaviors can or cannot be used depending on the memory space and real time constraints. This behavior exploits the tolerance for imprecision and learning capabilities. At this juncture, the principal constituents are fuzzy logic, neural computing, evolutionary computation machine learning and probabilistic reasoning.

The activation, dynamic parameterization and scheduling of behaviors (the rule engine is seen as a behavior) within an agent is performed by the dynamic planner. The dynamic planner decides which behaviors have to be active, when they have to be active and with which parameters. The dynamic planner detects changes in the situated view and occurrence of external/internal events; from there, it pilots the reaction of the agent to changes in the network environment.

Finally a policy repository is necessary for defining the rules associated with the physical and the virtual networks.

4 Experimentation

The autonomic algorithm we are using to turn off a maximum number of mesh access points is as follows. An access point AP_i receives from its situated view the number of virtual machines associated with each access point. When there are m virtual machines, this means that m different flows have to be forwarded in the AP. The machine AP_i detects the least loaded machine of its situated view, i.e. the physical machine embedding the smallest number of virtual machines, say AP_n. Eventually, $i = n$. AP_i also knows about the topology of the network within its situated view. With the information coming from its situated view, AP_i can decide what are the transfers to perform to empty the physical machine AP_n. When decided, AP_i sends a message to the member of its situated view to inform them of the moves. If any machine sends a message to indicate a better solution on their own environment, the transfers are executed. A better solution indicates that the physical machine n can be emptied in a more optimized way (total number of virtual machines to be moved because changing a path can demand to change more than one virtual machine). When the moves are performed, all nodes are executing again the same distributed algorithm.

The experiences we did on this algorithm showed that a situated view of two hops is the optimum: one hop is generally too short to find new routes and three-hop requests a too large volume of information. Indeed, the situated view depends on the topology of the networks and irregular situated views may lead to better performance. So we decided to move forward assuming a two-hop situated view for the network described below.

A first prototype of the environment was realized using machines developed in LIP6 and LRI labs. With this prototype a large number of new algorithms and paradigms have been tested but the algorithm described just above had the best results concerning energy consumption.

The platform assembles all the elements described in this paper: the virtualisation process, the autonomic plane, the customized virtual networks and the control scheme through the distributed piloting system using the situated view of two-hops. The platform contains 20 physical machines (industrial PC with quite a high potential). A physical machine is able of supporting 200 virtual machines. So for a total of 20 machines in the network, we have been able to experiment a global network with 4 000 virtual resources. The tests performed on this testbed show that the energy consumption decreases by a factor of 10% at peak hour, 50% between peak hours and 99% during the night.

5 Conclusion

In this paper we developed a new paradigm quite simple to understand: for decreasing the energy consumption of a mesh network we have to turn off a maximum number of machines without losing the quality of service of the different applications. To reach this goal, we are using virtualization. We move virtual machines with an autonomic algorithm allowing locally to determine what machines or resources have to be moved.

As a conclusion, we think that the future Internet architecture will contain a virtual plane and a piloting system able to optimize the placement of the virtual resource. A virtualized cloud will also necessary to permit the customer to get information in a quite simple and optimized manner.

References

1. Clausen, T., Jacquet, P.: Optimized Link State Routing Protocol (OLSR). IETF RFC 3626 (2003)
2. Hasan, Z., Boostanimehr, H., Bhargava, V.K.: Green Cellular Networks: A Survey, Some Research Issues and Challenges. IEEE Communications Surveys and Tutorials 13, 524–540 (2011)
3. Oh, E., Krishnamachari, B.: Energy Savings through Dynamic Base Station Switching in Cellular Wireless Access Networks. In: Proceedings of 2010 IEEE Global Telecommunications Conference, pp. 1–5 (2010)
4. Deruyck, M., Tanghe, E., Joseph, W., Martens, L.: Modeling and optimization of power consumption in wireless access networks. Computer Communications 34, 2036–2046 (2011)

Predictive Sink Mobility for Target Tracking in Sensor Networks

Joseph Rahmé, Lila Boukhatem, and Khaldoun Al Agha

LRI, Univ. Paris-Sud 11 - CNRS
Bât 490, 91405 Orsay, France
{Joseph.Rahme,Lila.Boukhatem,Khaldoun.Alagha}@lri.fr

Abstract. In sensor networks, the information is generated by sensors deployed in a geographic area, and sent to a node called "sink" (or gateway). Since the node's energy is battery limited, an efficient management of this resource affects the network's lifetime. Our work presents a new approach called RPL (Repositioning, Prediction, Localization), that aims to extend the lifetime of the sensor network for a target tracking application. This is realized by switching sensors between active/sleep states and moving the sink close to the target's future position. The movement of the sink reduces the energy needed for a packet transmission, and minimizes the number of hops between the sink and the emitting sensors. The proposed scheme is validated through simulations.

Keywords: sensor networks, target tracking, sink movement.

1 Introduction

Recent advances in electronics allowed the development of tiny sensors at low prices, capable of communicating for small distances. However, numerous constraints are still imposed on these devices and especially on their energy. Sensors are randomly deployed in an area of interest. They use incorporated protocols and algorithms allowing them to auto-configure and form a network. The information (temperature, humidity, vibration, etc.) captured by the sensors, is relayed to the sink (or gateway) using a hop-by-hop routing. Many applications exist for such networks (civil, medical and military domains), justifying the numerous research effort in this area.

As sensor nodes are battery-powered, their operational time is limited. Thus, energy efficiency is a critical design consideration of a wireless sensor network. To deal with this issue, several approaches have been proposed. The first approach considers the optimization at the MAC layer, where sleeping modes are considered to save energy [8–10]. The second approach acts at the network layer where efficient routing protocols help conserving the energy [11–13]. The last approach is based on data aggregation, which exploits data correlations to reduce the size of transmitted information. In our work, we focus on routing mechanisms combined with a new approach, based on the concept of sink mobility. In [6],

V. Guyot (Ed.): ICAIT 2012, LNCS 7593, pp. 283–295, 2013.

the notion of sink mobility has been introduced. The sink (gateway) is a mobile node with unlimited energy. The sink moves toward the zone of sensors generating most of the data, and sends the collected information to a central computing server. The sink could be a moving robot, a human with a laptop, etc. The sink's movement reduces the routing cost of the packets, by reducing the number of hops between the source sensor and the sink. This also conserves the remaining energy of the relaying nodes by reducing the number of sensors that participate in packets routing. Furthermore, the sink relocation can also be beneficial in real-time traffic applications. In such applications, the sink movement allows the use of shorter routes, which reduces end-to-end delay.

In the network, every sensor detecting a target generates a packet and forwards it to the sink. When the motion of the target is random, we have a random packet generation, that does not derive from a static zone of sensors. Thus, the solution presented in [6] could not be implemented in target tracking, since it only considers a static traffic, and moves the sink close to the nodes with high traffic loads. Moreover, the network needs to react fast to track the movement of targets without the need to activate all the sensors. Having this in mind, we use a prediction method, that estimates the future position of the target, and allows:

- an early movement of the sink toward the zones, expected to generate packets in the future
- an activation of the sensors in the zone between the current and estimated target positions. The sensors outside this zone are kept in a sleep mode in case the target's velocity is low.

As a consequence, the prediction method will introduce another degree of optimization in network's lifetime (besides sink mobility), since it restricts the number of active sensors. Finally, we propose a new method for target positioning that uses the information of the sensors detecting the target, and localizes the target in the monitored area.

The paper is organized as follows. In the next section, we detail a review of the main related work. In section III, we present our RPL scheme. Section IV describes the detection method used for target tracking. Performance evaluation and results are presented in section V. Finally, section VI presents the conclusions and some future works.

2 Related Work

This section presents a general overview of the previous work done in the target tracking domain.

The "Distributed Predictive Tracking algorithm" DPT [4] uses a distributed prediction to track moving targets in a sensor network. The protocol relies on a prediction method, that uses the old positions of the target, It activates only three sensors situated in the vicinity of the predicted position. The algorithm becomes inefficient if the target changes suddenly it's velocity or direction. In [2], the authors consider a sensor density that insures a minimum number of nodes near the target. The detection range of a sensor is rectangular. The position of the target in the network, is the intersection of the nodes' ranges detecting the target. This approach lacks of precision when, the number of sensors detecting simultaneously the target, is small.

In [5], the sensors monitor the environment and communicate the data periodically to the server. The server localizes the position of the target (the authors assume that the target continuously transmits a constant signal), using the triangulation method and the data generated by the sensors. This approach relies on the strength of the signal emitted by the target. However, the presence of noise or obstacles may attenuate the signal, resulting in an inaccurate localization of the target. The authors in [7] propose a target tracking mechanism called Dynamic Convoy Tree-Based Collaboration (DCTC). DCTC, is based on a tree structure called convoy tree. Each node in the tree, corresponds to a sensor near the mobile target. The tree is dynamically configured to add and delete nodes during the movement of the target. Based on the convoy tree, the root gathers information from the sensors, and refines it to obtain a complete and precise information about the target. DCTC becomes ineffective when the target movement is fast and random. Frequent tree updates are then necessary causing a significant increase in the sensor's energy consumption.

In [3], the authors present three protocols based on the distance between two random nodes. If the distance is lower than the detection diameter 2R, the detection ranges of the two nodes intersect and form a detection region. The line, formed by the intersection of the detection ranges of the active sensors, is moved to detect the target. Every geographic point in the field is scanned at minimum once. It may happen that a target enters the field from one side, while the active line is on the opposite side making the target invisible to the network for a moment.

In the literature, the approaches proposed for target tracking give good results for the case they were build for. Changing the initial assumptions of the tracking approach, leads to a significant decrease in the performance. In our work, we present a global tracking approach since no restriction is made on the targets movements. Moreover, our solution optimizes the energy consumption in the network, by moving the sink mobility, and using a prediction approach for a better management of the sensors energy states (active/sleep).

3 RPL Scheme

3.1 Assumptions

In our approach, we consider realistic assumptions independent from network's state and target movement. Recall that the sink (a laptop or an on-board computer in a car, for example) is not energy constrained and has the ability to move in the field with a limited speed. We assume that the nodes' positions are known at the sink level. This assumption does not present any particular constraint, since it is generally admitted that the nodes positioning problem can be solved [1]. Thus, the sink possesses a total view of the network and can use a centralized routing approach, allowing an efficient tracking of the target. Our approach can be considered as a virtual clustering approach, since the sink position is calculated for a specific zone of sensors. We assume that the sensors, at the borders of the monitored area, are always active. The target is detected once it enters the field and then, the tracking is launched. The network is capable of managing simultaneously several targets, and each time a new target enters the detection field, the sink associates to each target a single identifier.

3.2 Solution Description

Unlike above cited approaches [2, 3, 5, 7], our solution has the advantage to dynamically adapt to target and network dynamics: single or multiple targets with low and high velocity movement.

To achieve a maximum energy optimization, our solution merges the benefits of two distinct concepts

- Relocate the sink by considering the remaining energy of the nodes in its vicinity (see next section centroid formula)
- Predict the target's future position using previous positions, in order to activate a restricted number of sensors for the detection of the target

Optimal Sink Positioning. We can optimize the energy consumed in the network, by moving the sink toward the nodes with low remaining energies. This reduces the transmission distance, and preserves the energy consumed in the network, by reducing the number of sensors that participate in the routing of a packet.

Sink mobility has been introduced in [6] where a cost function is used to calculate the optimal position of the sink in the network but for applications different from target tracking. This function takes into account the state of the nodes balanced with the number of transmitted packets in the nodes close to the sink. The cost function introduced in [6] gives good results if used in a network where events are localized in static zones. But, when it comes for target tracking it gives poor performance since when the target moves fast, packets are generated randomly from different zones. In this case, the sink will not have enough time to move toward the position calculated by the cost function and if it does, the target will already be far from this calculated position. This leads to a frequent change in sink positions and a very high packet loss rate. Therefore, we introduce an *Energy centroid* (1) formula that finds the optimal positions of the sink with a fast moving target by considering the remaining energy of the neighboring sensors belonging to a prediction region (which will be defined in next subsections). For the best of our knowledge, this formula has never been used in this domain.

The energy centroid formula main goal is to move the sink closer to the nodes that will generate the traffic in the near future and more precisely toward the nodes with the minimum remaining energy. This movement is done with the help of the prediction method described in next section. The main advantage of moving the sink is the reduction of the packet's total power transmission: packets need less hops and less transmissions distance to reach the sink. This results in a reduction in the energy consumed per route and limits the number of sensors involved in the routing. Both results are beneficial to reduce the energy consumption in the network and hence increase its lifetime.

Let g be a target identified by sink j. The formula of the energy centroid is given as follows:

$$\begin{cases} X_j(t) = \dfrac{\sum_{i \in PR_j(t)} \frac{1}{Energy_i(t)} \cdot x_i(t)}{\sum_{i \in PR_j(t)} \frac{1}{Energy_i(t)}} \\ Y_j(t) = \dfrac{\sum_{i \in PR_j(t)} \frac{1}{Energy_i(t)} \cdot y_i(t)}{\sum_{i \in PR_j(t)} \frac{1}{Energy_i(t)}} \end{cases} \tag{1}$$

where $X_j(t)$ and $Y_j(t)$ are the coordinates (function of time) of the new calculated position of the sink. Index i represents the identifier of all the active sensors in the prediction region $PR_j(t)$. $x_i(t)$ and $y_i(t)$ are the coordinates of the active sensor i and $Energy_i$ it's remaining energy. As it can be noticed, the weight of the sensor position is inversely proportional to its remaining energy, which will make the centroid close to nodes with little remaining energy. Note that this formula requires the knowledge of the sensors' energy in the specific zone, the remaining energy of the nodes is simply updated by the sink upon packet reception. This is done using the routing table that identifies the sensors that participated in the routing.

Predict the Future Position of the Target. Our prediction method is based on the Kalman filter prediction which uses the former positions of the target to predict its future position. In our approach, this is done in order to activate only the sensors in the vicinity of the current and future target's positions, this region is called the prediction region (PR). The used model for target motion is linear and is as follows:

$$X(t_{n+1}) = \Phi X(t_n) + \Gamma w(t_n) \tag{2}$$

where:

$$X = \begin{pmatrix} x \\ y \\ x' \\ y' \end{pmatrix}$$

X is a state vector consisting of position and velocity which evolve at each time interval according to the model in (2)

$$\Phi = \begin{pmatrix} 1 & 0 & T & 0 \\ 0 & 1 & 0 & T \\ 0 & 0 & 1 & 0 \\ 0 & 0 & 0 & 1 \end{pmatrix}$$

$$\Gamma = \begin{pmatrix} 0\,0 \\ 0\,0 \\ 1\,0 \\ 0\,1 \end{pmatrix}$$

where w is zero-mean gaussian white noise with zero mean and covariance Q

$$Q = \begin{pmatrix} qT & 0 \\ 0 & qT \end{pmatrix}$$

T is the time step and q is a constant.

Prediction Implementation. In our solution, the velocity of the target is the key factor used by the network to allow an efficient detection of all the targets while reducing the energy consumption of the sensors. In case a single target enters the monitored area with a low speed, using the former position of the target, we can predict its future position. These two positions (current and future) enable us to define a rectangular zone called the prediction region PR contained in a circle of radius R, and all the nodes included in this zone are activated. The movement of the sink into the PR zone is made to (1) reduce the transmission power of the sensors. If the predicted position is in the PR zone, to avoid unnecessary updates of the sink position, we restrict the sink movement using the following condition:

$$dist(Sink, pos_{pred}) > 2 * Range) \wedge (min(Er(i)/i \in S_d) < \Delta) \quad (3)$$

where:

- S_d be the set of the nodes participating in the routing of the packets generated by sensors belonging to S1
- S_1 = set of sensors in the PR zone with a distance less than Range from the predicted position
- Range is the detection range of the sensor, Er(i) is the remaining energy of node i and Δ is an energy threshold (for example, 20% of the node's initial energy)

If the target increases dramatically its velocity, the sink becomes incapable of tracking efficiently the target and will not have enough time to reach the calculated optimal position. Therefore, we propose a solution to activate all the sensors in the network and place the sink according to the formula of the energy centroid (1). Note that the sink relocation phase will be executed periodically according to the speed of the target. We define a parameter p to represent this relocation periodicity.

4 Target Localization Method

In a target tracking application, the aim is to localize the position of the target. The network uses the packets received from the sensors which detected the target to compute the target's position. As mentioned previously, the sink knows all the positions of the sensors and possesses a total view of the network. When the target is simultaneously detected by several sensors at the same time, these sensors send the data packets to the nearest sink. The sink transfers these data to the command node which localizes the position of the target using our proposed localization method.

4.1 Localization Method Description

The method's main goal is to simplify target localization when the number of nodes n detecting the target is high. It reduces the number of nodes participating in the localization process for the computation of the real target's position.

If we consider the detection range of a sensor to be circular, the location of the target is the intersection of all the detection ranges (circles) of the sensors detecting the target. Note at this step, that the final target localization is the minimal intersection area of the detection ranges but not an exact position.

For a network with a high sensor density, target's location would be the intersection of numerous detection ranges corresponding to all the sensors having detected the target. This leads to computational complexity if we proceed using an iterative calculation method. To solve this problem, we introduce a new approach which to our knowledge does not exist in the literature. This approach reduces the computation for target position, from an intersection of n circles to an intersection of four circles, where n is the number of sensors which have detected the target. We assume that all the nodes have a circular detection range of the same radius.

Let us consider the following notations:

- Let Z be the minimum area containing the target
- Let D be the set of all nodes detecting the target
- Let (c_i),(c_j) and (c_k) be the circles having as centers N_i, N_j and N_k respectively

The goal of our method is to *minimize Z*. The method is summarized by the following algorithm:

Target localization algorithm

1. $\forall N_i, N_j \in D$, compute (d_1) the line formed by the points T_1 and T_2 such that $\{T_1, T_2\} = (c_i) \cap (c_j)$
2. For all nodes $N_k \in D - \{N_i, N_j\}$
   Find the circle(s) c_k that restrict(s) the zone between T_1 and T_2, T_1 and T_2 become the limit of this zone on (d_1)
3. Find nodes which detection ranges (circles) pass through T_1 and T_2
   3.1 If only one circle (c_s) passes by both T_1 and T_2 Then
   $\text{Z} = (c_s) \cap (c_i \cap c_j) \Rightarrow \text{END}$

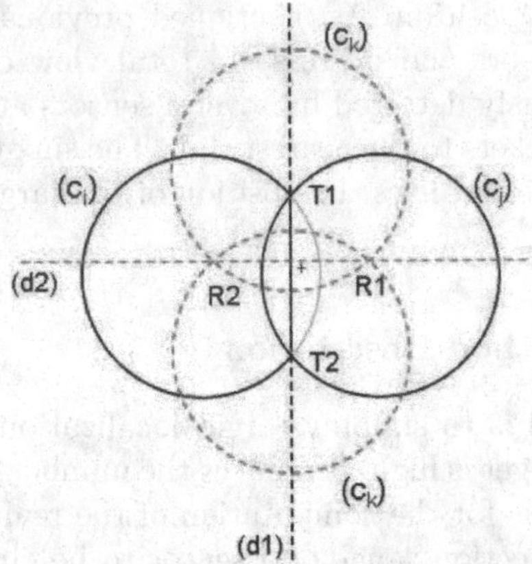

Fig. 1. The detection method

3.2 Two circles (c_l) and (c_m) pass through T_1 and T_2
- Compute points R_1 and R_2 such that $(\{R_1,R_2\} = (c_l) \cap (c_m))$
- Compute line (d2) passing through R_1 and R_2

4. For all nodes which detection range ($\neq (c_l, c_m)$) intersects (d_2) and restricts $[R_1R_2]$
   4.1 Execute (3.1) with $[R_1R_2]$ substituting $[T_1T_2]$
   - If two distinct circles exist passing by R_1, R_2
     Compute the intersection zone Z_1 of these two ranges $Z = (c_l) \cap c_m) \cap Z_1$
     $\Rightarrow$ END
   - else (one circular (c_r) range pass by R_1, R_2)
     $Z = (c_r) \cap (c_i \cap c_j) \Rightarrow$ END

This method tries to compute the minimum zone in which the target is located. First, two nodes detecting the target are chosen arbitrarily in order to calculate the line (d_1). Then, in an iterative way the circles that intersect and restrict $[T_1T_2]$ are found. After the second step, the method finds the circles passing by T_1 and T_2 and computes (d_2) which is the line formed by the points R_1 and R_2 resulting from the intersection of the circles passing by T_1 and T_2. The same method is used to restrict $[R_1R_2]$. At the end, the zone in which the target exists is the intersection of (c_j), (c_i) and (c_k) (k can be 1 or 2) as shown in figure 1 ('+' in figure 1 represents the target).

5 Performance Evaluation

The effectiveness of our RPL scheme with its repositioning, prediction and localization methods has been validated through simulations. In our experiments, we used Opnet simulator. The network is composed of 250 fixed nodes randomly distributed over a 100m x 100m square area. The detection range of a node is 20 meters and all nodes possess the same initial power estimated to 5000 unit (u). We consider that at any time only one event can occur in the network. Our simulation lifetime is considered as a series of rounds. A round represents the change of the target's position which is implemented by the routing of the packets generated by the sensors to the sink. A single event is generated per round of simulation which is fixed to every second. The target moves at a constant velocity of 1 m/s. The energy of the nodes in the network is updated after each packet routing. We considered two conditions to stop our simulations: the first is when 50 percent of the network nodes are depleted and the second is when the target becomes invisible to the network, i.e. all the packets generated by the sensors that detect the target are lost (do not reach the sink).

In figures 2 and 3, we consider that the simulation stops when 50 percent of the sensors are depleted.

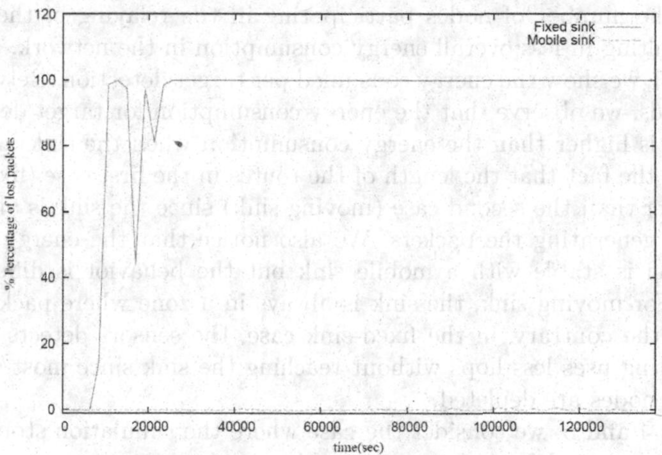

Fig. 2. Percentage of lost packets per detection

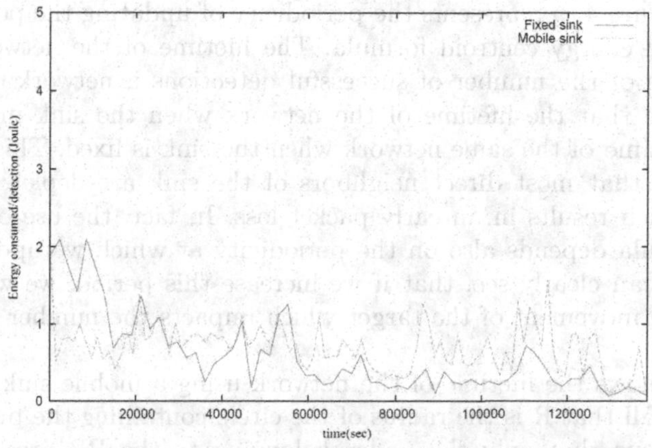

Fig. 3. Energy consumption per target detection

In figure 2, we plot the percentage of packet loss per detection for the cases where the sink is fixed and mobile. The x-axis represents the number of rounds in the network and each round corresponds to a target detection. We can notice from figure 2 that between 0 and 8761 seconds, the network have the same percentage of packet loss for both cases. But, this tendency changes for the fixed sink case because of the depletion of the 1-hop neighbors of the sink. Since these neighbors are used in the routing of all the packets generated by the sensors, they are statistically the first nodes to die which results in the lost of all the packets generated by the sensors after 22969 seconds as it can be seen in figure 2. When the sink moves toward the position calculated by the energy centroid formula, we can clearly notice that the percentage of lost packets per detection is very low. This result was expected since the sink is positioned close to the zone that generate the most number of packets. Thus, the transmission distance between the source and the sink is reduced preserving the energy of the sensors. Moreover, the number of nodes participating in the relaying of the packet is reduced resulting in less overall energy consumption in the network.

In figure 3, we show the energy consumed per target detection. Between 0 and 20000 seconds, we observe that the energy consumption for target detection for a fixed sink is higher than the energy consumption when the sink moves. This results from the fact that the length of the routes in the first case (fixed sink) is always higher than the second case (moving sink) since the sink is always close to the zone generating the packets. We also notice that the energy consumed per detection is stable with a mobile sink but the behavior is different for a fixed sink. For moving sink, the sink is always in a zone where packets can be routed. On the contrary, in the fixed-sink case, the sensors detects the target but the routing uses less hops without reaching the sink since most of the sink neighboring nodes are depleted.

In figures 4 and 5, we consider the case where the simulation stops when all the packets generated from a target detection are lost.

Figure 4 shows a lifetime comparison between the case where the sink is fixed and when the position of the sink is changed according to the energy centroid formula. In figure 4, p represents the periodicity of updating the position of the sink using the energy centroid formula. The lifetime of the network is calculated in terms of the number of successful detections a network can perform. We can notice that the lifetime of the network when the sink moves outperforms the lifetime of the same network when the sink is fixed. This also results from the fact that most direct neighbors of the sink are depleted in case of fixed sink which results in an early packet loss. In fact, the use of the energy centroid formula depends also on the periodicity at which we update the sink position. We can clearly see, that if we increase this period, we will not react rapidly to the movement of the target which impacts the number of successful detections.

Figure 5, shows the lifetime of the network using a mobile sink for different R values. Recall that R is the radius of the circle containing the predicted zone PR. This means that only the nodes belonging to the PR area are used in

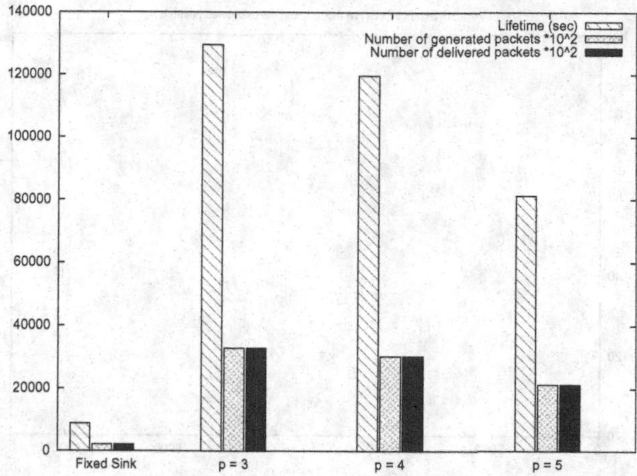

Fig. 4. Impact of updating parameter p

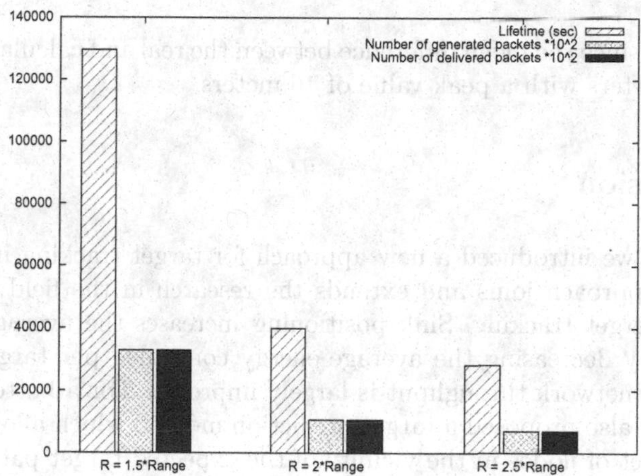

Fig. 5. Impact of updating parameter R

the calculation of the energy centroid. This figure shows that the choice of the nodes that participate in the calculation of our formula is crucial to extend network's lifetime. The lifetime duration using a radius R = 1.5 * Range where Range is the detection range of a single sensor (here Range= 20m), is significant compared to the same network where the centroid formula is calculated using a larger R.

Finally, to evaluate the performance of our detection method, we use the same previous simulation parameters. The obtained results are illustrated in figure 6. They show the difference between the real position of the target and the position computed by our detection method. This result proves the efficiency

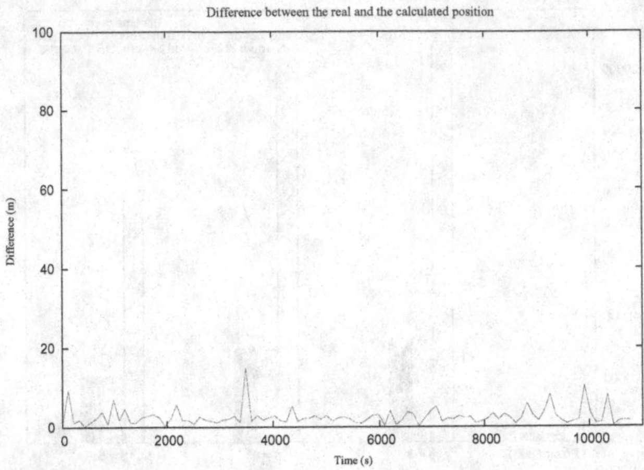

Fig. 6. Difference between the real and calculated positions

of our method since the mean difference between the real and calculated positions is around 3 meters with a peak value of 16 meters.

6 Conclusion

In this paper, we introduced a new approach for target tracking in sensor networks. This approach joins and extends the research in the field of sink positioning and target tracking. Sink positioning increases the average lifetime of the network by decreasing the average energy consumed per target detection. Moreover, the network throughput is largely improved. For a better energy optimization, we also proposed a target prediction method which allows activation of only a subset of nodes in the vicinity of the expected target path. We finally proposed an efficient algorithm to reduce computational complexity for target localization estimation. Simulation results have demonstrated the effectiveness of our approach in terms of energy consumption and network throughput.

References

1. Doherty, L., Pister, K., Ghaoui, L.: Convex position estimation in wireless sensor networks. In: Proceedings of IEEE INFOCOM, Alaska (2001)
2. Galstyan, A., Krishnamachari, B., Lerman, K., Pattren, S.: Distributed Online localisation in sensor networks using a moving target. In: Information Processing in Sensor Networks, USA (2004)
3. Ren, S., Li, Q., Wang, H., Zhang, X.: Design and analysis of wave scheduling Protocols for Object-Tracking applications. In: First IEEE International Conference Distributed Computing in Sensor Systems, Marina del Rey (2005)

4. Yang, H., Sikdar, B.: A protocol for tracking Mobile targets using Sensor Networks. In: Proceedings of IEEE Workshop on Sensor Network Protocols and Applications (2003)
5. Yu, X., Niyogi, K., Mehrotra, S., Venkatasubramanian, N.: Adaptive target tracking in sensor networks. IEEE Signal Processing Magazine (2002)
6. Younis, M., Akkaya, K.: Sink Repositioning For Enhanced Performance in Wireless Sensor Networks. The Elsevier Computer Networks Journal (November 2004)
7. Zhang, W., Cao, G.: DCTC: Dynamic Convoy Tree-Based Collaboration for Target Tracking in Sensor. IEEE Transactions on Wireless Communications (September 5, 2004)
8. Merrer, E.L., Gramoli, V., Vaina, A.C., Bertier, M., Kermarre, A.M.: Energy aware self-organizing density management in wireless sensor networks. In: ACM MobiShare, Los Angeles, CA (2006)
9. Carle, J., Simplot-Ryl, D.: Energy-efficient area monitoring for sensor networks. Computer 37(2), 40–46 (2004)
10. Cardei, M., Du, D.: Improving wireless sensor network lifetime through power aware organization. ACM Journal of Wireless Networks (2005)
11. Shah, R., Rabaey, J.: Energy aware routing for low energy ad hoc sensor networks. In: Proceedings of IEEE Wireless Communications and Networking Conference (WCNC), vol. 1, pp. 17–21 (2002)
12. Kwon, S., Shroff, N.B.: Energy-efficient interference-based routing for multi-hop wireless networks. In: IEEE INFOCOM 2006, Barcelona, Spain (2006)
13. Hassanein, H., Luo, J.: Reliable energy aware routing in wireless sensor networks. In: Second IEEE Workshop on Dependability and Security in Sensor Networks and Systems DSSNS (2006)

Backhaul Topology Design and Weighted Max-Min Fair Capacity Allocation in Wireless Mesh Networks

Abdelhak Farsi[1], Nadjib Achir[1,2], Khaled Boussetta[1], Gladys Diaz[1], and Arturo Gomez[1]

[1] L2TI – Institut Galilée – Université Paris 13, Sorbonne Paris Cité
99 Avenue J-B Clément, 93430 Villetaneuse, France
{farsi,nadjib.achir,khaled.boussetta,gladys.diaz, arturo.gomez}@univ-paris13.fr
[2] INRIA HiPERCOM
Rocquencourt B.P. 105, 78153 Le Chesnay, France
nadjib.achir@inria.fr

Abstract. In this paper we focus on the Multi-Channel, Multi-Radio Wireless Mesh Network design issue. We propose an effective planning approach which considers two folds. First, to determine the backhaul topology by interconnecting wirelessly the mesh routers (MRs). Second, to share based on the weighted max-min fair scheme the available capacity between connected mesh routers. We formulate both aspects as a global problem. Due to the high computational complexity, we deal with the global problem by decoupling it into two separated problems: bakhaul topology formation and the weighted max-min fair capacity allocation problems. These latter aspects are treated sequentially where we adopt local search heuristics in order to address the scalability issue. Numerical results are presented to demonstrate the effectiveness of our proposition. Thus, we evaluate the proposed heuristics according to the exact solution of the global problem, and we discuss their opportunities.

Keywords: Wireless mesh networks, topology formation, Max-Min fairness, capacity allocation.

1 Introduction

Wireless mesh networks (WMNs) have been adopted in different area network deployments due to the concept of achieving an extended coverage with much lower transmission power through multihop communications. They are widely used in a variety of application scenarios such as a last-mile broadband Internet access technology, broadband home networking, gaming, enterprise, community and neighborhood networks, etc. The WMN consists on connecting adjacent stationary wireless nodes, called mesh routers (MRs), to a wired network via the gateway. In order to improve coverage and enhance connectivity, the mesh router has been designed to provide two functionalities. Firstly, it operates as

V. Guyot (Ed.): ICAIT 2012, LNCS 7593, pp. 296–309, 2013.

a relay to forward traffic, in a multi-hop fashion, from neighbor mesh routers to the Internet gateway and vice versa. Secondly, it acts as an Access Point to the end-users within its coverage area. From this basic description, such network has been represented as two-tier architecture, consisting of a backhaul tier (mesh node to mesh node) and an access tier (mesh node to users).

Designing WMN is a key issue to optimize the network performance. Various works treated the WMN design problem have been presented in the literature, most of them such as [1-3] proposed clustering based gateway placement algorithms while considering as constraints the delay and the bandwidth. However, splitting up the backhaul tier entailes the deployment of additional gateways, and consequently increases the overall cost of the network. Besides, in most cases the clustering approach results in tree-based clusters with a few links. These mentioned works do not focus on the multipath feature of the WMN. Authors in [5] proposed to position a single gateway in WMN. Unfortunately, their approach based on a set of limited assumptions. They assume that nodes use the same frequency channel and communicate among them using a fixed modulation scheme, and each node has only one radio interface. Capacity per node in such solution drops significantly with the increase of the network size. In [8], authors formulate the problem of gateway and mesh routers placement to design the WMN based on the set covering problem. The objective here is to reduce the cost of the network while ensuring connectivity. However, the constraint limiting the number of radio interfaces is not taken into account.

Other works have investigated the topology formation and capacity maximization as a joint optimization problem [10],[11]. They start from a backhaul topology resulting from the deployment of mesh routers. In [10], the objective is to determine the logical links connecting the mesh routers while mitigating interferences. However the authors in [11] try to increase the network capacity by connecting MRs to their gateway through at most two path-disjoint links. For both works, aspect of fairness among shared links has been ignored.

The problem of WMN design is strongly related to the problem of channel assignment, which is proven to be NP-hard problem [7]. Thus, optimal channel allocation is needed to improve the performance of the WMN by mitigating the interference. Currently, many attractive approaches have been proposed to increase the capacity while reducing the interference in WMN. Typical examples have been detailed in [14] including the use of orthogonal channels, directional and smart antennas, MIMO systems, and multiradio/multichannel systems.

In our case, and regarding the propagation model of the 802.11-based 5GHz band, we have verified that the interference between wireless links forming the backhaul tier could be eliminated and all links can be simultaneously active when we determine the convenient mapping between the links forming the backhaul tier and the available 12-orthogonal channels. Even assuming this practical solution, it is worthy to clarify that the capacity of wireless links is not considered constant and it is estimated based on the perceived Signal-to-Interference plus Noise Ratio (SINR) as it is detailed hereafter.

The aim of this study can be summarized as follows. **First**, we formulate jointly the *backhaul topology formation* and the *weighted max-min fair capacity allocation* problems. **Second**, due to the mathematical complexity of this global optimization problem we propose to resolve it using two scalable heuristics: the first heuristic namely Backhaul Topology Formation Algorithm (BTFA) and the second heuristic is weighted max-min fair capacity allocation algorithm. It is important to note that we adapt the ϵ-approximation algorithm to our context in order to achieve a weighted max-min fair allocation.

The rest of this paper is organized as follows. Section 2 discusses the problem formulation. Section 3 details the used strategies to resolve the backhaul topology design problem and explains how can we optimize the concurrent flows at the backhaul tier. Section 4 shows the obtained numerical results. Finally, the paper is concluded in section 5.

2 WMN Design Problem Formulation

In this section, we formally define the backhaul topology design problem. We consider a 2D-geographical environment denoted as $\mathcal{A}$ in which a set of mesh routers have been installed according, for instance, to the methods in [3][4]. We assume only one gateway referred to as g, positioned in the barycenter of $\mathcal{A}$. Our choice is justified by the fact that, the barycenter location already endows existing internet connectivity. Besides, it allows to avoid forming long hops in the backhaul. Each mesh router participates to form the access tier using its dedicated radio interface to communicate with its associated wireless users. On the other hand, the mesh router uses its I radio interfaces to relay the traffic aggregated on behalf of other mesh nodes that may not be within direct wireless transmission range of their gateway. We assume that the I radio interfaces are directionals. For any two nodes u and v located within the radio communication range of each other, then there is a potential wireless link between them denoted (u, v). Considering all the potential wireless links among mesh nodes, we can model the backhaul tier by the physical topology graph $G = (R, L)$ where $R = \{g, s_1, \ldots, s_n\}$ is the set of mesh nodes, and L is the set of all potential undirected communication links.

For each mesh node $u \in R$, potentially linked to mesh node $v \in R$, we associate the $(I \times 1)$ interface assignment vector x_{uv}. If the mesh node u may communicate with mesh node v over the ith radio interface, then the ith element in the vector x_{uv} is set to 1. This definition is illustrated through the following example: We assume that $I = 4$, and the mesh node u uses its second radio interface to communicate with v, whereas node v uses its forth radio interface to communicate with u. This yields to the two following interface assignment vectors $x_{uv} = [0\ 1\ 0\ 0]^T$ and $x_{vu} = [0\ 0\ 0\ 1]^T$.

In general, to maintain a logical link among two mesh nodes located within the coverage area of each other, each node should assign one of its I radio interfaces to handle the link. This first constraint can be interpreted as:

$$1^T x_{uv} = 1, \quad \forall u, v \in R, \quad (u, v) \in L \tag{1}$$

Establishing the logical link between u and v if a pair of their interfaces are connected together:

$$1^T x_{uv} = 1^T x_{vu}, \quad \forall u, v \in R, \quad (u, v) \in L \tag{2}$$

We highlight that $1^T x_{vu}$ is interpreted as a binary variable constraint:

$$1^T x_{uv} \in \{0, 1\}, \quad \forall u, v \in R, \quad (u, v) \in L \tag{3}$$

Practically, each mesh router has a limited number of radio interfaces. One radio is intended to the access tier, however I radio interfaces are dedicated to form the backhaul tier network. This latter constraint is expressed as:

$$\sum_{v \in R} 1^T x_{uv} 1^T x_{vu} \leq I, \quad \forall u, v \in R, \quad (u, v) \in L \tag{4}$$

Another constraints to consider when using multiple radio interfaces is channel dependency and ripple effect [6]. To restrict the channel dependency, generally, an upper bound on the number of logical links that a radio interface may support has to be set. However, the ripple effect is caused when a radio interface monitors more than one logical link. Switching from the actual channel to another involves changing all concerned logical links. In order to deal with these two problems, we assign a radio interface exclusively to only one logical link. More explicitly, for a logical link (u, v) in node u, there is no additional link sharing a radio interface with the link (u, v). Based on this condition, we avoid determining the portion of time each logical link accesses the radio interface and consequently increasing the link capacity. Both of the two constraints are grouped as follows:

$$\sum_{k \in R, v \neq k, (u,k) \in L} x_{uv}^T x_{uk} = 0, \quad \forall u, v \in R, \quad (u, v) \in L \tag{5}$$

For improving the overall throughput in the backhaul network, we should maximize the amount of flows to be routed from sources to the gateway. We define a path p from the node s_i to the node g as a sequence $\{s_i = v_1, v_2, \ldots, v_q = g\}$ of vertices from R, where for all $1 \leq i \leq q$, v_{i+1} is adjacent to v_i in G. Let $f^{s_i g}$ denotes the amount of flow to be routed through a given path p connecting the mesh node s_i to the gateway g. Moreover, we define the binary variable $a_{uv}^{s_i g}$. It is set to 1 when the two following conditions are satisfied: first, the logical link $(u, v) \in L$ connecting mesh nodes u and v is kept. Second, the link (u, v) is used to rely the flow sending from s_i to g.

$$a_{uv}^{s_i g} \in \{0, 1\}, \quad \forall u, v, s_i, g \in R, \quad (u, v) \in L \tag{6a}$$

$$a_{uv}^{s_i g} \leq 1^T x_{uv} \tag{6b}$$

Thus, maximizing the flow of each pair referred as (s_i, g), where g is the destination, is achievable by exploiting the rich connectivity of the backhaul tier. For this reason, we consider more than one path between the sender and the receiver.

$$\sum_{u \in R} f^{s_i u} 1^T x_{s_i u} 1^T x_{u s_i} \geq 1, \quad \forall s_i, u \in R, \quad (s_i, u) \in L \tag{7}$$

In fact, the flow $f^{s_i g}$ characterizes the bandwidth allocated to the pair (s_i, g). We suppose that a minimum amount of flow noted d_i has to be transmitted between s_i and g. Let define the triplet (s_i, g, d_i) as commodity $i \in \mathcal{C}$, where $\mathcal{C}$ is the set of all commodities. Besides, we denote by c_{uv} the capacity of the logical link (u, v). Obviously, the total flow to be routed over a logical link (u, v) denoted as $f_{uv}^{s_i g}$, does not exceed the capacity of the link itself. This constraint ensures that no capacities are violated.

$$\sum_{i \in \mathcal{C}} f_{uv}^{s_i g} 1^T x_{uv} 1^T x_{vu} \leq c_{uv}, \quad \forall s_i, g, u, v \in R, \ (u, v) \in L \tag{8}$$

Since all mesh nodes send flow concurrently to the gateway, we define γ as the ratio of the flow supplied between a pair (s_i, g) to the predefined demand d_i for that pair. Considering fairness among all commodities implies maximizing γ where at least $\gamma f^{s_i g}$ amount of throughput can be routed from each mesh router s_i to the gateway g. This problem is implicitly coupled with the aforementioned constraints that determine routes. Let denote P_i the set of all paths that belong to the same commodity i, and $f^{s_i g}(p)$ denotes the bandwidth assigned to commodity i on the path $p \in P_i$.

$$\sum_{p \in P_i} f^{s_i g}(p) \geq \gamma d_i, \quad \forall s_i, g \in R \tag{9}$$

Define the objective function as maximizing the ratio γ and taking into account the constraints detailed above, allow us to summarize the WMN design as the following Mixed Integer Linear Programming (MILP) optimization problem.

$$\text{maximize} \quad \gamma \tag{10a}$$

subject to:

$$1^T x_{uv} = 1^T x_{vu} \leq 1, \tag{10b}$$

$$\sum_{k \in N, v \neq k, (u,k) \in L} x_{uv}^T x_{uk} = 0, \tag{10c}$$

$$\sum_{v \neq u, (u,v) \in L} x_{uv}^T x_{vu} \leq I, \tag{10d}$$

$$\sum_{u \in R} f^{s_i u} 1^T x_{s_i u} 1^T x_{u s_i} \geq 1, \tag{10e}$$

$$\sum_{i \in \mathcal{C}} f_{uv}^{s_i g} 1^T x_{uv} 1^T x_{vu} \leq c_{uv}, \tag{10f}$$

$$\sum_{p \in P_i} f^{s_i g}(p) \geq \gamma d_i \tag{10g}$$

Eliminating some constraints related to the backhaul topology formation simplifies the defined problem to be identical to the linear programming multicommodity concurrent flow problem, which is proven to be NP-hard problem [13].

The main limitation of this global formulation resides in its restriction to small sized instances. To deal with the complexity of the mesh backhaul design, we propose simple and efficient heuristic methods. In what follow we detail our proposed approach.

3 Our Approach

For many applications, it is more important to solve a given complex problem efficiently in fast manner than to solve it optimally. Therefore, we deal with the defined global problem by dividing it into two subproblems, and we propose a scalable heuristic for each subproblem. Description of both heuristics is given in the next subsections.

3.1 Backhaul Topology Formation Algorithm (BTFA)

The BTFA heuristic starts with the initial adjacency matrix A that corresponds to the connectivity graph $G = (R, L)$, where R is the set of mesh nodes and L is the set all potential links. We define the degree of a mesh node as the number of its assigned radio interfaces. The objective here is to connect all mesh nodes to the gateway in a multi-hop fashion while considering the constraints defined above. It is worth noting that our algorithm can be executed even when the environment contains a lot of clusters forming several wireless mesh networks. Our heuristic proceeds in two phases, and is summarized as follows.

The first phase consists in choosing a minimum-sized set of links that would connect all the mesh routers to the gateway while considering the following constraints: (1) a limited number of radio interfaces, (2) assigning each radio interface to one and only one link, and (3) maximizing the overall backhaul capacity by choosing the set of links among all potential links which offers high physical data rate, that is the shortest links. The idea behind this rational is to avoid saturating all radio interfaces without be able to connect certain mesh nodes. Based on the connectivity graph, we start first from the gateway g and determine its I nearest neighboring nodes, i.e. which are one hop away from it. We save them in the vector V_tmp. Initially all the mesh routers of G are unexplored. We start from some node belonging to V_tmp and choose a link to follow taking into account the constraints above. Traversing the link leads to a new node. We continue in this way; at each step we select a shortest and an unexplored link leading from a node already reached and we traverse this link. The link leads to some node, either new or already reached. Whenever we run out of links leading from old nodes, we choose some untreated node from the set V_tmp, and begin a new exploration from this node. This first phase outputs an initial tree topology where all mesh nodes are connected to g, and belong to the one of the determined brunches. Each brunch terminates in leaf node and represents one multi-hop path providing the maximum capacity.

In the second phase, we try to satisfy the constraint of redundancy for the paths determined in the first phase. Such purpose can be achieved by seeking for other paths, preferably disjoint paths, to either enhance reachability of the gateway or optimizing the capacity utilization by distributing the load over multiple paths. A classification of nodes according to their used radio interfaces is necessary to establish a priority when treating the mesh nodes. Considering this feature, we get at most I subsets, where the jth subset includes the nodes with j used interfaces, and $1 \leq j \leq I$.

The basic idea here is to interconnect the nodes with degree smaller than I. However, the algorithm this time proceeds in I steps. During the first step, it starts by the farthest leaf nodes according to the gateway position, i.e. the nodes of the first subset, and connect them together. Which means that the algorithm starts by enhancing connectivity of nodes position at the edge of each branch and consequently establishing a backup path for each mesh node belonging to the concerned branch in order to reach the gateway g. We mention that both of the number of used interfaces and the subsets differentiating between nodes have to be updated continuously after each link selection. At the end of the step i we look if it left some non treated nodes in the subset i. If so, we merge the subset i with the subset $i+1$ and treat the overall nodes in the current $i+1$ step. The process continues until all the I subsets are treated.

3.2 Weighted Max-Min Fair Capacity Allocation

An optimal WMN design has to guarantee that each mesh router has access to the gateway. An efficient way to achieve this purpose is to share fairly the overall network capacity among all mesh routers. Here, we explain briefly the Fully Polynomial Time Approximation Scheme (FPTAS) [9] that we have used with our minor modification . This algorithm allows to avoid the computational complexity when solving optimally the Multicommodity Concurrent Flow Problem (MCFP) [13]. We maintain the same definitions of the graph $G = (R, L)$ and a commodity (s_i, g, d_i). Resolving the MCFP problem in iterative way is achieved by using the dual problem namely the sparsest cuts problem [15]. Let denote two dual variables, the length $l(e)$ and the weight z_i, both of them are assigned to the edge $e \in L$ of capacity $u(e)$, and the demand d_i, respectively.

Let $D(l)$ denotes the dual objective function $\sum_e u(e)l(e)$, and $dist_i(l) = z_i$ denotes the length of the shortest path from s_i to g based on the length function l, and $\alpha(l) = \sum_i d(i)dist_i(l)$. Reference [9] explained that minimizing $D(l)$ under the dual constraints can also be viewed as computing the lengths $l(e)$, $\forall e \in L$, such that $\beta = \frac{D(l)}{\alpha(l)}$ is minimized. Therefore, [9] gave a time approximation algorithm that provides a final flow value at least $(1 - 3\epsilon)OPT$ and can be summarized as follows.

Initially, for all edges e, $l(e) = \frac{\delta}{u(e)}$, where δ is a small fixed value. The algorithm proceeds in phases. In each phase, there are $|R|$ iterations, where R is the set of mesh routers. In iteration j, the objective is to route d_j units of flow from s_j to the g. This is done in a series of steps. In each step, the shortest paths from s_j to g is computed based on the current length function. Let c be the minimum capacity of the edges on the shortest path. Then, an amount of flow that is equal to the smallest value of c and the remaining demand of the commodity being treated is sent from s_j along the shortest path. The amount of routed flow is deducted from the demand d_j, and both of the edge lengths on this shortest path and the flow routed through this path are updated. The entire procedure terminates when the dual objective function is greater than one.

The resulting flows are unfeasible and have to be scaled down at the end. Looking to the length associated to each edge, we have observed that there is always a link $e \in L$ higher than others. If we consider this edge as the bottleneck we can derive from which a scale value that we use to obtain the feasible flow of each edge in the network in such a way that its not possible to increase a flow of any commodity without decreasing a higher value allocated to another commodity. In another words, determining the scale value from the bottleneck link allows to increase the portion γ proportionally to the amount of demands, when the capacity is available. This weighted max-min feature has been verified by analyzing the obtained results for several topologies.

4 Numerical Results

Some key features will be investigated in this section. First of all, we compare for a small size topology our proposed heuristic approach to the exact resolution of the MILP formulation given in section 2. We note that the exact solution of the MILP formulation is obtained through two steps using the exhaustive search method. In the first step, we generate all valid topologies ensuring connectivity of all nodes using at most their I radio interfaces and selecting the links offering the higher physical data rate. Subsequently, in the second step, we resolve optimally and for each topology the LP problem of weighted max-min fair capacity allocation [13].

To compare the exact solution to the heuristic result, we consider an environment of size $50 \times 50m^2$, within it we deploy randomly 6 wireless mesh routers around a gateway. Each mesh node is equipped with $I = 3$ radio interfaces. To estimate the capacity of links, we assume that the backhaul tier uses the twelve 802.11a orthogonal channels with a physical data rate depending on the SINR level estimated using the free space propagation model. We note that our approach is independent of a specific propagation model, the major issue for us is to have a good estimation about each link capacity. In this paper we refer to the look-up table related to 802.11a Cisco Aironet wireless card to determine the capacity of a link based on its SINR level.

Figure 1 illustrates the mesh nodes and all possible links connecting them to each other. The resulting topology provided by the exact solution is the same as the topology obtained using our BTFA heuristic and is presented in figure 2, where we observe that the chosen links are those offering the maximum capacity i.e., they are the shortest. To illustrate the weighted max-min fairness aspect, we have compared the modified ϵ-approximative method (ϵ=0.2) with the exact method while considering different demand values. Figures 3 represents the required and the obtained bandwidths BWs for each mesh node. One can observe that the obtained bandwidths are proportional to the requested bandwidths.

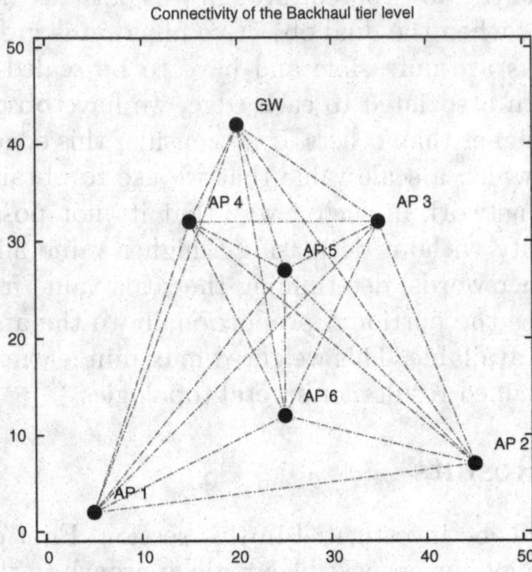

Fig. 1. Topology with all potential links

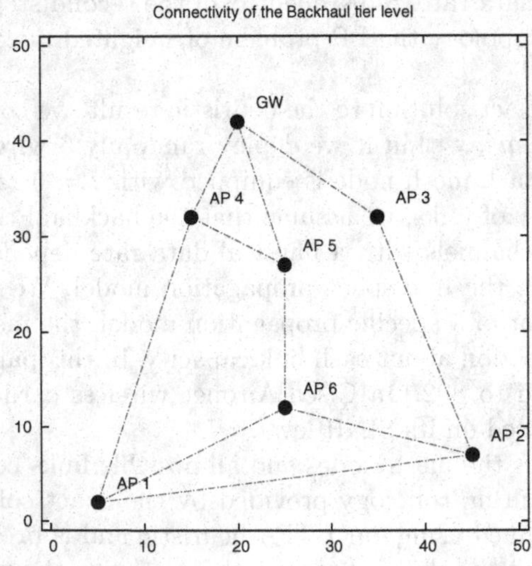

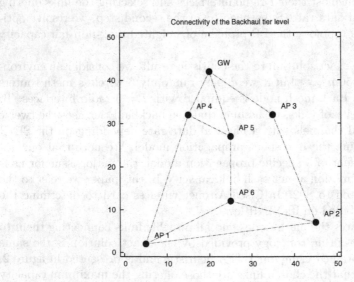

Fig. 2. Resulting logical topology for the exact and the heuristic methods

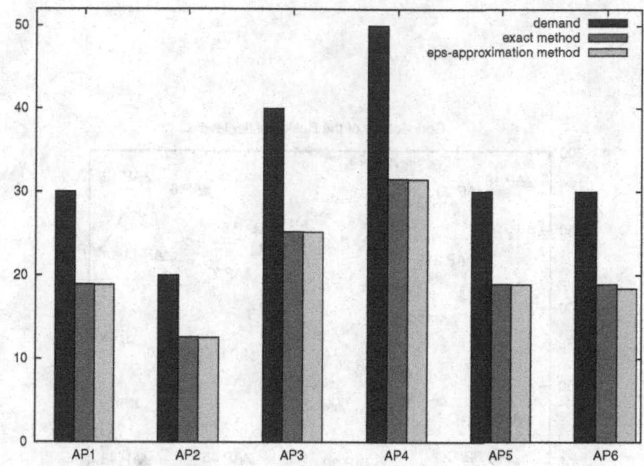

Fig. 3. The obtained bandwidth when the required BW is variable

To evaluate the performance of our proposition on large scale network, we consider environments with different sizes. In each environment we assume that there are a set of wireless users. For each environment we generate twenty scenarios by spreading out randomly the set of users and we cover them using mesh routers. The exact number of mesh routers to deploy depends on the number of users and their distribution, it may be determined using one of the method proposed in the literature such as [3][4]. Our environments have a size of $300 \times 300, 400 \times 400$ and $500 \times 500m^2$ where the average number of installed mesh routers is 50, 70 and 90 respectively. For each environment we ran our heuristics on twenty different scenarios. Each mesh router is equipped with four radio interfaces intended to the backhaul network.

Figure 4 shows a sample physical topology (among the twenty topologies) when all potential links are considered. Its corresponding logical topology, containing the chosen links and the radio interface assignment, is shown in figure 5. In addition to the negligible execution time to find the final topology, one can observe that mesh routers have from 2 to 4 disjoint links, which is the case for all the twenty scenarios.

To highlight the efficiency of the BTFA and the modified ϵ-approximative algorithms we proceed by considering that links are bi-directionals and the bandwidth assigned to a given commodity i can be used simultaneously or alternatively for downlink or uplink communications between s_i and the g. To estimate the demand of each commodity i associated to the pair (s_i, g) we assume that each mesh router covers a set of wireless stations operating on the 802.11b technology. We consider the upper and the lower demand bounds are estimated using the Bianchi's MAC model [12]. Based on this model, the upper bound is determined when the number of competing wireless stations is lower. In this case, the corresponding demand for each MR is up to $6Mbps$.

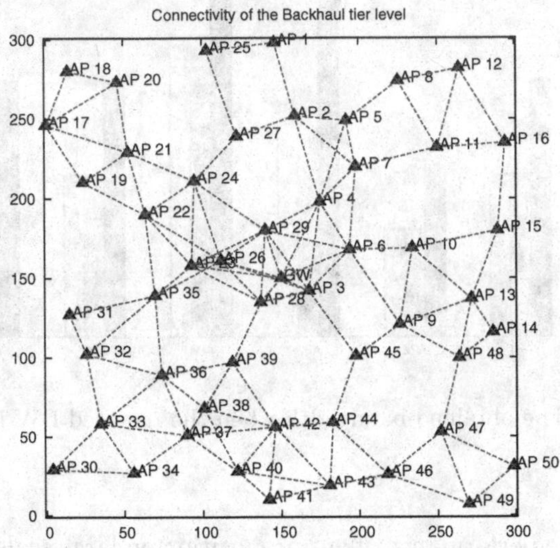

Fig. 4. Topology with all potential links

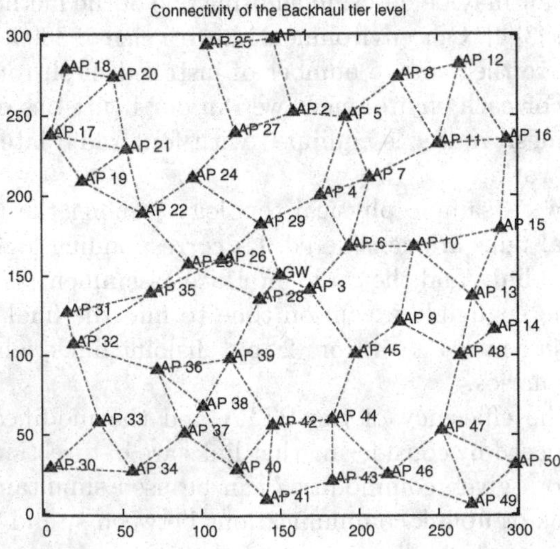

Fig. 5. Resulting logical topology using the BTFA algorithm

By analyzing the obtained results, we have noticed that the capacity allocated for each mesh router using the modified ϵ-approximative method is almost the same, with a standard deviation of 0.2%. This value is valid for all scenarios and what we present in the figures is the mean value.

Figure 6 shows the obtained bandwidths when all mesh routers require the maximum demand (i.e. 6Mbps). Here we compare three different metrics which are respectively, the path offering the maximum capacity, the shortest path in term of hop number and the adjacent paths. From this figure, we observe that the modified ϵ-approximative method produces the same results as the exact method (resulting from the MCFP formulation) because the ϵ-approximative's solution fall in the range $(1 - 3\epsilon)$ according to the exact solution. A second interesting feature that each MR has obtained the same portion of capacity whatever the metric used. In other words, the capacity is allocated fairly among nodes independently of the number of hops from the gateway. Finally, when all MRs select the path offering the maximum capacity to access the gateway, each of them get a small portion of bandwidth, because they share the same links. However, when only one path is used to join the gateway, the bandwidth is higher than the previous cases, which can be explained by the fact that the selected shortest path is shared among a small number of MR. The third metric provides an interesting solution because each mesh router uses all disjoint paths.

In another evaluation we try to determine the set of paths needed to exploit the overall capacity offered by the mesh network and sharing it in fair manner. For this purpose, we resolve the MCFP using the exact method when there is no huge number of paths connecting all pairs (s_i, g), and we use the modified ϵ-approximative method otherwise. for this time we do not fixed the number of paths, but we determine the set of paths for each MR based on the hop count metric. We choose all the set of paths connecting MRi to the gateway, where each path has at most respectively 8 hops, 10 hops and 12 hops. Figure 7 shows that

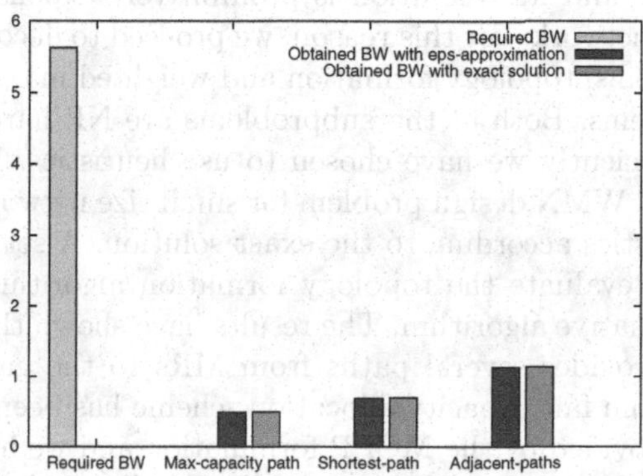

Fig. 6. The obtained BW for shortest path, maximum capacity path and disjoint paths respectively

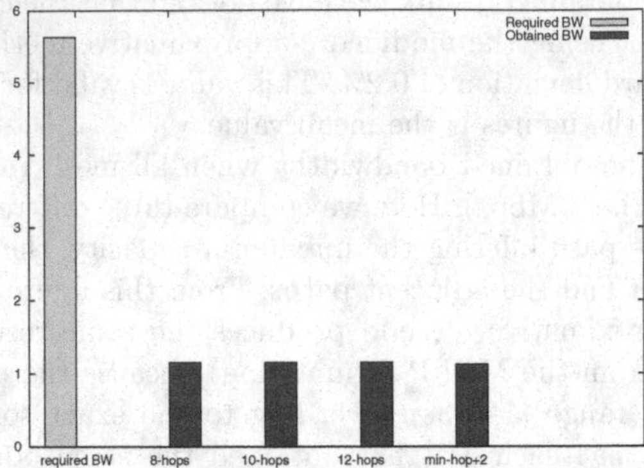

Fig. 7. The obtained BW versus the path length (in term of hop number)

all MRs get the same bandwidth (1,2Mbps). However we can get the same result when we select for each MR a set of paths by limiting the maximum number of hops to be the number of hops for the shortest path plus two additional hops (chosen arbitrarily value). conclusions done above, figure 6 expresses that even if the fairness property is maintained, the WMN has not a sufficient capacity to satisfy the demand of each MR. Figure 7 shows that the obtained bandwidth is $1.2Mbps$ and can be obtained by reducing the set of paths based on the metric of hop count constraint.

5 Conclusion

In this paper, we have formulated the design problem in multi-interface multi-channel wireless mesh network to jointly deal with the backhaul topology formation and the fair capacity assignment problems. The global WMN designing problem is NP-hard and its resolution is prohibitively expensive and does not scale beyond small network. For this reason, we proceed to decoupling it into two separated subproblems: topology formation and weighted max-min fair capacity allocation subproblems. Both of the subproblems are NP-hard and at the aim to resolve them efficiently we have chosen to use heuristics. We have resolved optimally the global WMN design problem for small size network to evaluate the results of our heuristics according to the exact solution. A set of scenarios have been considered to evaluate the topology formation algorithm BTFA and the modified ϵ-approximative algorithm. The results have shown that BTFA ensures connectivity and provides several paths from MRs to the gateway. Moreover, the weighted max-min fair capacity allocation scheme has been compared to the optimal solution provided by the MCFP formulation and we have shown that it ensures the access to the gateway from each MR. Our heuristics provide solutions instantly even for large scale networks.

References

1. Aoun, B., Boutaba, R., Iraqi, Y., Kenward, G.W.: Gateway Placement Optimization in Wireless Mesh Networks With QoS Constraints. IEEE Journal on Selected Areas in Communications (2006)
2. Drabu, Y., Peyravi, H.: Gateway Placement with QoS Constraints in Wireless Mesh Networks. In: International Conference on Networking (2008)
3. Benyamina, D., Hafid, A., Gendreau, M., Hallam, N.: Optimization models for planning wireless mesh networks: a comparative study. In: Conf. WCNC (2009)
4. Farsi, A., Achir, N., Boussetta, K.: Heuristic approaches for access points deployment and Frequency Assignment in WLANs. In: GIIS (2011)
5. Muthaiah, S.N., Rosenberg, C.: Single Gateway Placement in Wireless Mesh Networks. In: International IEEE Symposium On Computer Networks, ISCN (2008)
6. Raniwala, A., Chiueh, T.: Architecture and algorithms for an IEEE 802.11-based multi-channel wireless mesh network. In: Proc. of IEEE Infocom, Miami, FL (March 2005)
7. Brélaz, D.: New methods to color the vertices of a graph. Communications of the Assoc. of Comput. Machinery 22 (1979)
8. Amaldi, E., Capone, A., Cesana, M., Filippini, I., Malucelli, F.: Optimization models and methods for planning WMN. Computer Networks V. 52 (2008)
9. Fleischer, L.: Approximating Fractional Multicommodity Flow Independent of the Number of Commodities (2000)
10. Mohsenian Rad, A.H., Wong, V.W.S.: Logical topology design and interface assignment for multi-channel wireless mesh networks. IEEE Globecom (2006)
11. Chun, C., Chekuri, C., Klabjan, D.D.: Topology Formation for Wireless Mesh Network Planning. IEEE Infocomm (2009)
12. Bianchi, G.: Performance analysis of the ieee 802.11 distributed coordination function. IEEE Journal Selected Areas in Communications (2000)
13. Shahrokhi, F., Matula, D.W.: The maximum concurrent flow problem. J. ACM 37(2) (1990)
14. Hossain, E., Leung, K.K.: Wireless Mesh Networks: Architectures and Protocols. Springer (2008)
15. Shmoys, D.B.: Cut Problems And Their Application To Divide-And-Conquer. Approximation Algorithms for NP-Hard Problems (1996)

A Double Data Rate, Low Complexity 2 x 2 MIMO Scheme Based on a Combination of Alamouti System and Orthogonal Codes

Nizar Ouni and Ridha Bouallegue

Innov'COM Lab, Sup'Com, University of Carthage Tunis, Tunisia
nizar.ouni127@laposte.net,
ridha.bouallegue@supcom.rnu.tn

Abstract. Multiple-input multiple-output (MIMO) systems are an important element in the recent wireless communication. Space Time Codes (STCs) and Space Multiplexing (SM) are mandatory for the WIMAX systems. The Almouti's code has played an important role for the growth and development of these systems. But, the Alamouti's code is with low data rate (half rate). For this, some research activities aimed to increase the data rate have been made.

In particular, this paper deals with combining Alamouti's code and the orthogonal codes in order to benefit from the full diversity, to increase the data rate and to keep the system simple as much as possible.

Keywords: MIMO systems, STCs, Alamouti, Orthogonal codes.

1 Introduction

Multi-Input Multi-Output (MIMO) systems can give two types of gains: transmit diversity and spatial diversity [1]. In [2] Alamouti has presented a simple transmit diversity technique which is based on transmitting two symbols throw two antennas in two time slots. Unfortunately, this technique leads to a transmission rate of ½ which counterbalances its other attractive features. Whereas, constrictors objectives are to reach the maximum of data rate and to satisfy the users and applications increasing demands.

S. Sezginer and H. Sari [3] & [4] have presented a fast decidable full-rate space-time block code (STBC) scheme. This scheme is based on transmitting two symbols throw the same antenna, as mentioned in equation (1). It was explained that it will increase the data rate. But we consider that this will also add complexity to the system.

In fact, looking to the equation computation described in [3] and [4], we think that this remains very complex. In fact, at the receiver side, it should compute s_1, s_2, s_3 and s_4 and a, b, c and d with several loops. In general this is very costly in term of decoding time and the complexity of hardware/software (HW/SW) used.

In this paper we will start from the scheme described in [3] and [4] to propose a simple and low complex scheme with reduced decoding computation and simple mathematic analysis. We are looking to increase the data rate and reduce the system

V. Guyot (Ed.): ICAIT 2012, LNCS 7593, pp. 310–318, 2013.

complexity. In fact, our proposal is based on reducing the parameters of (1). Also, it exploits the orthogonal codes characteristics to reduce the computation at the receiver's side.

In coming section we will describe our proposal, for both transmitter and receiver side. After that, we will analyse its structure. Then will present some simulation results. Finally we will give a conclusion to this proposed scheme.

2 Proposed Scheme

2.1 Transmitted Symbols Presentation

Based on proposal in [3] & [4]; which proposed a scheme that can be described via equation (1):

$$X_{SSB} = \begin{bmatrix} a\times s_1 + b\times s_3 & -c\times s_2^* - d\times s_4^* \\ a\times s_2 + b\times s_4 & c\times s_1^* + d\times s_3^* \end{bmatrix} \tag{1}$$

With the recommendation that $|a| = |c| \quad and \quad |b| = |d|$, so, for our case and as a simple way to achieve these constraints, we can use $a = c \quad and \quad b = d$.

Now, exploiting the orthogonal codes to replace a,b, c and d by orthogonal codes as below: $a = c = C^1 \quad and \quad b = d = C^2$.

With $C^1 \quad and \quad C^2$ two orthogonal codes.

After this, we can re-write this equation as below:

$$X_{New} = \begin{bmatrix} C^1\times s_1 + C^2\times s_3 & -C^1\times s_2^* - C^2\times s_4^* \\ C^1\times s_2 + C^2\times s_4 & C^1\times s_1^* + C^2\times s_3^* \end{bmatrix} \tag{2}$$

For calculation simplicity reason, to be used in the coming sections, we would present (2) as:

$$X_{New} = C^1 \times \begin{bmatrix} s_1 & -s_2^* \\ s_2 & s_1^* \end{bmatrix} + C^2 \times \begin{bmatrix} s_3 & -s_4^* \\ s_4 & s_3^* \end{bmatrix} \tag{3-a}$$

With $C^1 \quad and \quad C^2$ the two orthogonal codes previously declared.

$$X_{New} = C^1 \times \underbrace{\begin{bmatrix} s_1 & -s_2^* \\ s_2 & s_1^* \end{bmatrix}}_{Alamouti} + C^2 \times \underbrace{\begin{bmatrix} s_3 & -s_4^* \\ s_4 & s_3^* \end{bmatrix}}_{Alamouti} \tag{3-b}$$

This means that the transmitted system keeps the same Alamouti representation.
So we can re-write (again) equation (3-b) as:

$$X_{New} = C^1 \times S_n^1 + C^2 \times S_n^2 \tag{4-a}$$

With S_n^m $(m = [1 \quad 2])$ is the Alamouti's matrix presentation for, respectively, s_1, s_2 and s_3, s_4.

2.2 Transmitter Scheme

Figure 1 presents the structure of the transmitter scheme already described in the above sections. From this figure, we can notice that X_1 *and* X_2 at the output of the system corresponds respectively to $C^1 \times S_n^1$ and $C^2 \times S_n^2$.

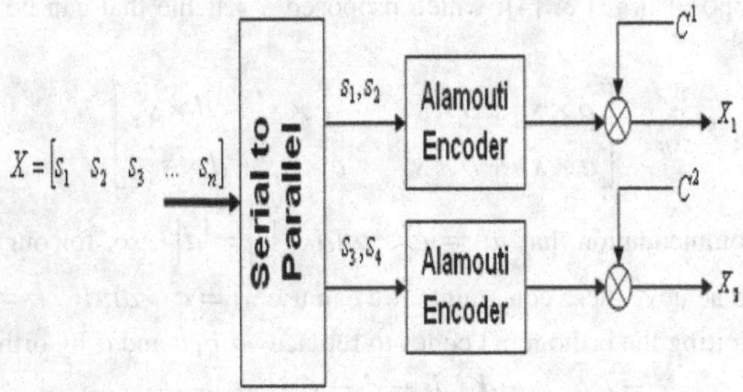

Fig. 1. Transmitter with two Alamouti encoder in parallel

At this level, we can re-write (4-a) as:

$$X_{New} = X_1 + X_2 \tag{4-b}$$

2.3 Receiver Computation

At the received side and due to the fact that C^1 *and* C^2 are orthogonal, so we can consider that the interference between the 2 equation systems X_1 *and* X_2 are obsolete.

Also, we can consider that we will get two Alamouti systems "protected" with two orthogonal codes. So at the receiver's side we can write the received signal as below:

$$Y = Y_1 + Y_2 + n \tag{5}$$

" n" is the received noise caused by the transmission throw the channel. And Y_1 *and* Y_2 are respectively:

$$Y_1 = H_1 \times X_1 \tag{6-a}$$

$$Y_2 = H_2 \times X_2 \tag{6-b}$$

We assume that the receiver is with full channel estimation and all channel details are known.

To get X_1 *and* X_2, we can use the following method:

$$C^1 \times Y = C^1 \times (Y_1 + Y_2 + n) \tag{7-a}$$

$$C^2 \times Y = C^2 \times (Y_1 + Y_2 + n) \tag{7-b}$$

So,

$$C^1 \times Y = C^1 \times ((H_1 \times (C^1 \times S_n^1)) + (H_2 \times (C^2 \times S_n^2)) + n) \tag{8-a}$$

$$C^2 \times Y = C^2 \times ((H_1 \times (C^1 \times S_n^1)) + (H_2 \times (C^2 \times S_n^2)) + n) \tag{8-b}$$

And so, if we exploit the C^1 *and* C^2 orthogonal characteristics [5]:

$$C^1 \times Y = C^1 \times ((H_1 \times (C^1 \times S_n^1)) + n_1) \tag{9-a}$$

$$C^2 \times Y = C^2 \times ((H_2 \times (C^2 \times S_n^2)) + n_2) \tag{9-b}$$

Where n_i 's are circularly symmetric additive Gaussian noise terms with spectral densityN_0.

Hence, this gives that we can generate X_1 *and* X_2 from received signal with a very simple way.

To decrease the decoding time we can use two Alamouti decoders in parallel (figure 2) or we can use only one but we increase the decoding frequency (double of

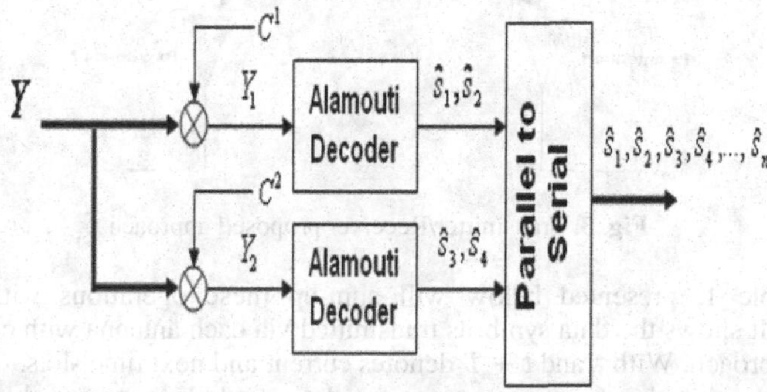

Fig. 2. Receiver with two Alamouti decoder in parallel

receiver sampling/buffering frequency). This will avoid the receiver complexity and cost and keep the decoding rate as expected.

Hence, we have been able to double the data rate of a 2x2 MIMO system by combining the famous Alamouti technique and the orthogonal codes and keeping the same number of antennas at both sides.

3 Global System Structure

3.1 Transmitter Side

For the transmitter side and after generating the symbols $s_1, \quad s_2, \quad s_3, \quad s_4$ it will generate the orthogonal codes $C^1, \quad C^2$. After that a symbol selection operation will happen to parse which symbols will be processed with the Alamouti encoder. After that, the "orthogonal code protection" operation will happen for each Alamouti encoder output. Finally the data will be transmitted; $X_1 = C^1 \times s_n^1$ for the first antenna and $X_2 = C^2 \times s_n^2$ for the second antenna. Figure 3 describes these operations.

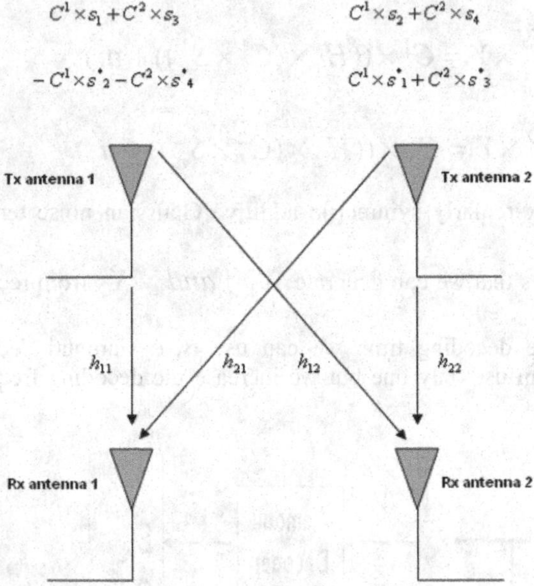

Fig. 3. Transmitter/Receiver proposed approach

The Table 1, presented below will sum-up these operations with time slots scheduling. It shows the data symbols transmitted via each antenna with corresponding time slot approach. With t and $t + T$ denotes current and next time slots.

This means that the system transmits for data symbols, respectivelys_1, s_2, s_3, s_4 over two antennas and at two time slots. Thus, the systems began full rate.

Table 1. The encoding and transmitted sequence of the proposed scheme

	Time t	*Time t + T*
Tx 1	$C^1 \times s_1 + C^2 \times s_3$	$-C^1 \times s^*_2 - C^2 \times s^*_4$
Tx 2	$C^1 \times s_2 + C^2 \times s_4$	$C^1 \times s^*_1 + C^2 \times s^*_3$

3.2 Receiver Side

At the receiver side, a reverse operation will happen. In fact, the received signal contains several elementary signals that are basically "protected" with two orthogonal codes.

Consequently, a simple multiplication with the two codes will allow us to separate the two sub-signals containing two symbols each. After that, an Alamouti decoding operation will happen to identify each symbols $[\widehat{s_1} \quad \widehat{s_3}]$ and $[\widehat{s_2} \quad \widehat{s_4}]$ respectively from each decoder. Finally, symbols will be re-ordered to the initial order$[\widehat{s_1} \quad \widehat{s_2} \quad \widehat{s_3} \quad \widehat{s_4}]$.

4 Simulation Results

4.1 Performance Results

From the IEEE 802.16e specifications [1], it has been specified two mandatory profiles to be use on the downlink. The first is called Matrix A, is based on the space–time code (STC) proposed by Alamouti [2]. In spite of the increasing diversity order given by this scheme it still a half-rate code, since it only transmits two symbols using two time slots and two transmit antennas. The second profile is called Matrix B, which uses two transmit antennas to transmit two independent data streams (spatial multiplexing). This scheme is full-rate, but it does not benefit from any spatial diversity at the transmitter. For future evolutions of the WiMAX standard, it is highly desirable to include new codes combining the respective advantages of the Alamouti code and the SM while avoiding their drawbacks. Such a code, referred to as Matrix C, actually exists in the IEEE 802.16e specifications [1].

We are now providing a performance results and comparison between the proposed scheme and the Alamouti scheme, as a first step. Then, we will present the same for the two MIMO schemes including the WiMAX system specifications, namely the SM (Matrix B) and the Matrix C.

For our simulations, two receive and two transmitter antennas were used in all of these schemes. The simulations were carried out for the BPSK signal constellations over an uncorrelated Rayleigh fading channel. And we used maximum-likelihood (ML) decoder and assumed perfect channel estimation at the receiver side.

Below figures show the BER performance as a function of E_s/N_0 (E_s is the average transmitted signal energy per antenna use).

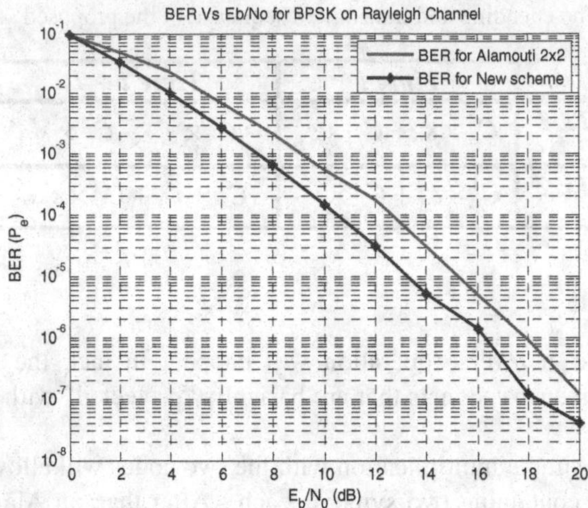

Fig. 4. BER result for the new scheme vs the ordinary Alamouti's scheme.

As seen above in Figure 4, the new scheme's bit error rate (BER) curve is asymptotic to the Alamouti 2x2 scheme but with better performance. Thus, we can remark the difference and the improvement in term of BER performance given by the new proposal. Knowing that our proposal is transmitting the double of symbols as per Alamouti, this makes the result interesting. That's important; our scheme doubles the data-rate and improves the BER performance while using the same antennas number at both sides of the systems.

Figure 5 shows the performances BER curves for respectively, our proposed scheme, the matrix B and C of WiMax system. It shows clearly the advantage of our proposal.

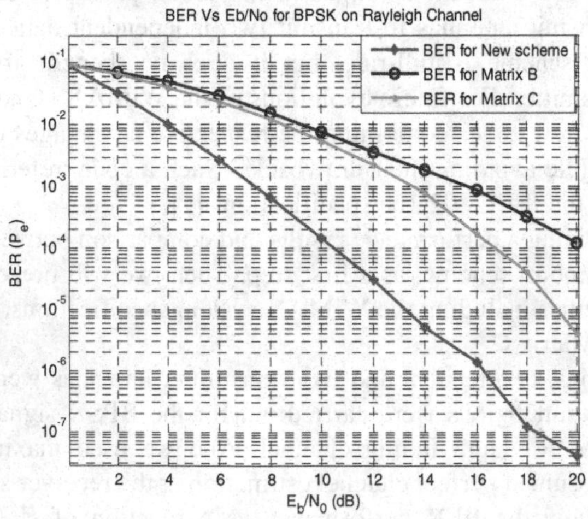

Fig. 5. BER result for the new scheme vs the Matrix B and C or Wimax

At this level, we can clearly notice that results for the new approach are better than the Matrix C or Wimax system, which is already better than the Matrix B [1]. Also, in [3] it was presented that Sezginer's approach result is quite similar to Matric C and better than Matrix B. Thus, we can consider that this approach outperforms Matrix C and so it exceeds all Sezginer's approachs in term of performance.

Consequently, our new scheme has an important added value and brings a considerable BER performance. Not only comparing to the starting approach indicated in [3] & [4], but also, comparing to the standard Alamouti's scheme and the Matrix B & C presented in [1]. As evidenced, the proposed approach doubles the bit rate and avoids the signal to noise ratio (SNR) loss.

4.2 Additional Benefits

In addition to the simple and easy system behaviour we can notice other benefits like:

- Increasing the data rate; this is multiplied in this case and can be more if we introduce more orthogonal codes. As it was shown, with a couple of codes, we achieved a double data rate. Also, we can easily remark that using an additional couple of codes will allow transmitting two other symbols. Consequently, this approach can be generalized for "*N*" couple of codes.
- Inter-symbols interference is automatically cancelled via the orthogonal codes which adds more performance to the system and brings some enhancement to the received signal treatment process. This is shown in the simulation results by the fact that the curve related to the new scheme is better than the normal Alamouti scheme's curve.
- Simple implementation and reduced complexity comparing to the Sezginer and Sari's proposal. This can be noticed by reducing the number of iterations at receiver side, as shown in [3] & [4]. Also, it can benefit from the reuse of existing systems and features like Alamouti encoder/decoder and orthogonal codes.

All the above described points take an important role for any mobile systems construction. And so, this attracts and interest systems designers.

5 Conclusion

The proposed scheme is showing a good BER performance curve (better comparing to the normal 2x2 Alamouti scheme and Matrix B/C). It shows, also, an important increase for the data rate comparing to the ordinary Alamouti scheme (double the data rate for this case), while keeping a constant transmitter/receiver antennas number.

In the meantime, this approach, based on the reuse of a well-known and confirmed features/technics such as Alamouti encoder/decoder and orthogonal code, doesn't increase the complexity of the system. But, in contrary it shows an important complexity reduction comparing to Sezginer and Sari's scheme presented in [3] & [4].

Also, there is a considerable performance improvement while keeping the same antennas numbers and data rate.

Therefore, current approach can bring a design simplicity, data rate improvement and robustness to MIMO systems. But, we should note that our proposal will require more channel bandwidth. This was not discussed in this paper; however it can be the subject of another paper to present the system behavior from this point of view.

Finally, in spite of all the benefits simplicities shown by this approach, it is still admitted that more improvements can be introduced and it can be considered as a starting point for simpler schemes.

References

1. IEEE 802.16-2005: IEEE Standard for Local and Metropolitan Area Networks–Part 16: Air Interface for Fixed and Mobile Broadband Wire-less Access Systems–Amendment 2: Physical Layer and Medium Access Control Layers for Combined Fixed and Mobile Operation in Licensed Bands (February 2006)
2. Alamouti, S.M.: A simple transmit diversity technique for wireless communications. IEEE Journal on Selected Areas in Communications 16(8) (October 1998)
3. Sezginer, S., Sari, H.: Full-rate full-diversity 2 x 2 space-time codes of reduced decoder complexity. IEEE Communications Letters 11(12), 973–975 (2008), doi:10.1109/LCOMM.2007.071388
4. Sezginer, S., Sari, H.: A High-Rate Full-Diversity 2x2 Space-Time Code with Simple Maximum Likelihood Decoding. IEEE International Symposium on Signal Processing and Information Technology (2007), doi:10.1109/ISSPIT.2007.4458067, ISBN:978-1-4244-1835-0
5. Hedayat, A.S., Sloane, N.J.A., Stufken, J.: Orthogonal Arrays: Theory and Applications. Springer, New York (1999)

GeoSUZ: A Geocast Routing Protocol in Sub-ZORs for VANETs

Salim Allal and Saadi Boudjit

Université Paris 13, Sorbonne Paris Cité,
Laboratoire de Traitement et Transport
de l'Information (L2TI), (EA 3043),
F-93430, Villetaneuse, France
{salim.allal,boudjit}@univ-paris13.fr
http://www-l2ti.univ-paris13.fr

Abstract. Vehicular Ad Hoc Networks (VANETs) are characterized by highly speed nodes, highly dynamic topology and frequent links disconnection. This raises a number of challenges especially in the field of data dissemination. In our work, we focus on Geocast routing in VANETs which consists of routing a message from a unique source vehicle to all vehicles located in a well geographically defined destination area called ZOR (Zone Of Relevance). In literature, ZORs are often assumed to be of any form and still chosen according to the scenarios and motivation needs of the authors. In this paper, we consider a ZOR as a set of sub-ZORs and we choose simple geometrical forms of sub-ZORs so that they will be easy to implement and to represent mathematically. We provide a geometrical vision angles based technique that allows to know if two sub-ZORs are in the same direction in order to send them a single message and hence, reduce the messages overhead. We then introduce a new routing protocol in Sub-ZORs (GeoSUZ) for VANETs based on our geometrical vision angles and greedy forwarding techniques. We compare GeoSUZ to GPSR routing protocol (Greedy Perimeter Stateless Routing for Wireless Networks) [11] and some numerical results show a significant gain in terms of number of messages sent over the network.

Keywords: Geocast routing, Sub-ZORs, VANETs.

1 Introduction

Vehicular Ad Hoc Networks, VANETs, provide one of the most important fields of research for the high interest that Intelligent Transportation Systems, ITS, can offer through them in both saving lives, time, energy and the planet. To ensure autonomous communication between vehicles on the road for the purpose of traffic management, safety alerting or infotainment, literature provides a large range of routing protocols for VANETs. In our work, we considered the geocast routing techniques which respond to different needs of ITS in terms of dissemination of safety information packets as well as traffic management and also comfort and mobility applications.

V. Guyot (Ed.): ICAIT 2012, LNCS 7593, pp. 319–329, 2013.

The remaining of this paper is organized as follow: in section 2 we present a brief overview of geocast routing protocols in VANETs. We then highlight our motivation behind splitting the destination area (ZOR) into a set of sub-ZORs, and considering simple geometrical forms to cover these destination areas. Section 3, presents a geometrical vision angles technique to define whether two sub-ZORs are in the same direction in order to send them a single message and hence, reduce the messages overhead. In section 4, we present our geocast routing protocol for VANETs based on our proposed geometrical vision angles and greedy forwarding techniques. Some numerical results which illustrate our protocol performances are presented in section 5 and finally, section 6 concludes the paper.

2 Background

Geocast routing in VANETs consists of routing a message generated from a single source vehicle to all vehicles belonging to a well geographically defined destination area ZOR (Zone of Relevance). Literature provides a large range of papers dealing with geocast routing in VANETs. We can cite IVG [1], cached Geocast [2], Abiding Geocast [3], DRG [4], ROVER [5], DG-CastoR [6], Mobicast [7], DTSG [8], constrained Geocast [9], Geocache [10], etc. These protocols could be classified according to different parameters as the used relay selection technique (beacon-based or beaconless-based), the used recovery mode strategy or the used forwarding strategy.

In most above mentioned geocast routing protocols, the forms of ZORs are assumed to be of circular or rectangular shape and confined in a unique geographical zone. This makes the representation of forms of ZORs, their origin and positioning arbitrary and are choosen according to the scenarios and to the motivation needs of authors. In our current work, we delegate affectation of geographic destination areas (ZORs) to a competent authority (as road safety services) which will provide when an event (accident for instance) occurs, the coordinates or designations of stretches of roads where vehicles will be likely affected by the event, as well as its nature, its location, its duration and why not periodic pictures or even videos. An appropriate algorithm on on-board unit inside vehicles can be implemented for the road accidents case. It will consider the position of the concerned vehicle, the rules of the circulation traffic and a digital map of the city, to process designations of relevant destination areas.

2.1 Zone of Relevance Shapes

Knowing that roads' forms are either simple geometrically taking the form of straight lines and turns in elliptical or circular arc, or can be in some places of any forms. In order to cover all forms of roads, we consider that the road network is represented by a two dimensional Euclidean plane geometry. Also, we choose simple geometrical forms of *ZOR*s, so that they will be easy to implement and to represent mathematically.

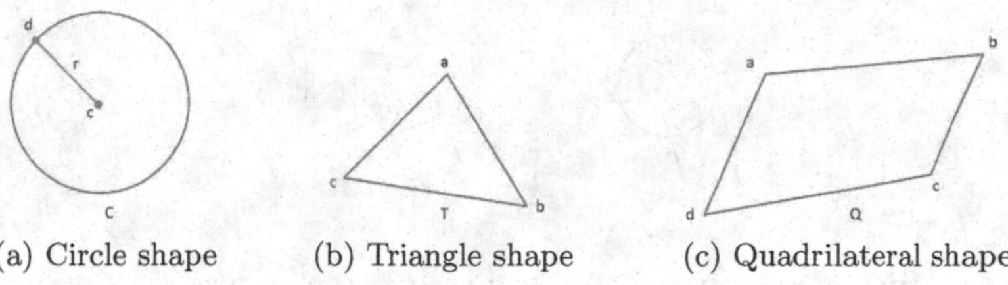

(a) Circle shape (b) Triangle shape (c) Quadrilateral shape

Fig. 1. Zone of Relevance shapes

Circle Shape. Simple geometrical form represented by the knowledge of two information: coordinates of the center and its radius. For the sake of implementation, we represent all the *ZOR*s' forms by their coordinates. So, we represent the circle shape by the coordinates of its center and the coordinates of one point of its contour. In Figure 1a, the circle C is represented by the coordinates of its center c and the point d where the distance between them is the radius r: $\{(x_c, y_c), (x_d, y_d)\}$.

Triangle Shape. As illustrated in Figure 1b, a triangle T is represented by the coordinates of its three corners: $\{(x_a, y_a), (x_b, y_b), (x_c, y_c)\}$.

Quadrilateral Shape. A quadrilateral Q is a polygon with four sides (or edges) and four vertices (or corners) represented by the coordinates of its corners: $\{(x_a, y_a), (x_b, y_b), (x_c, y_c), (x_d, y_d)\}$. Figure 1c, illustrates this shape.

We note here the use of only convex and concave forms, because the complex quadrilateral in our case can be represented by two triangles.

Some remarks:

- The naming of the corners of forms follows arbitrarily the clockwise.
- The choice of these three shapes is motivated by their simplicity of representation and by their identification through their number of coordinates.
- It is possible to enlarge our set of shapes to infinite by confining the space occupied by the *ZOR* to represent it as it is in reality. However, in implementation, more a form is represented by several coordinates, more the time spent in processing this form is longer. For this reason, we reduce the set of forms in our model to 3 simple geometrical ones.

The three considered shapes can cover several places and can be used in case of curved routes as illustrated in figure 2.

2.2 *ZOR* Is a Set of Sub-*ZOR*s

We consider the scenario illustrated by Figure 3. If the red star represents an accident that happens in lane B_l (the left lane of the road B after the junction), vehicles belonging to sections $A_l(Z_1)$, $A_r(Z_3)$ and $B_l(Z_2)$ at the entrance of the

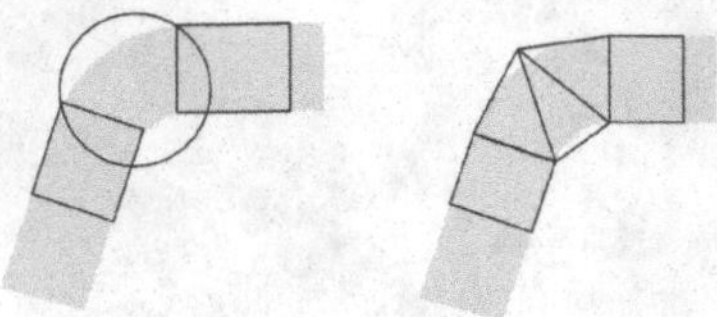

Fig. 2. Curved routes covered by the considered shapes

junction need to be informed about the accident. Thus, vehicles that want to take this road affected by the event can act to find an other path. This facilitates the flow at the level of the intersection.

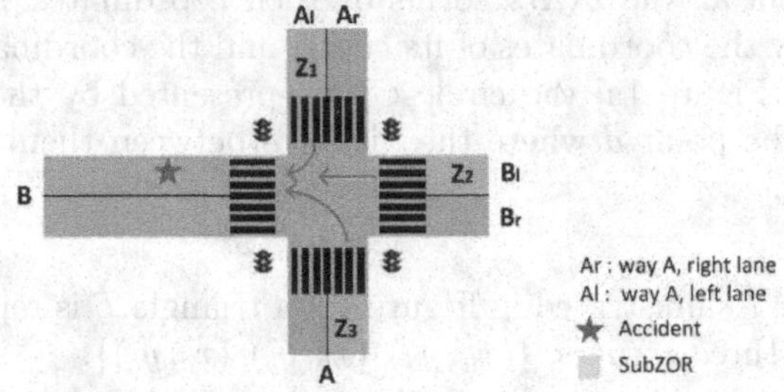

Fig. 3. Example of relevant Sub-*ZOR*s

We can also consider the scenario of an emergency vehicle that announces its arrival at a crowded place as it advances on the road.
We note that the intersection of some parts of the Sub-*ZOR*s is probable and acceptable. In this case, vehicles belonging to these few locations receive the same message twice; thus, they ignore the second.

2.3 Challenges and Idea of Resolution

After we have presented our coverage technique of sub-*ZOR*s using simple geometric shapes, we face the challenge of proposing an optimal technique to transmit messages from a single source to all vehicles located in different sub-*ZOR*s so that to cover the total *ZOR*. We consider the scenario of road network illustrated in Figure 4, where S represents a unique source vehicle and A, B, C sub-*ZOR*s composing the same *ZOR*. In this scenario, the same message will take approximately the same path to reach both A, B and C through vehicles p and q. In the case where S sends few messages to A, B and C, the problem of overloading the network does not arise. However, when S generates a considerable size of data (as video streaming), the use of greedy forwarding will generate three times the same stream (destined to A, B and C) at p-level and two times the same stream (destined to A and C) at q-level.

We previously mentioned that a geocast message is destined for all vehicules located in the same *ZOR* and in our illustration above, we proved that a *ZOR*

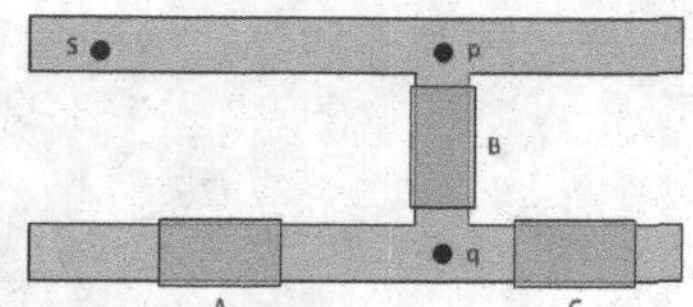

Fig. 4. Message Transmission Scenario

is a set of sub-*ZOR*s. Thus, the content of the same geocast message is destined to reach all vehicles in different sub-*ZOR*s. Also, we have noted in our state of the art the effectiveness of greedy forwarding technique through algorithms like IVG [1], DRG [4], etc. as well as the problem of local maximum and its solutions proposed in these papers. To obtain the best results in term of messages overhead and time processing, we provide in the next section a technique permitting us to determine whether some sub-*ZOR*s are in the same direction in order to address them the same message stream.

3 Vision Angle Routing Technique

Before a source S sends a geocast message, it calculates the distance between its own position and the nearest point of the ZOR (or the different sub-ZORs).

In two-dimentional plan, the distance between two points $A(x_A, y_A)$ and $B(x_B, y_B)$ is defined in (1).

$$d_{AB} = \sqrt{(x_B - x_A)^2 + (y_B - y_A)^2} \tag{1}$$

Depending on the form of the destination sub-ZOR, the distance between the source S and the sub-ZOR is calculated as following:

3.1 Circular Sub-ZOR C

$$d_{SC} = \min(d_{Sd}, d_{Sc}) = d_{Sd} \tag{2}$$

Where c, r and d are the center of the circular sub-ZOR C, its radius and the nearest point on its contour respectively. The radius $r = d_{Sc} - d_{Sd}$.

3.2 Triangular Sub-ZOR T

$$d_{ST} = \min(d_{Sa}, d_{Sb}, d_{Sc}) \tag{3}$$

Where a, b and c are the three corners of the triangular sub-ZOR T.

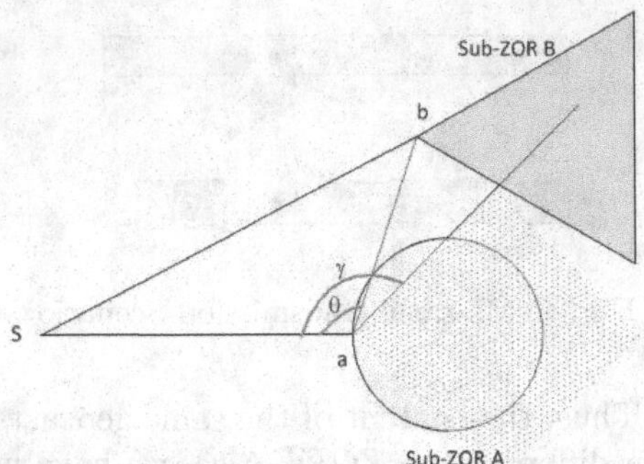

Fig. 5. Geometrical vision angles based routing technique

3.3 Quadrilateral Sub-ZOR Q

$$d_{SQ} = \min(d_{Sa}, d_{Sb}, d_{Sc}, d_{Sd}) \tag{4}$$

Where a, b, c and d are the four corners of the quadrilateral sub-ZOR Q.

Figure 5, illustrates our vision angle technique itself based on the distance between the source and the different sub-ZORs. We consider S as the source of the geocast message M, and A and B two sub-ZORs constituting the total ZOR. When S needs to inform the sub-ZORs A and B about an event, it first calculates the distances d_{Sa} and d_{Sb}. In our case, sub-ZOR A is closer to S than sub-ZOR B ($d_{Sa} < d_{Sb}$). Thus, S needs to know if sub-ZOR B is in the same direction as sub-ZOR A. In other words, is sub-ZOR B accessible via sub-ZOR A or, does B belongs to the vision angle of S through A. The angle θ represents the angle $S\hat{a}b$ of the triangle Sab. The angle γ, is an arbitrary vision angle fixed according to different parameters (speed of vehicles, number of vehicles, etc.). Applying the Formula (5) to the scenario above, we conclude that sub-ZOR B is not in the same direction as sub-ZOR A. So, source S sends two occurrences of the geocast message destined to A and B respectively.

$$\frac{Sa^2 + ab^2 - Sb^2}{2 * Sa * ab} \geq cos(\gamma) \tag{5}$$

Where $\frac{Sa^2+ab^2-Sb^2}{2*Sa*ab} = cos(\theta)$ (law of cosines in trigonometry).

If $\theta \leq 90°$, the source S sends two messages to the sub-ZORs A and B. If $\theta \in]90°, 180°]$, S sends one message intended to reach A and B (via A).

4 GeoSUZ Protocol

4.1 Position of the Source

We define S as the source vehicle and ZOR as the destination area. We can highlight two cases of geocast routing: either when S belongs to the ZOR or when S is out of the ZOR. We note that ZOR is a destination area of one of the three forms introduced above (C, T or Q) and can be in a confined area or in different geographical areas. We describe ZOR as :

$$ZOR = subZOR_1 \cup subZOR_2 \cup ... \cup subZOR_n \tag{6}$$

where $n \geq 1$

Source S in ZOR. Figure 6b, shows the case where the source belongs to the ZOR. In this case, a simple broadcast overcomes to the principal of delivering the geocast message to all the vehicles located in the ZOR. But, we can note that in the case of fragmented ZOR, the $subZOR_2$ will be covered while the $subZOR_1$ not, because in simple broadcast, each vehicle around the $subZOR_2$ limits the flooding to the same sub-ZOR surounding it ($subZOR_2$ in this case).

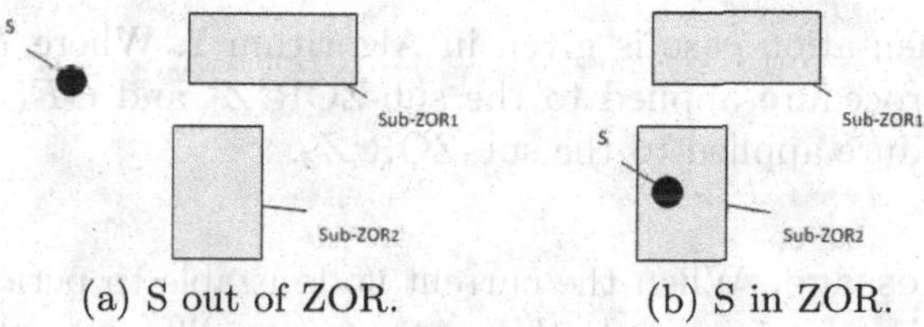

(a) S out of ZOR. (b) S in ZOR.

Fig. 6. Position of the source S with respect to ZOR

$$S \in ZOR \tag{7}$$

Source S out of ZOR. In the case of unique ZOR shape, geocast routing can be ensured either by GeoUnicast routing or by the use of zone of forwarding ZOF [4]. But in the case of multiple sub-ZORs, it is challenging to provide an optimal technique of routing to address the problem.

Figure 6a, shows the case where the source is out of the ZOR.

$$S \notin ZOR \tag{8}$$

4.2 Geocast Message Structure

The geocast message M is defined as :

$$M[m, S, Z] \tag{9}$$

Where $M[m]$ is the message content, $M[S]$ is the sender ID, and $M[Z]$ the coordinates of the destination area.

Pre-fragmented Message. When the same geocast message destined to two sub-ZORs Z_1 and Z_2 (or more) follows the same path due to the use of a recovery mode in greedy forwarding technique, the message M is pre-fragmented and defined as :

$$M_1[m, S, \{Z_1\}].M_2[m, S, \{Z_2\}] \tag{10}$$

We note that all the sub-ZORs are different in each pre-fragmented message.

Algorithm 1 . Pre_fragment($M[m, S, \{Z_1, Z_2\}]$)

IF [not($GF(Z_1)$) and $GF(Z_2)$ and $RM(Z_1)$==$GF(Z_2)$] or [$GF(Z_1)$ and not($GF(Z_2)$) and $GF(Z_1)$==$RM(Z_2)$] or [not($GF(Z_1)$) and not($GF(Z_2)$) and $RM(Z_1)$==$RM(Z_2)$]
THEN
return ($M_1[m, S, \{Z_1\}].M_2[m, S, \{Z_2\}]$) ;
ENDIF

The pre-fragmentation case is given in Algorithm 1. Where $RM(Z_1)$ is the recovery mode procedure applied to the sub-ZOR Z_1 and $GF(Z_2)$ the greedy forwarding procedure applied to the sub-ZOR Z_2.

Fragmented Message. When the current node is able to perform the greedy forwarding technique, it fragments the message into different sub-messages addressing the different sub-ZORs. The Formula 9 becomes :

$$M_1[m, S, \{Z_1\}], M_2[m, S, \{Z_2\}] \tag{11}$$

Here, we note that the two messages $M_1$and M_2 are forwarded separately in different paths.

The Algorithm 2 illustrates the fragmentation case.

Algorithm 2 . Fragment($M_1[m, S, \{Z_1\}].M_2[m, S, \{Z_2\}]$)

IF [$GF(Z_1)$ and $GF(Z_2)$ and $GF(Z_1)$=!$GF(Z_2)$] or [not($GF(Z_1)$) and $GF(Z_2)$ and $RM(Z_1)$=!$GF(Z_2)$] or [$GF(Z_1)$ and not($GF(Z_2)$) and $GF(Z_1)$==$RM(Z_2)$] or [not($GF(Z_1)$) and not($GF(Z_2)$) and $RM(Z_1)$==$RM(Z_2)$] THEN
return ($M_1[m, S, \{Z_1\}], M_2[m, S, \{Z_2\}]$);

Defragmented Message. Pre-fragmented messages can be defragmented in the case when the sub-ZORs are currently able to be addressed sequentially. The formula 9 becomes :

$$M[m, S, \{Z_1, Z_2\}] \tag{12}$$

We note that a fragmented messages cannot be defragmented.

Defragmentation case is presented as shown in Algorithm 3.

Algorithm 3 . Defragment($M_1[m, S, \{Z_1\}].M_2[m, S, \{Z_2\}]$)

IF [$GF(Z_1)$ and $GF(Z_2)$ and $GF(Z_1)$==$GF(Z_2)$] THEN
return($M[m, S, \{Z_1, Z_2\}]$);

4.3 GeoSUZ Algorithm

Algorithm 4, presents our GeoSUZ routing protocol and Algorithm 5 shows the pre-fragmentation procedure based on our vision angle technique.

Algorithm 4 . GEOSUZ algorithm

Define γ
Calculate all D_{SZ_i} where Z_i the sub-ZOR $i : i = 1, 2, ..., n$
Ascending order of D_{SZ_i} into D_{SZ_k} where $k = 1, 2, ..., n$
GENERATE($M[m, S, Z_k]$); // S generates or receives M
IF Current_Node in $M[Z[1]]$ THEN
GeoBroadcast($M[m, S, Z[1]]$);
SUB($Z[1]$, M); // $M[m, S, Z \setminus Current\_subZOR]$
PREFRAGMENT(M); //$M_1[m, S, Z].M_2[m, S, Z]$
END IF
\\ Pre-fragmentation
IF (pre_fragment(M)) THEN
GeoUnicast(M);
ELSE \\ Fragmentation
IF (fragment(M)) THEN
GeoUnicast(M_1);
GeoUnicast(M_2);
ELSE \\ Defragmentation
IF (defragment(M)) THEN
GeoUnicast(M, GF($M_1[Z[1]]$));
END IF
END IF
END IF

5 Numerical Results

Figure 7, presents numerical results of the application of two routing protocols to the scenario of figure 4. The first is GPSR (Greedy Perimeter stateless Routing for wireless networks) [11] based on Greedy Forwarding technique, and the second is our GeoSUZ protocol which is an adaptation of GPSR to the context of geocast routing with multiple sub-ZORs. In this scenario, we assumed that the source S sends 3000 different packets to sub-ZORs A, B and C. These packets cross p and q nodes since all sub-ZORs are in the same direction.

Algorithm 5 . Pre-fragment vision angle based procedure

$h = 1$; // Z_h the nearest sub-ZOR
$M_1[Z] = Z_h$;
$M_2[Z] = \phi$;
$j = 1$;
WHILE $j < k$ THEN
IF $S\hat{Z_h}Z_{j+1} \geq \gamma$ THEN
ADD(Z_{j+1}, M_1); // $M_1[m, S, \{Z_h, Z_{j+1}\}]$
ELSE // $S\hat{Z_h}Z_{j+1} < \gamma$
ADD(Z_{j+1}, M_2);
END IF
$j = j + 1$;
END WHILE

We note here that GeoSUZ allows a considerable gain of bandwidth compared to GPSR, by decreasing significantly the number of messages sent over the network.

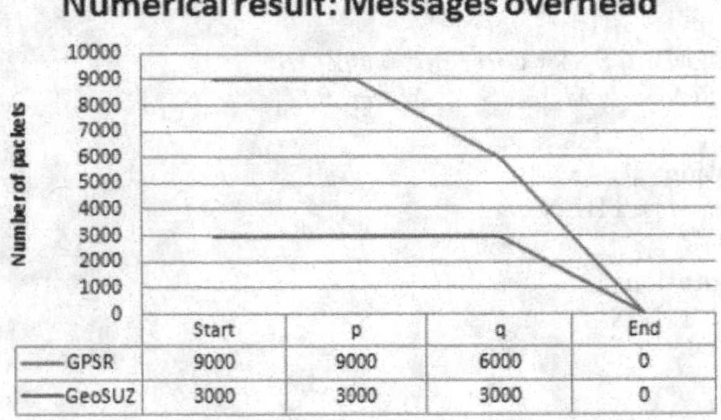

Fig. 7. Messages overhead

6 Conclusion

In this paper, we first presented different categories of routing protocols in Vanet networks and then focused on geocast routing techniques. We have introduced a new geocast routing protocol in Sub-ZORs (GeoSUZ) for VANETs based on a geometrical vision angles technique which allows to know whether two sub-ZORs are in the same direction in order to send them a single message and hence, reduce the messages overhead. For that purpose, we have choosed simple geometrical forms of sub-ZORs so that they will be easy to implement and to represent mathematically. Compared to a well known geocast routing protocol GPSR [11], the performances evaluation of GeoSUZ shows a significant gain in terms of number of messages sent over the network.

We are currently in phase of implementing GeoSUZ protocol on NS3 simulator in order to compare its performances to other known geocast protocols, and also to simulate the impact of some vehicles' parameters (speed of vehicles, number of vehicles, etc.) on the size of the vision angle γ. We are also considering some optimized broadcast techniques inside sub-ZORs.

References

1. Bachir, A., Benslimane, A.: A multicast protocol in ad hoc networks inter-vehicle geocast. In: The 57th IEEE Semiannual Vehicular Technology Conference, VTC 2003-Spring, vol. 4, pp. 2456–2460 (2003)
2. Maihöfer, C., Eberhardt, R.: Geocast in vehicular environments: Caching and transmission range control for improved efficiency. In: Proceedings of IEEE Intelligent Vehicles Symposium (IV), pp. 951–956 (2004)
3. Maihöfer, C., Leinmüller, T., Schoch, E.: Abiding geocast: time–stable geocast for ad hoc networks. In: Proceedings of the 2nd ACM International Workshop on Vehicular Ad Hoc Networks, pp. 20–29 (2005)
4. Joshi, H.P., Sichitiu, M.L., Kihl, M.: Distributed robust geocast multicast routing for inter-vehicle communication. In: Proceedings of WEIRD Workshop on WiMax, Wireless and Mobility, pp. 9–21 (2007)
5. Kihl, M., Sichitiu, M., Ekeroth, T., Rozenberg, M.: Reliable Geographical Multicast Routing in Vehicular Ad-Hoc Networks. In: Boavida, F., Monteiro, E., Mascolo, S., Koucheryavy, Y. (eds.) WWIC 2007. LNCS, vol. 4517, pp. 315–325. Springer, Heidelberg (2007)
6. Atechian, T.: DG-CastoR: Direction-based GeoCast Routing Protocol for query dissemination in VANET. In: 4th International Workshop on Localized Communication and Topology Protocols for Ad Hoc Networks (2008)
7. Chen, Y.S., Lin, Y.W., Lee, S.L.: A Mobicast Routing Protocol for Vehicular Ad Hoc Networks. ACM/Springer Mobile Networks and Applications (MONET) 15(1), 20–35 (2010)
8. Rahbar, H., Naik, K., Nayak, A.: DTSG: Dynamic Time-Stable Geocast Routing in Vehicular Ad Hoc Networks. In: IEEE Symposium on Computers and Communications, pp. 198–203 (2010)
9. Wolterink, W.K., Geert, H., Georgios, K.: Constrained Geocast to Support Cooperative Adaptive Cruise Control (CACC) Merging. In: 2010 IEEE Vehicular Networking Conference (VNC), pp. 41–48 (2010)
10. Lakas, M., Shaqfa, A.: Geocache: Sharing and Exchanging Road Traffic Information Using Peer-to-peer Vehicular Communication. In: 2011 IEEE 73rd Vehicular Technology Conference (VTC Spring), pp. 1–7 (2011)
11. Karp, B., Kung, H.T.: GPSR: greedy perimeter stateless routing for wireless networks. In: Proceedings of the 6th Annual International Conference on Mobile Computing and Networking, pp. 243–254 (2000)

Adaptive Contention Window for Zone-Based Dissemination of Vehicular Traffic

Arturo Gomez[1], Gladys Diaz[1], Khaled Boussetta[1], Nadjib Achir[1,2], and Abdelhak Farsi[1]

[1] L2TI – Institut Galilée – Université Paris 13, Sorbonne Paris Cité
99 Avenue J-B Clément, 93430 Villetaneuse, France
{arturo.gomez,gladys.diaz,khaled.boussetta,nadjib.achir,farsi}@univ-paris13.fr

[2] INRIA HiPERCOM
Rocquencourt B.P. 105, 78153 Le Chesnay, France
nadjib.achir@inria.fr

Abstract. Inter-Vehicular Communication (IVC) is very promising for advanced applications in traffic systems. However, current efforts and implementations still require more attention in order to turn such applications into reality. The data dissemination and the vehicular communication are two key concerns in order to make more feasible alternative traffic information systems. In this paper we focus on the traffic data dissemination and the inter-vehicle communication applied to our traffic guidance architecture presented in [5]. We present a twofold proposal: a mechanism for V2I, V2V traffic data dissemination and a simple but efficient mechanism to enhance broadcast communication. We show through extensive evaluations that our composite solution tends to be efficient under the design of our specific application guidelines.

Keywords: Traffic data dissemination, Broadcast enhancement, Intelligent Transportation Systems.

1 Introduction

Terrestrial transportation networks are able to provide a plethora of promising services. These niches are mainly oriented toward safety, entertainment and traffic efficiency services. In the case of traffic efficiency a pervasive data dissemination is highly demanded. Providing timely and useful information to specific receivers is a key concern for traffic applications.

Pioneer countries in the Intelligent Transportation Systems (ITS): the United States, Canada and Europe have allocated frequency spectrum in the 5.9GHz band. Japan, Korea in the 5.8GHz band for Dedicated Short Range Communication (DSRC). These efforts are forward to support further development in ITS infrastructure. Such government actions denote an increasing interest to impulse a new generation of motorway services based on V2I (Vehicle-to-Infrastructure), V2V (Vehicle-to-Vehicle). Despite the fact of these initiatives the costs due to

V. Guyot (Ed.): ICAIT 2012, LNCS 7593, pp. 330–339, 2013.

traffic bottlenecks are still climbing in the developed countries and the emerging economies with an important growth in the last decades (e.g. mega-cities in developing countries). This is because current economies are strongly dependent on the transportation of goods and persons. Even with the continuous advances in informatics and technologies oriented to the transportation, these technologies are partially or scarcely implemented because of the cost to acquire, deploy and maintain. This asseveration is true for cities with a large road infrastructure and budget constraint (e.g., big rural areas, developing countries).

The traffic information systems must comply with timely information to users (drivers). In this sense the users should be forewarned promptly regarding current traffic congestion ahead. The traffic data information is usually disseminated through *Variable Message Signs* (VMS), *Radio Data System-Traffic Message Channel* (RDS-TMC), mobile technology (UMTS). These technologies have been used typically to communicate traffic systems to drivers. Nevertheless, their utilization run under a cost base and their availability depends on the provider's coverage area. For implementation of large scale the price can become prohibitive. A different approach is to use the vehicle with communication capabilities in order to disseminate information in an opportunistic way.

Moreover, the dissemination among vehicles represents several challenges to be faced before exploiting their benign advantages. According to [11] the important issue to be resolved in VANET communications is the way to exchange communication among vehicles in a scalable design. The Vehicular network poses unique challenges because of dynamic changing conditions. Under these circumstances the communication based on broadcasting can degenerate from overburden to null connectivity because of the high or scarce levels of vehicular affluence.

We propose a decentralized method to complement the dissemination of information based on vehicles. We utilized a zone-based approach consisting in a delimited area around every junction where the Inter-Vehicle Communication can be exchanged. This is oriented to location based services where information is delivered to nodes within a defined geographic area and during a certain time [9].

Our second proposal relates to the IVC issues. The inter-vehicular application lies notably on the broadcast communication. One family standard widely used and accepted is the IEEE 802.11x WLAN family protocol. Because of the successful acceptance an approved amendment for Wireless Access in Vehicular Environments (WAVE) [1] has been released.

In this paper we present an adaptive contention window for zone-based dissemination of ITS data traffics based on 802.11p. In order to reduce frame losses due to contention at the MAC layer, our proposal is to add an adaptive delay into the application layer called *Application* CW_{min}. This delay is applied before to be delivered to the MAC layer in order to be transmitted. This application-layer delay provides an advantage of portability while avoiding considerable and costly changes in the large base of installed units (devices using IEEE 802.11).

The remainder of this paper is organized as follows. Section two provides the background and related work. Section three describes our solution. Section four makes reference to the evaluation process and section five concludes with the results obtained and the future work.

2 Background and Related Work

2.1 Traffic Data Dissemination

The concept of vehicular dissemination has been proposed in the literature with early implementations of traffic systems such as: TRAFFIC, SOTIS/SODA. In general terms the data transmission in V2I (push data) is conceived to broadcast information from the fixed infrastructure to vehicle (e.g., traffic condition, advertisements). Under V2V dissemination we can have flooding and dissemination method. Flooding is based on periodic broadcast information about the node itself and acting as merely repeaters of messages received from other peers. This mechanism can converge in faster dissemination but lacks of scalability. The dissemination method on the contrary can be addressed to all peers or some specific neighbours. In fact the broadcast pattern is governed by a specific set of rules. Nevertheless, there is no such thing of one-for-all solution. Every dissemination pattern aims to a specific goal or application guidelines. In [13] authors describe a dissemination zone based forwarding using less communication overhead among the nodes. This is based on defined road segments where an elected node is in charge to handle communications into the segment. In [4] authors propose a probabilistic VANET dissemination of traffic alerts by vehicles equipped with UMTS connexion. The objective is to retransmit these alerts from the equipped nodes to the unequipped nodes via opportunistic Wi-Fi communication.

Besides the current solutions, we have chosen a simpler approach that uses as criteria the road junctions as zone-base dissemination to exchange data among concurrent peers. We do not contemplate a node leader election, hence nor does further overhead communication occur. Rather, we focus on the broadcast enhancement for improving junction dissemination with the objective to maintain simplicity and promote scalability.

3 Proposed Solution

3.1 VPAIR Use Case

Our base architecture is called *Virtual Police Agent for ITS traffic Routing* (VPAIR). This is oriented toward a lighter, cost affordable and scalable version of traffic guidance service for driver assistance [5]. Its functionality is achieved through the road side units called *Virtual Police Agents* (VPA) distributed along the city. The VPA entity is a software entity aware of the traffic condition into a given sector. A sector is defined by geographic boundaries. The final objective is to assist drivers into the sector and giving to them up-to-date traffic information. The VPA in charge of the sector will transmit periodically the traffic data information called *Weight Map Sector* (WMS). This is the network map of the sector with the current travel time per arc (street).

For example, given a road network scenario this is segmented into a grid of sectors. Every sector is controlled by a VPA that is responsible to provide traffic guidance service for the vehicles navigating into the sector. The VPA is located at main junctions where the maximum number of users can be reached. However, in order to extend the VPA penetration to all possible corners of the sector, we have complemented a subsequent mechanism based on vehicle dissemination. The objective is to extend the VPA information beyond its communication range and up to the geographic limits of the sector.

This information can be transmitted either from the VPA or any other vehicle that already have received the sector information. This process occurs inside of every sector where the users will be able to access the system through regular smart-phones (with GPS, Wi-Fi capable). Further reference of our use-case architecture can be found in [6].

3.2 VPAIR Dissemination Algorithm

The algorithm 1 describes the main functions of the vehicle entity regarding the dissemination process. This is based on the periodic information beaconed from the VPA to the users in their transmission range. The scope of the communication is one-hop. The VPA location is taken into account in order to avoid overlap with another VPA transmission range. The transmission period for the VPA $Beacon_{vpa}$ and vehicle $Beacon_{veh}$ are fixed values. With the exception that beaconing time of the vehicle is composed of $Beacon_{veh}$ plus an extra delay called *Application* CW_{min} (explained in section 3.4).

Once the vehicles have acquired the VPA information they will carry this information with the objective to be disseminated afterwards. In fact, the vehicles become beacons themselves and retransmit the information that they just came to learn. The dissemination is achieved at every junction in the moment the vehicle found itself inside the junction area $Juncion_{radio}$ (via on-board GPS and local route map). In the case that other transmissions were heard before to transmit, the vehicle will reschedule the transmission attempt for the next time period. Also if the received information results to be up-to-date, the vehicle will replace the outdated information with the new one received.

3.3 IEEE 802.11p Collision

The implementation of legacy IEEE 802.11 WLAN protocols under emergent vehicular networks is well known to present scalable inconveniences that need to be addressed [12]. They have been designed to have a limited number of nodes with performance throughput as objective. In the broadcast communication the nodes can not agree to medium reservation because of CTS/RTS and acknowledgements absence. This also inhibits the activity for the *Binary Exponential Backoff* (BEB) algorithm. Under these circumstances the node's task is to allocate blindly the most of the messages in free slot times while avoiding stepping into another node transmission.

Algorithm 1. Traffic Data Dissemination

```
Application CW_min = DROP_ratio * (CW_max − CW_min) + CW_min
Vehicle.TimeToBeacon ← Beacon_vehicle + Application CW_min
VPA.TimeToBeacon ← Beacon_vpa
if Beacon_vpa is received or Beacon_vehicle is received then
  Vehicle.dissemination ← true
end if
if Vehicle.junction <= Juncion_radio then
  while Vehicle.dissemination = true do
    Vehicle.timer ← start
    if Vehicle.timer = 0 then
      Transmit Vehicle beacon
    else if other beacons are received then
      Vehicle.timer ← reset
      Vehicle.information ← update
    end if
  end while
end if
```

One mechanism used by the IEEE 802.11 to deal with MAC layer congestion control is the minimum contention window (CW_{min}) used in the backoff mechanism. This is the upper threshold limit used for the random function where the slot times are retrieved. Lower values for CW_{min} results in low delay transmissions but they risk to step into another node transmissions. A higher value for CW_{min} can avoid the transmission overlapping but it represents more delay to transmit. Under these conditions the objective is to manipulate the CW_{min} value in such a way that improve the number of messages successfully received.

The contention window has been researched extensively under WLAN scenarios. Current studies fall either in estimating the number of contending neighbours [8] or measuring the level of collisions and available free time in the medium [7]. Another interesting approach is observing the node's queue length called optimal CSMA (oCSMA). Here the contention window of every node can turn more aggressive (reducing CW_{min}) in function of the local queued data. This quite simple approach uses local information with good throughput results.

The studies related specifically to VANET scenarios are not so numerous. In [2] authors measure the number of lost beacons by adding a sequence number to the transmitted messages. The sequences revised on the receptors are counted as the number of successful receptions. In [10] the neighbour density is estimated and the CW_{min} is affected proportionally when the level of lost beacons increments. A simple but effective approach is studied in [15], here the authors observe the MAC layer and utilize the expired beacons as a point of reference to infer congestion situation. This information is accessible through the node's MAC layer.

3.4 Application Contention Window

The existing approaches to estimate the number of contending neighbours have usually an overhead cost. For the approach to estimate collision events, there exists no accurate mechanism able to detect effectively these events. In this regard we have adopted an approach of simple estimation that consists in observing the expired beacons on the local node [15]. Under this mode our application layer will listen to the number of unsuccessful or missing transmissions occurring in the MAC layer. In function to the ratio of missing transmission we estimate our *Application* CW_{min} value. This value is summed up as an extra delay to the message in the application layer before to be delivered downward to the MAC layer protocol. The resulting algorithm to calculate the node *Application* CW_{min} is inspired from [16] and is defined as:

$$Application\ CW_{min} = DROP_{ratio}(CW_{max} - CW_{min}) + CW_{min} \,. \tag{1}$$

4 Evaluation Results

4.1 Static Scenario Simulation

In our study we utilise a static and dynamic scenario. The static scenario is oriented to observe the impact of our application contention window approach under saturated conditions. This scenario includes 100 static nodes with 802.11p enabled in close proximity, within a grid of 5m by 10m. The network simulator selected is OMNET++ [17].

Under our application design we can expect a maximum rate transmission of one message per second generated for any entity. We take this into account in order to test the system behaviour under saturation. In the figure 1(a) the probability of reception for the protocol 802.11p increases according to higher values of the fixed CW_{min}. On the other hand our adaptive *Application* CW_{min} tends to be more homogeneous from the beginning with a good probability

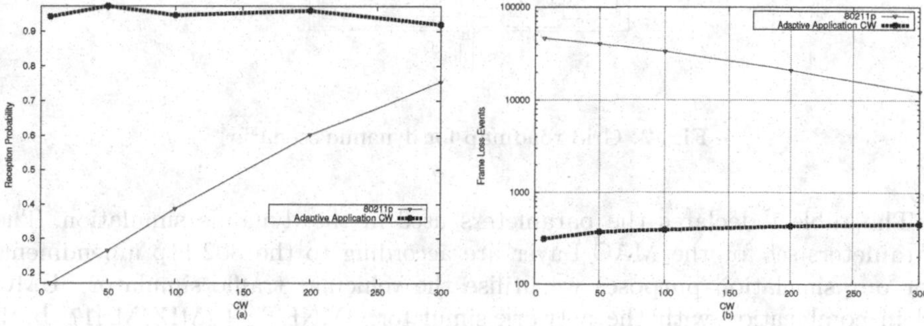

Fig. 1. Fig (a) representative response of the probability nodes' reception, fig (b) representation of the overall missing messages. This scenario uses 802.11p protocol under saturation conditions.

of reception among the node receptors. In the figure 1(b) the overall missing packets are represented, this is the overall loss of messages in the nodes. The losses for the protocol 802.11p result to be higher compared to our adaptive solution performance.

Even though our solution can provoke extra delay in the transmission because of big values in the *Application* CW_{min} and because of processing in the application layer. However, this is not to be an important drawback because our application type is not sensitive to delay. On the other hand what really matters for our purposes is the correct reception to the maximum number of nodes.

4.2 Dynamic Scenario Simulation

In order to evaluate our solution composed of our dissemination method and application contention window. We have evaluated our solution under mobile conditions. Our proposed road network scenario is depicted in the figure 2. Five sources of traffic flow toward one single direction. Five stop lights as traffic regulators with identical traffic light programming located around central junctions. For the simulation we start with a route assignation to every vehicle. This is calculated under the Dijkstra algorithm from the vehicle source S_i to the destination T_i. This is a typical approach as using a GPS to obtain a personal route plan. Under these parameters the road network can be an example of peak hours volume.

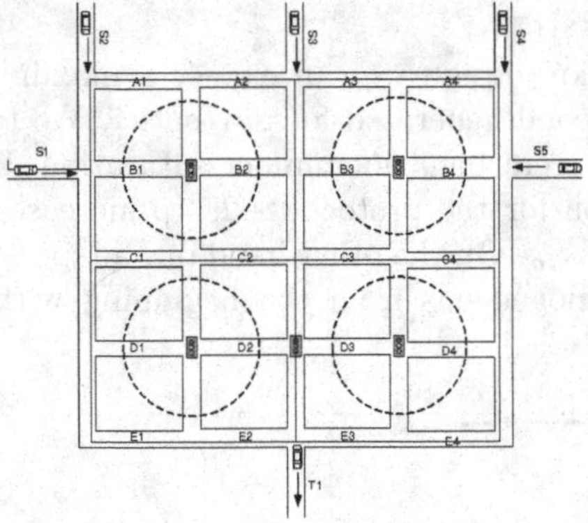

Fig. 2. Grid roadmap for dynamic scenario

The table 1 declares the parameters used in the dynamic simulation. The parameters set for the MAC Layer are according to the 802.11p amendment. For our simulation purposes we utilise the vehicular traffic simulator SUMO [3] in combination with the network simulator OMNET++/MIXIM [17] both simulators are coupled with the framework VEINS [14].

Table 1. Parameters of road network

Parameter	Value
Network grid	4 grid x 4 grid
Grid size	$400m^2$
Traffic light programming	Red 60s, yellow 10s, green 45s
Network grid	4 grid x 4 grid
Vehicle flow	Generated every 15s per source
Vehicle number	900
Communication protocol	IEEE 802.11p
Simulation time	600s
Propagation delay	True
$Beacon_{veh}$, $Beacon_{vpa}$, $Junction_{radio}$	5s, 10s, 20m

4.3 Single VPA Sector Scenario

In the first place we evaluate our composite solution with one sector and one VPA. The communication range of the VPA and vehicles are set to the maximum transmission range (1000m). At this level of coverage all entities can participate for the medium access contention concurrently. In the first observation we can verify that the vehicles using our *Application* CW_{min} are able to allocate more messages with a successful reception in relation to the fixed CW_{min} of protocol 802.11p. However, when the fixed CW_{min} >= 200 the difference tend to be short.

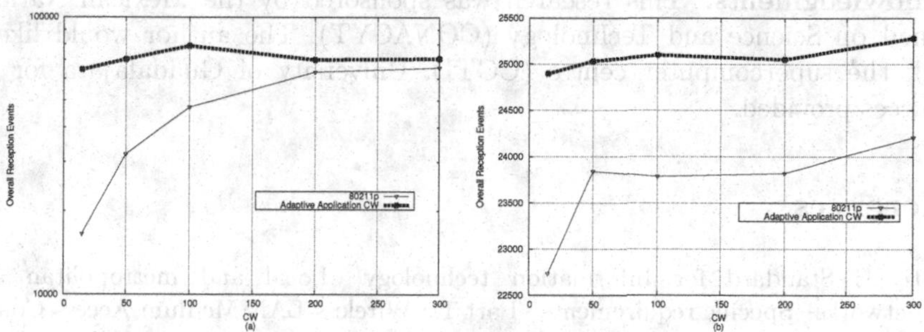

Fig. 3. Fig(a) overall message reception for one VPA scenario, fig(b) overall message reception with four VPAs (logarithmic scale)

4.4 Several VPA Sectors Scenario

Under the same scenario we evaluate our composite solution adding four sectors and four VPAs distributed homogeneously in our road network. The communication range of the VPA is around 300m and vehicles of 130m. In this scenario the collision domains are fractioned with fewer entities to contend simultaneously. With fewer vehicles contending we have less possibility of missing packets. However, according to our observations our *Application* CW_{min} still produces more successful receptions even if the improvements remains quiet modest in comparison to the static scenario. This is because of the number of missing messages observed in the MAC protocol turn to occur less frequently, therefore our algorithm will be less active.

Under these scenarios we have tested with high and low levels of contending nodes. Under these circumstances our application goal has been accomplished in the sense that our solution can be adapted in conditions of high and low contending nodes .

5 Conclusion

Here we have presented a specific application oriented to enhance data dissemination and inter-vehicular communication. Vehicular data dissemination and communication mechanism are key concerns of traffic information systems. The simplicity of our approach turns in costless and readily adaptable to vehicular network applications. This approach tends to achieve a good performance when high congestion happens. Under light congestion the impact of our solution is modest but still better compared with the performance of the protocol 802.11p. Our future work is looking forward to evaluate our architecture under large scale scenarios and to complement our algorithm to be more responsive under light traffic conditions.

Acknowledgments. This research was sponsored by the Mexican National Council on Science and Technology (CONACYT). The author would like to thank the supercomputer centre (CGTI), University of Guadalajara for the resources provided.

References

[1] IEEE Standard for Information technology– Local and metropolitan area networks– Specific requirements– Part 11: Wireless LAN Medium Access Control (MAC) and Physical Layer (PHY) Specifications Amendment 6: Wireless Access in Vehicular Environments (2010)

[2] Balon, N., Guo, J.: Increasing Broadcast Reliability in Vehicular Ad Hoc Networks. In: 3rd ACM International Workshop on Vehicular Ad Hoc Networks, pp. 104–105 (2006)

[3] Behrisch, M., Bieker, L., Erdmann, J., Krajzewicz, D.: SUMO - Simulation of Urban MObility, An Overview. In: Third International Conference on Advances in System Simulation (2011)

[4] Ferrari, G., Busanelli, S., Iotti, N., Kaplan, Y.: Cross-network information dissemination in VANETs. In: 11th Conference on ITS Telecommunications, pp. 351–356 (2011)

[5] Gomez, A., Diaz, G., Boussetta, K.: Virtual Police Agents for ITS Traffic Routing. In: 11th IEEE International Conference on Intelligent Transport Systems Telecommunications, pp. 152–157 (2011)

[6] Gomez, A., Diaz, G., Boussetta, K., Achir, N.: Use case description of VPAIR: Virtual Police Agents for traffic guidance. In: IEEE Global Information Infrastructure Symposium, pp. 1–6 (2011)
[7] Heusse, M., Rousseau, F., Guillier, R., Duda, A.: Idle Sense: An Optimal Access Method for High Throughput and Fairness in Rate Diverse Wireless LANs. In: Proceedings of the ACM SIGCOMM Conference on Data Communication, pp. 121–132 (2005)
[8] Kim, M.S., Kwon, D.H., Suh, Y.J.: MAC in Wireless Ad Hoc Networks. In: Proceedings of the 19th International Conference on Information Networking, pp. 31–40 (2005)
[9] Maihöfer, C., Franz, W., Eberhardt, R.: Stored Geocast. 58th Vehicular Technology Conference 5, 2901–2905 (2003)
[10] Mertens, Y., Wellens, M., Mahonen, P.: Simulation-based Performance Evaluation of Enhanced Broadcast Schemes for IEEE 802.11-based Vehicular Networks. In: IEEE 67th Vehicular Technology Conference, pp. 3042–3046 (2008)
[11] Nadeem, T., Shankar, P., Lftode, L.: A Comparative Study of Data Dissemination Models for VANETs. In: Third Annual International Conference on Mobile and Ubiquitous Systems: Networking and Services, pp. 1–10 (2006)
[12] Oliveira, R., Bernardo, L., Pinto, P.: The influence of broadcast traffic on IEEE 802.11 DCF networks. Computer Communications 32(2), 439–452 (2009)
[13] Singh, R.P., Gupta, A.: Information Dissemination in VANETs using Zone Based Forwarding. Wireless Days IFIP, pp. 1–3 (2011)
[14] Sommer, C., German, R., Dressler, F.: Bidirectionally Coupled Network and Road Traffic Simulation for Improved IVC Analysis. IEEE Transactions on Mobile Computing 10(1), 3–15 (2011)
[15] Stanica, R., Chaput, E., Beylot, A.L.: Enhancements of IEEE 802.11p Protocol for Access Control on a VANET Control Channel. In: IEEE International Communications, pp. 1–5 (2011)
[16] Stanica, R., Chaput, E., Beylot, A.L.: Local Density Estimation for Contention Window Adaptation in Vehicular Networks. In: IEEE 22nd International Symposium on Personal Indoor and Mobile Radio Communications (2011)
[17] Varga, A., Hornig, R.: An overview of the OMNeT++ simulation environment. In: Proceedings of the 1st International Conference on Simulation Tools and Techniques for Communications, Networks and Systems & Workshops, pp. 60:1–60:10 (2008)

Highway Preventive Congestion Control through Input Regulation in Vehicular Networks

Rola Naja[1,2,3]

[1] Laboratoire PRiSM (CNRS 8144), Université de Versailles,
45 avenue des Etats-Unis, 78035 Versailles Cedex
[2] Département Informatique, ESIEE Paris, 2 bd Blaise Pascal 93162 Noisy Le Grand Cedex
Versailles Cedex
[3] Electrical and Engineering Department, BAU University, P.O. Box 115020
r.naja@esiee.fr, rola.naja@prism.uvsq.fr

Abstract. In this paper, we developed some insights into the design of a preventive congestion control applied in vehicular network. The proposed mechanism, implemented at the highway entrances, regulates input traffic and performs vehicular traffic shaping. Our congestion control mechanism deals with different classes of vehicles and is based on a specific priority ticket pool scheme with queue-length threshold scheduling policy, tailored to vehicular networks. Mathematical model based on the embedded Markov chain method shows the benefits of the proposed scheme and highlights the impact of the system parameters on the overall performance. Our technique meets drivers expectations as they will experience bounded performance parameters and limited burst vehicular traffic size.

Keywords: Intelligent Transport system, queue-length-threshold scheduling, congestion control, quality of service.

1 Introduction

Intelligent Transportation Systems (ITS) have been attracting an increasing attention from car manufacturers as well as transportation authorities and communications standards organizations [1]. ITS were identified as a key technology to promote increased safety, improve the national transportation infrastructure, and provide sophisticated information service to road users. Since numerous information is exchanged between vehicles and roadside infrastructure, Vehicle to Vehicle Communications (V2V) and Vehicles to Infrastructure communications (V2I) become two important components of the ITS.

Of particular interest is the vehicular traffic congestion management in intelligent transportation systems. In fact, traffic congestion is recognized to induce transportation costs, incremental delay, driver stress, crash risk and pollution resulting from interference between vehicles in the traffic stream, particularly as a road system approaches its capacity.

Some research papers are devoted to tackle the vehicular congestion problem. The automated incident detection scheme proposed in [2] is based on information sent by

V. Guyot (Ed.): ICAIT 2012, LNCS 7593, pp. 340–356, 2013.

surveillance cameras: It makes use of a spatio-temporal Markov random field algorithm for tracking along with incident detection algorithms.

A technique proposed in [3] intercepts vehicles traffic congestion using information sent by satellite. The advantage with this technique is that satellites cover large areas addressing limitations in terms of spatial coverage. In [4], authors used the cell dwell time information provided by the network to obtain the information associated with vehicle traffic congestion.

The proactive traffic merging strategy [5] tries to solve the problem of traffic congestion in intersections where a ramp leads on to a highway. Each vehicle, equipped with sensors and communication devices, decides where and when it can merge onto the highway before arriving at the merging point. The technique proposed in [6] adopts traffic information sharing and route selection procedures. Based on the traffic information shared, a congestion free route is selected using the route selection procedure.

In [7], congestion is classified into three different threshold values based on vehicle speed: free flow, slow moving and heavily congested. According to the received information from video cameras and GPS devices, a threshold value is selected and reported to the vehicles. Authors in [8] proposed the adaptive proportional integral rate controller as the candidate algorithm to perform vehicle traffic management. This algorithm is a rate based controller that uses control theory to manage the problem of traffic congestion. The idea is that the road side unit controls the vehicles flow using up-to-date calculated vehicle rates.

In this paper, we designed a preventive congestion control based on input regulation and applied at highway entrances, part of a complex highway network. The originality of our work can be summarized as follows:

- The proposed algorithm shapes vehicular traffic on a highway and bounds the number of admitted vehicles to the maximum highway capacity.
- We consider that a certain range of vehicles (i.e. urgent vehicles: ambulances, police cars) has strict requirement and should receive special treatment. Thus, the proposed algorithm achieves service differentiation while still meeting the quality of service for vehicles with limited priority.

We performed a mathematical analysis and conducted an extensive set of numerical resolutions to examine the performance of the proposed preventive congestion control that strives to shape vehicular traffic in a specific highway scenario.

This paper is organized as follows. Section II defines the vehicular traffic congestion problem. Section III describes our proposed preventive congestion control. In section IV, we give a mathematical model of the congestion control based on an embedded Markov chain and we capture the relationship of maximum burst size, packet loss, allocated buffer size and mean waiting time to the parameters of ticket pool algorithm in closed form equations. Section V is devoted for the numerical results and the performance analysis. Final remarks are addressed in Section VI.

2 Vehicular Traffic Congestion Problem

An in-depth understanding of vehicular congestion and vehicular traffic model is necessary to provide the groundwork for minimizing vehicular congestion. In next sub-sections, we present these models before describing the preventive congestion control.

2.1 Vehicular Congestion Definition

The three fundamental characteristics of vehicle traffic are flow rate λ (vehicles/hour), speed v (km/h) and density d (vehicles/km). The average values of these quantities can be approximately related by the basic traffic stream model [11]:

$$v = \frac{\lambda}{d} \tag{1}$$

With few vehicles on the highway, density approaches zero and speeds approach free flow speed. As additional vehicles enter the highway, traffic density and flow rate increase until flow reaches a maximum. As additional vehicles continue to enter, the traffic stream density will continue to increase but the flow rate will begin to decrease. When demand exceeds roadway capacity, increasing traffic densities approach a "jam density" limit. At this limit, all vehicles are stopped (i.e. flow rate is zero) with vehicles tightly packed on the highway, leading to the vehicular congestion.

2.2 Vehicular Traffic Model

Two generic models exist for vehicular traffic: macroscopic and microscopic models. Macroscopic models study the vehicle traffic flow as a whole while microscopic models describe individual vehicle behaviour. Microscopic models are of greater interest in studying vehicular networks because they allow the capture of inter-vehicle interaction and the continuously changing distribution of vehicles among the traffic stream.

In [10], the authors classified vehicular mobility models in four different classes: synthetic models wrapping all models based on mathematical models, survey-based models extracting mobility patterns from surveys, trace-based models generating mobility patterns from real mobility traces and traffic simulators-based models where the vehicular mobility traces are extracted from a detailed traffic simulator.

The first and most well known class includes synthetic models. Fiore [11] wrote a complete survey of models falling into this category. According to [11], synthetic models may be separated into five classes: stochastic models, car following models, traffic stream models, behavioral models and queue models.

Stochastic models describe nodes mobility with constrain random movements of nodes on a graph contrarily to Random Walk or the Random waypoint [12]. The City Section mobility model introduced by Davies [13] constrain nodes movement on a grid road topology, where all edges are considered bi-directional, single-lane roads.

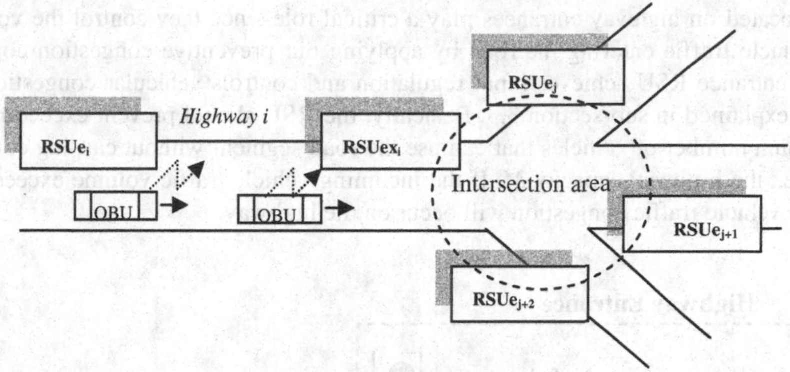

Fig. 1. Highway Model

In car following models, the behaviour of each driver is described in relation to the vehicle ahead. Most car following models compute the speed or acceleration of a car as a function of factors such as the distance to the front and the current speeds of both vehicles [10,14].

Vehicular traffic stream is modelled as a hydrodynamic phenomenon and try to relate velocity, density and flow. With behavioral models, each movement is determined by behavioral rules such as social influences rational decisions or actions following a stimulus-reaction process.

Finally, queue theory models the road as a queue and each vehicle as a queue client [15, 16]. Since queue models describe the movement of each vehicle in an independent way, they fall into an intermediate category with respect to macroscopic and microscopic description, which can be referred to as mesoscopic.

In this paper, we have undertaken our analysis based on queue models. In fact queue models lead to very good approximations of results obtained with much more complex microscopic mobility models [16]. Moreover, queue models have very low computational cost because they update the status of a vehicle only when a vehicle enters a new queue. This is performed even though queue models achieves reduced realism of the outcome.

3 Preventive Congestion Model

3.1 Highway Model Description

Fig. 1 illustrates the highway model where different types of vehicles circulate on a highway and approach from the highway exit. Highway wireless infrastructure consists of multiple road side units exchanging messages. In this study, we focus on highway entrances and exits which are equipped with road side units (RSUs) that communicate with other RSUs located on neighbouring highways entrances and exits. The RSU exchanged information is basically related to performance parameters, specifically the mean waiting time.

RSUs located on highway entrances play a critical role since they control the volume of vehicle traffic entering the road by applying our preventive congestion control: Each entrance RSU achieves input regulation and controls vehicular congestion as will be explained in sub-section 3.3. Basically, the RSU should prevent exceeding the maximum number of vehicles that can use the road segment without causing congestion, i.e., the highway capacity *M*. If the incoming vehicle traffic volume exceeds *M* then the vehicle traffic congestion will occur on the highway.

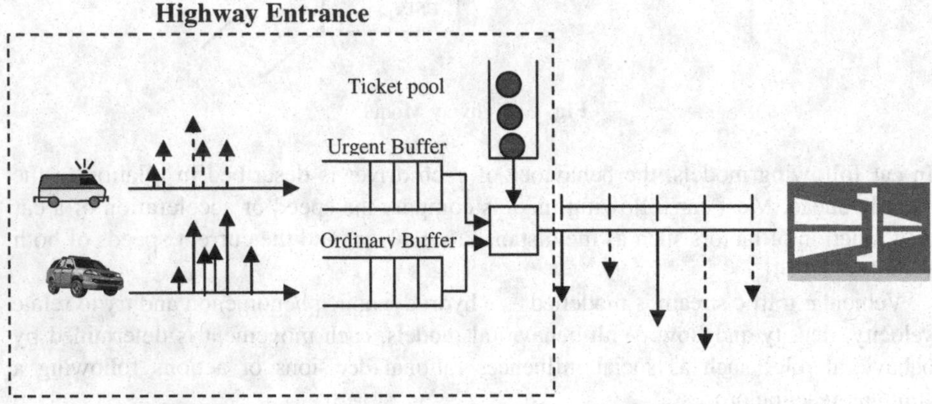

Fig. 2. Preventive congestion control

Capacity refers to the number of vehicles that could be accommodated in a highway. It depends on various design factors such as lane width and intersection configuration.

On the other hand, consider L_{high} as the highway length and L_{car} as the mean car dimension separating car front from the car back. We then derive the maximum number of vehicles, M , that circulate on a l lanes-highway as:

$$M \leq \frac{l.L_{high}}{L_{car} + SD} \tag{2}$$

Where *SD* is the minimum safety distance between two vehicles.

According to [19], congestion intensity at a particular location is evaluated using level-of-service (LOS) ratings, a grade from A (best) to F (worst), based on the volume-to-capacity ratio ratio. A V/C less than *0.85* is considered under-capacity, *0.85 to 0.95* is considered near capacity, *0.95 to 1.0* is considered at capacity, and over *1.0* is considered over-capacity.

3.2 Vehicular Classes and Vehicular Process

We distinguish between urgent vehicles and ordinary vehicles. As one can expect, urgent vehicles such as ambulances and police cars, should receive higher priority and special treatment from the vehicular wireless network. On the other hand, ordinary vehicles designate vehicles with limited priority.

The vehicle inter-arrival time is assumed to be an exponential random variable with arrival rate. This assumption has been shown valid in [17] because the Kolmogorov-Smirnov test can accurately approximate the statistics of vehicle inter-arrival time based on the empirical data for a real roadway into an exponential distribution. Thus we suppose that urgent and ordinary vehicular traffic arrive according to independent Poisson process with rates λ_1 and λ_2, respectively.

Vehicular traffic generated at the sources is generally bursty in nature and requires flow control for not congesting the highway as will be detailed in next section.

3.3 Proposed Preventive Congestion Control Model

We design an algorithm for preventing congestion control in a vehicular environment while taking into account the traffic burstiness and the priority classes of vehicles. The proposed congestion control achieves an input regulation and shapes vehicular traffic on highways.

The model consists of two waiting queues with finite capacities *K1* and *K2* that accommodate urgent and ordinary vehicles respectively (fig. 2). Vehicles arriving in a bursty pattern are first queued in the corresponding waiting queue.

At highway entrance, each single vehicle should acquire a ticket to be accepted on the highway, and the ticket following an acceptance is removed from the ticket pool with a finite capacity *M:* Tickets are generated at constant intervals every *T* (units) and stored in the pool. Vehicles drivers in the urgent or ordinary waiting queue can take the highway only if there are tickets in the pool.

In order to apply a service differentiation, we implement the Queue Length Threshold (QLT) scheduling policy by considering a threshold *L* in the ordinary buffer.

More precisely, the QLT works as follows:

1. Whenever there are any tickets in the ticket pool (this implies there are no vehicles waiting), the vehicle arriving, regardless of traffic type, is permitted to circulate.
2. If the number of ordinary vehicles is less than or equal to the threshold value *L* just before the ticket generation epoch, the vehicle (if any) in urgent traffic waiting queue is authorized to circulate.
3. If the number of vehicles of ordinary traffic exceeds the threshold value *L* or if the waiting queue of urgent traffic is empty just before the ticket generation epoch, the vehicle of ordinary traffic can circulate on the highway.
4. When a vehicle driver arrives to a full waiting queue, he/she will change his/her itinerary and choose another exit. The vehicle is then considered to be lost from the system.

3.4 Vehicular Burst Size

Given the shaping function provided by the token pool, the maximum burst of traffic will be *M* and the sustained mean data rate will be *R=1/T*. In other words, during any time period Δt, the amount of vehicular traffic on the highway sent cannot exceed $(\Delta t/T+M)$.

Based on this understanding, highway designer should dimension the ticket generation rate and pool size according to the following constraint:

$$R.\Delta t + M \leq \frac{l.L_{high}}{L_{car} + SD} \tag{3}$$

At this stage, we proceed with the mathematical analysis of the proposed model.

4 Mathematical Model Analysis

4.1 System State Distribution

In the following, we will refer respectively to the vehicles of urgent traffic and ordinary traffic as type 1 and type 2.

We apply the embedded Markov chain method to analyze the proposed scheme and quantify performance parameters. More precisely, we consider the system state at ticket generation instants *0,T,2T,...*

Let *N1(n)* and *N2(n)* be the number of type 1 vehicles and the number of type 2 vehicles, respectively, just after the nth ticket generation instant, where $0 \leq N1(n) \leq K1$ and $0 \leq N2(n) \leq K2$. As soon as the buffer occupancy statistics are known, the loss probabilities and other performance metrics can be found.

Let *T(n)* be the number of tickets in the ticket pool just after the nth ticket generation instant. In a steady state, a type 1 (or type 2) vehicle can be queued in the buffer leading to *N1(n)>0* (or *N2(n)>0*), only if the ticket pool is empty (*T(n)=0*). Otherwise, the vehicle would be accepted, one per ticket.

On the other hand, the ticket pool contains tickets (*T(n)>0*), only if the type 1 waiting queue and type 2 waiting queue are empty.

We express the state of the waiting queue for type 1 vehicles and the ticket pool as follows:

$$B_1(n) = N_1(n) + M - T(n) \tag{4}$$

We note that B1(n) has the following properties:

1. $0 \leq B1(n) \leq M+K1$,
2. In the range $0 \leq B1(n) < M$, N1(n)=0 and B1(n) = M – T(n),
3. In the range $M \leq B1(n) \leq M+K1$, T(n)=0 and B1(n) = N1(n) +M.

It is noteworthy that the relationship between the type1 waiting queue occupancy and the ticket pool occupancy is captured in the following condition:

$$N_1(n)\ .\ T(n) = 0 \tag{5}$$

The vehicular congestion control mechanism is described by the two dimensional Markov chain process *P(n)={(B1 (n), N2(n)) , n≥ 0}* which has the finite state space illustrated in fig. 3.

It can be seen that states *(M-i,0)* for $0 \leq i \leq M$ correspond to a system with empty urgent waiting queue and *i* tickets in the ticket pool. Whereas states *(M+j,l) for* $0 \leq j \leq K1-1$ and $0 \leq l \leq K2-1$ illustrate a system with an empty ticket pool, *j* vehicles waiting in the urgent waiting queue and *l* vehicles in the ordinary queue.

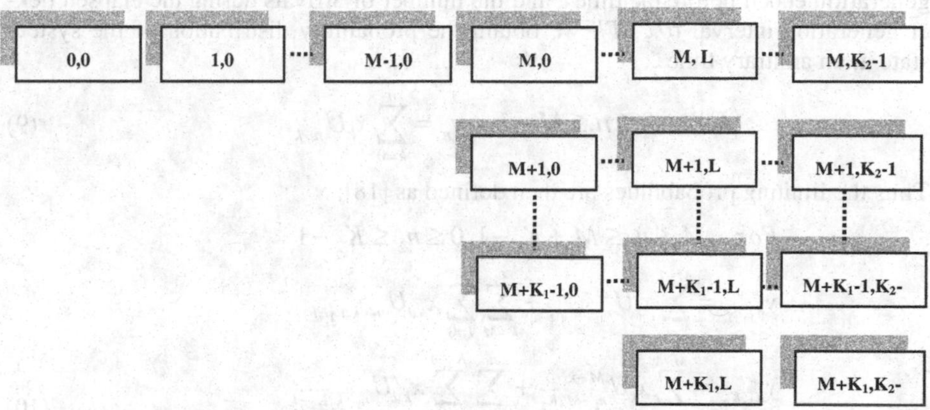

Fig. 3. Markov chain state space

When *n* tends towards infinity, the Markov chain *P(n)* will be described by the steady-state probability vector *X*:

X=(X0,0, X1,0,...,XM-1,0, XM,0, XM,1, ...,XM, L,...,XM,K2-1, XM+1,0, XM+1,1, ...,XM+1,L, ...,XM+1, K2-1,...,XM+K1-1,0, XM+K1-1,1, ..., XM+K1-1,L,...,XM+K1-1,K2-1, XM+K1,L,...,XM+K1,K2-1)

The probability vector *X* is obtained by solving the equations:

$$\begin{aligned} X.A &= X \\ X.e &= 1 \end{aligned} \tag{6}$$

where *e* denotes a column vector with all elements equal to one and *A* is the transition probability matrix which will not be exhibited in this paper due to lack of space.

At this stage, we derive the system state distribution at an arbitrary time. For this purpose, we define the limiting probabilities *yk* and *yk,l* as:

$$\begin{aligned} y_k &= \lim_{t\to\infty}\{B_1(t)=k, N_2(t)=0\}; 0 \leq k \leq M-1 \\ y_{k,l} &= \lim_{t\to\infty}\{B_1(t)=k, N_2(t)=l\}; M \leq k \leq M+K_1, \\ & 0 \leq l \leq K_2 \end{aligned} \tag{7}$$

where $N_1(t) = B_1(t) + M - T(t)$ and $N_2(t)$ the number of type 2 vehicles at time *t*.

Consider Um, the probability for having *m*-arrivals in total during the elapsed ticket generation interval *(0, ζ - ζT]* in the ticket generation interval including the time *ζ*.

We can then derive Um as:

$$U_m = \frac{1}{T}\int_0^T \frac{(\lambda T)^m}{m!} e^{-\lambda t} dt = \frac{1}{\lambda T}\{1 - e^{-\lambda T}\sum_{l=0}^{m}\frac{(\lambda T)^l}{l!}\} \tag{8}$$

with $\lambda = \lambda 1 + \lambda 2$ the total arrival rate of urgent and ordinary vehicles.

Consider an arbitrary time ζ, and let ζT, be the starting time of the ticket generation interval which includes the time ζ. By considering the system state at the last ticket generation epoch before the time ζ and the number of arrivals during the elapsed ticket generation interval *(0,ζ-ζT]*, we obtain the probability distribution of the system state at an arbitrary time ζ:

$$For \quad 0 \le n \le M-1 \quad y_n = \sum_{k=0}^{n} x_k U_{n-k} \tag{9}$$

Thus the limiting probabilities are then defined as [18]:

$$\begin{aligned}
&For \quad M \le n_1 \le M + K_1 - 1, 0 \le n_2 \le K_2 - 1 \\
&y_{n_1,n_2} = \sum_{k=0}^{M-1} x_k U^{M-k}_{n_1-M,n_2} + \sum_{k=M}^{n_1}\sum_{l=0}^{n_2} x_{k,l} U_{n_1-k,n_2-l} \\
&y_{n_1,K_2} = \sum_{k=0}^{M-1} x_k U^{M-k}_{n_1-M,\overline{K_2}} + \sum_{k=M}^{n_1}\sum_{l=0}^{K_2-1} x_{k,l} U_{n_1-k,\overline{K_2-l}} \\
&y_{M+K_1,n_2} = \sum_{k=0}^{M-1} x_k U^{M-k}_{\overline{K_1},n_2} + \sum_{k=M}^{M+K_1-1}\sum_{l=0}^{n_2} x_{k,l} U_{\overline{M+K_1-k},n_2-l} \\
&+\sum_{l=L}^{n_2} x_{M+K_1,l} U_{\overline{0},n_2-l} . 1_{\{n_2 > L\}}
\end{aligned} \tag{10}$$

At this stage, we define the probability $U^i_{k,l}$ for having i-arrivals in total during interval (*0, Xi]* and then *k* and *i* arrivals of type 1 and type 2 vehicles, respectively, during interval *(Xi, ζ - ζT]* in the ticket generation interval including the time ζ.

$$\begin{aligned}
&U^i_{k,l} = \binom{k+l}{l} . (\frac{\lambda_1}{\lambda})^k . (\frac{\lambda_2}{\lambda})^l . \frac{1}{\lambda T} . (1 - e^{-\lambda T}\sum_{m=0}^{i+k+l}\frac{(\lambda T)^m}{m!} \\
&U^i_{k,l} = \binom{k+l}{l} . (\frac{\lambda_1}{\lambda})^k . (\frac{\lambda_2}{\lambda})^l . \frac{1}{\lambda T} . (1 - e^{-\lambda T}\sum_{m=0}^{k+l}\frac{(\lambda T)^m}{m!}) \\
&U_{\overline{j},l} = \sum_{m=j}^{\infty} U_{m,l} \quad U_{j,\overline{l}} = \sum_{m=l}^{\infty} U_{j,m} \\
&U^i_{\overline{j},l} = \sum_{m=j}^{\infty} U^i_{m,l} \quad U^i_{j,\overline{l}} = \sum_{m=l}^{\infty} U^i_{j,m} \\
&y_{M+K_1,K_2} = 1 - \sum_{n=0}^{M-1} y_n - \sum_{n_1=M}^{M+K_1-1}\sum_{n_2=0}^{K_2} y_{n_1,n_2} - \sum_{n_2=0}^{K_2-1} y_{M+K_1,n_2}
\end{aligned} \tag{11}$$

4.2 Performance Parameters

Using the above probability distributions, we obtain the following performance parameters measured by mean queue length, mean waiting time, loss probability and maximum vehicular burst size of urgent and ordinary vehicular traffic.

➢ The maximum burst size corresponds to the maximum number of vehicles served during a ticket generation epoch. It is computed as follows:

$$N_s = \sum_{i=1}^{M}(M-i).y_{M-i,0} + \sum_{i=0}^{K_2}\sum_{n=0}^{K_2} M.y_{M+i,n} \tag{12}$$

➢ The loss probability of urgent vehicular traffic denotes the probability of an urgent vehicle driver finding a full waiting queue and is considered as lost from the system:

$$P_{loss1} = \sum_{n=0}^{K_2} y_{M+K_1,n} \tag{13}$$

➢ The loss probability of ordinary traffic denotes the probability of an ordinary vehicle driver finding a full waiting queue and is considered as lost:

$$P_{loss2} = \sum_{n=M}^{M+K_1} y_{n,K_2} \tag{14}$$

➢ The mean queue length of urgent vehicular traffic is easily obtained:

$$M_1 = \sum_{i=0}^{K_1}\sum_{n=0}^{K_2} i.y_{M+i,n} \tag{15}$$

➢ The mean queue length of ordinary vehicular traffic is derived as:

$$M_2 = \sum_{i=0}^{K_2}\sum_{n=0}^{K_1} i.y_{M+n,i} \tag{16}$$

➢ The mean urgent waiting time corresponds to the mean time observed by a vehicle driver in the urgent queue. It is obtained by applying Little's law:

$$W_1 = \frac{M_1}{\lambda_1(1-P_{loss}^1)} \tag{17}$$

➢ The mean ordinary waiting time is the mean time observed by a vehicle driver in the ordinary queue. (Little's law):

$$W_2 = \frac{M_2}{\lambda_2(1-P_{loss}^2)} \tag{18}$$

5 Performance Analysis

The mathematical model being intractable, we proceeded to the numerical resolution using Matlab and conducted an extensive batch of simulations in order to evaluate performance parameters. Numerical resolutions are achieved for a single lane highway and with equal mean input rate for urgent and ordinary traffic (i.e. $\lambda_1 = \lambda_2 = \lambda/2$).

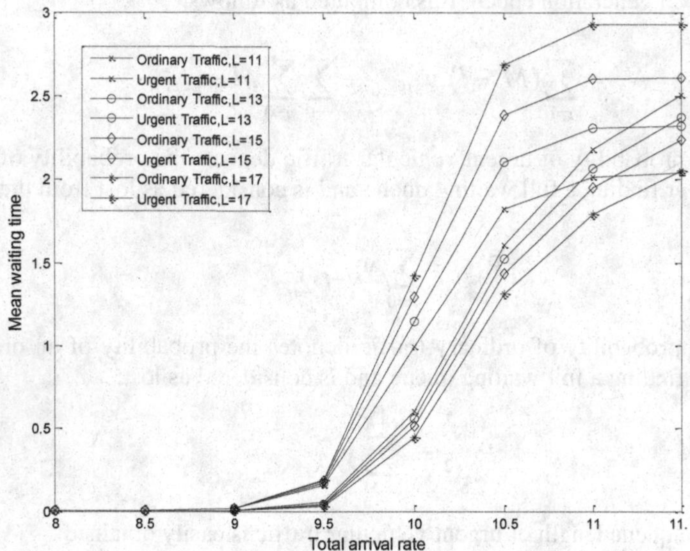

Fig. 4. Mean Waiting time(sec) $K_1=20$, $K_2=20$, $M=20$

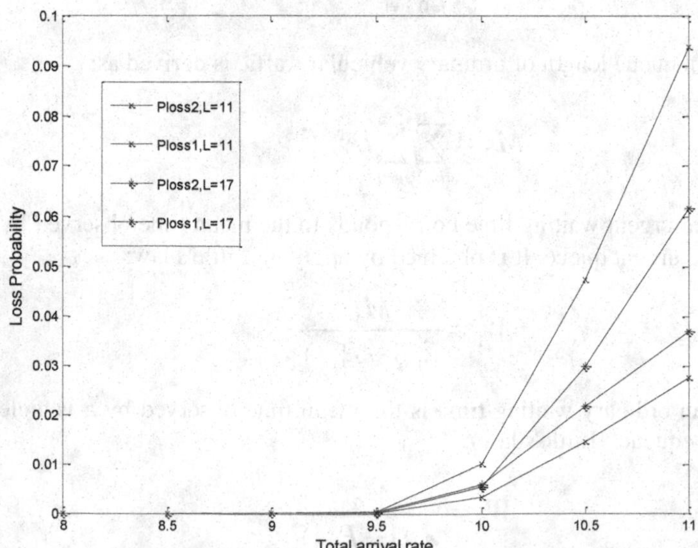

Fig. 5. Loss Probability $K_1=20$, $K_2=20$, $M=20$

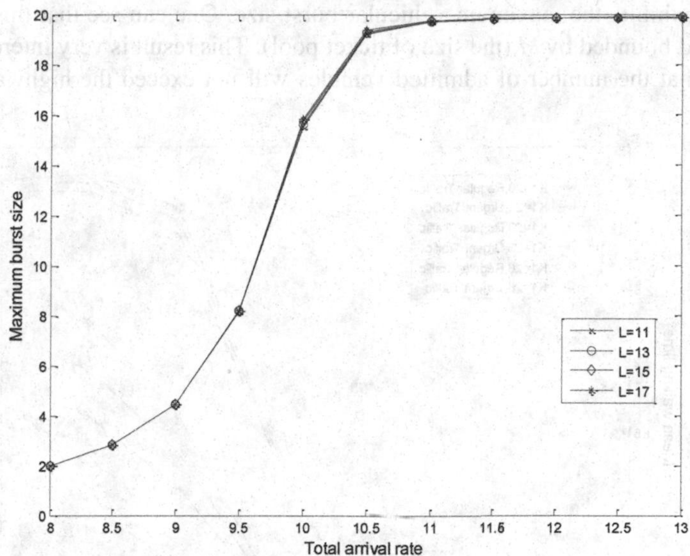

Fig. 6. Maximum burst size $K_1=20, K_2=20, M=20$

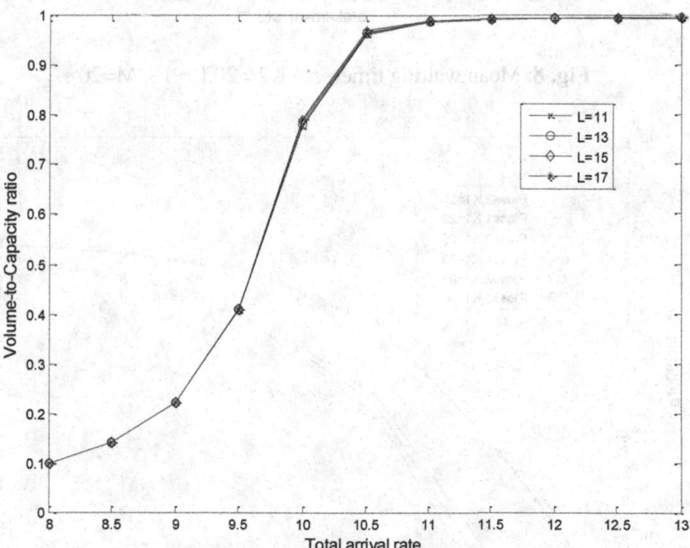

Fig. 7. Volume-to-Capacity ratio$(K_1, K_2, M)= (20,20,20)$

The first set of results showed in figures 4 and 5 illustrate the impact of different values of threshold L on the system performance. As L increases, ordinary traffic gets less priority and urgent traffic experiences higher priority. Thus, ordinary traffic waiting time W_2 and loss probability P_{loss2} (resp. urgent traffic waiting time W_1 and loss probability P_{loss1}) increase (resp. decrease) as L increases.

Fig. 6 exhibits the maximum vehicular burst size. One can see that this number is limited and bounded by M (the size of ticket pool). This result is very interesting since it shows that the number of admitted vehicles will not exceed the highway capacity.

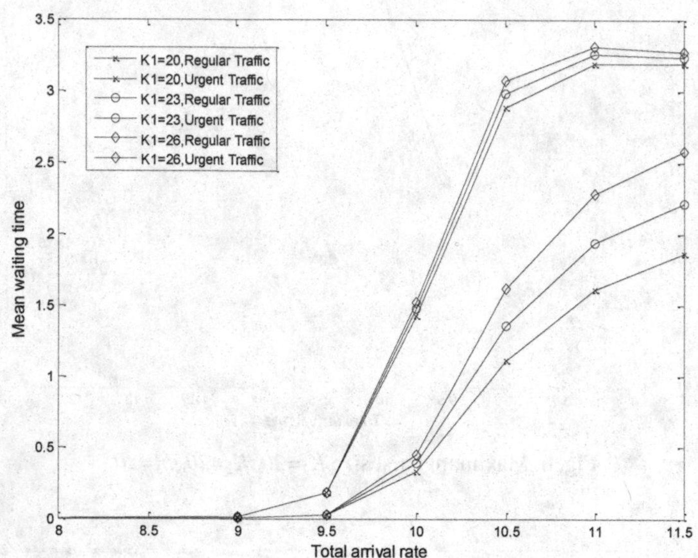

Fig. 8. Mean waiting time(sec) K2= 20,L= 18, M=20

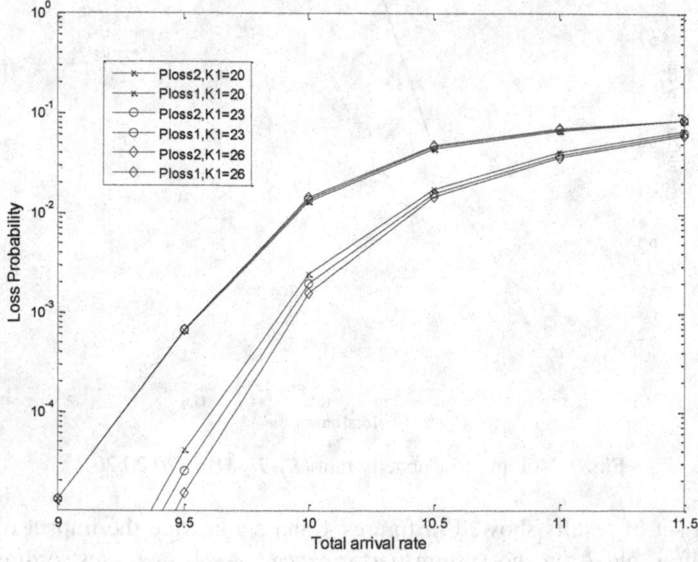

Fig. 9. Loss Probability K2=20,L=18, M=20

In fact, our model achieves congestion control by input rate regulation and by tightly controlling the vehicle input rate.

Fig. 7 depicts the volume-to-capacity ratio (*V/C*). The system is under capacity (resp. near capacity) for a total rate less (resp. greater) than *10.25 Er*.
The second set of results illustrated in figures 8 and 9 depict the impact of urgent traffic waiting queue size. One can see that urgent traffic is very sensitive to the change of its buffer size *K1*. As *K1* increases, the urgent traffic waiting delay increases (fig. 8) and loss probability decreases (fig. 9).

Ordinary vehicular traffic is less affected by urgent traffic queue size variation at low load. However, as load increases, ordinary traffic experiences more concurrency from higher priority traffic. Thus, its mean waiting time starts to increase. On the contrary, the ordinary traffic loss probability is not affected by *K1* variation.

Figs. 10 and 11 display performance parameters obtained with different values of ordinary traffic queue size *K2*. Numerical resolutions were conducted with *K1, L* and *M* respectively equal to 20, 10 and 20. The Threshold *L* equal to *10* has a significant impact on prioritizing ordinary traffic over urgent traffic and the set of values *K2(20,23,26)* does not have a major impact on loss probability. This explains the fact that ordinary traffic is not sensitive to the buffer size variation due to *L* small value. For low loads, mean waiting time is not affected by *K2*. As the total arrival rate increases, results show a slight increase in delays for both traffic types.

Figs. 12 and 13 depict the mean waiting time and the loss probability of each vehicular traffic type, respectively for various values of the ticket pool size. When *M*

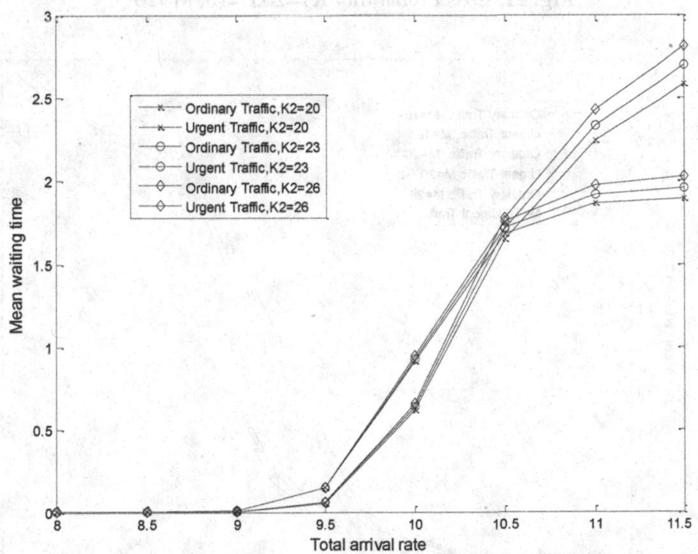

Fig. 10. Mean waiting time (sec)K1=20,L=10,M= 20

increases, urgent and ordinary vehicular traffic are served by a greater number of tickets. Therefore, the loss probability and the mean waiting time for each traffic decrease as the ticket pool size becomes large.

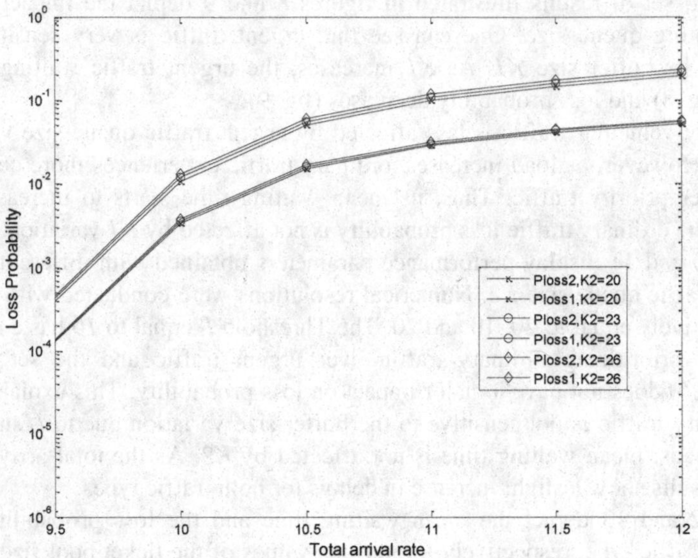

Fig. 11. Loss Probability K1=20,L=10, M=20

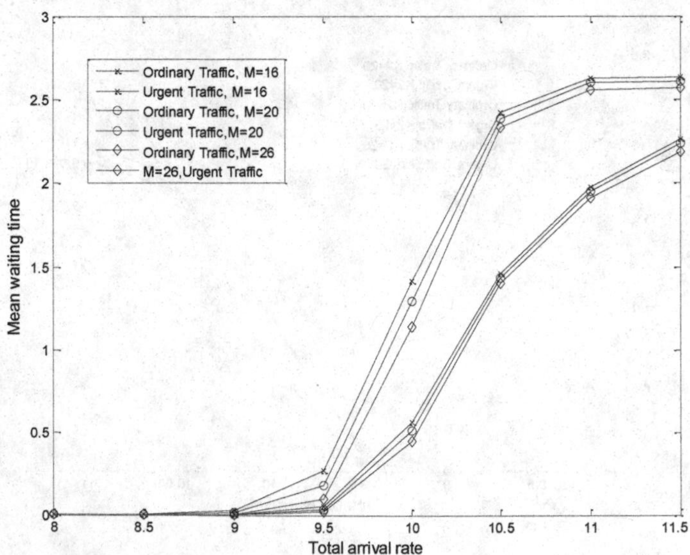

Fig. 12. Mean waiting time(sec) K1=20, K2=20, L=15

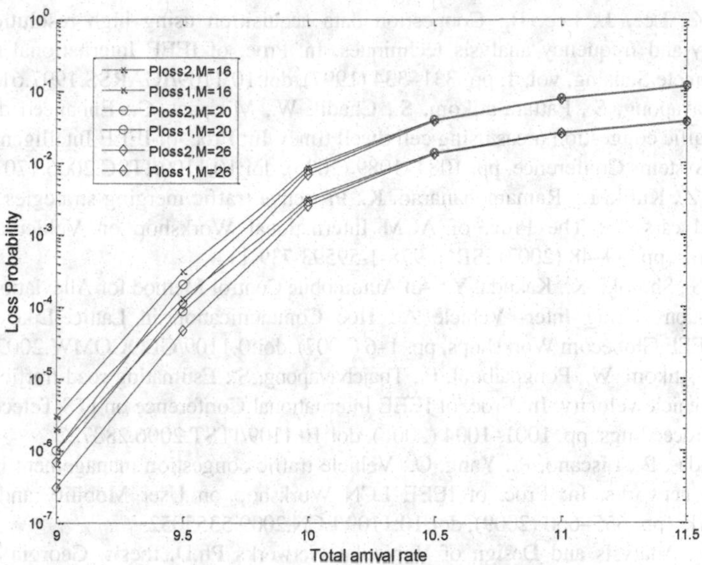

Fig. 13. Loss Probability K1=20, K2=20, L=15

6 Conclusion

Traffic monitoring is commonplace in most major urban areas. Given the importance of minimizing congestion, considerable attention should be oriented towards monitoring freeway speeds and flows in an effort to remedy from traffic jam and crash risks. Based on this understanding, we have designed a preventive congestion control applied in vehicular network architecture. The main purpose of the proposed scheme is to regulate the ordinary and urgent vehicular traffic as well as to shape the traffic.

We validated our model throughout an accurate mathematical model resolved numerically. Performance parameters were computed for various sets of input variables. Numerical results show the effects of the system parameters, such as the waiting queue sizes *K1* and *K2,* the ticket pool size *M* and the threshold value *L* on the overall performance. Numerical results show that our algorithms satisfies delay requirement of urgent traffic while providing improved quality of service for ordinary traffic.

Finally, the highway designer should set the ticket pool size according to the maximum highway capacity. This will guarantee that the number of vehicles circulating on the highway is bounded and will act as a vehicular traffic shaper on highways.

References

1. IEEE Vehicular Technology Society (VTS), IEEE Trial-Use Standard for Wireless Access in Vehicular Environments (WAVE)-Resource Manager. IEEE Std. 1609.1 (2006)
2. Kamijo, S., Koo, H., Liu, X., Fujihira, K., Sakauchi, M.: Development and Evaluation of Real-time Video Surveillance System on Highway based on Semantic Hierarchy and Decision Surface. In: Proc. of IEEE International Conference on Systems, Man and Cybernetics, vol. 1, pp. 840–846 (2005), doi:10.1109/ICSMC.2005.1571251

3. Kim, K., Lee, J., Lee, B.: Congestion data acquisition using high resolution satellite imagery and frequency analysis techniques. In: Proc. of IEEE International Geoscience and Remote Sensing, vol. 1, pp. 331–334 (1997), doi:10.1109/IGARSS.1997.615877
4. Thajchayapong, S., Pattara-atikom, S., Chadil, W., Mitrpant, C.: Enhanced detection of road traffic congestion areas using cell dwell times. In: Proc. of IEEE Intelligent Transportation Systems Conference, pp. 1084–1089 (2006), doi:10.1109/ITSC.2006.1707366
5. Wang, Z., Kulik, L., Ramamohanarao, K.: Proactive traffic merging strategies for sensor-enabled cars. In: The Proc. of ACM International Workshop on Vehicular Ad Hoc Networks, pp. 39–48 (2007) ISBN: 978-1-59593-739-1
6. Inoue, S., Shozaki, K., Kakuda, Y.: An Automobile Control Method for Alleviation of Traffic Congestions Using Inter- Vehicle Ad Hoc Communication in Lattice-Like Roads. In: Proc. IEEE Globecom Workshops, pp. 1–6 (2007), doi:0.1109/GLOCOMW.2007.4437828
7. Pattara-Atikom, W., Pongpaibool, P., Thajchayapong, S.: Estimating road traffic congestion using vehicle velocity. In: Proc. of IEEE International Conference on ITS Telecommunications Proceedings, pp. 1001–1004 (2006), doi:10.1109/ITST.2006.288722
8. Mohandas, B., Liscano, R., Yang, O.: Vehicle traffic congestion management in vehicular ad-hoc networks. In: Proc. of IEEE LCN Workshop on User Mobility and Vehicular Networks, pp. 655–660 (2009), doi:10.1109/LCN.2009.5355052
9. Wu, H.: Analysis and Design of Vehicular Networks Ph.D. thesis. Georgia Institute of Technology (2005)
10. Harri, J., Filali, F., Bonnet, C.: Mobility models for vehicular Ad hoc networls : a survey and taxonomy. Proc. of IEEE Commuications Surveys & Tutorials 11(4), 19–41 (2009), doi:10.1109/SURV.2009.090403
11. Fiore, M.: Mobility Models in Inter-Vehicle Communications Literature. Report (2006)
12. Johnson, D.B., Maltz, D.A., Broch, J.: DSR: The Dynamic Source Routing Protocol for Multi-Hop Wireless Ad Hoc Networks. In: Perkins, C.E. (ed.) Ad Hoc Networking, pp. 139–172. Addison-Wesley (2001)
13. Davies, V.: Evaluating Mobility Models within an Ad Hoc Network. MS thesis, Colorado School of Mines (2000)
14. Panwai, S., Dia, H.: Comparative evaluation of microscopic car-following behaviour. Proc. of IEEE Transactions on Intelligent Transportation Systems 6(3), 314–325 (2005), doi:10.1109/TITS.2005.853705
15. Cetin, N., Burri, A., Nagel, K.: A large-scale multi-agent traffic microsimulation based on queue model. In: Proceedings of Swiss Transport Research Conference, STRC (2003)
16. Gawron, C.: An iterative algorithm to determine the dynamic user equilibrium in a traffic simulation model. International journal of Modern Physics 9(3), 393–407 (1998)
17. Wisitpongphan, N., Bai, F., Mudalige, P., Tonguz, O.K.: On the Routing Problem in Disconnected Vehicular Ad Hoc Networks. In: Proc. of IEEE International Conference on Computer Communications, pp. 2291–2295 (2007), doi:10.1109/INFCOM.2007.267
18. Choi, D., Lee, S.: Performance analysis of the leaky bucket scheme with queue length dependent arrival rates. The Bull. Korean Math. Soc. 43(3), 657–669 (2006)

Author Index

Achir, Nadjib 296, 330
Ait Ouahman, Abdellah 16
Al Agha, Khaldoun 274, 283
Allal, Salim 319
Azizi, Mounir 25

Badache, Nadjib 177
Barthélémy, Éric 199
Benaini, Redouane 25
Ben Mamoun, Mouad 25
Binsztok, Henri 2
Bouallegue, Ridha 310
Boudjit, Saadi 319
Boughanmi, Najet 264
Boukhatem, Lila 283
Boussetta, Khaled 296, 330
Boutaba, Raouf 3
Brinis, Nour 231

Casolari, Sara 33
Chen, Sau-Gee 258
Chen, Yue-bin 151, 160
Cheng, Chih-Heng 83
Cheng, Jay 83
Choi, Hoon 75
Chou, Hsin-Hung 83
Colajanni, Michele 33

Desnos, Anthony 225
Diaz, Gladys 296, 330

El Mahdi Boumezzough, Mohamed 16
Erra, Robert 225
Esseghir, Moez 264

Famulari, Antonino 213
Farid, Farnaz 138
Farsi, Abdelhak 296, 330
Feng, Ji-hua 151
Feng, Sai-sai 160

Gao, Fei 151, 160
Gavish, Bezalel 1
Ghamri-Doudane, Yacine 4
Gomez, Arturo 296, 330
Guo, Qiang 109

Hao, Wu-bang 151
Hayashi, Yuki 5
Hecker, Artur 213
Hubbe, Allen 98
Hurfin, Michel 177

Idboufker, Noureddine 16

Jeong, Ok-Ran 169

Kawai, Eiji 47
Khoukhi, Lyes 264
Klein Junior, Valter 116
Krief, Francine 243

Lee, Eunseok 169
Lemlouma, Tayeb 128
Lin, Ying-Tsung 258
Liu, Yunqi 109

Merchant, Arif 98
Merghem-Boulahia, Leïla 264
Mihara, Hiroki 5
Minet, Pascale 231
Moise, Izabela 177

Naja, Rola 340

Oh, Jehwan 169
Orawiwattanakul, Tananun 47
Otsuki, Hideki 47
Ouni, Nizar 310

Park, Jong-Geun 75
Pedroso, Carlos Marcelo 116
Peres, Martin 243
Perier, Romain 243
Pujolle, Guy 274

Rahmé, Joseph 283
Robert, Jean-Marc 199
Ruan, Chun 138

Saidane, Leila Azouz 231
Shahrestani, Seyed 138

Shimojo, Shinji 47
Sousa, Pedro 61

Tosi, Stefania 33

Varki, Elizabeth 98

Wang, Tingyun 109

Yamamoto, Miki 5
Yang, Sheng-Hua 83
Yeh, Huan-Shun 258
Yoon, Eun-Jun 191

Zeghache, Linda 177
Zou, Jian 109